D1201474

SAMUEL DANIEL'S *The Civil Wars*

Published on a grant provided by Canisius College

THE CIVILE WARES
betweene the Howſes of Lancaſter
and Yorke corrected and continued
by Samuel Daniel one of the Groome
of hir Maieſties moſt honorable.
Priuie Chamber.

Ætas prima canat veneres
poſtrema tumultus.

PRINTED
AT LONDON
by Simon Waterſonne.
1609:

Cockſonus
ſculp:

THE CIVIL WARS

by

SAMUEL DANIEL

Edited with Introduction and Notes

BY LAURENCE MICHEL

Associate Professor of English, Canisius College
Sometime Fellow of Timothy Dwight College,
Yale University

NEW HAVEN: YALE UNIVERSITY PRESS

1958

PR 2241
. C4
1958

© 1958 by Yale University Press, Inc.
Printed in the United States of America by
George McKibbin & Son, Brattleboro, Vt.
All rights reserved. This book may not be
reproduced, in whole or in part, in any form
(except by reviewers for the public press),
without written permission from the publishers.
Library of Congress catalog card number: 58–5461

Preface

THIS VOLUME is the first of what is hoped will be a complete edition of Daniel. It is intended to supersede Grosart's version, which has the disadvantages of being limited in number of copies, generally unavailable, and textually untrustworthy. The great debt which all lovers of Daniel owe to Grosart, for keeping the poet alive and for his warm and generous advocacy of his worth, can best be paid by doing his work over again as well as one can. " 'My withers are unwrung,' " he said at the end of his labors, "I have done my level best." My correction of his text will, I hope, give him his *quietus;* and for my errors I will do my own wincing.

The *Civil Wars* was once Daniel's most highly thought-of work, by himself and his contemporaries, and Coleridge, Lamb, and Wordsworth singled it out for praise; but no attention has been paid it of late, except for an occasional snippet in anthologies. I have decided to begin with it for several reasons: A. C. Sprague's edition of Daniel's *Poems and A Defence of Ryme* (Cambridge, Mass., Harvard University Press, 1930; London, Routledge and Kegan Paul, 1950) will keep the shorter poetical works excellently provided for until they can take their places in this edition; an overdue revaluation and study of Daniel should begin with his major opus; and I intend to follow next with the prose *History* and the *Dramatic Works,* which with the *Civil Wars* will present a large block of various material for study of Daniel as a maker of history into literature.

The aim of the edition, as of now, is to provide readers, students, and scholars with a good text and with all its relevant surrounding materials; it is "critical" to that extent, but criticism as such is postponed until a final "the man and his works" volume. The variants contain, I believe, all the readings genuinely "variant"; the notes are compendious—factual, referential, expository, glossarial, (occasionally) appreciative. I will welcome suggestions for either enlarging or curtailing them. Writing about the *Civil Wars* has not been copious enough to warrant a variorum treatment, nor have I attempted anything like Grosart's "Memorial-Introduction: Critical." Most of the explicit comments have been referred to in footnotes, however, and I have inserted a small nosegay of allusions by Daniel's contemporaries early on in the notes. Coleridge's obiter dicta on the poem are uniquely interesting and important; they will be found, cross-referenced, in the

DEC 22 1958

notes and at the end of the Introduction. The section on Shakespeare is intended to present all the relevant facts and comes to only tentative conclusions; that on revision is chiefly descriptive, with some suggested approaches to analysis.

Two special acknowledgments must be made. The late Edwin Nungezer, professor of English at Cornell University, had conceived and begun work on a complete edition of Daniel some twenty years ago. As a Folger Library Fellow he spent a year collating and making photostats of most of the Daniel holdings there; he had amassed a large collection of materials and put together an extensive reference bibliography. Lack of free time had prevented him from commencing the actual edition, and when I applied to him in 1949 for a part in the work he handed over the editing of the *Civil Wars* to me, and with it all his resources and his personal support. On 29 September 1949, unknowingly prophetic, he wrote to me: "I expect that you will out-live me. On this assumption, I should like for you to be thoroughly acquainted with what I've tried to do. . . . In other words, I be-queath to you all of Daniel in my possession, with the hope that you will carry the project to completion." He died the next year; I am trying to carry out his bequest, and this edition (if indeed *I* complete it) will be a monument to his efforts and to my gratitude for his kind-ness. His materials and leads have considerably lightened my labors, but I alone am responsible for the texts below.

Cecil C. Seronsy has made many valuable studies of Daniel and has put all students of the *Civil Wars* in debt by searching out and pub-lishing manuscript material, especially the Coleridge and Wordsworth marginalia. He and I discovered at one point that our inquiries into the Shakespeare-Daniel question were almost uncannily similar: We published them in a joint paper, "Shakespeare's History Plays and Daniel—an Assessment," *Studies in Philology, 52,* no. 4 (1955), 549–77. The Coleridge material is reproduced here with the permission of the *Harvard Library Bulletin* (Seronsy, "Coleridge Marginalia in Lamb's Copy of Daniel's *Poetical Works,*" *HLB, 7,* no. 1 [1953], 105–12); the paper, with the permission of *SP,* has been incorporated with some changes on pp. 7–28 below.

The engraved title page of the 1609 edition of the poem is repro-duced, with permission, from the copy in the Sterling Memorial Library at Yale; excerpts from the manuscript (BM Sloane 1443) are interpolated into the text of the introduction with the sanction of the Trustees of the British Museum.

I should like to thank John C. Pope and Louis L. Martz for their friendly acts of reading the manuscript and of encouragement; and

Eugene Davidson and Norman V. Donaldson, editor and director of the Yale University Press, for their long-enduring faith in the project. The Administrators of Canisius College and its Committee on Faculty and Institutional Research have my gratitude for underwriting the costs of publication.

LAURENCE MICHEL

Buffalo, December 1957.

Contents

Introduction

As a gloss in the margin of what is in the present edition stanza 60 of Book I, Daniel states, "Froissart Pol. Virg. & Hall, deliuer it in this sort." Thus in 1595; in 1601 are added the words "but Walsinghame reportes it otherwise." The gloss is deleted in 1609. This is the only mention of sources in the text.

In the dedication to the edition of 1609 he mentions no names, citing as his authorities "the Historie," "our common Annalles," and "that publike Testimonie we haue."

In the same dedication he announces his intention to write, in prose, "the Historie of *England,* from the Conquest." The first part of this was printed in 1612, with "Certaine Aduertisements to the Reader" including the following: [1]

> Now for what I haue done, which is the greatest part of our History . . . I am to render an Account whence I had my furniture: which if I haue omitted to charge my Margin withall, I would haue the Reader to know, that in the Liues of *William* the First, *William* the Second, *Henry* the First, and *Stephan;* I haue especially followed *William Malmsbury, Ingulphus, Roger Houueden, Huntingdon,* with all such Collections, as haue beene made out of others for those times. In the Liues of *Henry* the Second, *Richard* the First, *Iohn,* and *Henry* the Third: *Giraldus Cambrensis, Rushanger, Mat Paris, Mat. Westminst. Nich. Triuet, Caxton,* and others. In the Liues of *Edward* the First, *Edward* the Second, and Third: *Froissart* and *Walsingham,* with such Collections as by *Pollidore Virgile, Fabian, Grafton, Hall, Holingshead, Stow* and *Speed,* diligent and Famous Trauailors in search of our History, haue beene made and diulged to the world. For forrayne businesses (especially with *France,* where we had most to doe) I haue for Authors, *Paulus AEmilius, Haillan, Tillet,* and others, without whom we cannot truely vnderstand our owne affayres. And where otherwise I haue had any supplyes extraordinary, either out of Record, or such Instruments of State, as I could procure, I haue giuen a true account of them in the

[1] Reproduced here in the form of the 1618 (?) edition, the last printed in Daniel's lifetime. There are only insignificant variations.

Margin. So that the Reader shall be sure to be payd with no counterfeit Coyne, but such as shall haue the Stampe of Antiquitie, the approbation of Testimony, and the allowance of Authority, so farre as I shall proceed herein.

And for that I would haue this Breuiarie to passe with an vninterrupted deliuery of the especiall Affaires of the Kingdome (without imbroyling the memory of the Reader) I haue in a body apart, vnder the Title of an *Appendix,* Collected all treaties, Letters, Articles, Charters, Ordinances, Intertainments, prouisions of Armies, businesses of Commerce, with other passages of State appertayning to our History . . . and to this *Appendix,* I haue made references in the Margin as occasion requires.

. . . For besides our owne faylings, wee must heere take vp many things vpon other mens credits, which often comes imperfect to our hands: As the summes of Monies, numbers of Souldiers, Shippes, the slayne in Battayle, Computation of Tymes, differences of Names and Tytles &c. wherein our Authors agree not.

. . . For besides our owne faylings, wee must heere take vp many things vpon other mens credits, which often comes imperfect to our hands: As the summes of Monies, numbers of Souldiers, Shippes, the slayne in Battayle, Computation of Tymes, differences of Names and Tytles &c. wherein our Authors agree not.

The appendix was never printed. There are abbreviated references in the text here and there, the only new ones possibly relevant to source material for *CW* being "Cambden Norf[olk].," "Lambert: *Freehold,*" "Geruasius Tilburnensis. Dialog. de Scaccario," "Coggis," "Chron. Lichfield"; and since the *History* goes only up to where *CW* begins in detail, these might have been useful only in that rapid survey of the times between William I and Richard II which is the subject of the first twenty stanzas of Book I.[2]

In the errata sheets following the *History* Daniel apologizes for mistakes, hopes to have plainer sailing in dealing with more modern

[2] Many of the medieval sources were not available in print in 1595; in fact, it may have been the spurt in editing them which came between then and, say, 1609 (especially Camden's work) which incited Daniel to write his prose *History.* (See May McKissack, "Samuel Daniel as Historian," *Review of English Studies,* vol. *23,* 1947, for a summary and evaluation. Rudolf B. Gottfried, who is presently preparing an edition of the *History,* has reported on his work in two articles: "Samuel Daniel's Method of Writing History," *Studies in the Renaissance,* vol. *3,* 1956, and "The Authorship of *A Breviary of the History of England,*" *Studies in Philology,* vol. *53,* 1956. The former especially is pertinent to a study of Daniel's use of sources.)

times, "and, I trust, haue more helpes of my frendes, and all worthy men that are furnisht with matter of this nature, whom I inuoke to assist mee, and who, seeing my honest ends, I trust will not deny their Country the knowledge of what they haue. And especially herein I rely vpon the ayde of the right worthy and well-deseruing knight, Sir Robert Cotton, who, out of his choyce and excellent store, can best furnish this worke."

Daniel's concern with sources is indicated by these statements. It remains to consider which and how much of them were probably used for *CW*. It is unlikely that he found it necessary or worth while to burrow into the primary materials of the records offices and the collections of Camden and Cotton for the subject matter of a historical poem; and indeed, such "numerary" facts as find their way into the poem were taken usually from the chronicles. Except for Speed's, whose *History* came out in 1611 and therefore was not available for any edition of *CW*, all those chronicles mentioned by Daniel which touch the period of *CW* were checked in making the present edition, and relevant citations will be found in the notes and elsewhere in the commentary. As a convenience, the editions used are listed here:

The Antient Chronicles of Sir John Froissart, tr. John Bourchier, Lord Berners, 1523–25. (4 vols., London, 1816), vol. *4*.

Robert Fabyan, *The New Chronicles of England and France,* 1516. Ed. Henry Ellis (London, 1811).

Richard Grafton, *A Chronicle at Large, and Meere History of the Affayres of Englande,* 1569. Ed. Henry Ellis (London, 1809).

Thomae Walsingham, quondam monachi S. Albani, Historia Anglicana, 1574. Ed. H. T. Riley (2 vols., London, 1863).

Polydori Vergilii Vrbinatis Anglicae Historiae Libri Vigintiseptem, Basileae, 1557.

Edward Hall, *The Vnion of the Two Noble and Illustre Famelies of Lancastre & Yorke,* 1548.

Raphaell Holinshed, *Chronicles,* 2d ed., 1587. (6 vols., London, 1807), vols. *2, 3*.

John Stow, *The Annales of England,* London, 1592.

It is difficult to say how Daniel made use of these materials, since the chroniclers themselves copy, translate, paraphrase, echo, and cross-reference each other and their predecessors: for example, one usual sequence is Polydore to Hall to Holinshed. There are certain points at which it can be ascertained that Daniel was looking particularly at Walsingham, or copying a gloss verbatim from Holinshed or Stow, or that, as with IV. 29–32, he revised in 1609 with Holinshed before him.

On the whole, it would seem that Holinshed supplied his base of operations for narrative, whence he ranged in search of corroborative detail or alternative versions.[3]

From Hall Daniel probably took the view of English history, and the value it might have for posterity, which had been slowly building up since the accession of Henry VII. E. M. W. Tillyard has traced this concept in great detail in *Shakespeare's History Plays* (New York, 1946). From his discussion it is evident that Daniel inherited it, and its concomitant moralizing tendency, almost intact from a long-founded tradition. It is, in brief, the "Tudor myth" which Henry VII had inspired; Daniel took it over, except for the *Arthur redivivus* aspect, as his statement in the 1609 dedication to *CW* shows. His purpose was

> to shewe the deformities of Ciuile Dissension, and the miserable euents of Rebellions, Conspiracies, and bloudy Reuengements, which followed (as in a circle) vpon that breach of the due course of Succession, by the Vsurpation of *Hen. 4;* and thereby to make the blessings of Peace, and the happinesse of an established Gouernment (in a direct Line) the better to appeare: I trust I shall doe a gratefull worke to my Countrie, to continue the same, vnto the glorious Vnion of *Hen. 7:* from whence is descended our present Happinesse.

As for his method, the statement continues, he has

> carefully followed that truth which is deliuered in the Historie; without adding to, or subtracting from, the general receiu'd opinion of things as we finde them in our common Annalles: holding it an impietie, to violate that publike Testimonie we haue, without more euident proofe; or to introduce fictions of our owne imagination, in things of this nature. *Famae rerum standum est.* Though I knowe, in these publike actions, there are euer popular bruites, and opinions, which run according to the time & the biass of mens affections: and it is the part of an Historian, to recite them, not to rule them; especially, otherwise then the circumstances may induce: according to that modest saying; *Nec affirmare sustineo de quibus dubito, nec subducere quae accepi.*

> I haue onely vsed that poeticall licence of framing speaches to

---

[3] Albert Probst (*Samuel Daniel's "Civil Wars . . ."* und *Michael Drayton's "Barons' Wars." Eine Quellenstudie,* Strassburg, 1902) would have Stow as the principal exemplar for the last six books of *CW*, but his arguments are not convincing to the present editor. Stow's chronicle is a compendium out of well over three hundred (according to his own list) writers and records of all sorts; it is nearly always shorter and less circumstantial than Hall or Holinshed.

the persons of men according to their occasions;[4] as *C. Salustius,* and *T. Liuius* (though Writers in Prose, yet in that kinde Poets) haue, with diuers other antient and modern Writers, done before me. . . . For the rest, setting-aside those ornaments, proper to this kinde of Writing; I haue faithfully obserued the Historie.

By "those ornaments" is meant, presumably, such epical episodes as that of the Genius of England appearing to Bolingbroke, or the provenance of the arts of printing and artillery from Nemesis through Pandora. The statement, I find, is a fairly exact description of Daniel's method, although it naturally takes no notice of the pervasive moralizing which by this time was considered an inherent part of historical writing,[5] nor of Daniel's perfervid patriotism. Sprague (Daniel's *Poems and A Defence of Ryme,* 1930, p. xxxiv) absolves Daniel of chauvinism; but a judgment on this matter will depend on each non-English reader's own mixture of Anglophilia and -phobia. The present editor's (perhaps querulous) reactions will be found at certain appropriate places in the notes.

Shakespeare as a source as well as a beneficiary of *CW* has been considered important enough to call for a separate section. As for other influences, the *Mirror for Magistrates,* Warner's *Albion's England,* Sidney's *Arcadia,* and Hayward's *Life of Henry IV* were examined and found to contain nothing which would warrant calling them sources in the strict sense. The *Mirror,* of course, was a precedent for many aspects of English historical verse writing: Perhaps Daniel found in its relative crudity an incentive to do the job more artistically (Sidney

---

[4] Daniel's creative or "myth-making" activity along these lines is discussed at various places in the introduction and notes, especially in the "Shakespeare" and "Revision" sections. "According to their occasions," although I believe not disingenuous, of course really begs the question.

[5] Miss McKissack has a high opinion of Daniel's historical judgments as found in the *History;* and they "afford striking evidence both of Daniel's eye for character and of his capacity for grasping the essentials of an historical situation" (p. 240). In *CW* he is also more concerned with moral and universal judgments, as befitted a "poet historical" who subscribed to the ideals of Sidney and Spenser. Or, to take his own words for it, he proposes to "discerne the true discourse"; "sacred *Virtue*" rather than any Muse, and "MEMORIE, preserv'resse of things done," will make him "these tumults rightly to rehearse." They shall be

> Vnintermixt with fictions, fantasies.
> I versifie the troth; not Poetize.

"Versification," in the interests of "vertue," was a good; "poetizing" was meretricious. All told, Daniel was more Aristotelian than Platonist. (See *CW,* I.4,6,7; and "To the Reader," 1607, ll. 61–2.)

could find it only "meetly furnished of bewtiful partes"). I have found no convincing instances of Daniel's having gone to the *Mirror* for his treatment of their common subjects. *Albion's England,* while perpetrating such gaffes as to call Bolingbroke's heir "Hot spur his Sonne, *Henry* the fifth," is carried by its galloping fourteeners at such breakneck speed over the road from Richard II to Richard III that I am sure our Daniel, thumped and dust-choked after a few jolting strides in company, turned indignantly off onto his leisurely byway.[6] Anything of Sidney's must be reckoned with in assessing Daniel, and *Arcadia,* with its background of civil war and its political commentary, was undoubtedly a formative influence; but it is not a source of matter or manner for *CW.* Hayward's book, the first installment of which was published in 1599, could have been used by Daniel only in his revisions; the only plausible example I have found concerns the 1601 revision of the Piers of Exton story (see below, p. 15n.).

One more document may be included here, for its general interest. John Speed, whose *History of Great Britaine* (London, 1611) was to be used by Daniel for his prose *History,* has the following on p. 601:

> The seedes (we say) of those fearefull calamities were then first here sowne, whose sum a flourishing* Writer in our age (willing neerely to haue imitated *Lucan,* as hee is indeed called our† *Lucan*) doth not vnfortunately expresse, though hee might rather haue said he wept them, then sung them; but so to sing them, is to weepe them.
>
> * *Sam. Dan.* in his ciuill warres.
> † *Remaines.*

Then follows quotation of *CW,* I.1. Camden, in his introductory section the excellencies of Britain, says (*Remaines concerning Britaine,* 2d ed., London, 1611):

> I will performe that I promised, in handling nothing seriously, and therefore I will bring you in some Poets, to speake in this behalfe for me. . . . But to conclude this, most truly our *Lucan* singeth of this our country.

[6] Gabriel Harvey wrote in his copy of Speght's *Chaucer* (1598) that "The Earle of Essex much commendes Albions England . . . The Lord Mountioy makes the like account of Daniels peece of the Chronicle, touching the Vsurpation of Henrie of Bullingbrooke. which in deede is a fine, sententious, & politique peece of Poetrie: as proffitable, as pleasurable . . ." (*Gabriel Harvey's Marginalia,* ed. G. C. Moore Smith, 1913, p. 232.) It seems appropriate that the headlong Essex should have preferred Warner to Mountjoy's politic Daniel.

The fairest land, that from her thrusts the rest,
As if she carde not for the world beside,
A world within her selfe with wonders blest.
[VI.42.2–4]

Sam. Daniel.

The kind of indebtedness Daniel lay in to Lucan is illustrated in the notes to I.1.1–3. (See also the citations under the note to I.5.4.)

THE *Civil Wars* AND SHAKESPEARE[1]

The likelihood that Daniel knew Shakespeare or any of his works before at least 1604 is small. There is no convincing external evidence, and what similarities in their writings can be mustered—the sonnets, *Rosamond* and *Lucrece*, plays on classical subjects, *CW* and Shakespeare's history plays—can all be instances of a one-way influence, if any, from Daniel to Shakespeare.[2] With regard to *CW* and the history plays, the parallels undoubtedly exist (they are cited in the notes below); but the conclusions drawn by commentators as to indebtedness have always been dictated by a prior conviction concerning the dates of Shakespeare's plays. Thus Probst and Moorman, following a line of critics going back to Malone in the belief that *Richard II* was written in 1593, are forced to find a radical difference between the connections of *CW* with that play and those with *Henry IV*.[3] These considerations, and all aesthetic arguments based upon them, would fall to the ground with the successful advent of a different theory of dates, e.g. that of another group of critics culminating with Dover Wilson, that *Richard II* was written in 1595.

It is safer, then, to begin with assumptions based on broad probability. Daniel's reputation was well established in 1595; he was giving authoritative literary expression to material and attitudes well known in the chronicles and the *Mirror for Magistrates;* he was following Spenser's lead as a poet historical; it is therefore probable that Shakespeare would have read his poem while contemplating or writing his series of plays covering the same period. Daniel was a self-conscious

[1] See Preface, p. vi above.

[2] For evidence of the general agreement that the *Complaint of Rosamond* (1592) influenced some of Shakespeare's earlier dramatic and nondramatic work see H. D. R. Anders, *Shakespeare's Books* (Berlin, 1904), pp. 85–9, and the summary by H. E. Rollins in the Variorum *Poems* (Philadelphia, 1938), pp. 425–6.

[3] F. W. Moorman, "Shakespeare's History Plays and Daniel's 'Civile Wars,'" *Shakespeare Jahrbuch, 40* (1904), 69–83. A. Probst, *Samuel Daniel's "Civil Wars . . . " und Michael Drayton's "Barons' Wars." Eine Quellenstudie.*

littérateur, a purist, and, scornful of the popular stage and its pur-
veyors, would not conceive of its productions, even when printed, as
literature.[4] It is therefore unlikely that he would have seen or read the
plays and even less likely that he would have considered them proper
source material. It is quite possible that this attitude had changed
somewhat by 1604, when he was appointed a licenser of plays—his revision of *Cleopatra* in 1607 and some of the extensive changes in the
1609 *CW* point to a knowledge of Shakespeare—but more than half of
the connections with the history plays involve the 1595 edition of *CW*.

Richard II

What bibliographical evidence there is, is all in favor of an earlier
date for *CW* than for *Richard II*. Daniel's poem was entered in the
Stationers' Register on 11 October 1594 and was published in 1595,
when a second issue also appeared. A manuscript version of the first
two books is probably of still earlier date.[5] Shakespeare's play was
entered on 29 August 1597 and was first published in quarto in the
same year.[6] It is not known when *Richard II* was first produced.
Internal evidences afforded by tests of rhyme, meter, and prose have
led some investigators to date the play as early as 1593, although more
recently scholars have placed the date around 1595.[7] Two facts are
clear: All the external evidence that we have points to the priority of
Daniel's poem, and there are a good many resemblances, not acci-
dental, in language and imagery and plot and idea between the two
works. Yet contrary to the implications of these facts another and
misleading view has long been held. According to this view a second
edition of *CW*, following close on the heels of *Richard II*, offers so
many parallels to the play not found in the first edition that Daniel
must be regarded as the borrower. This "edition" is a phantom, but it
has had an extraordinarily vigorous life; it may be instructive to trace
its history.

[4] E.g., "To her sacred Maiestie" (1601), ll. 29–30 (below, p. 65):

> Nor shall I hereby vainely entertaine
> Thy Land, with ydle shadowes to no end.

[5] See Cecil C. Seronsy, "Daniel's Manuscript *Civil Wars* with Some Previously
Unpublished Stanzas," *Journal of English and Germanic Philology, 52* (1953), 153–
60; and pp. 52, 55 below.

[6] For a detailed account see E. K. Chambers, *William Shakespeare* (Oxford,
1930), *1*, 348.

[7] Chambers, p. 270; J. Dover Wilson, New Cambridge ed., *Richard II* (1939),
pp. ix, xlii–xliii.

It all began when Charles Knight, in his *Pictorial Edition of Shakespeare* (New York, 1838–45), mentioned some parallels in his introduction to *Richard II;* "with some diffidence" he offered the conclusion that Shakespeare copied from Daniel, though for the rather curious reason that Daniel "was of a modest and retiring nature, and would purposely have avoided provoking a comparison" (5, 82–3), and also concluded that, since *CW* was published in 1595, *Richard II* was written shortly before the publication of the first quarto in 1597. H. N. Hudson (*Works,* Boston, 1857, 5, 6–7) added one more instance but refused to specify which way the obligation ran. The next editor, and the villain of this whole piece, was R. G. White (*Works,* Boston, 1859, vol. 6). He pointed out that two of the resemblances—concerning the quarrel between Bolingbroke and Mowbray and the Piers of Exton episode—showed changes in two different versions of *CW,* and he announced that these were a first and second edition in 1595: The second edition "was not a mere reimpression of the former, as appears by a comparison of the two." The conclusion was irresistible: Daniel had seen *Richard II* between these two editions; hence the play could be confidently dated "in the latter part of the year 1594 or the beginning of 1595" (pp. 138–42).

This were indeed a happy solution, if true, but the facts were false. As is shown on pp. 52–3, 56–7 below there were not two editions in 1595; there were two issues, with slightly different title pages bearing the same date, but with identical texts of books I–IV printed from a single setting. Later, when the fifth book was written, it was printed from two settings (one copied from the other); some of its sheets were bound up with the 1595 sheets and some with yet another title page when the poem was included in the 1599 *Poetical Essayes.* This may have been a source of White's confusion, although the fifth book is totally irrelevant to the story of Richard. White's "changes" actually did not occur until 1609 at the time of a thoroughgoing revision of the whole poem, although, to confuse some of his followers further, still other but nonsignificant changes had been made in 1601.

Among Shakespearean editors Charlotte Porter (*First Folio Edition,* 1903–10) should get the credit, apparently,[8] for correcting the basic "second-edition" error, although she states that there was only one issue in 1595. Hardin Craig carries on the correction in the introduc-

[8] Apparently only, because, although Smith (see below) cites her discussion as "First Folio Edition Richard II, Crowell, 1903–10, pp. xv–xvii; 125–6" and in his bibliography as of "New York, 1903," the Porter-Clarke "First Folio Edition" I have been able to find was put out by Harrap (London, n.d. [1906?]—and there the old error is perpetuated. That this kind of thing can happen now ought to reconcile us to edition and issue muddles in the 16th century.

tion to the Tudor Shakespeare *Richard II* (New York, 1912), although
he mentions Knight but not White as the source of the error. R. M.
Smith (*Froissart and the English Chronicle Play,* New York, 1915)
follows Miss Porter, and Grosart's rather misleading notions about
the setting problem, but he has got the important matter straight.
Llewellyn M. Buell, in the Yale Shakespeare (New Haven, 1921), again
finds White out but introduces the peripherally confusing misap-
prehension that "the modifications really date from 1599 and 1601"
(*Richard II*, p. 124). Now almost revived again, the truth in this
matter was dealt a crippling blow by E. K. Chambers in his *William
Shakespeare.* This work, which is likely to be an authoritative standard
to many people for some time to come, reverts all the way back to
White's error, although his list of modern editions omits White's but
does include Miss Buell's.[9] Kittredge (*Complete Works,* Boston, 1936)
dismisses the question, stating laconically that the parallels adduced
to date *Richard II* in 1595 "prove nothing" (p. 505).

At last Dover Wilson, in the New Cambridge Shakespeare (1939),
reviewed and correctly evaluated the whole matter:

> There are not two editions of *The Civil Wars* in 1595, but two
> issues with slight typographical differences, confined to the title-
> page, and though Daniel later revised the poem more than once,
> his changes first appeared in the successive editions of 1601, 1609
> and 1623 [1623 used sheets of 1609—they are identical except
> for one cancel]. Nor do the changes made in 1601 in any way
> indicate borrowings from the play. Some of those introduced in
> the far more drastic revision of 1609 do, however, suggest that
> Daniel had in the meantime been reading Shakespeare's play.
> (*Richard II,* pp. xlii–iii.)

[9] Chambers too believes in the "two editions in 1595," the second of which
"contains parallels to *Richard II,* which are not in the first." In support of this
view he adduces the supposed analogy of Daniel's later borrowing from *Antony
and Cleopatra* in the thorough revision of his own *Cleopatra* in 1607. Yet when
Chambers later discusses Shakespeare's supposed influence there (*1,* 477–8), he
falls back upon the analogy of Daniel's assumed borrowing from Shakespeare in
CW. Similarly, R. H. Case (Arden *Antony and Cleopatra,* London, 1934) makes
use of the same analogy in his claim that Daniel revised in 1607 in accordance
with Shakespeare's play. This is of course a possibility; but again the argument
starts from a hypothesis assumed for the purpose of dating Shakespeare. In addition the argument rests, save for some verbal echoes, on dramatic considerations
appropriate to a play of Daniel; they probably would not be of the same weight
in an epic poem. J. Schütze, "Daniel's *Cleopatra* und Shakespeare," *Englische
Studien,* vol. *71,* 1936, disapproves of the whole theory. See Michel and Seronsy,
pp. 569–76, for further evaluation.

E. M. W. Tillyard accepts this view in his *Shakespeare's History Plays* (New York, 1936, p. 331), and it is hoped that Wilson's account in his edition of the play, and this discussion in an edition of the poem, will lay the poor ghost for good.[10]

The over-all philosophical conception lying behind both Daniel and Shakespeare in their studies of English history has been well described by Tillyard.[11] This attitude, as well as most of the details of the action, is to be found in the chronicle sources used by both authors, so that it is chiefly material not to be found in these sources which is relevant for a discussion of influence. R. M. Smith (pp. 143–57) adduces twelve such parallels which he says differ from the chronicle sources,[12] and these parallels may be commented on as a convenient means of beginning the present discussion.

1. *Bolingbroke's popularity with the common people is given as the reason for his banishment.* But materials for this idea are found in Hall and Holinshed as well as in Froissart; indeed some episodes in Shakespeare (II.ii) may well have been suggested by a passage in Holinshed: "The lord tresuror, Bushie, Bagot, and Greene, perceiuing that the commons would cleaue vnto, and take part with the duke, slipped awaie . . ."

2. *Queen Isabel is presented as a mature woman, exhibiting understanding and passion beyond the scope of a lass of eleven.* Hall, Holinshed, and Stow give her age and emphasize her youth. Froissart, however, as Smith points out, had drawn a picture of her demeanor as quite pleasing to the English ambassadors in spite of her tender years, and it seems likely that Daniel elaborated his portrait from this and that Shakespeare took it from Daniel. Daniel had recognized that the Queen was "young," in his first editions (I.40, II.66);[13] his apology for "not suting her passions to her yeares," in the dedication to the edition of 1609, was perhaps the result of his being taken to task for the discrepancy; possibly, as Wilson suggests (p. xliii), he had by then become aware that Shakespeare had followed him.

[10] It has kept raising its head fitfully in various pocket editions, school texts, the old Arden, and even the New Clarendon (ed. J. M. Lothian, Oxford, 1938–49).

[11] See also above, "Sources," p. 4.

[12] P. 153. Here Smith apparently means Shakespeare's sources, and he does not include Froissart among them (p. 147), in unawareness or defiance of 1 *Henry VI*, I.ii.29.

[13] Citations from Daniel in this and the following section are given in the wording, spelling, punctuation, etc. of the relevant early editions. Book, stanza, and line numbers, however, are those of the present edition, for ready reference. A cross-reference table will be found on pp. 59–60 below. Shakespeare citations are taken from the relevant early edition (usually a facsimile).

3. Bolingbroke and Richard enter London tandem-style, the one triumphantly in the lead, the other following unnoticed or reviled. Daniel's scene (II.61 ff.) is greatly elaborated from mere hints in Holinshed and Stow, and the likeness between the poem and the play (V.ii) is remarkable, in detail and sentiment.

4. Isabel watches Richard enter London, is dismayed at his aspect, and later procures a meeting with him.[14] There is no warrant for any of this in any source. Apart from the incident itself, there do not appear to be many resemblances in language or ideas between the corresponding passages in the two works; this need not, however, militate against the theory of influence. Daniel's passage is the most elaborated showpiece of his characteristic pathetic mode; Shakespeare finds the incident itself sufficient for his dramatic purposes and reserves pathos for his characterization of Richard.

5. In both works Bolingbroke courts the favor of the common people, and his growing power is described by Daniel thus:

> All turn'd their faces to the rising *sunne*
> And leaues his setting-fortune *night begun.* (II.1)

by Shakespeare:

> Discharge my followers; let them hence awaie,
> From Richards *night* to Bullingbrookes *faire daie.* (III.ii.217 ff.)

The first item may have been easily found in the chronicles, as stated above; the verbal parallel is dubious evidence as are all such coincidences. Shakespeare is really closer to Daniel's metaphor in his reference to "the sunne of Bullingbrooke" (IV.i.261). Indeed the sun image is Shakespeare's all through *Richard II,* and in the summer-winter imagery it is carried into the opening lines of *Richard III.* Moreover, the sun image is found elsewhere in Daniel too, for instance in the 1594 *Cleopatra,* where the young Caesario is called "the rising Sunne of our declining state."

6. Similar portents in the heavens. The occurrence of the portents is in the chronicles; Shakespeare picks up withered bay trees from Holinshed, Daniel omits them; Daniel puts in more than Shakespeare; what they have in common, "Meteors" and "Stars," is common indeed.[15]

---

[14] Here Smith's text is confused, quoting part of the latter scene to illustrate a reference to the former.

[15] W. H. Clemen ("Anticipation and Foreboding in Shakespeare's Early Histories," *Shakespeare Survey 6,* Cambridge, 1953, p. 35) argues that it is "characteristic of Shakespeare's use of omen, that he does not take over the miraculous apparitions like Daniel's 'Red fiery dragons in the aire doe flie.'" They were, of course, the chroniclers' before they were Daniel's.

7. *The adoption of the familiar name "Bullingbrooke," and the spelling of "Herford."* Shakespeare may have accepted Daniel's familiarity (converting it into an epithet of scorn in the mouth of Hotspur later), although the name is mentioned in Hall. But surely spellings are insignificant.

8. *Richard delivers the crown to Bolingbroke with his own hand.* Miss Buell also adduces this, as "not in Holinshed" (p. 122). But it is in Froissart, and even relatively laconic Hall says "And then with a lamentable voyce and a sorrowful countenance, [Richard] deliuered his sceptre and croune to the duke of Lancastre . . ." Yet the dramatization of the idea in the two poems is close. Daniel thus relates Richard's abdication: "Tis said with his owne hands he gaue the crowne" (II.111); Shakespeare's Richard says, "With mine owne handes I giue awaie my crowne" (IV.i.208).

9. *The plotters against Henry reassure each other by swearing on the Sacrament.* Although this circumstance may be corroboratory in context, the practice itself was a commonplace.

10. *The hints given by Henry IV for the murder of Richard by Sir Piers of Exton.* Shakespeare's use of "rid" and "feare" would seem to indicate that he supplemented Holinshed from Daniel, who actually affords more hints for Henry's remark, quoted by Exton, "Haue I no friend will rid me of this liuing feare?" than has been hitherto recognized. First comes Daniel's reflection on how Richard is at the mercy of his enemies, "And they rid quite of feare, he of the crowne" (II.47). Later the same idea, similarly phrased, suggests itself to Henry who "wisht that some would so his life esteeme As rid him of these feares wherein he stood" (III.57). Hardin Craig adds the detail of Henry's eyeing Piers meaningfully, and Wilson adds the corroboration of "wishtly" in Shakespeare and "wisht" in Daniel. This is perhaps the strongest of the verbal concomitances.

11. *Richard muses on kings and commoners in his cell, just before a servant* [perhaps Ienico d'Artois, of whom Daniel makes much?] *rushes in to warn him, followed by Exton and his fellow assassins.* The parallel here is rather close. The scene is set in *CW,* III.64:

> The morning of that day, which was his last,
> After a weary rest rysing to paine
> Out at a little grate his eyes he cast
> Vppon those bordering hils, and open plaine,
> And viewes the towne, and sees how people past,
> Where others libertie makes him complaine
> The more his owne, and grieues his soule the more
> Conferring captiue-Crownes with freedome pore.

In *Richard II*, V.v:

> I haue beene studying how I may compare
> This prison where I liue, vnto the world:
>
> .   .   .   .   .
>
>   sometimes I am a King,
> Then treasons make me wish my selfe a beggar,
> And so I am: then crushing penurie
> Perswades me I was better when a king . . .

There are some tantalizing echoes, difficult to fit in but insistent to the ear, as is again the case in *CW*, III.65:

> O happie man, saith hee, that lo I see
> Grazing his cattel in those pleasant fieldes!
> If he but knew his good, how blessed hee
> That feeles not what affliction greatnes yeeldes,
> Other then what he is he would not bee,
> Nor chaung his state with him that Scepters weildes

which recalls the last line of Shakespeare's Sonnet 29, "That then I Skorne to change my state with Kings." Indeed it recalls the whole tenor of Sonnets 29 and 30 (with the further echo in the latter, "And with old woes new waile my deare times waste," with "I wasted time and now doth time waste me" in line 49 of this scene). Stanza 66 of *CW*

> Thou sit'st at home safe by thy quiet fire
> And hear'st of others harmes, but feelest none;
> And there thou telst of kinges and who aspire,
> Who fall, who rise, who triumphs, who doe mone:
> Perhappes thou talkst of mee, and dost inquire
> Of my restraint, why here I liue alone,
> O know tis others sin not my desart,
> And I could wish I were but as thou art.

and the incantatory use of the word "Death" spoken of in stanzas 69 and 70 seem to find a counterpart in the famous speech of *Richard II*, III.ii.155 ff.:

> For Gods sake let vs sit vpon the ground,
> And tell sad stories of the death of Kings,
>
> .   .   .   .   .   .
>
>   for within the hollow crowne
> That roundes the mortal temples of a king,
> Keeps death his court

and in Richard's valediction to Isabel in V.i.38 ff.:

> Thinke I am dead, and that euen here thou takest
> As from my death bed thy last liuing leaue;
> In winters tedious nights sit by the fire,
> With good old folks, and let them tell the tales,
> Of woeful ages long agoe betidde:
> And ere thou bid good night to quite their griefes,
> Tell thou the lamentable tale of me,
> And send the hearers weeping to their beds.

We are on slippery ground here, and indeed perilously close to the quicksands of the sonnet-dating question and the influence of Daniel's *Delia*. Perhaps it is best to say that the complex of ideas and images seems to be quite thick, and that Daniel has been caught up in it somewhere.

12. *Exton is repudiated by Henry IV after the murder.* "Shakespeare must have taken this from *The Civil Wars*" (Smith, p. 153). Here Smith has fallen into the error (and Wilson does not pick him up on it) of assuming that Daniel's passage was in the 1595 edition. The parallel is close, there is no mention in the chronicles; but this is one instance where it seems incontrovertible that Daniel borrowed from Shakespeare rather than vice versa. The 1595 version does not raise the point of Exton's relationship with Henry; the 1601 version revises, substituting a stanza on the theme of Exton's infamy with posterity,[16] but still not adverting to his repudiation by Henry; the 1609 version revises again, taking this out to make room for the repudiation idea. It seems probable that by 1609 Daniel had been forced to recognize Shakespeare as a serious writer on historical subjects and revised, especially those parts of his poem concerning Henry IV, in the light of Shakespeare's treatment.

As for Shakespeare's precedent in this matter, no one seems to have remarked the very close similarity between Henry-Exton-Richard,

[16] This Cain-curse idea was in the chronicles all the time, but perhaps Daniel's attention was drawn to it by the account in *The First Part of the Life and Raigne of King Henrie the IIII* . . . written by I[ohn] H[ayward], London, 1599. Hayward himself may here be combining what he found in Hall and Shakespeare:

> For Sir Pierce, expecting great fauour and rewards for his vngracious seruice, was frustrated of both, and not only missed that countenance for which he hoped, but lost that which before he had: so odious are vices euen when they are profitable.
>
> Heereupon hee grew at the first discontented, and afterwardes mightely turmoyled and tormented in conscience, and raging against himselfe would often exclaime, that to pleasure one vnthankfull person, he had made both himselfe and his posteritie, hatefull and infamous to all the world.

and John-Hubert-Arthur in *King John*, although somewhat the same impulse is found behind the two plays written very close together (and Wilson notes similarities in imagery, going back ultimately to Daniel!): John leers and hints to Hubert that he would like to have Arthur out of the way, and repudiates him when he thinks Arthur is dead.

Of the twelve citations, items 1, 5, 6, 7, and 9 are not sufficiently independent of common sources to have significance as parallels. Item 4 remains doubtful; item 12 is actually a case of Daniel's probably following Shakespeare in a later edition;[17] items 2, 3, 8, 10, and 11

[17] The last of Smith's citations was also one of White's big points (pp. 141–2); the other one (pp. 139–41) errs similarly (though in the other direction), as his whole argument stems from an ignorance of marginal notes by Daniel, and what the present editor considers the misreading of a line. Daniel disagrees with Shakespeare on the Bolingbroke-Mowbray quarrel, making Mowbray the accuser. His gloss reads, in the 1595 version, "Froissart Pol. Virg. & Hall, deliuer it in this sort." That is, that Mowbray went to the king with Bolingbroke's confidences; further-more, all three chroniclers impute malice to Mowbray. In 1601 the stanza remains the same except for verbal polishing, but the gloss is augmented with the words "but Walsinghame reports it otherwise." (To add to the ensuing confusion Grosart, whom most commentators following his edition used, has no mention of this addendum; it has not been printed since 1602.) What this indicates, in conjunction with the gloss to stanza 64 (which retails a comment found only in Walsingham), is that Daniel checked his sources when revising in 1601. He found Walsingham's brief statement, that Bolingbroke appealed Mowbray for words he had spoken prejudicial to the king, sufficient to require marginal notice but not to change his version of the story or his estimate of Mowbray's motive. In 1609 he omits the gloss altogether and, while maintaining Mowbray as the talebearer, deletes the epithet "faithles Duke" and shifts the onus of misconstruing Boling-broke's words from Mowbray to the king himself. (Hall, practically translating Polydore, had been insistent on Mowbray's being "bothe a depe dissimuler and a pleasaunte flaterer . . . as tell tales and sicophantes bee"; but Froissart, though stating that Mowbray told his tale "to please the King," tones down the impeach-ment by saying that Mowbray "thought in himself that the earl of Derby [Boling-broke] was likely to create much trouble in England." In his reconsideration Daniel apparently reverted from Hall to Froissart for Mowbray's character.) Richard's anger is agreed upon by all, but Daniel accounts for it in two different ways: in 1595, Mowbray

> Hastes to the King, peruerting what was told,
> And what came of good minde he makes it hate

that is, Mowbray tells the king that Bolingbroke's criticisms show hatred of the king. In 1609 Mowbray relates the whole discourse to the king,

> Who, not conceipting it, as it was told,
> But iudging it proceeded out of hate

calls Bolingbroke to account. That is, the king, not accepting Mowbray's straight-forward relation, judges for himself that it betrays hatred for him, the king, on

appear to be reasonably convincing instances of Daniel's influence on *Richard II*. To these are now added some hitherto unnoticed resemblances, offered as further proof that *CW* was an important source for *Richard II*.

The idea of a Nemesis dogging Henry IV for his impiety in rebelling against and usurping the crown of an anointed king is an important point of contact but difficult to pin down.[18] It, and horror at the vision of the wounds of civil war which are its instruments of revenge, are pervasive in both the whole *CW* and Shakespeare's cycle, transcending the bounds of any reign because the curse works itself out in the whole Lancastrian dynasty. The link in *Richard II* is Carlisle's speech, with its insistence on the invalidity of subjects' passing sentence on a king. In Daniel's poem the Bishop of Carlisle protests against the deposition of Richard and abhors the thought that the lawful king

> Should here be iudg'd vnheard, and vnarraignd
> By subiects two [*sic*]: Iudges incompetent
> To iudge their king vnlawfully detaind,
> And vn-brought forth to plead his guiltles cause,
> Barring th'annointed libertie of lawes. (III.23)

Shakespeare's bishop speaks in similar language:

> What subiect can giue sentence on his King:
> And who sits here that is not Richards subiect?
> Theeues are not iudgd but they are by to heare,
> Although apparant guilt be seene in them,
> And shall the figure of Gods Maiesty,
> His Captaine, steward, deputy, elect,

Bolingbroke's part. Now White interprets the change thus: "For hatred of the king attributed by one appellant to the other, we have a suspicion by the King of hatred of one appellant by the other." And, finding this second view similar to Shakespeare's "If he appeal the Duke on ancient malice?" and the reference to "rival-hating envy," he concludes that Daniel revised after having seen Shakespeare.

The position taken here is that this particular "parallel" is of no consequence in the indebtedness question. That the two authors chose and stuck to different versions of who accused whom and that Daniel, in revising, called attention to his use of a chronicler not used (so far as it is known) by Shakespeare seems sufficient warrant for discounting White's reading of the lines and his conclusions therefrom. The shifting of the onus to Richard in 1609 was doubtless part of Daniel's large-scale "reconsideration" of Richard discussed below (pp. 29–35).

[18] See note to VI.30 ff. below.

> Annointed, crowned, planted, many yeares
> Be iudgd by subiect and inferiour breath,
> And he himselfe not present?   (IV.i.121–9)

The whole speech abounds in echoes of Daniel. Perhaps the most striking one is

> Peace shall go sleepe with turkes and infidels,
> And in this seat of peace, tumultuous warres,
> Shall kin with kin, and kinde with kind confound.
>   (IV.i.138–41)

This argues for Shakespeare's recognition of Daniel as a spokesman for the central idea, by borrowing from his thematic opening stanza:

> I Sing the ciuil warrs, tumultuous broyles,
>
>   .   .   .   .
>
> Whil'st Kin their Kin, brother the brother foyles,
> Like Ensignes all against like Ensignes band:
> Bowes against bowes, the Crowne against the crowne,
> whil'st all pretending right, all right throwen downe.
>   (I.1)

Tillyard (pp. 238–42) has assembled a number of points of over-all resemblance between Daniel's poem and Shakespeare's two tetralogies beginning with *Richard II* and ending with *Richard III* (if we accept the authorship of all or most of the *Henry VI* trilogy). Both poets (as do Hall and the *Mirror for Magistrates*) begin at the same point in the reign of Richard II, and in political philosophy they are identical, showing the evils of civil dissension and the curse of rebellion. Tillyard further points out that they are "at one in their sense of history repeating itself, of history educating through the example, of one crime leading to another," and that they agree in seeing all this misery as a prelude to the glorious times of the Tudors. These common aims, along with the surprising concurrence of their choice of incidents, whatever their difference in execution, are probably more than mere coincidence.

It remains to set out whatever other parallels have been noticed by others or by the present editor.

An interesting correspondence is shown by the way in which both poets envisage woe and destruction as a consequence of Bolingbroke's ambition and ultimate usurpation of the crown. At the end of Book I, Daniel looks back at the ungodly beginnings of the plot against Richard and the impious warfare which has marred "The flowre of

thy chiefe pride, thou fairest Ile" (I.118); the Genius of England has
sounded the ominous note to Bolingbroke as he returns from exile:

> The babes vnborne, shall ô be borne to bleed
> In this thy quarrell if thou doe proceede   (I.89)

and when the usurpation is accomplished, the poet exclaims,

> What mourning in their ruin'd houses now?
> How many childrens plaints and mothers cryes?
> How many wofull widowes left to bow
> To sad disgrace? what perisht families?   (III.54)

Shakespeare seems to elaborate on this theme of general bloodshed and
slaughter that awaits those yet unborn. Richard foretells the fate
that the conspirators are bringing down upon England:

> Yet know, my maister God omnipotent,
> Is mustering in his cloudes on our behalfe,
> Armies of pestilence, and they shall strike
> Your children yet vnborne, and vnbegot,
>
>   .   .   .   .
>
> But ere the crowne he lookes for, liue in peace,
> Ten thousand bloudy crownes of mothers sonnes,
> Shall ill become the flower of Englands face (III.iii.85–97)

and later in the play, after the deposition, the Bishop of Carlisle
prophesies,

> The woe's to come, the children yet vnborne,
> Shall feele this day as sharp to them as thorne.

The resemblances in circumstance and, to some extent, in language
between the poem and the play in these prophecies of woe to come
are not found in Holinshed and Hall. Characteristically, Daniel exploits the pathos and sentiment of the situation in "childrens plaints,"
"mothers cryes," and "wofull widowes." All these touches are
neglected by Shakespeare, who seizes upon the "babes vnborne"
phrase as a means to intensify his account of the iron tragedy of war.

Gaunt's famous speech, celebrating England's insularity as a defense against foreign infection, has echoes of Daniel's apostrophe to
Neptune in Book IV, and the sea-spurning-shore imagery (a link,
incidentally, with *King John*) may have come from Daniel's description of the ambush of Richard II in Book II.

The image of a river in flood running over its banks is, of course,
common in both poets; but an influence seems pretty certain here

since the image is employed to describe the same thing—the freshet of rebellion that greeted Bolingbroke when he returned to England from exile—and since both poets employ this image to play on the name of the usurper. After showing how Henry's forces have been augmented like the Thames, Daniel adds,

> So flocke the mightie with their following traine
> Vnto the all-receiuing *Bullingbrooke*. (II.8)

And Shakespeare offers a somewhat more furious and dynamic punning image:

> So high aboue his limits swels the rage
> Of Bullingbrooke couering your feareful land.
>   (III.ii.109–10)

Richard's reproaches to Northumberland, his prophecy of Bolingbroke's spurning Northumberland once he has used him for a ladder to the throne, and the vision of ensuing corruption (V.i.55–68) are very close to the sentiments inaugurated by Daniel in II.2 ff. This may serve as one more illustration of the different quality of the two poets: Daniel first moralizes in his own person, then transfers the theme to Richard as a "complaint" soliloquy; his image is suggestive rather than concrete:

> "Th'aspirer once attaind vnto the top
> "Cuts off those meanes by which himselfe got vp. (II.15, 7–8)

Whereas Shakespeare has Richard blurt out his bitter lines as a direct response to being checked and rated by the blunt Northumberland; he makes the image simultaneously concrete and insulting: "Northumberland, thou ladder . . ." And he thought well enough of the idea to re-use it (and in a rare direct quotation) in the new dramatic situation of the prophecy's apparent operation in 2 *Henry IV* (III.i. 57 ff.).

The reiteration of the idea that Richard was betraying his patrimony by not prosecuting glorious foreign conquests, and the impiety of England's "shameful conquest of itself," find a continuous counterpart in Daniel from the beginning of his poem.

Richard's "senseless conjuration" of the stones of the castle when he returns from Ireland,

> This earth shall haue a feeling, and these stones,
> Proue armed souldiers ere her natiue King,
> Shall faulter vnder foule rebellions armes, (III.ii.24–6)

may well derive from Salisbury's eloquent plea in Daniel that Richard should stay where he is:

> Here haue you craggy rockes to take your part
> That neuer will betray their faith to you;
>
> . . . . .
>
> If men will not, these verie cliffes will fight
> And be sufficient to defend your right. (II.29)

I am convinced that the totality of evidence presented here makes it certain that the two treatments of Richard II are intimately connected. The verbal coincidences take on incomparably greater importance than is usual because they occur in the same contexts. And indeed, once it were established that Shakespeare followed Daniel, it would be more than likely that even much of the treatment for which there is precedent in the sources common to both men would be found to have taken its shaping impulse from the poet rather than the historians: It is not unreasonable to believe that, as Wilson puts it, "Shakespeare had his head full of the poem while he was engaged upon the play" (p. lxiv). In establishing the question of indebtedness, clearing up the date muddle helps considerably, but final conviction still rests on the "broad probabilities" mentioned at the beginning. The net result, it is hoped, is that *CW* will be recognized as the most illuminating background reading yet found for a full appreciation of *Richard II,* and a companion piece not unworthy to stand beside it, in its own right.

Henry IV

Once it has been accepted (as I think it universally has) that *Henry IV* was written around 1597–98 and that it has unmistakable links of continuity with *Richard II,* there is not much need for argument that here Daniel's contribution is clear. He often appears to anticipate Shakespeare in introducing changes from the chronicle sources.[19] The chief resemblances to the 1595 *CW*—not found in the sources—are these:

The idea of Nemesis is taken up and developed, and its impact upon the character and actions of Henry is emphasized; it becomes a kind of retributive justice, working through all the political action and forcing Henry to express remorse over his past conduct. Daniel "furnished his great disciple with the interpretation of the character

---

[19] Most of the resemblances cited here have been pointed out by Moorman.

of King Henry IV, as he had done in the case of the same man as Bolingbroke in the earlier play."[20] (It is interesting in this connection to speculate that Shakespeare later built his character of Claudius much upon the pattern of King Henry IV, while, I think it can be shown, shaping Hamlet in no small degree on the mold of Prince Henry.)

Hotspur is made a contemporary of Prince Henry, whereas historically he was older than the king. The prince, becoming a glorious knight of war at seventeen, encounters Hotspur at the Battle of Shrewsbury and saves his father from death or capture by the Douglas.

Glendower and the Welsh forces fail to appear at the Battle of Shrewsbury. The usual chroniclers say they were there; Daniel derived his information from some other source as yet undescried; Shakespeare took it from him; modern historians bear them out.

Henry's interview with the prince shortly before he dies is to be found in the chroniclers, but Daniel introduced the theme of regret for the "blot of foul attaining" on the crown he was about to pass on to his son and for not having been able to erase it by a crusade. When Daniel begins the narrative of the downfall of the House of Lancaster (with York starting to "looke Into their right"), he enters a reservation:

> Nere three score years are past since *Bullingbrooke*
> Did first attaine (God knows how just) the crowne. (V.45)

In Shakespeare the remorse is more directly felt by the king:

> God knowes (my sonne)
> By what by-paths and indirect crookt waies,
> I met this crowne.   (Pt. 2, IV.v.184–6)

This, and the advice he gives the prince to keep his subjects in hand by busying them with foreign conquest, may be confidently assigned as taken by Shakespeare from Daniel. They are in the latter's usual and characteristic vein.[21]

A rather striking piece of evidence[22] that Shakespeare followed

---

[20] J. D. Wilson, "The Origins and Development of Shakespeare's 'Henry IV,' " *The Library*, 26 (1945), 6.

[21] See also, however, G. R. Waggoner, "An Elizabethan Attitude toward Peace and War," *Philological Quarterly, 33*, (1954), 20–33, for the view that the notion of healthy foreign war was widespread in certain circles.

[22] Theobald in 1733 seems to have been the first to be struck by it; Malone picked it up (see Wilson's discussion, *The Library*, p. 5); Waller used it (see Lowell's comment, note to IV.84 below); the *New Variorum Shakespeare* records it.

Daniel very closely at times is the image both poets use to describe the
bodily feebleness of King Henry just before the arrival of death,

> Whose harald sicknes, being sent before
> With full commission to denounce his end,
> And paine, and griefe, enforcing more and more,
> Besiegd the hold that could not long defend,
> And so consum'd all that imboldning store
> Of hote gaine-striuing bloud that did contend,
> Wearing the wall so thin that now the mind
> Might well looke thorow, and his frailty find.   (IV.84)

> No, no, he cannot long hold out these pangs,
> Th'incessant care and labour of his mind
> Hath wrought the Mure that should confine it in,
> So thin that life lookes through.   (Pt.2, IV.iv.117–20)

There is much mention in 2 *Henry IV* of gunpowder, shot, artillery,
cannon, culverins, pistols (even the use of explosives to change the
course of the river Trent?) at the time of Homildon Hill and Shrewsbury. This anachronism was avoided by Daniel; in his long, fanciful
derivation of the arts of printing and artillery (VI.26 ff.) he puts the
first use of both, properly, in the time of Henry VI. However, his
vivid description of the devilish provenance of artillery, and its in-
strumentality in the decline of personal valor in battle, may well have
so impressed itself upon Shakespeare's mind as to be the source of
Hotspur's angry paraphrase of the pestering popinjay:

> And that it was great pitty, so it was,
> This villanous saltpeeter should be digd
> Out of the bowels of the harmeless earth,
> Which many a good tall fellow had destroyed
> So cowardly, and but for these vile guns
> He would himselfe haue been a souldior. (I.iii.59–64)

It may be some corroboration that Milton, who evidently knew
Daniel's works,[23] also seems to have been struck by this passage. (See

---

[23] See notes to VI.26 ff. below; also Cecil C. Seronsy, "Daniel and Milton,"
Notes and Queries, 197 (March 29, 1952), 134–5; (May 24, 1952), 239. The whole
idea, however, had been found viable for literature since (at least) Ariosto; see
Orlando Furioso, Book IX, stt. 24–7, 83–4 (trans. Sir John Harington, 1591).
Ariosto derives cannon and gunpowder from hell, but Harington, in the "Historie" appended to Book IX, records "our writers" as saying they were invented
in Germany in the time of Richard II!

Might this be a modicum to add to our apprehension of the "double vision"
of the English Renaissance? On the one hand, a sober allegorical-moral fraternity

the notes to VI.26–40, Book V originally. This book was presumably not written by the time I–IV were printed in 1595, but was later bound up with copies of the latter and sold with the 1595 title page. It is a good possibility that this may have been before 1597. See pp. 56–7 below.)

King Henry's nocturnal soliloquy, followed by his justification of his actions to Warwick and Surrey in Pt. 2, III.i,

> ô sleepe! o gentle sleep!
> Natures soft nurse, how haue I frighted thee,

and

> (Though then (God knowes) I had no such intent,
> But that necessitie so bowed the state,
> That I and greatnesse were compeld to kisse   (III.ii)

may owe something to Daniel's invention of the Genius of England's appearing to Bolingbroke in a nightly vision and his defense of his action in breaking exile. Daniel himself comments,

> And let vnwresting charitie beleeue
> That then thy oth with thy intent agreed,
> And others faith, thy faith did first deceiue,
> Thy after fortune forc'd thee to this deed:
> And let no man this idle censure giue
> Because th'euent proues so, twas so decreed:
> For ô what counsels sort to other end
> Then that which frailty did at first intend?   (I.98)

Mention has been made above of the pervasive presence of Nemesis in Daniel's account of the struggle between the rival houses. The fact that Nemesis is named for the first time in the poem in Book V (printed after 1595 and some time before 1599) has induced scholars to regard Daniel's explicit idea of Nemesis as having been available as a suggestion to Shakespeare for use in *Henry IV* but not for *Richard II*. But Daniel's *Cleopatra* (1594), which may well have been read by Shakespeare,[24] can fill the gap. The chorus at the end of Act III apostrophizes,

---

including Harington, sage and serious Spenser, Daniel, and Milton; and on the other, gentle-witty Shakespeare laughing *with* Ariosto at this Osric-like attempt to disinfect one's person from evil with civet, snuff, and lady-terms, to pretend that cannon-carriages are sword-hangers, and to make the devil responsible for villainous saltpeter. Coleridge called Daniel's passage "a cowardice of present evil."

24 See Michel and Seronsy, pp. 569–76.

> O Fearefull-frowning Nemesis,
> Daughter of Iustice, most severe.[25]

Here already is the kernel of Daniel's (and Shakespeare's) conception of English history, as the chorus, elaborating on the necessity of righting wrongs and of reversing evil trends and insisting on the alternate course of weal and woe, points the way to the philosophic notion behind *CW*. And the idea is worked out in some detail in Daniel's tragedy. Caesario, just before he goes to his death, prophesies,

> And thou Augustus that with bloody hand,
> Cutt'st off succession from another's race,
> Maist find the heavens thy vowes so to withstand,

and looks ahead to the time when Augustus himself will have no issue to succeed him, and the wheel of retribution will have come full cycle (ll. 1029 ff.). The tone and form of this utterance is not unlike that of Richard's warning to Bolingbroke, though the actual prophecy takes a different turn.[26]

Wilson, in the New Cambridge edition of *Henry IV*, points out resemblances in diction and imagery, plays on words, etc., which may or may not add to the conviction that Daniel's poem was in Shakespeare's mind as he wrote these plays. They are cited in the notes below.

On the other hand, the direction of influence seems to have been reversed in Daniel's revision of *CW* in 1609. (We should recall the possibility that he was attracted to Shakespeare's work earlier, after his appointment as a licenser of plays in 1604, particularly in his drastic revision of *Cleopatra* in 1607.) A considerable amount of new and revised material indicates that Daniel checked back over his presentation of Henry IV and Richard II after having seen Shakespeare's. Book III was split into III and IV, and much matter expanded. III.82, which had announced that with Richard's death Henry was now secure, was changed to introduce twenty-four new stanzas showing that the deed did *not* free Henry from care or fear. This theme is the burden of the opening scene of 1 *Henry IV*, the link with *Richard II*. Stanzas 17–19 of Book IV, added at this time, describe the friction between Henry and the Percies treated in I.iii of the play; Daniel confuses the two Mortimers, as had Shakespeare; 26–7 introduce the Percies' bill of complaint; 49–52 shift the emphasis from the two Blunts at the Battle of Shrewsbury to Douglas' difficulties in

---

[25] In 1607 the first line was revised to "Sterne and imperious *Nemesis*."
[26] See note to VI.30 ff. below.

encountering so many King Henrys. Stanza 56, added, tells of Douglas' capture and his pardon for "noble valour" shown, and introduces twenty-six new stanzas which summarize the political content of 2 *Henry IV*. Two new stanzas (IV.41–2) give the circumstances of Worcester's concealing from Hotspur the king's peace proposal and urge that Henry, by conceding much in making the peace overture, was moved to do so by a real horror of bloodshed. Daniel's shift from an earlier and harsher view of Henry, noticeable in a few such passages as these, may well have been influenced by Shakespeare.

In many places it is evident that Daniel felt in 1609 that he had allowed Richard altogether too much wisdom and good intention in earlier versions of the poem. In confirmation of this more sober view he added in 1609 a "character" of Richard at the end of Book III, in which his engaging manners, his generosity, and his personal charm are balanced against the excesses and defects of his character which had been dealt with rather lightly in the earlier editions. There had already been some toning down of his early sympathies for Richard, in successive revisions, but the shift in view is considerably more extensive in 1609.

All this is not to say that Daniel could not have found most of these things in the chronicles, and such inadvertencies as that he does not *describe* the meeting between Prince Henry and Hotspur are indicative that he was not copying Shakespeare.[27] The bulk of new material is impressive, however, and fits extremely well with what Daniel would have found treated by Shakespeare if he had become familiar with the play by 1609. It is perhaps significant that nine-tenths of the whole-line substitutions and all of the complete-stanza additions in the whole poem of 1609 concern Henry IV.

[27] Yet one is confronted by one of the many elusive single-word changes by Daniel, so hard to pin down: IV.34.1–2 read, up until 1609,

> There shall young *Hotspur*, with a fury led,
> Meete with thy forward sonne, as fierce as hee:

Daniel changed line 2 of this to "Ingrapple with thy sonne . . ." Had he encountered and been impressed by 1 *Henry IV*, V.ii.74?

> [*Hot.*] *I* will imbrace him with a souldiours arme,
> That he shall shrinke vnder my curtesie,

Or IV.47.3, which until 1609 described Hotspur's eagerness, "Whose young vndaunger'd hand now rash, makes way" but then reverses to "Whose forward hand, inur'd to woundes, makes way." Perhaps Daniel had been struck by Shakespear's insistence on Hotspur's experience in war and talk about wounds.

Henry VI

Since the controversy over the authorship of *Henry VI* is still undecided, this notice is perforce tentative. Relying on the basic probability asserted above, we may assume that Daniel did not know the original plays of which *The Contention* and *The True Tragedy* are generally considered to be some kind of distorted versions. Consequently, it is only the Folio version of *Henry VI* (and especially Part 3 which, it has been argued, Shakespeare revised) that concerns us. The difficulty is that there is no indication of when this revision, if any, took place. Daniel's Book VIII was first published in 1609, and we can be reasonably certain that Shakespeare would not be concerned with rehashing an old play on Henry VI after that date, and consequently that he was not the debtor in this instance; but when Daniel got hold of it must remain a matter of conjecture. If the supposition be good that he became interested in Shakespeare after 1604 and made use of him in the revision of 1609, then we may further suppose that he sought out the same dramatist's treatment of material he was about to work up for the first time—the incidents of Book VIII. (Incidentally, while this sheds no light on the time of the "Shakespeare revision," it may strengthen the argument that the ascription to Shakespeare is true. Daniel was a very discriminating critic, and having recognized Shakespeare's value in *Henry IV* he might very well have sought out a version of Henry VI's reign by the same pen when he continued his poem in 1609.)

Probst has pointed out some of the resemblances, although he seems unaware of any difference between the Folio version of Part 3 and *The True Tragedy*. Two scenes afford similarities: the wooing of Lady Grey by Edward IV; and King Henry on the molehill at Towton (Pt. 3. II.v.20–54)—"little hill" in Daniel (VIII.22)—which, in its general scheme of a slighted monarch comparing his situation with that of a common man and its preoccupation with the time image of dials, minutes, and hours, harks back to (or was the exemplar for?) Richard's soliloquy. The second scene is without detailed precedent in the chronicles; and the first, while reported rather fully by Hall and Holinshed, is still further elaborated by the play in details which are picked up by the poem—such as the *double-entendre* on "pleasure," for example. Incidentally, Daniel's estimate of Edward's character underwent some change in 1609—he omitted a whole stanza of glowing praise of the new king (VI.113) first introduced in 1601—but this fact need not be attributed solely to the influence of Shakespeare's unflattering presentation of Edward. Other concomitances cited by

Probst, such as the reference to Margaret as a modern Helen and giving Warwick the epithet "king-maker," are doubtful; the elaboration of the Amazon-like character of Margaret, however, and especially having her upbraid the weak Henry on behalf of herself and their son, are strikingly similar in the poem and the play—and it is just these passages that are not to be found in *The True Tragedy*.[28] On the whole, however, the evidence that in 1609 Daniel drew upon *Henry VI* is less extensive and convincing than that he adapted some of the other two plays.

In summary

As might have been expected, Shakespeare knew, valued, and drew upon Daniel's poem for the historical plays he wrote, shortly after the poem's first publication, about the same times and leading characters: Richard II and Henry IV.

As might have been hoped, Daniel, while supercilious toward and consequently ignorant of Shakespeare's plays until about 1604, saw the light thereafter and knew, valued, and drew upon the plays for his important revisions and continuation in 1609 of the figures of Richard II, Henry IV, Henry VI, and Edward IV.

The two poets shared the same view of English history and its interpretation, and Shakespeare drew upon Daniel's formulation of it and his making of it a vehicle for literature.

Although no evidence has been added to suggest any personal intimacy or even acquaintance between the two contemporaries, it is concluded here that there did exist a fruitful interaction between their brain children—and that both of them, and we, have profited by it.

REVISION

As the epistle "To the Reader" (1607) and his various dedications amply testify, Daniel was an inveterate reviser, who did "but long To liue t'amend." A complete analysis of his revisions is properly the function of the student; here an attempt will be made only to describe some of the kinds of changes made in the several editions of *CW* which such a student will find recorded in the textual variants. The large structural changes in *CW* noted below (pp. 55–60) will be broken down somewhat here, first with a listing, in chronological order of

---

[28] Margaret's speech occurs in Book VII, which was added to the poem (as Book VI) in 1601. If, then, there be any indebtedness here, Daniel's putative "interest in Shakespeare" would be pushed back that far.

editions, of changes that involve the deletion, addition, or complete
rewriting of a whole stanza or group of stanzas. No systematic attempt
to categorize or explain these revisions is made; some discussion of
reasons behind them will be found on pp. 7–27 above.

The stanzas in manuscript omitted from Book II in 1595 are in
three sections. Stanzas [17–18] are not much different from the context
of nine stanzas devoted to Richard II's complaint soliloquy; they do
however emphasize Richard's self-centeredness and his attempts to put
the blame for waste on his officers. Stanzas [62] and [64] are part of
another such soliloquy (six stanzas, the other four of which were expunged in 1609), and again were perhaps removed as being repeti-
tious. Stanzas [92–3] were part of Isabel's soliloquy on seeing Richard
enter London a captive; they break up the lyrical, personal tone with
rather prosaic explanatory details. All six stanzas have been character-
ized as "noticeably sympathetic to Richard," and their omission has
been held to "indicate that as early as 1595 the poet had begun to
modify his opinion of Richard."[1] But they show Richard as unappeal-
ingly sympathetic to himself; taking them out removes part of an *un*-
flattering presentation.

The 1595 edition also enlarged the manuscript. I.93–9 interpolates
an apology for Bolingbroke's motives in proceeding against King
Richard. II.67 gives more explanation and fuller background in the
introduction of Isabel, connecting her emotion with the situation.
The manuscript ends with what is stanza 96 in 1595, in the middle of
the meeting scene between Richard and Isabel. Book II is thus
obviously unfinished, but still the scribe has written "Finis" and his
ornamental squiggle just as at the end of Book I.

Three stanzas relating to Richard were added and three deleted
in 1601. I.55,57–8 expand the methods and the consequences of
Richard's treacherous destruction of Gloucester, Warwick, and
Arundel; this is made even more explicit in 1609 by the addition of
marginal glosses. III.67–8,70 in 1595 presented Richard bemoaning
his state, this time in prison; these stanzas are omitted in 1601, perhaps
because they again interjected self-pity into an otherwise philosophical
musing. II.126–7 constituted a laudatory apostrophe, in 1595, to
Essex (and in stanza 130 Essex was coupled with Mountjoy as "O you
two worthies, bewties of our state"); all three stanzas are taken out in
1601, for obvious reasons. Mountjoy's stanza (128) is allowed to remain, though with significant changes (see pp. 312, 348–9). The

---

[1] Cecil C. Seronsy, "Daniel's Manuscript *Civil Wars* with Some Previously Unpublished Stanzas," *Journal of English and Germanic Philology*, 52 (1953), 159–60.

whole passage was to be deleted in 1609, both Elizabeth and Mountjoy being then dead.

In 1609 such stanza changes were many and drastic. In Book I
stanzas 9 and 15–18 of 1601 were eliminated in the interests of tightening up the rapid chronicle of English kings and deleting comparative
reference to foreign states. Stanza 61 (mutual recriminations between
the rival dukes before Richard) was added in consequence of the
change in stanza 60, where the onus of misconstruing Bolingbroke's
words was shifted in 1609 from Mowbray to Richard (see p. 16, n.
17; pp. 300, 344–5). Stanzas 122–3, allowed to stand until now, had
speculated on how one should account for portents and evil omens
and had concluded that "terror must be our knowledge, feare our
skill"; perhaps later Daniel felt this to be unmanly or un-English. In
Book II the deletion of stanza 21 carries further the pruning of
Richard's maudlin personal appeal, already seen at work in 1595, and
likewise stanzas 58–61. Now perhaps the dropping of the two manuscript stanzas is felt not to be enough, and this whole one-sided self-
characterization of Richard comes out, to be replaced by the balanced
appraisal by the author inserted at the end of Book III. Stanza 100 was
an almost lyrical indictment of Bolingbroke and Parliament for ruining Richard's reputation in order to justify his deposition; 109–10
carried this even further, putting into the mouths of some choric
"lookers-on" eloquent indignation at the insolence and impiety of
subjects calling majesty into judgment. All this fire went out of the
poem with Daniel's more considerate evaluation of Henry IV's actions. (The last two lines of the preceding stanza were changed in
1609 and openly ascribed "excuse and pittie" to the onlookers for
Richard's "defects.") Stanzas 113–14 and half of 115 were added in
1609. They are a paraphrase, sustained by a text gloss, of the Archbishop of Canterbury's Machiavellian sermon justifying power.
Daniel went back to the chronicles for this episode, evidently to get
holy backing for his later pragmatic view of the usurpation. But the
last half of stanza 115 and stanza 116, though tinkered with somewhat,
remain as an unexorcised misgiving—if Henry IV's cause "had had as
lawfull and as sure a ground" as had his virtues and his noble heart,
none of the bloody strife would have ensued; and Book II ends on
that note. But previously there had been nine stanzas more of wistful
peroration, claiming further that by Elizabeth's time England would
have been ruler of the whole world, with Essex and Mountjoy as its
ornaments and Daniel as its triumphant poet laureate. Essex' stanzas
came out in 1601, as we have seen; Mountjoy's was subtly changed in
1601 and maybe deleted altogether at his death in 1606; and finally

Daniel sacrificed the whole thing, perhaps feeling that such a celebration of the Tudor dream would not be grateful to King James. Daniel was taking himself out of the poem by this time, anyway.

Books III and IV carry out extensively the new emphasis on the doctrine of might makes right. Stanzas 10–11, added in 1609, cap a process of modifying all the stanzas from the beginning of Book III: They condone pragmatism as against ideal "right," but the modification is not completely accomplished—the earlier emphasis is still to be perceived here and there. III.79, part of the description of Richard's death scene, had already been tinkered with somewhat in 1601— Daniel was not sure where he wanted to put "sacred"—but now all of Richard's sacredness, holiness, hallowedness, comeliness, gracefulness, and sweetness were sacrificed to the new emphasis; and the excision reverberated both backward and forward for two stanzas, causing almost complete revision. The nine stanzas at the end of Book III, with the documentary glosses Daniel often used to back up his reconsiderations, were added to balance off Richard's account and give him his quietus.

The new Book IV immediately substitutes Henry IV as a sympathetic protagonist; stanzas 1–14, added in 1609, point out all the foreign and domestic troubles he has incurred. 17–19 give more particulars of the insubordination of the Percies; 26–7 take the place of what had been stanza 91 of the old Book III—facts and particulars of the Percies' bill of complaint (with an identifying gloss added to stanza 25) instead of an intrusive moralizing stanza. Stanzas 29–32 are added to give Henry's reply in detail—arguments and evidence to vindicate his actions later. (The influence of—or upon—Shakespeare's presentation of all this is discussed at length elsewhere in this introduction, pp. 22–6. Here we might just notice that Daniel's treatment, unlike Shakespeare's dramatic clash of personalities, tends to explain and objectify the causes of Henry's feud with the Percies.) Stanzas 41–2 provide some psychological and moral filling-in on Henry's attempts at a truce before the Battle of Shrewsbury; whereas another stanza (the old III.103) is removed perhaps because it moralizes, and describes Shrewsbury as a stalemate, a mistake, in which both sides were bloodguilty. Stanzas 50–2 substitute for the story of the Blunts that of Douglas' vain search for the king, who had provided himself with three alter egos; Daniel praises and rationalizes this stratagem and ends by stating baldly that Henry at Shrewsbury proved the tenure of his right "By that especial right of kings: the *Sword;*" in 53.2 what had been paradoxically called "a loosing victorie" now is seen to be "a sauing victorie" in spite of the cost of much good blood. Stanza 54, added, provides material for considering Hotspur a worthy antogonist and introduces, with a revamped 55, twenty-eight new stanzas which retail Henry's struggle with Northumberland, Glendower, and foreign enemies, and his efforts to train his sons—especially the prince—to maintain his dynasty. The revival of rebellion in the north and suspicion of Prince Henry's ambition illustrate the cares of "the King (who neuer had his brow Seene free from sweat, nor hart from trouble rid)," and modulate nicely into the concluding scene, where (in stanza 84) Daniel salvages the image of Henry's body as a castle whose walls have been worn thin so that "th'illightned soule" can now see its way clear. It is a good image (Shakespeare borrowed it; see above, p. 23) in that it pulls together the personal and the dynastic elements which have been operating, and provides a focus for the ending of the book. The old III.117 is deleted as emphasizing too much the dying Henry's remorse about his crown: "clyming care" had led him to "passe those bounds," and he hated to think *how* the crown was gained; old III.119–20 likewise, having imputed to Henry the deathbed idea of getting pardon for his sins by giving back the crown "to whom it seem'd to appertaine." Daniel wants to keep the idea of remorse, but the question of hereditary right versus conquest is too important a tension in the ensuing struggle to be prejudiced at this point.

The book (as Book III) had ended with a stanza appealing to the Muse and to his patron for help to continue the poem. In 1601 the "worthy" addressed was increased to "great Wortheys"; the whole stanza is deleted in 1609; see note to IV. (129.5) below.

Book V begins by leaving out one of two stanzas introducing Henry V's upbraiding the poet for not telling the good things of his reign: The deleted stanza had focused attention on what "*I* feele here now in passing by These blessed times." Stanza 36 had been the first of a series moralizing on the mischief of doing wrong with good cause, but it is turgid and contorted and was properly blue-penciled. Three stanzas are pulled out of Queen Margaret's speech (102–5, in 1609); why these three were thought worse than the rest is hard to say, unless because they have Daniel telling the reader what Margaret surmised that Suffolk would have said. Coleridge reacted strongly to this passage, even without knowing that it had been cut in half (see note to V.102 ff. below).

The remaining books of the poem did not seem to call for any major reconsideration: Daniel was apparently satisfied with his handling of the political situation. Book VI provides some stylistic alterations. After stanza 7 two stanzas had been devoted to a Spenserian attempt at extended simile—Jack Cade's mob likened to a "greedy

Pyrat." By themselves they are vivid and effective, but Daniel's later eye doubtless saw the difficulty of viewing an unwieldly crowd under the aspect of a trim and speedy pirate ship. After stanza 12 another simile-stanza had drawn upon Daniel's recollections of "thousand-branched Po" to illustrate the ramifications of "that mighty Familie, The faire distended stock of Neuiles kind;" 1609 deleted it—is it just because of a toning down of ornamentation or is this another example of Daniel's later reversion to insularity, with an unwilling-ness to celebrate a foreign river or his erstwhile "sweete Lombardie"? After 45 a stanza had been devoted to the elaboration of Elizabeth's unique immunity to Pandora's implementation of Nemesis' strife-stirrings; its context is left in, but this, saying that Elizabeth was "secure (as intimate with fate)," comes out, together with the substitu-tion of "dignitie" for "eternitie" in 47–8 (see also note to VI.(49.4)).

VII.10 had incorporated another river simile into the over-all water imagery of its context, that of the Rodon at Wansted, Mountjoy's country place; it was deleted in 1609.[2] After 99 there had been two

[2] (See also the notes to I.5.1, II.(126), and VII.10.) This is an interesting deletion. The image of a river, springing obscurely but strengthened with tributaries until it becomes mighty and powerful, destined to lose its sovereignty in the ocean but sometimes giving battle before submitting, is a favorite one of Daniel's in describing the rise of rebellious factions. One finds the same treatment given to the Thames, the Severn, and the Rhine. But the use of the image is also indicative of Daniel's never resolved dichotomy of feeling about the sacredness of kingship on the one hand and the magnanimity of some of the engulfed nobles on the other. Here stanzas 9, 11, and 13 back up the image—or, rather, in 1601 Daniel dared to illustrate the dryness of York's hopes with a personal allusion:

> So humble *Rodon, Wainsteedes* sweete delight,*
> That waters *Mountioyes* solitarie rest,
> Be'ing checkt with Sommers heate, shrinkes out of sight
> Downe in his narrow bed, as quite supprest,
> That lately Swolne with forrayne-ayding might,
> Ran boundlesse ouer all, and all possest:
> And now so feeble growne, hath left no more
> Then scarse sustaynes his variable store.
> * *Rodon the Riuer by Wainsteed.*

(Mountjoy had bought Wansted from Essex in 1599; Daniel's references elsewhere to its "solitary brooke" and its "quiet shore" suggest that he was invited there to recreate and to write by both owners.) But is there also a cryptic topical allusion? Remembering Spenser's "Somers-heat" pun in *Prothalamion* (1596), we note that Edward Somerset, Earl of Worcester, had been in the Essex-Mountjoy-South-ampton clique but apparently saw the danger far enough ahead to leave it and consolidate his position with the loyalist faction: he took an active part in Essex' capture and testified against him at the trial. Had Somerset also "checked" Mountjoy between 1599 and 1601? Had something happened to enable Somerset to "quite suppress" Mountjoy's rising reputation as a successful and beloved

stanzas describing Henry VI's momentary triumph at being recaptured by Queen Margaret, and defending his "agreeing" with the other faction when they held him captive. Perhaps Daniel changed his mind about this; perhaps he just felt that it was irrelevant to the context and intrusive. The stanza following 109 had had an important statement. After praising the royal qualities of the Earl of March (shortly to be Edward IV), Daniel seemed here to be coming to a conclusion about at least one of his doubts: "This is my side, my Muse must hold with kings." He was tempted to end the poem here and be satisfied with Edward's approximation of a perfect right to the crown ("all Maiesties best partes Both pers'nage, bloud, vertue, powre and wit"). But in 1609 he wrote Book VIII, which again raises the dilemma between right and peace, and Daniel sadly took out the stanza.

Book VIII was never revised. It will perhaps repay some comparative study, in evidence that Daniel's spirits were freshened in 1609. Book VII (added in 1601 as Book VI) was perhaps the dullest in the poem—Daniel felt bogged down in the frustrations of his subject. But such a 1609 revision of VII.12.7 as "thus t'wards kings abus'd their swordes" to "thus against their Kings draw swords" seems to indicate that Daniel became more of a Yorkist and was thus able to find some hope for continuing toward the eventual reconciling union. In 1601 near the end of Book VI his Muse was "but in the midst of her long way"; in 1609 not only did Book VI become Book VII, thus leaping the classical halfway hurdle, but in vision too his Muse could be said to be "but little past halfe her long way" (VII.111.1).

These large structural changes and the shifting about of whole stanzas or blocks of stanzas are the most striking but also the "coarsest" examples of revision. Daniel also habitually implemented his large changes by reworking smaller units: parts of stanzas, lines, sentences,

administrator of Irish affairs ("lately Swolne with forrayne-ayding might")? The context of the stanza—York's uprising against Henry VI—was, as not unusual, fatally tempting to Daniel in its pat resemblance: a gloss added in 1601 to VI. 11 points it up: "This Rebellion was thought to be fostred by some friend of the Duke of Yorke, who at this time was in Ireland, sent thither to appease a Rebellion: which hee effected in such sort, as got him and his linage exceeding loue & liking with that people euer after . . ." And to make it more interesting, there was of course that other Somerset who was York's mortal enemy. But Mountjoy seems to have been riding the crest of the wave, retained the queen's favor, and was made Earl of Devonshire by James in 1603; the only specific indication of a possible "checking" is the refusal of his request for recall from Ireland in October 1600. Daniel got himself in trouble with Mountjoy by implicating him in the *Philotas* Star Chamber inquiry of 1605; he may have determined to delete this hazardous stanza then. At any rate it came out in 1609, even after Daniel's *Funeral Poeme* on Mountjoy had claimed to "settle his account."

clauses, phrases, single words, even single letters and punctuation marks. Some categories of these will be attempted below; taking just one of his areas of change, the general progression toward a cooler approach to both Richard II and Henry IV, we note here the following:

I.84.1 in both the manuscript and the 1595 edition picked up, from the preceding description of "home broyles," with "And all this makes for thee, ô *Bullingbroke*"—the coordinating conjunction rather connecting him with detestable anarchy. 1601 simply changed "And" to "But," and this somehow changes the feeling, mitigates Bolingbroke's responsibility. I.85.1 called Richard "this absent King"; it was changed in 1609 to "this absent Lord"—does this subtly indicate that Richard wasn't enough of a king? Perhaps it is a reverberation, in rereading, from 84.6: "Who, crowned a King, a King yet must not die." II.108.8 had said that Richard's glory and name, at his deposition, were buried, "Intomb'd for euermore in others blame"; it became "Intomb'd both in his owne and others blame." One of the most persuasive ways of partially exculpating Henry was to present his deeds as *faits accomplis* rather than in the process: III.7.8, "Seeking all meanes t'oppresse the aduerse part" becomes "And rayses them [his partisans], by crushing th'aduerse part." III.6.1 even goes into the pluperfect construction, with other subtle changes: from "But well he *thought* his *powre* made all *seem* plaine" to "But, *after, hauing made* his *title* plaine." In both the manuscript and the 1595 edition I.86.2 had said that what Bolingbroke does "He doth with cunning traine and pollicy"; in 1601 the whole climate of sympathy is verbally changed to "Relying on his friends fidelitie." In the manuscript I.100.1 had, after Bolingbroke's nightly vision, "The morning sonne he first salutes wth blood"; new stanzas were inserted in 1595, and their impact is helped by the change of this line to "But, by degrees he ventures now on blood." IV.87.8 is a neat example of economy: the dying Henry addresses his crown, "which with blood I got" (1601); the simple change of "got" to "held" mitigates the blood shed, from that of an anointed king to that of the rebellious Percies. II.110.7–8,

> And all this did he but t'haue leaue to liue,
> The which was all he crau'd that they would giue

became in 1609

> To testifie his act, and doth professe
> To do the same with most free willingnesse,

shifting Richard's plea for life (which Daniel had apparently invented) to willing acquiescence in the deposition. And III.66.7–8, in
1595, has Richard exonerate himself:

> O know tis others sin not my desart
> And I could wish I were but as thou art.

In 1601 this disturbing implication is modulated into

> And pittiest this my miserable fall:
> For pittie must haue part, enuie not all

—we can still pity Richard even if we must pin the blame on him.
III.2 and 3 will repay close examination into the numerous changes,
small but cumulative, which help alter the reader's general feeling.
Daniel had a sensitive ear for these overtones; it was perhaps his version of the poet's ear for the *mot juste*. Finally, II.59–60 provide
examples of stanzas almost wholly rewritten: Bolingbroke's truculent
and insolent tone is metamorphosed into sorrowful firmness;
Richard's reply is changed around a bit but not much altered. It
should be noted that Daniel is "framing" all these speeches—he is
creating character, not reporting history. And the myth-maker has the
right to change his myth.

As to the more technical aspects of the craft of revision, analysis will
have a large field for exercise in *CW*. A broad generalization is that
there was a conscientious progression toward consolidation and organ-
izational unity, and consistency of form; but the implementation of
this program takes many and intricate shapes.

The corrections made by Daniel in the manuscript itself, and
changes from the manuscript reading in 1595, provide some interesting data possibly pointing to dictation, or more probably to the
author's reading his own holograph to the fair-copy scribe. It is difficult
to see how a copyist would *read* "ought" for "oft," "their" for

(I.72.1)

"far," "And" for "Had"; but they are sufficiently similar in sound,
or unaccented, to explain the error in hearing. It is probable that
Daniel pronounced "outwardly" something like "uttardly"—in I.55.4

the scribe wrote "vttwardlie" for it—so that the "vtterlie" which
Daniel had to change to "vttwardlie" in I.[44].4 (economically not
disturbing the first and last syllables) would be more plausible as

an audio than a visual error. Omitted words, especially those connectives or relatives slurred over in speech, point the same way;
likewise past participles with a written "-ed" which Daniel corrected
to the elided " 'd." Perhaps the best of these is in II.69.6: the scribe
wrote "sits vpright"; Daniel corrected to "sits s'vpright" (that is, "sits
so upright"). Daniel evidently failed to catch all such errors in manuscript, for he changed a good many more in 1595: "require" to "repine"; "lightlie" to "likely"; "thvniustest" to "the iustest"; "dissolation" to "desolation"; "choose" to "chose"; "the" to "those"; "In" to
"On"; "by" to "buy"; "The whilst" to "The whiles"; "a man" to "a
name."[3] II.68.5 in the manuscript, "Then backe she stands, and then
desire was faine," was half-corrected to "desires was faine" in 1595 and
1601, and the 1609 version "and then desires as faine" seems likely to
have been what Daniel originally spoke. A "w^{ch}" lined through and
followed by "y^{t}" seems to point to either the scribe's immediate correction of a wrongly anticipated relative, or Daniel's revision while dictat-
ing—perhaps his ear warned him of the cacophony in "which vanisht"
that had escaped detection because of never having been sounded
before. None of these examples is decisive, of course; but the likelihood of some form of dictation somewhere in the transmission of the

---

[3] This (I.22.7) is a borderline case. The context introduces Richard II:

> Then when this Richard first the crowne possest
> Second of name a man in two accurst
> And well we might haue mist all but the first.

"name, a name" is obviously correct, and it appears so in 1595. Seronsy (p. 154)
seems to think that "man" was Daniel's original term and that his correction in
1595 is of his own original "obscurity"; this is, I think, unlikely. But was it mis-
read, or misheard, by the scribe? The words do not sound too much alike; but on
the other hand in the manuscript "name" has a clear "e" on the end, and "man"
just as clearly has not. It seems improbable that a copyist would mis*read* a word
which he had just written correctly. The present editor opts for dictation.

II.17.6 in MS has clearly "appiers," which is changed to "aspires" in 1595. The
former could be a sound-error or a misreading of a long "s" as the first "p"; the
difference in the form of the written letters is perhaps of more weight than the
making of nonwords out of like sounds: Scribes (like some modern typists)
apparently were often indifferent to the sense of what they wrote. In II.60.4 this
one wrote "never" for "ever," with no qualms about reducing the line to nonsense.

author's thought to the reader should be kept in mind and may resolve certain cruces unexplainable otherwise.[4]

The wholesale deletion of expletives and exclamatives to which Daniel subjected all his works took place for *CW* in 1601, but several times "O" in 1595 became "Ah" in 1601 before being expunged in 1609. For the most part, each subsequent edition was provided with more copious marginal glosses than its predecessor, both in identification of historical persons and places and in explanatory expansion of the text—a beginning of this practice is to be found even in the manuscript. Often the gloss assimilated material omitted when the text was changed. Some selectiveness was exercised, however. The gloss to I.60 in 1595 was expanded in 1601 and deleted wholly in 1609; II.27 in 1595, shortened in all subsequent editions. III.68 glossed the name of the monarch mentioned in the text, 1595; the name was inserted in the text in 1601 so the gloss was deleted; the incident was quoted in Latin in 1609. In IV.34, 47, 49, 50, 53 glosses were omitted or substituted for in 1609 when the accompanying text was changed; in V.11 the identification in 1595 was deleted in 1601.

There is evidence that Daniel took some pains to check his facts—names, rank, places, dates, differences among his sources—but not that he made any exhaustive re-examination. He did, of course, try to keep up with the times: During the published career of *CW* his patrons died or changed, political events had their repercussions on his interpretation of history, and, most far-reaching of all, the "glory of Eliza's days" came to an end, and the celebrant of the Tudor dynasty had to make his way in a Stuart court. Such revisions range from obvious changes from present or present perfect to simple past tenses, to a toning down of Elizabethan hyperbole: I.3.8, "That glorie, which no age could euer showe," became in 1609 "which few Times could euer showe"; the next lines, which in 1595 began "O sacred Goddesse, I no Muse, but thee, Inuoke," were changed only to "Thou sacred Goddesse" in 1601 (in line with the general excision of "O's"); but in

---

[4] One is tempted to hypothecate reading or dictation to the compositor in the print shop, too, to account for certain homonyms or near-homonyms: "wakened" (VII.29.1) in 1601 became "weakened" in 1609, whereas the 1601 version is the better reading; "infect" (VII.30.3) in 1601 became "infest," producing no significant change in meaning. Changes in spelling from one edition to another, especially consistent ones, seem psychologically more understandable if the compositor were being read to than if he had a picture of the word before his eye. Finally, there is the curious facility for "economical" revision mentioned below. But all these are unsupported guesses and merely add a few illustrations to R. B. McKerrow's discussion of the topic (*Introduction to Bibliography*, Oxford, 1927, pp. 241–6).

1609 we have "Come sacred *Virtue*"—a dea-fication perhaps more pleasing to James, and certainly to Daniel's new royal patroness, Anne of Denmark. Likewise, in VI.47.8 Elizabeth had been endowed with a "large Patent of eternitie"; now it is "of her dignitie."

Making a decision on the reason for a change is rendered very difficult by Daniel's concern with technical minutiae, and what a sympathetic analyst would call nicety and precision, an unsympathetic one fussiness and pedantry. We have no holograph or working manuscript, ✗ so there is no question of watching his original creative process at work; I doubt that much of a palimpsest would show up if we had such a manuscript, because of Daniel's welling fluency. But he began almost immediately to tinker, to file, to try new combinations; our corrected fair-copy manuscript here is a good example. Besides the correction of the scribe's errors (even in spelling, punctuation, elision) and omissions, there are revisions, chiefly single-word substitutions.

(II.6.5)

And, as the variants recorded below show at large, he kept up this process throughout his publishing career,

> Like to the curious builder who this yeare
> Puls downe, and alters what he did the last
> As if the thing in doing were more deare
> Then being done, & nothing likes thats past.
>   ("To the Reader," 1607, ll. 7–10.)

I do not believe that it is concern for the mot juste, such as we are accustomed to celebrate in modern symbolists, imagists, or metaphoricians (nor even the need for apostrophic adequacy of Daniel's admirer Wordsworth, who spent a morning searching for an epithet for the cuckoo), so much as exactness in expression, "neatness of dress." The changes rarely startle us with luminous inevitability—often we have to puzzle out why the new version is better, and are at a loss to ascribe it to a feeling for diction, for rhythm, for euphony, for conciseness, for contextual relevance, for formal accuracy, for syntactical or grammatical precision, for emphasis, and so on and on. Daniel seems to have had an increasing fondness for antithesis as one of several means of tightening up his expression. One can see a diminution of his earlier penchant for elaborate plays on words, puns, and "turns," as well as the reduction of apostrophic address which accompanied the removal of himself from the poem. But except for the systematic deletion of "O's" and "Ah's," and such wholesale changes as of "that" to "who," each revision must be examined for itself; and usually some genuine amelioration, however slight, can be perceived.

The *Defence of Ryme,* first published in 1603, provides some doctrine which shows that Daniel *thought* he was working by principles, at least of metrics. He asks rhetorically, for example,

> who knows not that we cannot kindely answere a feminine number with a masculine Ryme . . . as *Weaknes* with *Confesse, Nature* and *Indure* . . . this change of number in a Poem of one nature sits not so wel, as to mixe vncertainly, feminine Rymes with masculine, which, euer since I was warned of that deformitie by my kinde friend and countriman Maister *Hugh Samford,*[5] I haue always so auoyded it, as there are not aboue two couplettes in that kinde in all my Poem of the Ciuill warres: and I would willingly if I coulde, haue altered it in all the rest, holding feminine Rymes to be fittest for Ditties, and either to be set certaine, or else by themselues . . .

Just what "femininity" means here is a bit confused. "Feminine number" seems to go along with the identification of it elsewhere in the *Defence* with a trochaic or falling accent, and to concern only dissyllabic words. And Daniel has followed his precept: I have not found even the two couplets which mix a feminine and masculine *rhyme.* But another dictum, that we should not "raise the last sillable, which falles out very vnnaturall in *Desolate, Funerall, Elizabeth, Prodigall,* and in all the rest sauing the Monosillables," does not fare so well in his practice. There are fifty-six couplets violating this principle in the poem as it appeared in 1601, and nineteen more in Book VIII when it was added in 1609. In 1609, in some cases, he actually changes the couplet but leaves the mixture of rhymes—"head: pittiéd" to "head: colouréd"; and there are even some of his own *exempla horrenda:* "fate : fortunate," "Elizabeth : death," "wretchednesse : successe," "generall : all." In the more than three hundred mixtures in the A and B rhymes of his *ottava rima* stanzas, changes have been very seldom made and as often as not in the "wrong" direction. Considerations of exactness sometimes overcame the rule: V.17.5 in 1595, "Yet he those vnordred troupes so led," becomes "Those long vnordred

[5] Just when Master Samford performed this office we cannot tell, at least from *CW,* since there is no significant quantity of alterations of this sort in the revisions of 1601. E. H. Miller, "Samuel Daniel's Revisions in *Delia," Journal of English and Germanic Philology, 53* (1954), claims that it must have been about 1594, "for, until that time, Daniel had shown no interest in effecting changes in his feminine rhymes" (p. 59).

troupes so marshalléd"—one corrects unorderedness in troops by marshalling not leading. The only consistent attempt to ameliorate concerns the "raised" ending "-ĭón," especially in polysyllabic words. Several times Daniel adds a monosyllabic word in order that these last three letters may be pronounced as a single short syllable; but even here the mixture does not bother him so much as the ending, and once he even revises in the opposite direction. Finally, a single stanza will illustrate many failures to follow his own doctrine: II.110 rhymes (A) "generall : all : call"; (B) "fealtie : dignitie : hie"; (C) "professe : willingnesse"; and the couplet was a change in 1609 from the previous "liue : giue."

All of this goes to show that with regard to *one* of the mechanics of poetry (of which Daniel considered himself sufficiently a master to write a treatise against the eminent Campion) our reviser adhered to no system which will stand confrontation with the facts.[6] We are to

---

[6] T. S. Omond (*English Metrists*, Oxford, 1921, p. 30) comes to much this same conclusion about the *Defence of Ryme*. But should we hold Daniel to his theory? The testimony of a practicing poet should have at least equal weight with that of a critical analyst, and Coleridge ignores the *Defence* to focus his almost empathic understanding of Daniel upon the *CW* itself:

> It is perhaps worth noticing as an excellence suited to the style of the Poetry (whatever may be thought of that) that the accents and scansion of Daniel's Lines more assist the reading of the sense, than in any work, I know. If the Line runs ill to you, you may be sure, you have not read it in it's exact sense. The whole represents a grave easy man talking seriously to his friends. Sometimes too he breaks up, for a moment, the feeling of versification; but never by a *contradiction to* it, but by heightening the feeling of conversation . . .

> Is it from any hobby-horsical Love of our old writers . . . or is it a real Beauty, the interspersion I mean (in stanza poems) of rhymes from polysyllables—such as Eminence, Obedience, Reverence [see VII.5, below]? To my ear they convey not only a relief from variety, but a *sweetness* as of repose—and the understanding they gratify by reconciling Verse with the whole wide extent of good Sense. Without being distinctly conscious of such a notion, having it rather than reflecting it, (for one may think in the same way as onè may see and hear), I seem to be made to know that I need have no fear; that there is nothing excellent in itself which the Poet cannot express accurately and naturally, nay no good word. . . .

> [Cf. Daniel's phrase, "verse and vertue," quoted below. There was an anticipation of it in Southwell's prefatory epistle to *Saint Peter's Complaint* (1595): "wherein it may be seene how well, verse and vertue sute together."]

> See [VI.46.4]—where there are 3 emphatic and 3 subemphatic words. . . .

> In the first Line of Stanza 16 of [Bk. VI] is a Pun in it's right place & passion. [See below, p. 51.]

look pragmatically, then, at each revision, at least the isolated and less extensive ones.

Daniel's penchant for what I have called tinkering may be considered the natural expression of an almost prehensile sense of "justness," which we may observe operating in a fascinatingly economical fashion.[7] Analogies might be the coordination of eye and hand of the compositor justifying a line of type, the mosaic-worker or puzzle-fitter using substitutions and slight pressures to accomplish the final tightness of the work, the stone-wall builder weighing and turning his

---

This kind of remark, by the deviser of the "new principle" of accent-versification exhibited in *Christabel*, should make us wary of limiting our appreciation of Daniel's metrics to the scruples induced in the poet by such as Master Samford (perhaps while Daniel was still smarting from one of "snarling Ben Jonson's" sneers, and cowed to boot by rumblings in his direction from the Star Chamber); he had recovered his self-confidence sufficiently in 1607 to write these lines:

> I know I shalbe read, among the rest
> So long as men speake english, and so long
> As verse and vertue shalbe in request
> Or grace to honest industry belong:
> And England since I vse thy present tongue
> Thy forme of speech thou must be my defence
> If to new eares, it seems not well exprest
> *For though I hold not accent I hold sence.*
>   And since the measures of our tong we see
> Confirmd by no edict of power doth rest
> But onely vnderneath the regencie
> Of vse and fashion, which may be the best
> Is not for my poore forces to contest
> But as the Peacock, seeing himselfe to weake
> Confest the Eagle fairer farre to be
> And yet not in his feathers but his beake.
> Authoritie of powerful censure may
> Preiudicate the forme wherein we mould
> This matter of our spirite, but if it *pay*
> *The eare with substance,* we haue what wee wold
> For that is all which must our credit hold.
> The rest (how euer gay, or seeming rich
> It be in fashion, wise men will not wey)
> *The stamp will not allow it, but the touch.*
> ("To the Reader," ll.59–82; italics mine.)

Most of this seems to be directed at Jonson; perhaps Daniel showed a covert distaste for the man who called his output "Works," by changing in 1609 "this great worke" to "this great labour" (*CW*, I.4.2).

[7] Dayton N. Dennett, in his edition of *Cleopatra* (unpublished Cornell dissertation, 1951, p. cxlviii) uses the rather more pejorative term "parsimonious" and ascribes it to meagerness of resources.

shapes until they lock into place. We have examined the larger revisions, in which the radicalness of the new idea requires a new start
and a complete restatement. But more often, and more characteristically, I think, do we find Daniel retaining the original materials
which flowed so readily from his pen, and then setting himself the task
of putting the best words in the best order with the least number of
moves, almost as in a chess problem. This economy is illustrated at its
most thrifty in the manuscript corrections, where even in a fair copy
Daniel salvages parts of wrong words instead of rewriting them: in
II.53.8 the scribe had telescoped the line, and ended "dreames was
trueth." Daniel careted in the missing phrase, then took the medial
"e" out of "trueth" and added it on the end, "truthe"; and changed
"was" to "were" by erasing the "s" to substitute "re" but salvaged the
"w" and overwrote the "a" into an "e," using part of the original
letter.[8] There are several of these salvagings in the manuscript.

Shifts in word order are perhaps the commonest examples of this
final twisting of the line into shape. Sometimes it is just for smoother
rhythm or in the interests of an iamb instead of a trochee or spondee:
VII.61.4 "Onley a feeble body and a Crowne" to "A feeble body onley,
and a Crowne"; often for syntactical precision, to put modifiers or
auxiliaries or subjects where they bear most properly: II.64.2, "what
he never thought could bee" to "what hee thought could neuer be";
sometimes to clear up a possible ambiguity: VII.72.8, "Seemes as re-

[8] How these minutiae can be operative may be seen in a difference of opinion
about a manuscript reading. Seronsy (p. 158) accepts "inerr" (II.[62].3), although
it is an unsatisfactory reading for several reasons; I read "marr" on the grounds
that Daniel has caught the scribal anomaly and has changed the middle letter to
"a," letting the original "in" stand for his "m," as well it might. (This can-

not be checked against the compositor's reading, for the word is in one of the
manuscript stanzas omitted in 1595.) My reading is given weight, I believe, by the
fact that in the line immediately preceding the scribe had written "coyce";
Daniel has interpolated a new "c" as first letter and has written an "h" over the
original "c," using it as part of the new letter.

seru'd to be for something wrought" to "Reserued seemes, for some
thing to be wrought" (where "to be" is tied down to one meaning);
sometimes to avoid internal rhyme: II.75.1, "What might hee be saide
shee" to "What might he be she sayd"; sometimes to achieve more
complex effects: IV.45.6, "Thundring confused, murmurs horrible"
is a fairly tame parallelism; "Confused thundring-murmurs horrible"
is more onomatopoetic, really confused and piled up.

The same basic technique may be found in more extensive revisions. V.53.4, "Seeking his bountie, not his powre t'haue knowne," is
in the middle of a stanza wrought almost entirely of Popean antitheses;
to avoid too many zeugmas (and/or to use a more vivid word without
padding the line, or to insure that "have" be not taken for an auxili-
ary?), Daniel changes to "He chokes his powre, to haue his bountie
knowne." The verbal activity thus generated then spills over into the
first line of the next stanza, where "With such a weake, good, feeble,
godly King" becomes, with a simple orthographic stroke, the much
more complex "weake-good, feeble-godly." I.10.2 attempted a zeugma,
an antithesis, and a paradox: "The great outworne with Warre, or
slaine in peace"; a less ambitious but more sensible version comes
out of the refitting to "The great men spent in peace, or slaine in
fight," which perhaps began as required by the new rhyme-word. III.
5 dilated upon the undermining-water image of stanza 4; Daniel did
some (rather rare) good blue-penciling here—the whole stanza is telescoped into a new capping couplet of stanza 4, tying the metaphor in
where it belongs, as a climax and not diluted by repetition in a whole
stanza.

The necessity for rhyming makes the salvaging of sounds in revision
obvious, but this kind of economy also shows up as a suggestive re-
source elsewhere than at the end of the line. Daniel apparently wished
to tone down Richard's responsibility in I.30.6, so he changed "presumed to take the raigne" to "and so assum'd the raine," where some
echo of the sound perhaps gave him a short cut to the new word he
wanted. He can even economize on a complete reversal. In IV.53.2, as
part of his general shift in attitude toward Henry IV's actions at
Shrewsbury, Daniel wants to say that it *was* a famous victory despite
heavy losses, because it established Henry as undisputed sovereign.
He had first called it a "loosing victory"—why beat about the bush to
state his change of mind? He just picks up the antonym with the same
metric value—"sauing" will fit as well as "loosing." "Repriz'd" in VII.
Argument.1 better describes the shuttling back and forth of captive
Henry VI than "repriu'd" (its cognate but already shifting form), and
is in accord with Daniel's practice here of being descriptive rather

than judicial—whether it is sound or etymology working is hard to
say. Daniel sometimes substitutes a Latin equivalent: "auersiue" for
"a way-ward" for greater precision; "Martiall *Worster*" for "warlike
Worster" to avoid alliteration. Or he will change the syntax for greater
precision while preserving the form: "Vnwilling would proceed" to
"Vnwilling to proceed"; "H'is . . . set" to "hee . . . set." Or salvage
part of a word by using a more exact form, substituting a finite form
for a participle, or a derivative for a gerund to be more definitely passive: "his committing" to "his commitment." There are quite a few
examples, too, of what might be a kind of economy, the elimination of
padding or tautology in order to get more ideas in the same space
(sometimes this is done by, or in conjunction with, putting the over-
flow in a marginal gloss): I.30.7–8, "but as now he lendes his eare And
youthfull counsell willingly doth heare" to "now his eare he lends To
youthfull counsell, and his lustes attends." These are all miniscule
points, but Daniel does make the changes; and *CW* provides a quarry
for the useful exercise of one's powers of distinction and assessment.

There is considerable evidence that Daniel grew more cautious, or
conservative, or noncommittal, or objective (deleting first-person pro-
nouns, for example), or tentative in his judgments. As early as 1595
he was changing "Neuer" to "Hardlie," "would" to "could," "only"
to "chiefly," "all the rest" to "most of all the rest"; this proceeds to an
attitude of explanation rather than of moral or emotional censure:
I.37.1–2:

>   (MS) Which soone, with many others had their ende,
>   Cruelly slaine without the course of right
>
> (1595, 1601) Who soone, with many others had their ende,
>   All put to death without the course of right
>
>   (1609) And here had many worthy men their ende,
>   Without all forme, or any course of Right.

It shows up sometimes in assessing facts or motives. In I.47.8, up to
1609, Count St. Paul's advice about Gloucester was "Strangled or
poison'd secret let him be," but then it became "In secret sort, let him
dispatched bee"; Queen Margaret (V.64.3), who in 1601 could "Haue
matcht the worthiest that the world hath knowne," in 1609 could
"Haue beene among the Worthies of renowne." The anti-Richard
parliament (II.97.1) gathers "And now doth Enuie articles obiect"
against him; but in 1609 it is only "they" who bring in "diuerse articles." A transitional change may be observed in I.59.3: Henry is first
described as "worthily great Iohn of *Gaunt's* first sonne"; the change

of emphasis, "sonne and heire to mighty *Iohn* of *Gaunt*," shows perhaps the direction Daniel is taking in his evaluation of the actions of the principals in the civil war—from a feeling for motives and personal worth to judicious assessment of legal claims to the crown.

Yet generalization on this point is as hazardous as elsewhere. In many revisions one reacts first to what seems to be a feeling for exactness of diction, only to perceive that some kind of judgment is involved too: I.33.6, "this confus'd disordering" becomes "such confus'd misgouerning," and tautology is removed with an increment of judgment. "Disorder" is one of Daniel's favorite words, but this example and I.116.2, where "Disordered mortalitie" becomes "Disorder'd proud mortalitie," might show that even he came to recognize that a term gets trite through indiscriminate and unqualified use. But he can return to its effective use: in VII.1.1 York's precarious ascendency was first described as "Vnnatural Authoritie"; in 1609, as the long added gloss points up, Daniel realized that the condition was essentially political or legalistic rather than in the realm of moral law and changed to "Disordinate Authoritie."

Another circumstance accounts for a good many changes which refuse to fit into any reasonable category: reverberation. The most obvious kind is in rhyme, where a change in one word requires new rhymes in its partners. Daniel began the practice already in the fair-copy manuscript: II.[35] shows how any one of the three B-rhyme words might have started the shift. The reverberation has been car-

ried through mechanically, for the most part, as two exceptions prove. In III.16.5 Daniel has his eye on the wrong sequence and supplies a B instead of an A rhyme; in VII.58 he has changed "disobedience" to "disobediencie" and "reuerence" to "iollitie" but has forgotten about "defence." Much the same are the shifts in agreement (number, tense, person, etc.) called for by the initial revision. The addition or deletion of a stanza or stanzas requires new transitions and connectives. But this kind of thing has pervasive though often unaccountable conse-

quences. The change of a single word upsets the syllabic balance:
V.19.5–6

> Ease was not suffered with a greedy eye
> T'examine states, or priuate wealthes to rate

becomes

> Exactors did not, with a greedy eye,
> Examine states, or priuate riches rate.

"Exactors" is the stronger word, but its three syllables require a chain
of syllabic adjustments which in turn require grammatical shifts, in-
terchange of particles, and word substitution. Many stanzas are found
to be more or less rewritten without any significant change in idea.
What starts the chain reaction? Sometimes one can trace it back to its
apparent source, but more often it seems to be no more than momen-
tum, the aftermath of adding or deleting a stanza. Within a stanza we
get this kind of thing (VII.63.4–6):

> Ambition fayles not, to be here in poost
> And comes with greater glory to appeare
> Which seemes to be made more, by be'ing long lost

changed to

> Ambition (still on horse-backe) comes in poost,
> And seemes with greater glory to appeare;
> As made the more, by be'ing so long time lost.

Perhaps the horseback image started the reverberations, forcing
"comes" into the main-verb position and the economical moving-up
of "seems" to a coordinate verb; perhaps it was the shift from "comes"
to "seems" in the emphatic position of line 5, promoting the idea of
seeming from a trailing subordinate clause to the main predication,
and, coupling "comes" now with "in poost," generating the horseback
image. Three stanzas of Book VII (54–6) will repay some investiga-
tion. The passage begins

> *Muse,* what may we imagine was the Cause
> That *Furie* workes thus vniuersally?

and goes on to present several alternative explanations. In revision
some of the ideas, words, and constructions are transposed, causing reverberations backward and forward. The result seems to reflect Daniel's mental habit, a constant turning over of ideas in search of the
ultimate neatness of dress for the lodgings of his affections, "As if
there were no saboath of the minde."

The hundreds of single-word changes offer almost as many separate opportunities for speculation of all sorts; they are recommended here for study in order to mitigate the received opinion that Daniel was *only* a tinkerer—Miller for example (p. 68), with reference to the *Delia* revisions, says that "he polished rather than recreated. . . . he attempted to perfect his lines, in sterile academic fashion according to an evolving poetic theory rather than to recapture imaginatively the original emotion." But there can be a re-creativeness of expression as well as of emotion. Coleridge gave Daniel credit for a feeling for words which nonpoet critics have not generally perceived; and the instinct to seek for the optimum image of the mind is an extension of that poetic feeling.

Coleridge on the *Civil Wars*

THE CIVIL WARS of Daniel is an instructive, and even interesting work; but take the following stanzas (and from the hundred instances which abound I might probably have selected others far more striking: [quotes I.7–9].

Will it be contended on the one side, that these lines are mean and senseless? Or on the other, that they are not prosaic, and for *that* reason unpoetic? This poet's well-merited epithet is that of the "well-languaged Daniel;" but likewise, and by the consent of his contemporaries no less than of all succeeding critics, the "prosaic Daniel." Yet those, who thus designate this wise and amiable writer from the frequent incorrespondency of his diction to his metre in the majority of his compositions, not only deem them valuable and interesting on other accounts; but willingly admit, that there are to be found throughout his poems, and especially in his EPISTLES and in his HYMEN'S TRIUMPH, many and exquisite specimens of that style which, as the *neutral ground* of prose and verse, is common to both.

[For more of Coleridge on "well-languaged," see note to VI.99.]

—*Biographia Literaria*, ch. 18

. . . Read Daniel—the admirable Daniel—in his "Civil Wars," and "Triumphs of Hymen." The style and language are just such as any very pure and manly writer of the present day—Wordsworth, for example—would use; it seems quite modern in comparison with the style of Shakespeare.

—*Table Talk,* 15 March 1834

. . . Drayton is a sweet poet. . . . Daniel is a superior man; his diction is pre-eminently pure—of that quality which I believe has always existed somewhere in society. It is just such English, without any alteration, as Wordsworth or Sir George Beaumont might have spoken or written in the present day.

—Table Talk, 11 September 1831

Tuesday, Feb. 10th, 1808 (10th or 9th)

DEAR CHARLES,

I think more highly, far more, of the "Civil Wars" than you seemed to do on Monday night, Feb. 9th, 1808. The verse does not tease me; and all the while I am reading it, I cannot but fancy a plain England-loving English country gentleman, with only some dozen books in his whole library, and at a time when a "Mercury" or "Intelligencer" was seen by him once in a month or two, making this his newspaper and political Bible at the same time, and reading it so often as to store his memory with its aphorisms. Conceive a good man of that kind, diffident and passive, yet *rather* inclined to Jacobitism; seeing the reasons of the revolutionary party, yet by disposition and old principles leaning, in quiet nods and sighs, at his own parlour fire, to the hereditary right—(and of these characters there must have been many)—and then read this poem, assuming in your heart his character —conceive how grave he would look, and what pleasure there would be, what unconscious, harmless, humble self-conceit, self-compliment in his gravity: how wise he would feel himself, and yet after all how forbearing. How much calmed by that most calming reflection (when it is really the mind's own reflection). Ay, it was just so in Henry VI's time, always the same passions at work, &c. Have I improved thy book —or wilt thou like it the better there*fore?* But I have done as I would gladly be done by—thee at least.

S. T. COLERIDGE.

—Raysor, Coleridge's Miscellaneous Criticism, p. 235

Second letter—five hours after the first.

DEAR CHARLES,

You must read over these "Civil Wars" again. We both know what a *mood* is. And the genial mood will, it shall, come for my soberminded Daniel. He was a tutor and a sort of steward in a noble family in which form was religiously observed, and religion formally; and yet there was such warm blood and mighty muscle of substance within, that the moulding irons did not dispel, tho' they stiffened the vital

man within. Daniel caught and recommunicated the spirit of the
great Countess of Pembroke, the glory of the North; he formed her
mind, and her mind inspirited him. Gravely sober in all ordinary
affairs, and not easily excited by any—yet there is one, on which his
blood boils—whenever he speaks of English valour exerted against
a foreign enemy. Do read over—but some evening when we are quite
comfortable at your fire-side—and oh! where shall I ever be, if I am
not so there—that is the last altar on the horns of which my old feelings hang, but alas! listen and tremble. Nonsense!—well! I will read
it to you and Mary. The 205, 206, and 207th page [VI.87–106]; and
above all, that 93rd stanza; and in a different style the 98th stanza, p.
208; and what an image in 107, p. 211! Thousands even of educated
men would become more sensible, fitter to be members of Parliament
or ministers, by reading Daniel—and even those few who, *quoad in-
tellectum,* only gain refreshment of notions already their own, must
become better Englishmen. O, if it be not too late, write a kind note
about him.

S. T. COLERIDGE.

—Raysor, *Coleridge's Miscellaneous Criticism,* pp. 236–7

[These two letters, written on the fly-leaves of volume 2 of Lamb's
copy of Daniel's *Poetical Works* (1718), have been reprinted (with
various small errors) in *Notes and Queries,* volume 7, no. 145, 7 August 1852, pp. 117–18; in W. C. Hazlitt, *The Lambs . . .* (London,
1897), pp. 220–4; in Grosart, *4,* xxi–iii; as well as by Raysor. They are
described, with valuable background material, in Seronsy (see Preface,
p. 6 above). The rest of Coleridge's marginalia in the Lamb copy of
Daniel and in the Anderson's *British Poets* copy are taken from
Seronsy or Raysor and incorporated in the notes below where they
pertain: V.101.4 (gloss), V.102 ff., V.113–14, VI.2.5, VI.16.1, VI.22 ff.,
VI.34–41, VI.42.8, VI.46.4, VI.93, VI.99, VI.101.5, VI.105.4, VI.106.6,
VII.1 ff., VII.5.1,3,5, VII.8.2, VII.14.5. To complete the dossier, on
Grosart's grounds that "a Coleridge's dust is dust of gold," Hartley
Coleridge's comment on VIII.35.1–4 is reprinted in the notes, and
herewith his verses on Daniel (preceded by a poem on Donne):

> Not such was DANIEL, gentle, bland, and good,
> The wisest monitor of womanhood;
> Plain morals utter'd in plain mother tongue,
> And flat historic facts he plainly sung.
> And yet by earnest faith bestow'd a grace
> On bald event and ancient common-place.

The oldest truths to him were ever new;
No wonder, for he always felt them true.
The bootless battles of the red and white,
Which few can read, he patiently could write.
                    —*Poems* (London, 1851), 2, 322.]

BIBLIOGRAPHICAL DATA

Manuscript (no date)

No title page. Head-title: The ciuile warrs~ / betweene the hou= / ses of york & Lanaste[r] [*sic*]

4°. 37 numbered folios, unsigned. No Arguments, no stanza numbers, no running titles. 3 stanzas to a page, within marginal rules, except: fol. 1[r] (head-title and 2 stanzas); fol. 20[r] (1 stanza, *finis*, ornamental squiggle); fol. 20[v] blank; fol. 37[v] (2 stanzas, *finis*, squiggle), followed by unnumbered leaf, with "*37. folios*" written in center of recto; verso blank.

Foll. 1–20, head-title, 114 stanzas [Book I]; foll. 21–37[v], head-title: "The second Canto," 101 stanzas [Book II].

British Museum P. 9954 Sloane 1443; Sellers, p. 49 (III).[1] Designated hereafter as MS. Copy used: photostat, Yale University Library.[2]

Entry in Stationers' Register:[3] "xj octobris. [1594] Symon waterson / Entred for his copie vnder the wardens handes, a booke intituled, *The discention betwixt the houses of YORKE and LAN-CASTER in verse* penned by SAMUELL DANIELL, vppon Condicon that before yt be printed he shall procure sufficient aucthority for the printinge of yt. . . . vj[d]" (Arber, 2, 661).

1595

THE / FIRST FOWRE / Bookes of the ciuile / warres betweene the / two houses of / *Lancaster and* / *Yorke.* / By SAMVEL DANIEL. / *AEtas prima canat veneres* / *postrema tumultus.* / Printed at London by *P. Short* / for *Simon Waterson.* / 1595 /

---

[1] H. Sellers, "A Bibliography of the Works of Samuel Daniel 1585–1623," *Oxford Bibliographical Society Proceedings and Papers*, vol. 2 (1927).

[2] L. J. Gorton, assistant keeper, Department of Manuscripts of the British Museum, has kindly examined the manuscript and reports that the binding is of the late 18th or early 19th century; that the numbers 3 and 4 which appear in the top margin of folios 9 and 11 respectively appear to be in the same ink as the text, but that the folio numbers 1–37 and the words "*37. folios*" are later additions.

[3] E. Arber, ed., *A Transcript of the Registers of the Company of Stationers of London, 1554–1600* (London, private printing, 1875–77).

Border McKerrow 160,[4] with initial B cut out. 4°. [A2], B-Z4, 2 leaves. Foll. 88 (20, 26, 31, 35, 79, 85, 87 misnumbered 17, 21, 24, 21, 80, 86, 88). STC[5] 6244; Sellers, p. 34 (III); Corser,[6] pp. 22, 28. Designated hereafter as 95. Copy used: Yale University Library.

Another issue:

THE / FIRST FOWRE / Bookes of the ciuile wars / between the two hou- / ses of *Lancaster* / and *Yorke.* / By SAMVEL DANIEL. / *AEtas prima canat veneres postrema tumultus.* / AT LONDON, / Printed by *P. Short* for *Simon* / *Waterson.* 1595. /

Border McKerrow 177. Copy used: Folger 6244a (Huth copy, cs. 82). *N.B.:* Some copies have added Aa-Ee4, 1 leaf (foll. 89–108): The fyft Booke of the Ciuill / VVarres betweene the two Houses of / *Lancaster and Yorke.* Yet others have: The fift Booke of the Ciuill warres / betweene the two Houses of *Lancaster* / and *Yorke.* This latter setting is designated hereafter as 95a. See below, under 1599, and notes.

1599

THE / CIVILL WARS / OF ENGLAND, BE- / tweene the two Houses of / *Lancaster* and *Yorke.* / (***) / *AEtas prima canat veneres, postrema tumultus.* / SAM. DANIELL: / [Device McKerrow 278,[7] with motto "Et Vsque Ad Nubes Veritas Tua."] / AT LONDON / Printed by P. S. for Symon Waterson. / 1599. / [On verso: Mountjoy's arms, within a Garter, all enclosed by a square border.]

This is part of:

THE / POETICALL / ESSAYES / OF / SAM. DANYEL. / Newly corrected and aug- / mented. / *AEtas prima canat veneres,* / *postrema tumultus.* / AT LONDON / Printed by P. Short for Simon / Water- son. 1599. / [On verso: Mountjoy's arms within a Garter, and "The Argumentes of these / *Essayes following.*"]

Border McKerrow 179. 4°. [A4], B-Z4, Aa-Ee4, 1 leaf. Foll. 108, 1 leaf (20, 26, 31, 35, 79, 85, 87 misnumbered 17, 21, 24, 21, 80, 86, 88).

[4] R. B. McKerrow and F. S. Ferguson, *Title-Page Borders Used in England and Scotland, 1485–1640* (London, 1932).

[5] A. W. Pollard and G. R. Redgrave, eds., *A Short-Title Catalogue of Books Printed in England, Scotland, and Ireland, and of English Books Printed Abroad, 1475–1640* (London, London Bibliographical Society, 1926).

[6] Thomas Corser, "Collectanea Anglo-Poetica," Pt. V, *Publications of the Chetham Society,* vol. *91* (1873).

[7] R. B. McKerrow, *Printers' and Publishers' Devices in England and Scotland, 1485–1640* (London, 1913).

STC 6261; Sellers, p. 35; Corser, pp. 29, 30. Designated hereafter as 99. Copy used: Folger 6261 (HH copy ["The fift Booke . . ."]; Manwood copy ["The fyft Booke . . ."]).

1601–02

THE / WORKS / of / SAMVEL DANIEL / Newly augmented. / *AEtas prima canat veneres* / *postrema tumultus.* / LONDON / Printed for Simon Waterson. / 1602. /

Border McKerrow 229. No title page for *CW*. Folio in sixes. A2, B-O6, P-T4. Foll. 97. STC 6237; Sellers, p. 36; Corser, p. 41. Designated hereafter as 01. Copy used: Yale University Library. *N.B.:* This is a reissue of the presentation-copy issue, which has the title page except for the date, which is 1601. STC 6236.

1609

THE CIVILE WARES / *betweene the Howses of Lancaster* / *and Yorke corrected and continued* / *by Samuel Daniel one of the Groomes* / *of hir Maiesties most honorable Priuie Chamber,* / *AEtas prima canat veneres* / *postrema tumultus,* / [portrait] / PRINTED / AT LONDON / *by Simon Watersonne,* / 1609; / *Focksonius,* / *sculp:* / [Engraved.]

4°. A2, B-C4, D-Q8, R4. Pp. 231. STC 6245; Sellers, p. 41; Corser, pp. 55–7. Designated hereafter as CT (copy-text), except where different from 23; see below, Notes on Editions. Copy used: Yale University Library.

1623

THE / WHOLE / WORKES OF / SAMVEL DANIEL Esquire / *in Poetrie.* / [ornament] / LONDON, / Printed by NICHOLAS OKES, for / SIMON WATERSON, and are to be / sold at his shoppe in *Paules* Church- / yard, at the Signe of the Crowne. / 1623. /

No title page for *CW*. 4°. B-C4, D-Q8, R4. Pp. 231. STC 6238; Sellers, pp. 44, 45; Corser, pp. 64, 65. Designated hereafter as CT (copy text), except where different from 09; see below, Notes on Editions. Copy used: Yale University Library.

1717–18

Volume title page (Vol. *1*):
THE / Poetical Works / OF / Mr. Samuel Daniel, / AUTHOR of the *English* History, / To which is prefix'd, / MEMOIRS / OF HIS LIFE *and* WRITINGS. / Vol. I / LONDON: / Printed for R. GOSLING, against *St. Dunstan's* / Church in *Fleet-street,* W. MEARS, at the /

Lamb, and J. BROWNE, at the *Black Swan,* / without *Temple-Bar.* MDCCXVIII. *CW* begins Vol. 2.

1885–96

Samuel Daniel, *Complete Works in Verse and Prose,* A. B. Grosart, ed. (5 vols., London, Hazell, Watson, & Viney; vol. 2, 1885). Printed for private circulation only. Referred to throughout as Grosart.

NOTES ON EDITIONS

MS. "Written in a conventional book-hand, but marginalia are added in the handwriting of Daniel's letter to Devonshire" (Sellers, p. 49). Also, there are many corrections, in the same hand, of a sort attributable only to the author: word substitutions, additions, contractions *metri causa,* and the like. There are a few corrections made by the copyist, and some nine errors undetected by either reader. Daniel's corrections and the errors are noted in the appropriate places in the notes. I have taken no notice of the usual manuscript abbreviations such as w^{ch}, y^t, y^{or}, x for ten, or the cross barred "p" for "per," "par," or "pre," except that they have been reproduced when included in a variant recorded for another reason.

I have not been able to determine whether MS was intended for private circulation, for printer's copy, or for first one and then the other. The variants from 95 are many and radical; yet the corrections and the addition of glosses may be evidence of prepublication editing. Perhaps this was the first finished draft of the first two books; perhaps Daniel showed it around to his friends, was encouraged to print it, prepared it for copy, then immediately began that process of correcting, augmenting, and deleting which was his regular practice. He was especially intimate with his publisher, Waterson, and undoubtedly maintained a close liaison with the printing house.

The punctuation of MS is curious. For the most part there was no line-end punctuation at all, except at the end of the stanza; and there are some sixty-one stanzas where even this is not visible. Often the period is tossed in only approximately near the last word, giving the impression that such was merely formal—not grammatical or rhetorical—punctuation. Faint marks—mostly commas but often colons or question marks—have, however, been scattered throughout the MS. L. J. Gorton reports that they do not appear to be in the same ink as the text; who put them in, or when, or why, it seems impossible to state. They do not correspond consistently with the punctuation of any of the printed editions. Sometimes they are supererogatory, as a comma in addition to an original colon (fol. 6ᵛ, st. 1, l. 2) or comma and original period (fol. 10ᵛ, st. 2, l. 4). They *may* have been the work of Daniel as he proofread the fair copy; or that of the printing-house stylist (assuming that MS was used as copy); but the present editor's conjecture is that they represent the notions of a later owner of MS, who had strong feelings about punctuation and was outraged by the lack of seemly pointing.

95–99. The text of Books I–IV is the same setting throughout the various issues of these two editions, with only these variations: P2, l. 7, "thought smust," "thoughts must"; Q2ᵛ, st. no. "8o," "o8"; V4, l. 1, "years," "yeares"; sig. F2 given as "E2," corrected to "F2." All these, which are assorted in the six copies I have checked, are susceptible of explanation as incidental changes made by the printer in running off a second impression from the same type and do not affect the description of the text as one setting. In all six copies the running title for Book IV is given as "THE THIRD BOOKE." on V1ᵛ, X1ᵛ, X2ᵛ, Z3ᵛ. Book V (Aa-Ee4ᵛ, 1 leaf), however, had two settings: one with head-title "The fyft Booke . . ." and the almost constant use of "vv" for "w"; the other with head-title "The fift Booke . . ." and the almost constant use of "y" for "i." There are a few orthographical differences: The one has "beatifies" for "beautifies" (Aa3ᵛ, l. 12), which was picked up by the compositor of o1; and on Dd1ᵛ, l. 1, the one has "Thus" and the other has "Thys," which might be a variant or might be merely an error. Otherwise one setting is a close copy of the other, even to unusual spellings ("coullor") and the reproduction of the error "mimens" for "immens." It is hard to say which came first or even why there *were* two settings. Copies of 95 and of 99 have survived, (1) containing Books I–IV only; (2) with a complete assortment of the two 95 title pages and the two Book V settings; and (3) with the 99 title page and either of the two Book V settings. The errata sheet (unsigned, after Ee4) covers all five books but was not bound into all surviving copies of either 95 or 99.

An explanation for such an assortment is still to seek. Possibly the sequence was as follows: Books I–IV were published in 1595 in two issues. (Why? Did the first impression sell out, and Short, having put border 160 to other use, print up some more title pages with border 177? Or, as Corser [p. 23] suggests, did it sell slowly, causing the publisher to try a new title page? This latter seems unlikely, as the second title page is no more attractive than the first; yet there were still some first-issue title pages left to be bound up with the addition of Book V.) Book V was written sometime before 1599, and two settings were made then. The remaining sheets of Books I–IV were checked and a list of "Faults Escaped" made for all five books. The two settings of Book V were then bound up indiscriminately with the remainders of the two issues of 1595, some having the errata sheet and some not. When the 1599 *Poeticall Essayes* was compiled, what was left of this mixture was incorporated until at some point a new title page was printed up and inserted with the date 1599 and the title "The Civill Wars of England" instead of "The First Fowre Bookes."

At all events, there is nothing textually important about these matters (but see the discussion of *CW* and Shakespeare, pp. 8–11 above). In the variants and notes 95 stands for 95–99; in the fifth book 95 stands for the "fyft Booke" setting and 95a stands for the "fift Booke" setting. A dedicatory sonnet to Mountjoy appears on the recto of the leaf following the volume title page in 99.

01–02. There are no setting variations between these two issues except for the last digit in the date on the title page. The first issue was printed on large paper, presumably for presentation copies; few have survived (see Sellers, p. 35). There is no separate title page for *CW;* a dedicatory epistle to the queen prefaces the text, and Book VI appears for the first time.

09–23. 23 incorporates sheets of 09 except for the title page; there is no separate *CW* title page in 23. The sheets were undoubtedly remainders. Grosart's assumption that "1609 must have been kept standing in type" (2, [2]) does not do justice to the limitations of type supply in Jacobean print shops. Some copies of both 09 and 23 have page number 192 given erroneously as 162. There are at least three states of leaf E4 (pp. 39–40), which are designated in the variants as 09 (Yale 09, copy 2); 09a, 23a identical; Yale 09, copy 1; Folger 09 [6245, Crawford copy, cs. 4027]; and Folger 23); and 23 (Yale 23). Since 09 has "all" for "call" on E4^v, l. 24, and the error is one of the three noticed in "Faults Escaped," 09 is presumably the first state and the others are cancels. 09a was a poor substitute, beginning four lines with lower-case letters, omitting the period from the running titles, and changing spelling capriciously; so it in turn became a cancel and was replaced by 23. The variations, except for spelling, punctuation, and running titles, are recorded in the variants. For purposes of identification the following table shows differences:

Stanza	Line	09	09a, 23a	23
22,	1	iustice . . . be	Iustice . . . be	Iustice . . . bee
	3	And . . . remov'd	and . . . remov'd	And . . . remoou'd
	4	cosin *Henrie* . . . hee	cosin *Henry* . . . he	cousen *Henry* . . . hee
	7	And . . . restor'd	and . . . resto'rd	And . . . restor'd
23,	1	enterparle	enterparle	interparle
	2	And . . . Princely	and . . . princely	And . . . Princely
	6	And . . . be	and . . . be	And . . . bee
	7	oth	Oath	Oath
24,	6	Maiestie	Maiesty	Maiesty
	7	choyces . . . be	choyses . . . be	choyses . . . bee
25,	1	standes he'in	standes he'in	stands he in
gloss		*Salisburie*	*Salisbury*	*Salisbury*
26, gloss		(Omitted)	sir . . . Cheshire	Sir . . . Cheshire,
	6	In darkenesse . . . fidelitie	in darknesse . . . fidelitie	In darknesse . . . fidelity
27, gloss		*Ienico d'Artois a Gascoin.*	*Ienico d'Artois a Gascoin*	*Ienico d'Artois a Gascoyne.*
	2	memorie . . . trustie	memorie . . . trusty	memory . . . trusty
	3	Gasconie	Gasconie	*Gascoyne*
	5	companie	companie	Company
28, gloss		*The E. of Salsburie*	*The Earle of Salsbury*	*The Earle of Salisbury*
	2	either	either	eyther
	6	their	theyr	their
	8	And . . . all	and . . . call,	And . . . call,
29,	1	Rockes	Rocks	Rocks
	3	trustie . . . here	trusty . . . here	trusty . . . heere
	4	t'vpbrayd . . . shame,	t'vpbraid . . . shame	t'vpbraid . . . shame
	6	Against . . . crew‡	against . . . Crew:	Against . . . Crew:
	8	And be	and be	And bee

In all copies collated, "Book." is given anomalously for "Booke." in the running titles on O7, O8, O8ᵛ, P, P1ᵛ, P6ᵛ, P7ᵛ, P8ᵛ, Q, Q2, Q6, Q6ᵛ, Q7ᵛ, Q8ᵛ, R, R4. Although there is an apparent parallel in the inner and outer formes of the second gatherings of P and Q, there is not enough of a pattern here to postulate any procedure. There were probably two sticks of "Book." type which were mixed in with the "Booke." sticks, both at the end of Book VII and all through Book VIII.

INTERRELATIONSHIP OF EDITIONS—MAKE-UP

MS consists of Books I and II only. 95 and 99 add Books III, IV, and V. 01 adds dedicatory epistle "To her sacred Maiestie" and Book VI. 09 and 23 substitute prose dedication to the Countess of Pembroke for dedicatory epistle, split Book III into III and IV, make Books IV, V, and VI into V, VI, and VII, and add Book VIII. Every version has stanzas not in the others. Kinship of stanzas is indicated at the appropriate places in the variants and in the following table:

	MS	95, 99	01	09, 23 (CT)	
I	[1–9]	1–9	1–9	1–8	
	[10–18]	10–18	10–18	9–13	
	[19–54]	19–54	19–55	14–50	
	[55–6]	55–6	56–9	51–4	
	[57–62]	57–62	60–5	55–61	
	[63–94]	63–101	66–104	62–100	
	[95–113]	102–20	105–23	101–17	
	[114]	121	124	118	
II	[1–19]	1–17	1–17	1–17	
	[20–3]	18–21	18–21	18–20	
	[24–62]	22–59	22–59	21–56	
	[63–4]	60	60		
	[65]	61	61		
	[66–74]	62–72	62–72	57–67	(67 ff. misnumbered 66 ff. in 09, 23)
	[75–91]	73–88	73–88	68–83	
	[92–101]	89–96	89–96	84–91	
		97–100	97–100	92–4	
		101–10	101–10	95–102	
		111–21	111–21	103–15	
		122–7	122–5	116	
		128–30	126–7		(130 misnumbered 136 in 95, 99)
		131	128		
III	1–5	1–5	1–4		
	6–10	6–10	5–11		
	11–68	11–66	12–67	(11 misnumbered 17 in 95, 99)	
	69–70	67	68		
	71–82	68–79	69–79		
	83–5	80–2	80–91		
IV			1–14		
	86–7	83–4	15–19		
	88–94	85–91	20–7	(87 ff. misnumbered 97 ff. in 01)	
	95	92	28–32		
	96–103	93–100	33–42		
	104–6	101–3	43–4		
	107–12	104–9	45–52		
	113	110	53–4		
	114	111	55–82		
	115–20	112–17	83–7		
	121–3	118–20	88		
	124–32	121–9	89–96	(131 misnumbered 113 in 95, 99)	
IV	1–2	1–2	V 1		
	3–36	3–36	2–34		
	37–109	37–109	35–104		
	110–21	110–21	105–16	(110 misnumbered 114 in 95, 99)	

V	1–9		1–9	*VI*	1–7
	10–15		10–15		8–12
	16–49		16–49		13–45
	50–118		50–118		46–114

	VI	1–10	*VII*	1–9	
		11–102		10–99	(35, 78 misnumbered 34, 77 in 01;
		103–13		100–9	50 ff. misnumbered 49 ff. in 09,
		114–15		110–11	23)
			VIII	1–112	(26 ff. misnumbered 24 ff.)

MS is fragmentary and was already departed from in no small degree by 95. Its chief interest is in evidences of author correction, evidence of possible dictation instead of copying, and in having a total of six stanzas (Bk. II, stt. [17, 18, 62, 64, 92, 93]) omitted from 95.[1] Twice 09 appears to be going behind 01 and 95 to MS: I.78.7, "But now he was" MS, 09; "But being now" 95, 01; and II.43.8, "Since farther actions, further but vnrest" MS, 09; "Since farther actions farther but vnrest" 95, 01. These may be merely coincidental or they may show that *a* manuscript was at hand in the revisions.

Although revision was extensive at each new edition, and especially at 09, the basic copy for each new version was its immediate predecessor. Thus 09 normally follows 01 where 01 differs from 95; I have found only one clear example of 09 going behind 01 to 95: I.38.4, "But blame the course held in the managing" 09; "But onely blame the course held in the thing" 01; "But onely blame the course of managing" 95. II.5.5 read "amazing" in 95 but was corrected to "amuzing" in its "Faults Escaped"; 01 reads "amazing," 09 again "amuzing." This may be evidence of 09 checking back (at least on the errata) to 95, or it may simply be ascribable to Daniel's careful revision of 09. A continued error may be seen in V.109.1: after "T'attempt" in 95 the end of a space quad stuck up and printed something like an apostrophe; 01 has "T'attempt' " and 09 follows 01.

Since 09 is the most complete version of the poem and was the last one revised and published in Daniel's lifetime, it is the copy-text,[2]

---

[1] These stanzas were printed for the first time by Cecil C. Seronsy, "Daniel's Manuscript *Civil Wars* with Some Previously Unpublished Stanzas," *Journal of English and Germanic Philology*, 52 (1953), 153–60; a subsequent version appeared in the same journal (p. 594), incorporating transcription corrections and some, but not all, of the present editor's different readings of the text. The stanzas will be found in the variants below, and some comment on the readings on p. 43 above.

[2] According an author the right to be officially represented by his latest version is justified in Daniel's case by his own scrupulosity in revising and proofreading. Progressive deterioration of the text has been held to a minimum.

and all preceding rejected or changed material is relegated to the variants. Both dedications, however, have been preserved in the preliminaries; and the sonnet to Mountjoy, although it applies to the whole of the *Poeticall Essayes* of 99, is printed here because of Mountjoy's special connection with *CW* (see I.5). For leaf E4 of O9 and 23, the version of 23 is adopted; see above, pp. 57–8.

The edition of 1718 is of interest (for *CW*) only in that it was the version of the poem read by such people as Lamb, Wordsworth, and Coleridge. Lamb's copy, now in the Harvard College Library, contains many textual corrections and emendations in his own hand and some important commentary by Coleridge in the margins.[3] The editor is unknown.

The edition of our indefatigable but not indefectible Grosart, while less culpable with regard to *CW* than to some other of Daniel's works, still does things sufficiently queer that I have ignored it except on a few occasions.

Methods Used in the Text and Variants

1. The reading of the copy-text is adopted at all times, except for misprints, which are noted and changed, and obvious errors, which are corrected from the other collated editions. Running titles are corrected silently where wrong and otherwise normalized.

2. Punctuation, spelling, capitalization, italics follow the copy-text, with the exception that long *s* is replaced with square *s*, and *vv* with *w*. Where there is no doubt that the copy-text stanza-end punctuation is in error, it is replaced by that of the next preceding edition with a possible reading. Brackets in other editions than the copy-text are noted where they change sense or emphasis but not where they merely substitute for commas or are used parenthetically where the copy-text has nothing. Quotation marks, both for reported speech and for *sententiae*, appear first generally in the copy-text; their absence in previous editions is not noted. Likewise mere differences in punctuation, spelling, etc. in other editions, not being considered genuine variants, are ordinarily ignored; a few unusual spellings and punctuation and italic anomalies are mentioned in the variants.

[3] The copy is fully described and the Coleridge marginalia reproduced by Cecil C. Seronsy in the *Harvard Library Bulletin*, 7 (1953), 105–12. These latter are incorporated where they pertain in the notes below, identified as "Coleridge note" and with reference to the page in the Lamb copy where they occur.

3. Since all the printed editions have book numbers as running titles, and stanza numbers, no listing of page numbers or gathering signatures is made in the variants. Page numbers are those of the present edition. Daniel's italicized marginalia have been brought down to the foot of the page. I have inserted the asterisks, daggers, etc. into the text, normally at the end of a line unless the gloss seems to refer to a single word or phrase or to the stanza as a whole. The lemma for a variant is in the form of stanza and line numbers separated by a period: 29.3. Where whole stanzas which are not present in the copy-text are given, the version of the latest edition including them is quoted; variants from it in preceding editions follow the stanza, indented, and introduced by a square bracket. Sigla for the various editions have been explained above; unless otherwise indicated they are MS, 95 (signifies both 1595 and 1599), 01 (signifies both 1601 and 1602), and CT, copy-text (signifies both 1609 and 1623). For indicating stanza-number correspondence, the equality sign and various brackets are used, as follows: 118(=124=<121=[114]) that is, stanza 118 in CT corresponds to 124 in 01, 121 in 95, and (unnumbered) 114 in MS.

4. A variant standing alone without sigla means "so all editions preceding the copy-text." Variants are given in inverse chronological order. Where variants differ in nonsignificant matters such as spelling, punctuation, etc. the version of the latest varying edition is adopted; and here *vv* for *w* and the manuscript contractions are retained. Normally no punctuation is included in the variants unless it is significant, internal, or at the end of a whole variant line. Author corrections in MS are given with the correction first: I.4.4 "the<that MS-D" indicates that Daniel has scratched out "that" and substituted "the."

5. Despite a conscientious canvassing of concordantial sources available to me, and the advice of my classicist friends in searching texts, some five Latin citations remain unaccounted for, although I am sure they are right under our noses. If and when they are reported they shall be ensconced in their proper niches in the notes in any subsequent printing.

THE CIVIL WARS

TO HER SACRED MAIESTIE

HEre sacred Soueraigne, glorious Queene of Peace,
The tumults of disordred times I sing,
To glorifie thy Raigne, and to increase
The wonder of those blessings thou doost bring
5 *Vpon thy Land, which ioyes th'intire release*
From bloud and sorrowes by thy gouerning,
That through affliction we may see our ioyes,
And blesse the glory of Elizaes *dayes.*

Happier then all thy great Progenitors,
10 *That euer sate vpon that powerfull throne;*
Or all thy mightiest neighbour-Gouernors,
Which wonder at the blessings of thy Crowne,
Whose Peace more glorious farre then all their warres,
Haue greater powres of admiration showne;
15 *Receiue these humble fruites of mine increase,*
Offred on th'Altare of thy sacred Peace.

I, who by that most blessed hand sustain'd,
In quietnes, doe eate the bread of rest:
And by that all-reuiuing powre obtain'd,
20 *That comfort which my Muse and me hath blest,*
Bring here this worke of Warre, whereby was gain'd
This blessed Vnion which these wounds redrest,
That sacred Concord which prepar'd the way
Of glory for thee onely to enioy.

25 *Whereto if these my Labors shall attaine,*
And which, if Fortune giue me leaue to end,
It will not be the least worke of thy Raigne,
Nor that which least thy glory shall commend,
Nor shall I hereby vainely entertaine
30 *Thy Land, with ydle shadowes to no end;*
But by thy Peace, teach what thy blessings are,
The more t'abhorre this execrable warre.

Samuel Daniel.

To the Right honorable, Sir *Charles Blunt*
    Knight, Lord *Mountioy,* and Knight of the most
        Noble order of the Garter, and his
            most worthy Lord.

I Do not plant thy great respected name
    Here in this front, to th'end thou shouldst protect
    These my endeuors from contempt or blame,
    Which none but their own forces must effect:
Nor do I seeke to win thy more respect,
    Most learned Lord, by these Essaies of mine,
    Since that cleere iudgement that did first elect
    To fauor me, will alwaies keepe me thine:
Nor do *J* this more honor to assigne,
    Vnto thy worth that is not more hereby,
    Since th'offrings made vnto the powers deuine,
    Enrich not them but shew mens pietie:
But this I do to th'end if destinie
    Shall any monument reserue of me,
    Those times should see my loue, how willing I
    That liu'd by thee, would haue thee liue with me.
                                                    S. D.

TO THE RIGHT NOBLE

Lady, the Lady Marie, *Countesse*
Dowager of Pembrooke.

MADAME:

THis Poëm of our last Ciuile Warres of England, *(whereof the*
many Editions shewe what kinde of intertainement it hath had with
the world) I haue now againe sent-forth, with the addition of two
bookes: the one, continuing the course of the Historie; the other,
5 *making-vp a part, which (for haste) was left vnfurnisht in the*
former Impressions. And, hauing nothing else to doo with my life,
but to worke whil'st I haue it; I held it my part, to adorne (the
best I could) this Prouince, Nature hath allotted to my Charge:
and which I desire to leaue, after my death, in the best forme I
10 *may; seeing I can erect no other pillars to sustaine my memorie,*
but my lines, nor otherwise pay my debts and the recknings of my
gratitude to their honour who haue donne me good, and furthered
this Worke.

And, whereas this Argument was long since undertaken (in a
15 *time which was not so well secur'd of the future, as God be blessed*
now it is) with a purpose, to shewe the deformities of Ciuile Dissen-
sion, and the miserable euents of Rebellions, Conspiracies, and
bloudy Reuengements, which followed (as in a circle) vpon that
breach of the due course of Succession, by the Vsurpation of Hen.
20 4; *and thereby to make the blessings of Peace, and the happinesse*
of an established Gouernment (in a direct Line) the better to
appeare: I trust I shall doo a gratefull worke to my Countrie, to
continue the same, vnto the glorious Vnion of Hen. 7: *from whence*
is descended our present Happinesse.

25 *In which Worke, I haue carefully followed that truth which*
is deliuered in the Historie; without adding to, or subtracting
from, the general receiu'd opinion of things as we finde them in
our common Annalles: holding it an impietie, to violate that pub-
like Testimonie we haue, without more euident proofe; or to intro-
30 *duce fictions of our owne imagination, in things of this nature.*
Famae rerum standum est. *Though I knowe, in these publike ac-*
tions, there are euer popular bruites, and opinions, which run
according to the time & the biass of mens affections: and it is the
part of an Historian, to recite them, not to rule thē; especially,

67

35 *otherwise then the circumstances may induce: according to that*
   modest saying; Nec affirmare sustineo de quibus dubito, nec sub-
   ducere quae accepi.

   I haue onely vsed that poeticall licence, of framing speaches
   to the persons of men according to their occasions; as C. Salustius,
40 *and* T. Liuius *(though Writers in Prose, yet in that kinde Poets)*
   haue, with diuers other antient and modern Writers, done before
   me. Wherein, though they haue incroched vpon others rights, and
   vsurpt a part that was not properly theirs: yet, seeing they hold so
   iust a proportion, with the nature of men, and the course of affayres;
45 *they passe as the partes of the Actor (not the Writer) and are*
   reciu'd with great approbation.

   And although many of these Images are drawne with the pencil
   of mine owne conceiuing: yet I knowe, they are according to the
   portraiture of Nature; and carrie a resemblance to the life of
50 *Action, and their complexions whom they represent. For I see,*
   Ambition, Faction, and Affections, speake euer one Language,
   weare like colours (though in seuerall fashions) feed, and are fed
   with the same nutriments; and only vary but in time.

   Man is a creature of the same dimension he was: and how great
55 *and eminent soeuer hee bee, his measure and height is easie to be*
   taken. And all these great actions are openly presented on the
   Stage of the World: where, there are euer Spectators, *who will*
   iudge and censure how men personate those parts, which they are
   set to perform; and so enter them in the Records of Memorie.

60   *And if I haue erred somewhat in the draught of the young*
   Q. Isabel *(wife to* Ric. 2.) *in not suting her passions to her yeares:*
   I must craue fauour of my credulous Readers; and hope, the young
   Ladies of England *(who peraduenture will thinke themselues of*
   age sufficient, at 14 *yeares, to haue a feeling of their owne estates)*
65 *will excuse me in that point. For the rest, setting-aside those orna-*
   ments, proper to this kinde of Writing; I haue faithfully obserued
   the Historie. Wherein, such as loue this Harmony of words, may
   finde, that a Subiect, of the greatest grauitie, will be aptly exprest:
   howsoeuer others (seeing in what sort Verse hath beene idly abused)
70 *hold it but as a language fitting Lightnes and Vanitie.*

   For mine owne part, I am not so far in loue with this forme of
   Writing (nor haue I sworne Fealtie onely to Ryme) but that I may
   serue in any other state of Inuention, with what weapon of vtter-
   ance I will: and, so it may make good my minde, I care not. For,
75 *I see, Iudgement and Discretion (with whatsoeuer is worthy)*
   carry their owne Ornaments, and are grac't with their owne beau-

ties; be they apparayled in what fashion they will. And because I finde the common tongue of the world is Prose; I purpose in that kinde to write the Historie of England, *from the Conquest: being* 80 *incouraged thereunto, by many noble & worthy Spirits. Although Madame, I must not neglect to prosecute the other part of this Worke; being thus reuiued by your Goodnes: to whome, and to whose Noble Family, I hold my selfe euer bound; and will labour to doo you all the honor, and seruice I can.*

SAM. DANYEL.

The First *Booke*

THE ARGVMENT.

What times fore-goe Richard *the seconds Raigne,*
The fatall causes of this ciuile Warre,
His Vncles pride, his greedy Minions gaine,
Glosters *reuolt, and death, deliuered are.*
Herford, *accus'd, exil'd, call'd-back againe,*
Pretendes t'amend what others Rule did marre.
The King from Ireland *hastes, but did no good;*
Whil'st strange prodigious signes fore-token blood.

1

I Sing the ciuill Warres, tumultuous Broyles,
And Bloody factions of a mightie Land:
Whose people hautie, proud with forraine spoyles,
Vpon themselues turn-backe their conquering hand;
Whil'st Kin their Kin, Brother the Brother foyles;
Like Ensignes all against like Ensignes band;
Bowes against Bowes, the Crowne against the Crowne;
Whil'st all pretending right, all right's throwne downe.

2

What furie, ô what madnes held thee so,
Deare *England* (too too prodigall of blood)
To waste so much, and warre without a foe,
Whilst *Fraunce,* to see thy spoyles, at pleasure stood!
How much might'st thou haue purchast with lesse woe,
T'haue done thee honour and thy people good?
Thine might haue beene what-euer lies betweene
The *Alps* and vs, the *Pyrenei* and *Rhene.*

3

Yet now what reason haue we to complaine?
Since hereby came the calme we did inioy;
The blisse of thee *Eliza;* happie gaine
For all our losse: when-as no other way
The heauens could finde, but to vnite againe
The fatall sev'red Families, that they

71

Might bring foorth thee: that in thy peace might growe
That glorie, which few Times could euer showe.

4

Come sacred *Virtue:* I no *Muse,* but thee,
Inuoke, in this great labour I intend.
Doo thou inspire my thoughts, infuse in mee
A power to bring the same to happie end.
Rayse vp a worke, for later times to see,
That may thy glorie, and my paynes commend.
Make me these tumults rightly to rehearse:
And giue peace to my life, life to my verse.

5

And thou *Charles Montioy* (who didst once afford
Rest for my fortunes, on thy quiet shore;
And cheer'dst mee on, these measures to record
In grauer tones, then I had vs'd before)
Beholde: my gratitude makes good my word
Ingag'd to thee (although thou be no more)
That I, who heretofore haue liv'd by thee,
Doo giue thee now a roome to liue with me.

6

And MEMORIE, preserv'resse of things done,
Come thou, vnfold the woundes, the wracke, the waste:
Reueale to me how all the strife begunne
Twixt *Lancaster* and *Yorke,* in ages past:
How causes, counsels, and euents did runne,
So long as these vnhappie times did last,
Vnintermixt with fictions, fantasies.
I versifie the troth; not Poetize.

7

And to the ende wee may with better ease
Discerne the true discourse; vouchsafe to showe,
What were the times foregoing, neere to these,
That these we may with better profit knowe:
Tell, how the world fell into this disease,
And how so great distemperature did growe.
So shall we see, by what degrees it came,
"How things, at full, do soone wex out of frame.

8

Ten Kings had, from the *Norman* Conqueror, raign'd,
With intermixt and variable fate,*
When *England* to her greatest height attain'd
Of powrè, dominion, glorie, wealth, and State;
After it had, with much adoo, sustain'd
The violence of Princes, with debate
For titles, and the often mutinies
Of Nobles, for their ancient liberties.

9

For, first, the *Norman,* conquering all by might,†
By might was forc't to keepe what he had got;
Mixing our Customes and the forme of *Right*
With foraine Constitutions he had brought:
Maistering the mightie, humbling the poorer wight
By all seuerest meanes that could be wrought:
And, making the succession doubtful, rent
This new-got State, and left it turbulent.

10

William his sonne, tracing his fathers wayes‡
(The great men spent in peace, or slaine in fight)
Vpon depressed weaknes onely preyes,
And makes his force maintaine his doubtful right:
His elder brothers clayme, vexing his dayes,
His actions and exactions still incite:
And giuing Beastes, what did to Men pertaine
(Tooke for a Beast) himselfe in th'end was slaine.

11

His brother *Henrie* next commands the State:§
Who, *Roberts* title better to reiect,

* *Which mat in the space of 260. years.*

† *1067. Williã I. surnamed the Conqueror, the base sonne to Robert the sixt Duke of Normandie, raigned 20. yeares and 8. monthes, and left the Crowne of England to William his third sonne; contrary to the custome of succession.*

‡ *1087. Williã 2. had wars with his elder brother Robert D. of Normandie: with whom his Vncle Otho, and many of the Nobilitie of Eng. tooke part. Hee was slaine hunting in the new forrest by Sir Walter Tirell, shooting at a Deere, when he had raigned 13. yeares.*

§ *1100. Hen. I: the youngest sonne of William I. raigned 35. yeares, & 4 monthes, whose sonnes Will. & Ric. being drowned on the Seas, he leaves the Crow. to Maude first married to the Emperour, Hen. 4 and after to Geffrey Plantagenet E. of Aniou.*

Seekes to repacifie the peoples hate;
And with faire shewes, rather then in effect,
Allayes those grieuances that heauie sate:
Reformes the lawes, which soone hee did neglect;
And reft of sonnes, for whom he did prepare,
Leaues crowne and strife, to *Maude* his daughters care.

12

Whom *Stephen* his nephew (falsifying his Oath)
Preuents, assayles the Realme, obtaines the Crowne;*
Such tumults raysing as torment them both,
Whil'st both held nothing certainely their owne:
Th'afflicted State (diuided in their troth
And partiall faith) most miserable growne,
Endures the while, till peace, and *Stephens* death,
Gaue some calme leasure to recouer breath.

13

When *Henrie,* sonne to *Maude* the Empresse, raignes,†
And *England* into forme and greatnes brought,
Addes *Ireland* to this Scepter, and obtaines
Large Prouinces in *Fraunce;* much treasure gote,
And from exactions here at home abstaynes:
And had not his rebellious children fought
T'imbroyle his age with tumults, he had beene
The happiest Monarch that this State had seene.

14

Him, Richard followes in the gouernment:‡
Who much the glory of our Armes increast;
And all his fathers mighty treasure spent,
In that deuoutfull Action of the *East:*
Whereto, whiles he his forces wholly bent,
Despight and treason his designes opprest;

---

* *1135. Stephen son to the E. of Bloys & Adela daughter to Wil. I. inuades the kingdōe cōtēdes with Maude the Empresse for the succession, and raigned tumultuarily 18. yeares and 10. monethes.*

† *1154. Hen. 2. sonne of Geffry Plantagenet E. of Aniou & Maude the Empresse associated his sonne Hen. in the Crowne and gouerment: which turned to his great disturbance, and set all his sonnes, Henry, Richard, Geffry, & Iohn against him. He raigned 34. yeares & 7. months.*

‡ *1189. Richard went to the Holy warres, was king of Ierusalem whiles his brother Iohn by the help of the King of France vsurpt the crown of England. Hee was detained prisoner in Austria, redeemed, and reigned nine years. 9. months.*

A faithlesse brother, and a fatall King,
Cut-off his growth of glory, in the spring.

15

Which wicked brother, contrary to course,
False *Iohn* vsurpes his *Nephew Arthurs* right:*
Gets to the Crowne by craft, by wrong, by force;
Rules it with lust, oppression, rigour, might;
Murders the lawfull heire without remorse:
Wherefore procuring all the worlds despight,
A tyrant loath'd, a homicide conuented,
Poysoned he dyes, disgrac't and vnlamented.

16

Henrie his sonne is chosen King, though young,†
And *Lewes* of *France* (elected first) beguil'd;
After the mighty had debated long,
Doubtfull to choose a straunger or a child:
With him, the Barrons (in these times growne strong)
Warre for their auncient Lawes so long exil'd.
He graunts the *Charter* that pretended ease;
Yet kept his owne, and did his State appease.

17

Edward, his sonne, a Martiall King, succeedes;‡
Iust, prudent, graue, religious, fortunate:
Whose happy ordered Raigne most fertile breedes,
Plenty of mighty spirits to strength his State:
And worthy mindes, to manage worthy deedes,
Th'experience of those times ingenerate:
For, euer great imployment, for the great,
Quickens the blood, and honour doth beget.

18

And had not his mis-led lasciuious Sonne,
Edward the second,§ intermitted so

* *1199. K. Iohn vsurps the right of Arthur, sonne to Geffery his elder brother; and raignes 17 yeares. Hee had warres with his Barons; who elected Lewis, sonne to the K. of France.*

† *1216. Hen. 3. at 9. yeares of age, was Crowned King: and raigned 56. yeares.*

‡ *1272. Ed. I. had the dominion ouer his whole Iland of Britaine: and raigned gloriously 34. yeeres. 7. Moneths.*

§ *1307. Edward 2. abused by his Minions & debaushed by his owne weaknesse, was deposed frō his gouernment, when he had reigned 19. yeares 6. moneths; and was murthered in prison.*

The course of glory happily begunne
(Which brought him and his fauorites to woe)
That happy current without stop had runne
Vnto the full of his sonne *Edwards* flowe:
But, who hath often seene, in such a State,
Father and Sonne like good, like fortunate?

19

But now, this great Succeeder, all repaires,*
And reinduc't that discontinued good:
He builds vp strength & greatnes, for his heires,
Out of the virtues that adornd his blood:
He makes his Subiects Lords of more then theirs;
And sets their bounds farre wider then they stood.
His powre, and fortune, had sufficient wrought,
Could but the State haue kept what he had got.

20

And had his heire surviu'd him in due course,†
What limits *England* hadst thou found? what barre?
What world could haue resisted so great force?
O more then men! (two thunderbolts of warre)
Why did not Time your ioyned worth diuorce,
T'haue made your seueral glories greater farre?
Too prodigall was Nature, thus to doe;
To spend in one Age, what should serue for two.

21

But now the Scepter, in this glorious State,
Supported with strong powre and victorie,
Was left vnto a Child,‡ ordain'd by fate
To stay the course of what might growe too hie:
Here was a stop, that Greatnesse did abate,
When powre vpon so weake a base did lie.
For, least great fortune should presume too farre,
Such oppositions interposed are.

22

Neuer this Iland better peopled stood;
Neuer more men of might, and minds addrest:

---

* *1326. Edw. 3.*
† *Edward the black prince who died before his father.*
‡ *Richard. 2. being but 11. yeares of age, was crowned K, of England. 1377.*

Neuer more Princes of the royall blood,
(If not too many for the publique Rest)
Nor euer was more treasure, wealth and good;
Then when this *Richard*, first, the Crowne possest;
The second of that name, in two accurst:
And well we might haue mist all, but the first.

23

In this mans Raigne, began this fatal strife
(The bloudie argument whereof we treate)
That dearely cost so many'a Prince his life;
And spoyld the weake, and euen consum'd the great:
That, wherein all confusion was so rife,
As Memory euen grieues her to repeat,
And would that time might now this knowledge lose;
But that tis good to learne by others woes.

24

Edward the third, being dead, had left this child,
(Sonne of his worthy sonne deceast of late)*
The Crowne and Scepter of this Realme to wield:
Appointing the protectors of his State
Two of his sonnes, to be his better shield;
Supposing, Vncles, free from guile or hate,
Would order all things for his better good,
In the respect and honour of their bloud.

25

Of these, *Iohn,* Duke of *Lancaster,* was one,†
(Too great a Subiect growne, for such a State.
The title of a King, and glorie wonne
In great exploits his mind did eleuate
Aboue proportion kingdomes stand vpon:
Which made him push at what his issue gate)
The other *Langley:*‡ whose mild temperatness
Did tend vnto a calmer quietnesse.

* *Richard the 2. son to the blacke prince.*
† *The D. of Lancaster intitled K. of Castile in the right of his wife Constance eldest daughter to K. Peter.*
‡ *Edmond Langly Earle of Cambridge; after created D. of Yorke.*

26

With these, did *Woodstock* interpose his part;*
A man, for action violently bent,
And of a spirit averse, and ouer-thwart;
Which could not sute a peace-full gouernment:
Whose euer-swelling, and tumultuous heart
Wrought his owne ill and others discontent.
And these had all the manage of affayres,
During the time the King was vnder yeares.

27

And in the first yeares of his gouernment,
Things past, as first; the warres in *France* proceed,
Though not with that same fortune and euent,
Being now not followed with such carefull heed;
Our people here at home, growne discontent,
Through great exactions, insurrections breed:
Priuate respects hindred the Common-weale:
And idle ease doth on the mighty steale.

28

Too many Kings breed factions in the Court:
The head too weake, the members growne too great.
Which euermore doth happen in this sort,
When Children rule; the plague which God doth threat
Vnto those Kingdomes which he will transport
To other Lynes, or vtterly defeat:
"For, the ambitious, once inur'd to raigne,
"Can neuer brook a priuate state againe.

29

"And Kingdomes euer suffer this distresse,
"Where one, or many, guide the infant King:
"Which one or many (tasting this excesse
"Of greatnesse & command) can neuer bring
"Their thoughts againe t'obay, or to be lesse.
"From hence, these insolencies euer spring;
"Contempt of others, whom they seek to foyle:
"Then follow leagues, destruction, ruine, spoyle.

* *Thomas of Woodstocke after made D. of Glocester.*

30

And whether they, which vnder-went this charge,
Permit the King to take a youthfull vaine,
That they their priuate better might inlarge:
Or whether he himselfe would farther straine
(Thinking his yeeres sufficient to discharge
The gouernment) and so assum'd the raine:
Or howsoeuer, now his eare he lends
To youthfull counsell, and his lustes attends.

31

And Courts were neuer barren yet of those
Which could with subtile traine, and apt aduice,
Worke on the Princes weakenesse, and dispose
Of feeble frailtie, easie to entice.
And such, no doubt, about this King arose,
Whose flatterie (the dangerous nurse of vice)
Got hand vpon his youth, to pleasures bent:
Which, led by them, did others discontent.

32

For, now his Vncles grew much to mislike
These ill proceedings; were it that they saw
That others, fauour'd, did aspiring seeke
Their Nephew from their counsels to withdraw,
(Seeing him of nature flexible, and weake)
Because they onely would keepe all in awe;
Or that indeede they found the King and State
Abus'd by such as now in office sate.

33

Or rather else, they all were in the fault;
Th'ambitious Vncles, th'indiscreete young King,
The greedie Councell, and the Minions naught;
And altogether did this tempest bring:
Besides, the times, with all iniustice fraught,
Concurr'd, with such confus'd misgouenring,
That wee may truely say, This spoyld the State,
"Youthfull Counsaile, priuate Gaine, partiall Hate.

34

And then the King, besides his iealousies
Which nourisht were, had reason to be led

To doubt his Vncles for their loyalties;
Since *Iohn* of *Gaunt* (as was discouered)
Had practised his death in secret wise;
And *Gloster* openly becomes the head
Vnto a league, who all in armes were bent
T'oppose against the present gouernement;*

35

Pretending to remoue such men as were
Accounted to abuse the king, and State.
Of whome, the chiefe they did accuse, was *Veere,*
Made Duke of *Ireland,* with great grace of late;†
And diuers else, who for the place they beare
Obnoxious are, and subiect vnto hate.
And these must be sequestred with all speed:
Or else they vow'd, their swordes should doo the deed.

36

The King was forc't in that next Parliament,
To grant them what he durst not well refuse.
For, thither arm'd they came, and fully bent
To suffer no repulse, nor no excuse:
And here they did accomplish their intent;
Where Iustice did her sword, not Ballance, vse.
For, euen that sacred place they violate,
Arresting all the Iudges as they sate.‡

37

And here had many worthy men their ende,
Without all forme, or any course of Right.
"For, still these broyles, that publike good pretend,
"Worke most iniustice, being done through spight.
"For, those, aggrieued euermore do bend
"Against such as they see of greatest might:

---

* *Ann. Reg. 11. the D. of Gloster with the EE. of Darby, Arũdel, Nottingham, War-wicke, & other LL. hauing forced the K. to put from him all his officers of Court, at this Parliamẽt, caused most of thẽ to be executed: as, Iohn Beauchamp L. Steward of his house, Sir Simon Burley, L. Chamberlaine, with many other.*

† *Robert Veere Duke of Ireland.*

‡ *Also the L. chief Iustice was here executed, and all the Iudges condēned to death, for maintaining the kings prerogatiue against these LL. & the constitutions of the last Parliament, in Ann. 10.*

"Who, though they cannot helpe what will go ill;
"Yet, since they may doo wrong, are thought they will.

38

And yet herein I meane not to excuse
The Iustices, and Minions of the King
(Who might their office and their grace abuse)
But blame the course held in the managing.
"For, great-men, ouer-grac't, much rigor vse.
"Presuming fauorits discontentment bring.
"And disproportions harmonie do breake.
"Minions, too great, argue a king too weake.

39

Now, that so much was granted, as was sought;
A reconcilement made, although not ment,
Appeas'd them all in shewe, but not in thought,
Whilst euery one seem'd outwardly content:
Though hereby king, nor peeres, nor people got
More loue, more strength, or easier gouernment;
But euery day, things still succeeded worse.
"For good from Kings is seldome drawne by force.

40

And thus it loe continued, till by chaunce
The Queene (which was the Emperours daughter) di'de: *
When-as the King, t'establish peace with *Fraunce*,
And better for home-quiet to prouide,
Sought by contracting marriage to aduance
His owne affayres, against his Vncles pride;
Tooke the young daughter of King *Charles* to wife:†
Which after, in the end, rays'd greater strife.

41

For, now his vncle *Gloster* much repin'd,
Against this French alliance and this peace:
As either out of a tumultuous minde;
(Which neuer was content the warres should cease:)
Or that he did dishonorable find
Those articles which did our State decrease;

---

* *Ann. Reg. 18.*
† *Ann. 20. Isabel, daughter to Charles, 6.*

And therefore storm'd because the Crowne had wrong:
Or that he fear'd, the King would growe too strong.

42

But whatsoeuer mov'd him; this is sure,
Hereby he wrought his ruine in the end;
And was a fatall cause, that did procure
The swift approaching mischiefes that attend.
For loe, the King no longer could indure
Thus to be crost in what he did intend;
And therefore watcht but some occasion fit
T'attache the Duke, when he thought least of it.

43

And Fortune, to set forward this intent,
The Cont S. *Paule,* from *France,* doth hither bring: *
Whom *Charles* the sixt imploy'd in complement,
To see the Queene, and to salute the King.
To whom he shewes his Vncles discontent,
And of his secret dangerous practising,
How he his Subiectes sought to sulleuate,
And breake the league with *Fraunce* concluded late.

44

"To whom the Cont, most cunningly replies;
"Great Prince, it is within your power, with ease
"To remedy such feares, such iealousies,
"And rid you of such mutiners as these;
"By cutting off that, which might greater rise:
"And now at first, preuenting this disease,
"And that before he shall your wrath disclose.
"For, who threats first, meanes of reuenge doth lose.

45

"First take his head; then tell the reason why:
"Stand not to finde him guiltie by your lawes.
"You easier shall with him your quarrell trie
"Dead then aliue, who hath the better cause.
"For, in the murmuring vulgar, vsually
"This publique course of yours compassion drawes;
"Especially in cases of the great:
"Which worke much pitty, in the vndiscreat.

* *Valeran E. of S. Paule who had maried the kings halfe sister.*

46

"And this is sure, though his offence be such:
"Yet doth calamitie attract commorse:
"And men repine at Princes blood-shed much,
"(How iust-soeuer) iudging tis by force.
"I know not how, their death giues such a touch,
"In those that reach not to a true discourse;
"As so shall you, obseruing formall right,
"Be held still as vniust, and win more spight.

47

"And, oft, the cause may come preuented so:
"And therefore when tis done, let it be heard.
"For, thereby shall you scape your priuate wo,
"And satisfie the world too, afterward.
"What neede you weigh the rumors that shall go?
"What is that breath, being with your life compar'd?
"And therefore, if you will be rul'd by me,
"In secret sort, let him dispatched bee.

48

And then arraigne the chiefe of those you finde
Were of his faction secretly compact:
Who may so well be handled in their kinde;
As their confessions, which you shall exact,
May both appease the aggrieued peoples minde,
And make their death to aggrauate their fact.
So shall you rid your selfe of dangers quite;
And shew the world, that you haue done but right.

49

This counsell, vttred vnto such an eare
As willing listens to the safest wayes,
Workes on the yeelding matter of his feare;
Which easily to any course obayes.
For, euery Prince, seeing his daunger neere,
By any meanes his quiet peace assaies.
"And still the greatest wrongs, that euer were,
"Haue then been wrought, when Kings were put in feare.

50

Call'd in with publique pardon, and release,
The *Duke* of *Gloster,* with his complices;*
All tumults, all contentions seem to cease,
The land rich, people pleas'd, all in happinesse;
When sodainely *Gloster* came caught, with peace;
Warwicke, with profered loue and promises:
And *Arundell* was in, with cunning brought:
Who else abrode, his safetie might haue wrought.

51

Long was it not, ere *Gloster* was conuayd
To *Calice,* and there strangled secretly:†
Warwicke and *Arundell* close prisoners laid,
Th'especiall men of his confederacie:
Yet *Warwickes* teares and base confessions staide
The doome of death; and came confin'd thereby,
And so prolongs this not long base-begg'd breath:
But *Arundell* was put to publique death.

52

Which publique death (receiv'd with such a cheare,
As not a sigh, a looke, a shrink bewrayes
The least felt touch of a degenerous feare)
Gaue life to Enuie, to his courage prayse;
And made his stout-defended cause appeare
With such a face of Right, as that it layes
The side of wrong t'wards him, who had long since
By Parliament forgiuen this offence:‡

53

And in the vnconceiuing vulgar sort,
Such an impression of his goodnes gaue
As Sainted him, and rays'd a strange report
Of miracles effected on his Graue:

* *At the parliament, in Anno 11. the LL. of the league with Gloster, being pardoned for their opposing against the kings proceedings, were quiet till Anno 21; when vpon report of a new conspiracie, they were surprised.*

† *Mowbray E. Marshal, after made Duke of Norfolke, had the charge of dispatching the D. of Gloster, at Calice.*

‡ *The K. had by Parliament before pardoned the D. and those two Earles: yet was the pardon reuoked.*

Although the Wise (whome zeale did not transport)
"Knew, how each great example still must haue
"Something of wrong, a taste of violence;
"Wherewith, the publique quiet doth dispense.

54

The King foorth-with prouides him of a Guard;
A thousand Archers daily to attend:
Which now vpon the act he had prepar'd
As th'argument his actions to defend:
But yet the world hereof conceiu'd so hard,
That all this nought auaild him in the end.
"In vaine, with terror is he fortified,
"That is not guarded with firme loue beside.

55

Now storme his grieued Vncles, though in vaine;
Not able better courses to aduise.
They might their grieuance inwardly complaine;
But outwardly they needes must temporise.
The King was great; and they should nothing gaine
T'attempt reuenge, or offer once to rise:
This league with *Fraunce* had made him now so strong,
That they must needes as yet indure this wrong.

56

For, like a Lion that escapes his boundes,
Hauing beene long restrain'd his vse to stray,
Ranges the restless woods, stayes on no groūd,
Riots with blood-shed, wantons on his praie;
Seekes not for neede, but in his pride to wound,
Glorying to see his strength and what he may:
So this vnbridled King (freed of his feares)
In liberty, himself thus wildely beares.

57

For, standing now alone, he sees his might
Out of the compasse of respectiue awe;
And now beginnes to violate all right,
While no restraining feare at hand he saw.
Now he exacts of all, wastes in delight,

Riots in pleasure, and neglects the law:
He thinkes his Crowne is licenst to do ill.
"That lesse should list, that may do what it wil.

58

Thus b'ing transported in this sensuall course;
No friend to warne, no counsell to withstand,
He still proceedeth on from bad to worse,
Sooth'd in all actions that he tooke in hand,
By such as all impietie did nurse,
Commending euer what hee did command.*
"Vnhappie Kings! that neuer may be taught
"To know themselues, or to discerne their fault.

59

And whilst this course did much the kingdome daunt,
The Duke of *Herford* being of courage bolde,
As sonne and heire to mighty *Iohn* of *Gaunt*,†
Vtters the passion which he could not holde
Concerning these oppressions, and the want
Of gouernment: which he to *Norfolke*‡ told;
To th'end, he (being great about the king)
Might do some good, by better counselling.

60

Herof doth *Norfolke* presently take hold,
And to the king the whole discourse relate:
Who, not conceipting it, as it was told,
But iudging it proceeded out of hate;
Disdeigning deepely to be so controwl'd,
That others should his Rule preiudicate,
Charg'd *Herford* therewithall: who re-accus'd
Norfolke, for words of treason he had vs'd.

61

Norfolke denies them peremptorily.
Herford recharg'd, and supplicates the king,
To haue the combate of his enemie;
That by his sword hee might approue the thing.

* —*Nihil est quod credere de se, non possit, cùm laudatur, dijs aequa potestas.*
† *Hen. Bollingbroke of Hereford.*
‡ *Tho. Mowbray D. of Norfolke.*

Norfolke desires the same, as earnestly:
And both with equall courage menacing
Reuenge of wrong; that none knew which was free:
For, times of faction, times of slaunder bee.

62

The combate granted, and the day assign'd,
They both in order of the field appeare,
Most richly furnisht in all Martiall kinde,
And at the point of intercombate were;
When (lo) the king chang'd sodainly his minde,
Casts downe his warder to arrest them there;
As being aduis'd a better way to take,
Which might for his more certaine safetie make.

63

For, now considering (as it likely might)
The victorie should hap on *Herfords* side
(A man most valiant and of noble sprite,
Belov'd of all, and euer worthy tri'd)
How much he might be grac't in publique sight,
By such an act, as might aduance his pride,
And so become more popular by this;
Which he feares, too much he already is.

64

And therefore he resolues to banish both,
Though th'one in chiefest fauour with him stood,
A man he dearely lov'd; and might be loth
To leaue him, that had done him so much good: *
Yet hauing cause to do as now he doth,
To mitigate the enuie of his blood,
Thought best to lose a friend, to rid a foe;
And such a one, as now he doubted so.

65

And therefore to perpetual exile hee
Mowbray condemnes; *Herford* but for ten yeares:
Thinking (for that the wrong of this decree,
Compar'd with greater rigour, lesse appeares)

---

* *Mowbray was banished the very day (by the course of the yeere) whereon he murthered the D. of Glocester.*

It might of all the better liked bee:
But yet such murmuring of the fact he heares,
That he is faine foure of the ten forgiue,
And iudg'd him sixe yeares in exile to liue.

66

At whose departure hence out of the Land,
How did the open multitude reueale
The wondrous loue they bare him vnder-hand!
Which now, in this hote passion of their zeale,
They plainely shew'd; that all might vnderstand
How deare he was vnto the common weale.
They feard not to exclaime against the King;
As one, that sought all good mens ruining.

67

Vnto the shore, with teares, with sighes, with mone,
They him conduct; cursing the bounds that stay
Their willing feete, that would haue further gone,
Had not the fearefull *Ocean* stopt their way:
"Why *Neptune;* Hast thou made vs stand alone
"Diuided from the world, for this, say they?
"Hemd-in, to be a spoyle to tyrannie,
"Leauing affliction hence no way to flie?

68

"Are we lockt vp, poore soules, heere to abide
"Within the waterie prison of thy waues,
"As in a fold, where subiect to the pride
"And lust of Rulers we remaine as slaues?
"Here in the reach of might, where none can hide
"From th'eye of wrath, but onely in their Graues?
"Happie confiners you of other landes,
"That shift your soyle, and oft scape tyrants hands.

69

"And must we leaue him here, whom here were fit
"We should retaine, the pillar of our State?
"Whose vertues well deserue to gouerne it,
"And not this wanton young effeminate.
"Why should not he in Regall honour sit,
"That best knowes how a Realme to ordinate?

"But, one day yet, we hope thou shalt bring backe
"(Deare *Bullingbrooke*) the Iustice that we lacke.

70

"Thus muttred, loe, the malecontented sort;
"That loue Kings best, before they haue them, still;
"And neuer can the present State comport,
"But would as often change, as they change will.
For, this good Duke had wonne them in this sort
By succ'ring them, and pittying of their ill,
That they supposed streight it was one thing,
To be both a good Man, and a good King.

71

When-as the grauer sort that saw the course,
And knew that Princes may not be controld,
Lik't well to suffer this, for feare of worse;
"Since, many great, one Kingdome cannot hold.
For, now they saw, intestine strife, of force,
The apt-diuided State intangle would,
If he should stay whom they would make their head,
By whom the vulgar body might be led.

72

"They saw likewise, that Princes oft are faine
"To buy their quiet, with the price of wrong:
And better 'twere that now a few complaine,
Then all should mourne, aswell the weake as strong:
Seeing still how little, Realmes by chaunge do gaine;
And therefore learned by obseruing long,
"T'admire times past, follow the present will,
"Wish for good Princes, but t'indure the ill.

73

For, when it nought auailes, what folly then
To striue against the current of the time?
Who will throwe downe himselfe, for other men,
That make a ladder by his fall to clime?
Or who would seeke t'imbroyle his Country, when
He might haue rest; suffering but others crime?
"Since wise men euer haue preferred farre
"Th'vniustest peace, before the iustest warre.

74

Thus they considered, that in quiet sate,
Rich or content, or else vnfit to striue:
Peace-louer wealth, hating a troublous State,
Doth willing reasons for their rest contriue:
But, if that all were thus considerate,
How should in Court, the great, the fauour'd thriue?
Factions must be, and these varieties:
And some must fall, that other-some may rise.

75

But, long the Duke remain'd not in exile,
Before that *Iohn* of *Gaunt,* his father, dies.
Vpon whose state the king seis'd now, this while,
Disposing of it, as his enemies.
This open wrong no longer could beguile
The world, that saw these great indignities.
Which so exasperates the mindes of all,
That they resolv'd, him home againe to call.

76

For, now they saw, t'was malice in the King
(Transported in his ill-conceiued thought)
That made him so to prosecute the thing
Against all law, and in a course so naught.
And this aduantage to the Duke did bring
More fit occasions; whereupon he wrought.
"For, to a man so strong, and of such might,
"He giues him more, that takes away his right.

77

The King in this meane time* (I know not how)
Was drawne into some actions, foorth the Land,
T'appease the *Irish,* that reuolted now:
And, there attending what he had in hand,
Neglects those parts from whence worse dangers growe;
As ignorant, how his affayres did stand:
Whether the plot was wrought it should be so,
Or that his fate did draw him on to go.

* *An. Reg. 22.*

78

Most sure it is, that hee committed here
An ignorant and idle ouersight;
Not looking to the Dukes proceedings there,
Being in the Court of *Fraunce,* where best he might;
Where both the King and all assured were
T'haue stopt his course, being within their right:
But now he was exil'd, he thought him sure;
And, free from farther doubting, liv'd secure.

79

So blindes the sharpest counsels of the wise
This ouershadowing Prouidence on hie;
And dazleth all their clearest sighted eyes,
That they see not how nakedly they lie.
There where they little thinke, the storme doth rise,
And ouercasts their cleare securitie:
When man hath stopt all wayes saue onely that,
Which (as least doubted) Ruine enters at.

80

And now was all disorder in th'excesse,
And whatsoeuer doth a change portend;
As, idle luxurie, and wantonnesse,
Proteus-like varying Pride, vaine without ende:
Wrong-worker *Riot* (motiue to oppresse)
Endless Exactions, which the idle spend,
Consuming Vsurie, and credits crackt,
Call'd-on this purging Warre, that many lackt.

81

Then Ill-perswading want, in Martiall mindes,
And wronged patience (long opprest with might)
Loosenes in all (which no religion bindes)
Commaunding force (the measure made of *Right*)
Gaue fuell to this fire, that easie findes
The way, t'inflame the whole indangerd quite:
These were the publique breeders of this Warre;
By which, still greatest States confounded are.

82

For, now this peace with *Fraunce* had shut in here
The ouergrowing humours Warres do spend.

For, where t'euacuate no imployments were,
Wider th'vnwieldy burthen doth distend.
Men, wholly vs'd to warre, peace could not beare;
As knowing no other course, whereto to bend:
For, brought vp in the broyles of these two Reames,
They thought best fishing still, in troubled streames.

83

Like to a Riuer, that is stopt his course,
Doth violate his bankes, breakes his owne bed,
Destroyes his bounds, and ouer-runs, by force,
The neighbour-fieldes, irregularly spred:
Euen so this sodaine stop of Warre doth nurse
Home broyles, within it selfe, from others led:
So dangerous the change hereof is tri'd
Ere mindes 'come soft, or otherwise imploid.

84

But, all this makes for thee, ô *Bullingbrooke,*
To worke a way vnto thy Soueraintie.
This care, the Heauens, Fate, and Fortune tooke,
To bring thee to thy Scepter easily.
Vpon thee fall's that hap, which him forsooke,
Who, crownd a King, a King yet must not die.
Thou wert ordaind, by Prouidence, to rayse
A quarrell, lasting longer then thy dayes.

85

For, now this absent Lord, out of his Land
(Where though he shew'd great sprite and valor then;
Being attended with a worthy band
Of valiant Peeres, and most couragious men)
Gaue time to them at home, that had in hand
Th'vngodly worke, and knew the season when:
Who faile not to aduise the Duke with speed;
Solliciting to what hee soone agreed.

86

Who presently, vpon so good report,
Relying on his friends fidelitie,
Conueyes himselfe out of the French Kings Court,
Vnder pretence to go to *Britannie:*

And, with his followers, that to him resort,
Landed in *England:** Welcom'd ioyfully
Of th'altring vulgar, apt for changes still;
As headlong carried with a present will.

87

And com'n to quiet shore, but not to rest;
The first night of his ioyfull landing here,
A fearefull vision doth his thoughts molest:
Seeming to see in reuerent forme appeare
A faire and goodly woman all distrest;†
Which, with full-weeping eyes and rented haire,
Wringing her hands (as one that griev'd and prayd)
With sighes commixt with words, vnto him said;

88

"O! whither dost thou tend, my vnkinde Sonne?
"What mischiefe dost thou go-about to bring
"To her, whose *Genius* thou here lookst vpon,
"Thy Mother-countrey, whence thy selfe didst spring?
"Whither thus dost thou, in ambition, run,
"To change due course, by foule disordering?
"What bloodshed, what turmoyles dost thou commence,
"To last for many wofull ages hence?

89

"Stay here thy foote, thy yet vnguilty foote,
"That canst not stay when thou art farther in.
"Retire thee yet vnstain'd whil'st it doth boote:
"The end, is spoyle, of what thou dost begin:
"Iniustice neuer yet tooke lasting roote,
"Nor held that long, Impietie did win.
"The babes, vnborne, shall (ô) be borne to bleed
"In this thy quarrell, if thou do proceede.

90

This said, she ceast: when he in troubled thought
Griev'd at this tale and sigh't, and thus replies;
"Deare Countrey, ô I haue not hither brought

* *The D. being banished in Septēber, landed in the beginning of Iulie, after, at Rauenspurre, in Yorkeshire, some say but with 60. men, other with 3000 and 8. shippes set forth and furnished by the Duke of Brittaine Ann. Reg. 22.*
† *The Genius of England appeares to Bullingbrooke.*

"These Armes to spoyle, but for thy liberties:
"The sinne be on their head, that this haue wrought;
"Who wrongd me first, and thee do tyrannise.
"I am thy Champion, and I seeke my right:
"Prouok't I am to this, by others spight.

91

    "This, this pretence, saith shee, th'ambitious finde
"To smooth iniustice, and to flatter wrong.
"Thou dost not know what then will be thy minde,
"When thou shalt see thy selfe aduanc't and strong.
"When thou hast shak't off that, which others binde;
"Thou soone forgettest what thou learnedst long.
"Men do not know what then themselues will bee,
"When-as, more then themselues, themselues they see.

92

    And herewithall, turning about he wakes,
Lab'ring in spirit, troubled with this strange sight:
And mus'd a while, waking aduisement takes
Of what had past in sleepe and silent night:
Yet hereof no important reck'ning makes,
But as a dreame that vanisht with the light:
The day designes, and what he had in hand
Left it to his diuerted thoughts vnscand.

93

    Doubtfull at first, he warie doth proceed;
Seemes not t'affect that, which he did effect:
Or else perhaps seemes, as he meant indeed,
Sought but his owne, and did no more expect.
Then, Fortune, thou art guiltie of his deed:
That didst his state aboue his hopes erect:
And thou must beare some blame of his great sinne;
That leftst him worse, then when he did beginne.

94

    Thou didst conspire with Pride, and with the Time,
To make so easie an ascent to wrong,
That he who had no thought so hie to clime
(With fauouring comfort still allur'd along)
Was with occasion thrust into the crime;

Seeing others weakenes and his part so strong.
"And who is there, in such a case that will
"Do good, and feare, that may liue free with ill?

95

We will not say nor thinke, O *Lancaster,*
But that thou then didst meane as thou didst sweare
Vpon th'Euangelists at *Doncaster,*
In th'eye of heauen, and that assembly theare,
That thou but as an vpright orderer,
Sought'st to reforme th'abused Kingdome here,
And get thy right, and what was thine before;
And this was all; thou would'st attempt no more:

96

Though we might say, and thinke, that this pretence
Was but a shadow to the intended act;
Because th'euent doth argue the offence,
And plainely seemes to manifest the fact:
For that hereby thou mightst win confidence
With those, whom else thy course might hap distract,
And all suspicion of thy drift remoue;
"Since easily men credit whom they loue.

97

But, God forbid wee should so neerly pry
Into the lowe-deepe-buried sinnes long past,
T'examine and conferre iniquitie,
Whereof faith would no memorie should last:
That our times might not haue t'exemplifie
With aged staines; but, with our owne shame cast,
Might thinke our blot the first, not done before;
That new-made sinnes might make vs blush the more.

98

And let vnwresting Charitie beleeue
That then thy oath with thy intent agreed;
And others faith, thy faith did first deceiue,
Thy after-fortune forc't thee to this deed.
And let no man this idle censure giue,
Because th'euent proues so, 'twas so decreed.
"For, oft our counsels sort to other end,
"Then that which frailtie did at first intend.

99

Whil'st those that are but outward lookers on
(Who sildome sound these mysteries of State)
Deeme things were so contriv'd as they are done,
And hold that policie, which was but fate;
Imagining, all former acts did run
Vnto that course they see th'effects relate;
Whil'st still too short they come, or cast too far,
"And make these great men wiser then they ar.

100

But, by degrees he ventures now on blood;*
And sacrifiz'd, vnto the peoples loue,
The death of those that chiefe in enuie stood:
As, th'Officers (who first these dangers proue)
The Treasurer, and those whom they thought good,
Bushy and *Greene,* by death he must remoue:
These were the men, the people thought, did cause
Those great exactions, and abus'd the lawes.

101

This done, his cause was preacht with learned skill,
By *Arundel,* th'Archbishop:† who there show'd
A Pardon sent from *Rome,* to all that will
Take part with him, and quit the faith they ow'd
To *Richard;* as a Prince vnfit and ill:
On whom the Crowne was fatally bestow'd.
And easie-yeelding zeale was quickly caught,
With what the mouth of grauity had taught.

102

O that this power, from euerlasting giuen
(The great alliance made twixt God and vs;
Th'intelligence that earth doth hold with heauen)
Sacred Religion; ô that thou must thus
Be made to smooth our wayes vniust, vneuen;‡
Brought from aboue, earth-quarrels to discusse!

* *The D. put to death Williā Scroope E. of Wiltshire, Treasurer of Eng. with Sir Hen. Greene, & Sir Iohn Bushy, for misgouerning the king and the Realme.*
† *Th. Arundel Archbish. of Canterburie.*
‡ *Bis peccat, qui pretextu Religionis peccat.*

Must men beguile our soules, to winne our wils,
And make our Zeale the furtherer of ils?

103

But, the ambitious, to aduance their might,
Dispense with heauen, and what Religion would.
"The armed will finde right, or els make right;
If this meanes wrought not, yet an other should.
And this and other now do all incite
To strength the faction that the Duke doth hold:
Who easily obtained what he sought;
His vertues and his loue so greatly wrought.

104

The King, still busied in this *Irish* warre
(Which by his valour there did well succeed)
Had newes, how here his Lords reuolted are,
And how the Duke of *Herford* doth proceede:
In these affaires he feares are growne too farre;
Hastes his returne from thence with greatest speed:
But was by tempests, windes, and seas debarr'd;
As if they likewise had against him warr'd.

105

But, at the length (though late) in Wales he lands:
Where, thoroughly inform'd of *Henries* force,
And well aduertis'd how his owne case stands
(Which to his griefe he sees tends to the worse)
He leaues t'*Aumarle,** at *Milford,* all those bandes
He brought from *Ireland:* taking thence his course
To *Conway†* (all disguis'd) with fourteene more,
To th'Earle of *Salisburie,* thither sent before:

106

Thinking, the Earle‡ had rays'd some Armie there;
Whom there he findes forsaken all alone:
The forces, in those parts which leuied were,
Were closely shrunke away, disperst and gone.
The king had stayd too long; and they, in feare,

---

* *Edward D. of Aumerle Sonne to the D. of Yorke.*
† *Conway Castle in Wales.*
‡ *Montague E. of Salisburie.*

Resolued euerie man to shift for one.
At this amas'd, such fortune he laments;
Foresees his fall, whereto each thing consents.

107

In this disturb'd tumultuous broken State,
Whil'st yet th'euent stood doubtfull what should bee;
Whilst nought but headlong running to debate,
And glittering troupes and armor men might see:
Furie, and feare, compassion, wrath, and hate,
Confus'd through all the land, no corner free;
The strong, all mad, to strife, to ruine bent;
The weaker waild: the aged they lament,

108

And blame their many yeeres that liue so long,
To see the horrour of these miseries.
Why had not we (said they) di'd with the strong,
In forraine fieldes, in honourable wise,
In iust exployts, and noble without wrong,
And by the valiant hand of enemies?
And not thus now reserued, in our age,
To home-confusion, and disordered rage.

109

Vnto the Temples flocke the weake, deuout,
Sad wayling Women; there to vow and pray
For husbands, brothers, or their sonnes gone out
To blood-shed: whom nor teares, nor loue could stay.
Here, graue religious Fathers (which much doubt
The sad euents these broyles procure them may)
As Prophets warne, exclaime, disswade these crimes,
By the examples fresh of other times.

110

And (ô!) what, do you now prepare, said they,
Another Conquest, by these fatall wayes?
What, must your owne hands make your selues a pray
To desolation, which these tumults rayse?
What *Dane,* what *Norman,* shall prepare his way
To triumph on the spoyle of your decayes?
That, which nor *Fraunce,* nor all the world, could do
In vnion, shall your discord bring you to?

111

Conspire against vs, neighbour nations all,
That enuie at the height whereto w'are growne:
Coniure the barbarous North, and let them call
Strange furie from farre distant shores vnknowne;
And let them altogether on vs fall,
So to diuert the ruine of our owne:
That we, forgetting what doth so incense,
May turne the hand of malice, to defence.

112

Calme these tempestuous spirits, O mighty Lord;
This threatning storme that ouer-hangs the Land.
Make them consider, ere they'vnsheath the sword,
How vaine is th'earth, this point whereon they stand;
And with what sad calamities is stor'd
The best of that, for which th'Ambitious band:
"Labor the ende of labor, strife of strife;
"Terror in death, and horrour after life.

113

Thus they in zeale, whose humbled thoughts were good,
Whil'st in this wide-spread volume of the skies,
The booke of Prouidence disclosed stood,
Warnings of wrath, foregoing miseries
In lines of fire and characters of blood,
There fearefull formes in dreadfull flames arise,
Amazing Comets, threatning Monarchs might,
And new-seene Starres, vnknowne vnto the night,

114

Red fierie Dragons in the ayre do flye,
And burning Meteors, pointed-streaming lightes:
Bright Starres in midst of day appeare in skie,
Prodigious monsters, ghastly fearefull sights:
Strange Ghostes, and apparitions terrifie:
The wofull mother her owne birth affrightes;
Seeing a wrong deformed infant borne,
Grieues in her paines, deceiv'd in shame doth mourne.

115

The earth, as if afeard of blood and wounds,
Trembles in terrour of these falling bloes:

The hollow concaues giue out groning sounds,
And sighing murmures, to lament our woes:
The Ocean, all at discord with his boundes,
Reiterates his strange vntimely flowes:
Nature all out of course, to checke our course,
Neglects her worke, to worke in vs remorse.

116

So great a wracke vnto it selfe doth, lo,
Disorder'd proud mortalitie prepare,
That this whole frame doth euen labour so
Her ruine vnto frailty to declare:
And trauailes to fore-signifie the wo
That weake improuidence could not beware.
"For heauen and earth, and ayre and seas and all,
"Taught men to see, but not to shun their fall.

117

Is man so deare vnto the heauens, that they
Respect the wayes of earth, the workes of sinne?
Doth this great All, this *Vniuersall,* weigh
The vaine designes that weakenesse doth begin?
Or doth our *feare,* father of zeale, giue way
Vnto this errour ignorance liues in?
And deeme our faults the cause that moue these powres,
That haue their cause from other cause then ours?

118

But, these beginnings had this impious Warre,
Th'vngodly blood-shed that did so defile
The beautie of thy fields, and euen did marre
The flowre of thy chiefe pride, thou fairest Ile:
These were the causes that incenst so farre
The ciuill wounding hand inrag'd with spoyle;
That now the liuing, with afflicted eye,
Looke back with griefe on such calamitie.

The end of the first Booke.

The Second *Booke*

THE ARGVMENT

King Richard *mones his wrong, and wails his raigne:*
And here betrayd, to London *he is led,*
Basely attyr'd, attending Herfords *traine:*
Where th'one is scornd, the other Welcomed.
His Wife, *mistaking him, doth much complaine;*
And both togither greatly sorrowed:
In hope to saue his life and ease his thrall,
He yeelds up state, and Rule, *and Crowne, and all.*

1

IN dearth of faith, and scarcitie of friendes,
The late great mighty Monarch, on the shore
In th'vtmost corner of his Land, attendes
To call backe false obedience, fled before;
Toyles, and, in vaine, his toyle and labour spendes:
More harts he sought to gaine, he lost the more: /
All turn'd their faces to the rising sunne,
And leaue his setting-fortune, night begunne. /

2

Percy,* how soone, by thy example led,
The household traine forsooke their wretched Lord!
When, with thy staffe of charge dishonoured,
Thou brak'st thy fayth, not steward of thy word,
And tookst his part that after tooke thy head;
When thine owne hand had strengthned first his sword.
"For, such great merits do vpbraid, and call
"For great reward, or thinke the great too smal.

3

And Kings loue not to be beholding ought:
Which makes their chiefest friends oft speed the worst.

* *This Percie was Earle of Worster, brother to the Earle of Northumberland, and steward of the Kings house.*

101

For, those, by whom their fortunes haue bin wrought,
Put them in minde of what they were at first.
Whose doubtfull faith if once in question brought,
Tis thought they will offend because they durst:
And taken in a fault are neuer spar'd;
"Being easier to reuenge, then to reward.

4

And thus these mightie actors, sonnes of change,
These partizanes of factions, often tri'd;
That, in the smoake of Innouations strange,
Builde huge vncertaine plots of vnsure pride:
And, on the hazard of a bad exchange,
Haue ventur'd all the stocke of life beside;
"Whilst Princes, rais'd, disdaine to haue bin rais'd
"By those whose helpes deserue not to be prais'd.

5

But thus is *Richard* left, and all alone
Saue with th'vnarmed title of his right;
And those braue troupes, his fortune-followers gone,
And all that pompe (the complements of might)
Th'amuzing shadowes that are cast vpon
The state of Princes, to beguile the sight,
All vanisht cleane, and only frailty left;
Himselfe, of all, besides himselfe, bereft:

6

Like when some great *Colossus,* whose strong base
Or mightie props are shrunk or sunke away,
Fore-shewing ruine, threatning all the place
That in the danger of his fall doth stay,
All straight to better safetie flocke apace;
None rest to helpe the ruine, while they may.
"The perill great, and doubtfull the redresse,
"Men are content to leaue Right in distresse.

7

And looke, how *Thames,* inricht with many a Flood,
And goodly Riuers (that haue made their Graues,
And buried both their names and all their good
Within his greatnes, to augment his waues)

Glides on, with pompe of Waters, vnwithstood,
Vnto the *Ocean* (which his tribute craues)
And layes vp all his wealth, within that powre,
Which in it selfe all greatnes doth deuowre:

8

So flocke the mighty, with their following traine,
Vnto the all-receiuing *Bullingbrooke:**
Who wonders at himselfe, how hee should gaine
So many harts as now his partie tooke;
And with what ease, and with how slender paine,
His fortune giues him more then he could looke:
What he imagind neuer could be wrought
Is powrd vpon him, farre beyond his thought.

9

So, often, things which seeme at first in showe,
Without the compasse of accomplishment,
Once vent'red on, to that successe do growe,
That euen the Authors do admire th'euent;
So many meanes which they did neuer knowe
Do second their designes, and do present
Straunge vnexpected helps, and chiefly then
When th'Actors are reputed worthy men.

10

And *Richard,* who lookt Fortune in the backe,
Sees headlong-lightness running from the right,
Amazed standes to note how great a wracke
Of faith, his riots caus'd, what mortall spight
They beare him, who did law and iustice lacke;
Sees how concealed hate breakes out in sight,
And feare-depressed enuie (pent before)
When fit occasion thus vnlockt the dore.

11

Like when some mastiue whelpe, dispos'd to play,
A whole confused heard of beastes doth chace,
Which with one vile consent run all away;

* *The D. of Yorke, left Gouernour of the Realm in the absēce of the king, hauing leuied a great Army, as if to haue opposed against Bullingbrooke, brought most of the Nobilitie of the kingdome to take his part.*

If any hardier then the rest in place
But offer head, that idle feare to stay,
Backe straight the daunted chaser turnes his face,
And all the rest (with bold example led)
As fast run on him, as before they fled:

12

So, with this bold opposer, rushes-on
This many-headed monster, *Multitude:*
And he, who late was feard, is set vpon,
And by his owne (Actæon-like) pursu'd;
His owne, that had all loue and awe forgone:
Whom breath and shadowes onely did delude,
And newer hopes, which promises perswade;
Though rarely men keepe promises so made.

13

Which when he saw; thus to himselfe complaines:
"O why do you, fond, false-deceiued, so
"Run headlong to that change that nothing gaines,
"But gaine of sorrow, onely change of wo?
"Which is all one, if he be like who raignes:
"Why will you buy, with blood, what you forgoe?
"Tis nought, but shewes, that Ignorance esteemes:
"The thing possest is not the thing it seemes.

14

"And when the sinnes of *Bullingbrooke* shall be
"As great as mine, and you vnanswered
"In these your hopes; then may you wish for me
"Your lawfull Sov'raigne, from whose faith you fled;
"And, grieued in your soules, the error see
"That shining promises had shadowed:
"As th'humorous sicke, remouing, finde no ease,
"When changed Chambers change not the disease.

15

"Then shall you finde this name of Libertie
"(The watch-word of Rebellion euer vs'd;
"The idle eccho of Vncertaintie,
"That euermore the simple hath abus'd)
"But new-turned Seruitude and Miserie;

"And euen the same and worse, before refus'd.
"Th'aspirer once attaind vnto the top,
"Cuts off those meanes by which himselfe got vp.

16

"And with a harder hand, and streighter raine,
"Doth curbe that loosenes he did finde before;
"Doubting th'occasion like might serue againe:
"His owne example makes him feare the more.
"Then, ô iniurious Land, what dost thou gaine
"To aggrauate thine owne afflictions store?
"Since thou must needs obay Kings gouernement;
"And no rule, euer yet, could all content.

17

"What if my youth hath offered vp to lust
"Licentious fruites of indiscreet desires,
"When idle heate of vainer yeeres did thrust
"That furie on: yet now when it retires
"To calmer state, why should you so distrust
"To reape that good whereto mine age aspires?
"The youth of Princes haue no boundes for sinne,
"Vnlesse themselues do make them boundes within.

18

"Who sees not, that sees ought (wo worth the while)
"The easie way, that Greatnesse hath to fall?
"Enuirond with deceit, hemm'd-in with guile,
"Sooth'd vp in flatterie, fawned on of all:
"Within his owne, liuing as in exile;
"Heares but with others eares, or not at all:
"And euen is made a prey vnto a fewe,
"Who locke vp grace that would to other shewe:

19

"And who (as let in lease) do farme the Crowne,
"And ioy the vse of Maiestie and might;
"Whil'st we hold but the shadow of our owne,
"Pleas'd with vaine shewes, and dallied with delight:
"They, as huge vnproportion'd mountaines, growne
"Betweene our land and vs, shadowing our light,
"Bereaue the rest of ioy, and vs of loue,
"And keepe downe all, to keepe themselues aboue.

20

"Which wounds, with griefe, poore vnrespected zeale,
"When grace holdes no proportion in the parts;
"When distribution, in the Common-weale,
"Of charge and honour due to good desarts
"Is stopt; when others greedie hands must deale
"The benefite that Maiestie imparts:
"What good we meant, comes gleaned home but light,
"Whilst we are robd of prayse, they of their right.

21

Thus he complaind; when, lo, from *Lancaster*
(The new intit'led Duke) with order sent
Arriv'd *Northumberland,* as to conferre
And make relation of the Dukes intent: *
And offred there, if that he would referre
The controuersie vnto Parlement,
And punish those that had abus'd the State,
As causers of this vniuersall hate;

22

And also see that Iustice might bee had
On those the Duke of *Glosters* death procur'd,
And such remoou'd from Councell as were bad;
His cousen *Henry* would, hee there assur'd,
On humble knees before his Grace, bee glad
To aske him pardon, to bee well secur'd
And haue his right and grace restor'd againe:
The which was all hee labour'd to obtayne.

23

And therefore doth an interparle exhort,
Perswades him leaue that vnbeseeming place,
And with a Princely hardinesse resort
Vnto his people, that attend his Grace:
They meant his publique good, and not his hurt;
And would most ioyfull bee to see his face:
He layes his soule to pledge, and takes his Oath,
The ost of Christ, an ostage for his troth.

* *The E. of Northũberland sent to the king from Hen. Bullingbrooke now D. of Lancaster.*

24

This proffer, with such protestations, made
Vnto a King that so neere danger stood,
Was a sufficient motiue to perswade,
When no way else could shewe a face so good:
Th'vnhonourable meanes of safety, bade
Danger accept, what Maiesty withstood.
"When better choyses are not to bee had,
"We needes must take the seeming best of bad.

25

Yet stands he in doubt, a while, what way to take;
Conferring with that small remaining troope
Fortune had left; which neuer would forsake
Their poore distressed Lord, nor neuer stoope
To any hopes the stronger part could make.
Good *Carlile*,* *Ferby* and Sir *Stephen Scroope*,
With that most worthy *Montague*,† were all
That were content with *Maiesty* to fall.

26

Time, spare, and make not sacrilegious theft
Vpon so memorable constancy:
Let not succeeding Ages bee bereft
Of such examples of integrity:
Nor thou magnanimous *Leigh*‡ must not be left
In darknesse, for thy rare fidelity;
To saue thy faith, content to lose thy head:
That reuerent head, of good men honoured.

27

Nor will my Conscience I should iniury
Thy memory most trusty *Ienico*,§
For b'ing not ours; though wish that *Gascoyne*
Claym'd not, for hers, the faith we reuerence so;
That England might haue this small Company
Onely to her alone, hauing no moe:
But let's diuide this good betwixt vs both,
Take she thy birth, and we will haue thy troth.

* *The Bishop of Carlile.*
† *Montague Earle of Salisbury.*
‡ *This was Sir Peter Leighs Auncitor of Lime in Cheshire, that now is.*
§ *Ienico d'Artois a Gascoyne.*

28

"Graue *Montague,* whom long experience taught
"In eyther fortune, thus aduis'd his King:*
"*Deare Soueraigne* know, the matter that is sought
"Is onely now your Maiesty to bring
"(From out of this poore safety you haue got,)
"Into their hands, that else hold euery thing
"For, now, but onely you they want, of all;
"And wanting you, they nothing theirs can call,

29

"Here haue you craggie Rocks to take your part;
"That neuer will betray their faith to you:
"These trusty Mountaines heere will neuer start,
"But stand t'vpbraid their shame that are vntrue:
"Here may you fence your safety with small art,
"Against the pride of that confused Crew:
"If men will not, these very Cliffes will fight,
"And bee sufficient to defend your right.

30

"Then keepe you here, and here shall you behold,
"Within short space, the slyding faith of those
"That cannot long their resolution hold,
"Repent the course their idle rashnesse chose:
"For, that same mercenarie faith (they sold)
"With least occasions discontented growes,
"And insolent those voluntarie bands;
"Presuming how, by them, he chiefly stands.

31

"And how can he those mightie troupes sustaine
"Long time, where now he is, or any where?
"Besides, what discipline can he retaine
"Whereas he dares not keepe them vnder feare,
"For feare to haue them to reuolt againe?
"So that it selfe when Greatnesse cannot beare,
"With her owne waight, must needes confus'dly fall,
"Without the helpe of other force at all.

* *The Earle of Salisbury his speech to K. Richard.*

32

   "And hither to approche hee will not dare;
"Where deserts, rockes, and hilles, no succours giue;
"Where desolation, and no comforts are;
"Where few can do no good, many not liue.
"Besides, we haue the *Ocean* to prepare
"Some other place, if this should not relieue:
"So shall you tire his force, consume his strength,
"And weary all his followers, out, at length.

33

   "Doe but referre to time, and to small time;
"And infinite occasions you shall finde
"To quaile the Rebell, euen in the prime
"Of all his hopes, beyond all thought of minde:
"For, many (with the conscience of the crime)
"In colder blood will curse what they design'd;
"And bad successe, vpbrayding their ill fact,
"Drawes them, whom others draw, from such an act.

34

   "For, if the least imagin'd ouerture
"But of conceiv'd reuolt men once espie;
"Straight shrinke the weake, the great will not indure,
"Th'impatient run, the discontented flie:
"The friend his friends example doth procure,
"And all togither haste them presently
"Some to their home, some hide; others, that stay,
"To reconcile themselues, the rest betray.

35

   "What hope haue you, that euer *Bullingbrooke*
"Will liue a Subiect, that hath tri'd his fate?
"Or what good reconcilement can you looke,
"Where he must alwayes feare, and you must hate?
"And neuer thinke that he this quarrell tooke
"To reobtaine thereby his priuate state.
"T'was greater hopes, that hereto did him call:
"And he will thrust for all, or else lose all.

36

   "Nor trust this suttle *Agent,* nor his oth.
"You knowe his faith: you tri'd it before hand.

"His fault is death: and now to lose his troth,
"To saue his life, he will not greatly stand.
"Nor trust your kinsmans proffer; since you, both,
"Shew, blood in Princes is no stedfast band.
"What though he hath no title? he hath might:
"That makes a title, where there is no right.

37

Thus he: when that good Bishop* thus replies,
Out of a minde that quiet did affect:
"My Lord, I must confesse, as your case lies,
"You haue great cause your Subiects to suspect,
"And counterplot against their subtelties,
"Who all good care and honestie neglect;
"And feare the worst what insolence may do,
"Or armed fury may incense them to.

38

"But yet, my Lord, feare may aswell transport
"Your care, beyond the truth of what is meant;
"As otherwise neglect may fall too short,
"In not examining of their intent:
"But, let vs weigh the thing which they exhort.
"Tis Peace, Submission, and a Parlement:
"Which, how expedient 'tis for either part,
"Twere good we iudg'd with an vnpartiall hart.

39

"And first, for you my Lord, in griefe we see
"The miserable case wherein you stand;
"Voyde here of succour, helpe, or maiestie,
"On this poore promontorie of your Land:
"And where how long a time your Grace may be
"(Expecting what may fall into your hand)
"Wee know not; since th'euent of things do lie
"Clos'd vp in darkenes, farre from mortall eye.

40

"And how vnfit it were, you should protract
"Long time, in this so dangerous disgrace?
"As though that you good spirit and courage lackt
"To issue out of this opprobrious place:

* *The Bishop of Carlile.*

"When euen the face of Kings do oft exact
"Feare and remorse in faultie subiects base;
"And longer stay a great presumption drawes
"That you were guilty, or did doubt your cause.

41

"What Subiects euer so inrag'd would dare
"To violate a Prince, t'offend the blood
"Of that renowmed race, by which they are
"Exalted to the height of all their good?
"What if some things by chaunce misguided were,
"Which they haue now rebelliously withstood?
"They neuer will proceed with that despight
"To wracke the State, and to confound the right.

42

"Nor doe I thinke that *Bullingbrooke* can bee
"So blind-ambitious, to affect the Crowne;
"Hauing himselfe no title, and doth see
"Others, if you should fayle, must keepe him downe.
"Besides, the Realme, though mad, will neuer gree
"To haue a right succession ouerthrowne,
"To rayse confusion vpon them and theirs,
"By preiudicing true and lawfull heires.

43

"And now it may be, fearing the successe
"Of his attemptes, or with remorse of minde,
"Or else distrusting secret practises,
"He would be glad his quarrell were resign'd;
"So that there were some orderly redresse
"In those disorders which the Realme did finde:
"And this, I thinke, he now sees were his best;
"Since farther actions further but vnrest.

44

"And, for th'impossibilitie of peace
"And reconcilement, which my Lord obiects;
"I thinke, when doying iniurie shall cease
"(The cause pretended) then surcease th'effects:
"Time and some other Actions may increase
"As may diuert the thought of these respects;

"Others law of forgetting iniuries*
"May serue our turne in like calamities.

45

"And for his oath, in conscience, and in sense,
"True honour would not so be found vntrue,
"Nor spot his blood with such a foule offence
"Against his soule, against his God, and you.
"Our Lord forbid, that euer with th'expence
"Of heauen and heauenly ioyes, that shall insue,
"Mortalitie should buy this little breath,
"T'indure the horror of eternall death.

46

"And therefore, as I thinke, you safely may
"Accept this proffer; that determine shall
"All doubtfull courses by a quiet way,
"Needfull for you, fit for them, good for all.
"And here, my Sov'raigne, to make longer stay
"T'attend for what you are vnsure will fall,
"May slippe th'occasion, and incense their will:
"For, Feare, that's wiser then the truth, doth ill.

47

Thus he perswades, out of a zealous minde;
Supposing, men had spoken as they ment:
And, vnto this, the King likewise inclin'd;
As wholly vnto peace, and quiet bent:
And yeeldes himselfe to th'Earle, goes, leaues-behind
His safetie, Scepter, Honor, Gouernement:
For, gone, all's gone: he is no more his owne;
And they rid quite of feare, he of the Crowne.

48

A place there is, where proudly rais'd there stands
A huge aspiring Rock, neighb'ring the Skies;
Whose surly brow imperiously commaunds
The Sea his boundes, that at his proud feete lies:
And spurnes the waues, that in rebellious bands
Assault his Empire, and against him rise:
Vnder whose craggy gouernment, there was
A niggard narrow way for men to passe.

* *Lex Amnestiæ.*

49

And here, in hidden cliffes, concealed lay
A troope of armed men, to intercept
The vnsuspecting King, that had no way
To free his foote, that into danger stept.
The dreadfull *Ocean*, on the one side, lay:
The hard-incroching Mountaine th'other kept.
Before him, he beheld his hatefull foes:
Behind him, trayterous enemies inclose.

50

Enuiron'd thus, the Earle begins to cheere
His al-amased Lord, by him betrayde;
Bids him take courage, ther's no cause of feare,
These troopes, but there to guard him safe, were layd.
To whom the King; What neede so many here?
This is against your oath, my Lord, he said.
But, now hee sees in what distresse he stood:
To striue, was vaine; t'intreat, would do no good.

51

And therefore on with carefull hart he goes;
Complaines (but, to himselfe) sighes, grieues, and freats;
At *Rutland* dines, though feedes but on his woes:
The griefe of minde hindred the minde of meats.
For, sorrow, shame, and feare, scorne of his foes,
The thought of what he was, and what now threats,
Then what he should, and now what he hath done,
Musters confused passions all in one.

52

To *Flint*, from thence, vnto a restless bed,
That miserable night, he comes conuayd;
Poorely prouided, poorely followed,
Vncourted, vnrespected, vnobayd:
Where, if vncertaine sleepe but hoouered
Ouer the drooping cares that heauy weigh'd;
Millions of figures, fantasie presents
Vnto that sorrow, wakened griefe augments.

53

His new misfortune makes deluding sleepe
Say 'twas not so (False dreames the trueth denie).

Wherewith he starts; feels waking cares do creepe
Vpon his soule, and giues his dreame the lie;
Then sleepes againe: and then againe, as deepe
Deceites of darknes mocke his miserie.
So hard believ'd was sorrow in her youth:
That he thinks truth was dreams, & dreams were truth.

54

The morning light presents vnto his view
(Walking vpon a turret of the place)
The trueth of what hee sees is prov'd too true;
A hundred thousand men, before his face,
Came marching on the shore, which thither drew:
And, more to aggrauate his great disgrace,
Those he had wrongd, or done to them despight,
(As if they him vpbrayd) came first in sight.

55

There might hee see that false forsworne vile crue,
Those shameless agents of vnlawfull lust,
His *Pandars, Parasites* (people vntrue
To God and man, vnworthy any trust)
Preacing vnto that fortune that was new,
And with vnblushing faces formost thrust;
As those that still with prosperous fortune sort,
And are as borne for Corte, or made in Cort.

56

There hee beheld, how humbly diligent
New Adulation was to be at hand;
How ready Falsehood stept; how nimbly went
Base pick-thank Flattery, and preuents Command:
Hee saw the great obay, the graue consent,
And all with this new-rays'd Aspirer stand;
But, which was worst, his owne part acted there,
Not by himselfe; his power, not his appeare.

57

Which whilst he view'd, the Duke he might perceiue
Make towards the Castle, to an interview.
Wherefore he did his contemplation leaue,
And downe into some fitter place withdrew;
Where now he must admitte, without his leaue,

Him, who before with all submission due
Would haue beene glad, t'attend, and to prepare
The grace of audience, with respectiue care.

58

Who now being come in presence of his king
(Whether the sight of Maiestie did breed
Remorse of what he was incompassing,
Or whether but to formalize his deed)
He kneeles him downe with some astonishing,
Rose; kneeles againe (for, craft will still exceed)
When-as the king approch't, put off his Hood,
And welcomd him, though wisht him little good.

59

"To whom, the Duke began: My Lord, I knowe
"That both vncall'd, and vnexpected too,
"I haue presumed in this sort to showe
"And seeke the right which I am borne vnto:
"Yet pardon I beseech you, and allow
"Of that constraint, which driues me thus to doo.
"For, since I could not by a fairer course
"Attaine mine owne, I must vse this of force.

60

"Well: so it seemes, deare Cosin, said the King;
"Though you might haue procur'd it otherwise:
"And I am here content, in euery thing,
"To right you, as your selfe shal best deuise:
"And God voutsafe, the force that here you bring
"Beget not *England* greater iniuries.
And so they part: the Duke made haste from thence:
It was no place to ende this difference.

61

Straight towards *London*, in this heate of pride,
They forward set; as they had fore-decreed:
With whom, the *Captiue King* constraind must ride,
Most meanely mounted on a simple Steed:
Degraded of all grace and ease beside,
Thereby neglect of all respect to breed.

For, th'ouer-spreading pompe of prouder might
Must darken weaknes, and debase his sight.

62

Approaching neere the Cittie, hee was met
With all the sumptuous shewes ioy could deuise:
Where new-desire to please did not forget
To passe the vsuall pompe of former guise.
Striuing applause, as out of prison let,
Runnes-on, beyond all bounds, to nouelties:
And voyce, and hands, and knees, and all do now
A strange deformed forme of welcome showe.

63

And manifold confusion running greetes,
Shoutes, cries, claps hands, thrusts, striues and presses neere:
Houses impovrisht were, t'inrich the streetes,
And streetes left naked, that (vnhappie) were
Plac't from the sight where ioy with wonder meetes;
Where all, of all degrees, striue to appeare;
Where diuers-speaking zeale one murmure findes,
In vndistinguisht voyce to tell their mindes.

64

He that in glorie of his fortune sate,
Admiring what hee thought could neuer be,
Did feele his blood within salute his state,
And lift vp his reioycing soule, to see
So many hands and hearts congratulate
Th'aduancement of his long-desir'd degree;
When, prodigall of thankes, in passing by,
He resalutes them all, with chearefull eye.

65

Behind him, all aloofe, came pensiue on
The vnregarded King; that drooping went
Alone, and (but for spight) scarce lookt vpon:
Iudge, if hee did more enuie, or lament.
See what a wondrous worke this day is done;
Which th'image of both fortunes doth present:
In th'one, to shew the best of glories face;
In th'other, worse then worst of all disgrace.

66

Now *Isabell*, the young afflicted Queene
(Whose yeares had neuer shew'd her but delights,
Nor louely eyes before had euer seene
Other then smiling ioyes, and ioyfull sights;
Borne great, matcht great, liv'd great, and euer beene
Partaker of the worlds best benefits)
Had plac't her selfe, hearing her Lord should passe
That way, where she vnseene in secret was;

67

Sicke of delay, and longing to behold
Her long-mist Loue in fearefull ieoperdies:
To whom, although it had, in sort, beene told
Of their proceeding, and of his surprize;
Yet thinking they would neuer be so bold
To lead their Lord in any shamefull wise,
But rather would conduct him as their King;
As seeking but the States reordering.

68

And foorth shee lookes, and notes the formost traine;
And grieues to view some there she wisht not there:
Seeing the chiefe not come, stayes, lookes againe;
And yet she sees not him that should appeare:
Then backe she stands, and then desires as faine
Againe to looke, to see if hee were neere:
At length a glittering troupe farre off she spies,
Perceiues the throng, and heares the shouts and cries.

69

Lo, yonder now at length he comes, sayth shee:
Looke, my good women, where he is in sight:
Do you not see him? yonder; that is hee,
Mounted on that white Courser, all in white,
There where the thronging troupes of people bee;
I know him by his seate, he sits s'vpright:
Lo, now he bowes: deare Lord, with what sweet grace!
How long, haue I longd to behold that face!

70

O what delight my hart takes by mine eye!
I doubt me, when he comes but something neere,

I shall set wide the window: what care I
Who doth see me, so him I may see cleare.
Thus doth false ioy delude her wrongfully
(Sweete Lady) in the thing she held so deare.
For, neerer come, she findes she had mistooke;
And him she markt, was *Henrie Bullingbrooke.*

71

Then *Enuie* takes the place in her sweet eyes,
Where Sorrow had prepar'd her selfe a seat:
And words of wrath, from whence complaints should rise,
Proceed from egre lookes, and browes that threat:
Traytor, saith shee; ist thou, that, in this wise
To braue thy Lord and King, art made so great?
And haue mine eyes done vnto me this wrong,
To looke on thee? for this, staid I so long?

72

Ah, haue they grac't a periur'd Rebell so?
Well; for their errour I will weepe them out,
And hate the tongue defil'd, that praysde my foe,
And loath the minde, that gaue me not to doubt:
What? haue I added shame, vnto my woe?
Ile looke no more: Ladies looke you about,
And tell me if my Lord be in this traine;
Least my betraying eyes should erre againe.

73

And in this passion turnes her selfe away:
The rest looke all, and carefull note each wight;
Whil'st she, impatient of the least delay,
Demaundes againe; And what, not yet in sight?
Where is my Lord? What, gone some other way?
I muse at this. O God, graunt all goe right:
Then to the window goes againe at last,
And sees the chiefest traine of all was past;

74

And sees not him her soule desir'd to see:
And yet hope, spent, makes her not leaue to looke.
At last, her loue-quicke eyes, which ready be,
Fastens on one; whom though she neuer tooke

Could be her Lord; yet that sad cheere which hee
Then shew'd, his habit and his woful looke,
The grace he doth in base attire retaine,
Caus'd her she could not from his sight refraine.

75

What might he be, she said, that thus alone
Rides pensiue in this vniuersall ioy?
Some I perceiue, as well as we, do mone:
All are not pleas'd with euery thing this day.
It may be, he laments the wrong is done
Vnto my Lord, and grieues; as well he may.
Then he is some of ours: and we, of right,
Must pittie him, that pitties our sad plight.

76

But stay: ist not my Lord himselfe I see?
In truth, if 'twere not for his base aray,
I verily should thinke that it were hee;
And yet his basenes doth a grace bewray:
Yet God forbid; let me deceiued be,
And be it not my Lord, although it may:
Let my desire make vowes against desire;
And let my sight approue my sight a lier.

77

Let me not see him, but himselfe; a King:
For so he left me; so he did remoue.
This is not he: this feeles some other thing;
A passion of dislike, or else of loue.
O yes; 'tis he: that princely face doth bring
The euidence of Maiestie to prooue:
That face, I haue conferr'd, which now I see,
With that within my heart, and they agree.

78

Thus as she stood assur'd, and yet in doubt;
Wishing to see, what seene she griev'd to see;
Hauing beliefe, yet faine would be without;
Knowing, yet striuing not to know 'twas hee:
Her heart relenting, yet her heart so stout
As would not yeeld to thinke what was, could be:

Till, quite condemn'd by open proofe of sight,
She must confesse; or else denie the light.

79

For, whither loue in him did sympathize,
Or chaunce so wrought, to manifest her doubt;
Euen iust before, where she thus secret pries,
He stayes, and with cleare face lookes all about;
When she: Tis, ô, too true; I know his eyes:
Alas, it is my owne deare Lord cries out:
And, with that crie, sinks downe vpon the flore.
Abundant griefe lackt words to vtter more.

80

Sorrow keepes full possession in her heart,
Lockes it within, stops vp the way of breath,
Shuts senses out of doore from euerie part;
And so long holdes there, as it hazardeth
Oppressed Nature, and is forc't to part,
Or else must be constrain'd to stay with death:
So by a sigh, it lets in sense againe;
And sense, at length, giues words leaue to complaine.

81

Then, like a torrent had beene stopt before,
Teares, sighes, and words, doubled togither flowe;
Confus'dly striuing whether should do more,
The true intelligence of griefe to showe.
Sighes hindred words: words perisht in their store:
Both, intermixt in one, together growe.
One would do all: the other, more then's part;
Being both sent equall Agents, from the hart.

82

At length, when past the first of sorrowes worst,
When calm'd confusion better forme affordes;
Her heart commands, her words should passe out first,
And then her sighes should interpoint her words;
The whiles her eyes out into teares should burst:
This order with her sorrow she accordes;
Which, orderless, all forme of order brake:
So, then began her wordes, and thus she spake;

83

What? dost thou thus returne againe to mee?
Are these the triumphs, for thy victories?
Is this the glorie thou dost bring with thee,
From that vnhappie Irish enterprise?
And haue I made so many vowes to see
Thy safe returne, and see thee in this wise?
Is this the lookt-for comfort thou dost bring?
To come a Captiue, that wentst out a King?

84

And yet, deare Lord, though thy vngratefull Land
Hath left thee thus; yet I will take thy part:
I doo remaine the same, vnder thy hand;
Thou still dost rule the kingdome of my hart:
If all be lost, that gouernment doth stand;
And that shall neuer from thy rule depart:
And so thou bee, I care not how thou bee:
Let Greatnes goe; so it goe without thee.

85

And welcome come, how-so vnfortunate;
I will applaud what others do despise:
I loue thee for thy selfe, not for thy State:
More then thy selfe, is what without thee lies:
Let that more goe, if it be in thy fate:
And hauing but thy selfe, it will suffize:
I married was not to thy Crowne, but thee;
And thou, without a Crowne, all one to mee.

86

But what do I, heere lurking idlie, mone
And wayle apart, and in a single part
Make seuerall griefe? which should be both in one;
The touch being equall of each others hart.
Ah, no: sweet Lord, thou must not mone alone.
For, without me, thou art not all thou art;
Nor my teares, without thine, are fully teares:
For thus vnioyn'd, sorrow but halfe appeares.

87

Ioyne then our plaints, and make our griefe full griefe:
Our state being one, let vs not part our care.

Sorrow hath onely this poore bare reliefe,
To be bemon'd of such as wofull are.
And should I rob thy griefe, and be the thiefe
To steale a priuate part, and seuerall share,
Defrawding sorrow of her perfect due?
No, no, my Lord; I come to helpe thee rue.

88

Then foorth she goes, a close concealed way
(As grieuing to be seene not as she was);
Labors t'attaine his presence all she may:
Which, with most hard a-do, was brought to passe.
For, that night, vnderstanding where he lay,
With earnest 'treating she procur'd her Passe
To come to him. Rigor could not denie
Those teares, so poore a suite, or put her by.

89

Entring the chamber, where he was alone
(As one whose former fortune was his shame)
Loathing th'vpbrayding eye of any one
That knew him once, and knowes him not the same:
When hauing giuen expresse command that none
Should presse to him; yet hearing some that came,
Turnes angerly about his grieued eyes:
When, lo, his sweete afflicted Queene he spyes.

90

Straight cleares his brow; and with a borrowed smile,
What, my deare Queene? welcome, my deare, he sayes:
And (striuing his owne passion to beguile,
And hide the sorrow which his eye betrayes)
Could speake no more; but wrings her hands, the while:
And then, Sweet Lady; and againe he stayes:
Th'excesse of ioy and sorrow both affordes
Affliction none, or but poore niggard wordes.

91

Shee that was come with a resolued hart,
And with a mouth full stor'd, with wordes well chose;
Thinking, This comfort wil I first impart
Vnto my Lord, and thus my speach dispose:

Then thus Ile say, thus looke, and with this art
Hide mine owne sorrow to relieue his woes:
When being come, all this prov'd nought but winde;
Teares, lookes, and sighes, do only tell her minde.

92

Thus both stood silent and confused so,
Their eyes relating how their hearts did morne:
Both bigge with sorrow, and both great with wo
In labour with what was not to be borne:
This mightie burthen, wherewithall they goe,
Dies vndeliuered, perishes vnborne;
Sorrow makes silence her best Orator,
Where words may make it lesse, not shew it more.

93

But he, whom longer time had learn'd the art
T'indure affliction, as a vsuall touch,
Straines foorth his wordes, and throwes dismay apart,
To rayse vp her, whose passions now were such
As quite opprest her ouercharged hart
(Too small a vessell to containe so much)
And cheeres and mones, and fained hopes doth frame,
As if himselfe beleeu'd, or hop't the same.

94

And now, the while these Princes sorrowed,
Forward ambition (come so neere her ende)
Sleepes not, nor slippes th'occasion offered,
T'accomplish what it did before intend:
A Parlement is foorthwith summoned
In *Richards* name; whereby they might pretend
A forme, to grace disorder, and a showe
Of holy right, the right to ouerthrowe.

95

Order, how much predominant art thou!
That if but onely thou pretended art;
How soone, deceiv'd mortalitie doth bow
To follow thine, as still the better part!
Tis thought, that reuerent forme will not allow
Iniquitie, or sacred right peruart.

Within our soules, since then thou dwell'st so strong;
How ill do they, that vse thee, to do wrong!

96

So ill did they, that in this formall course
Sought to establish a deformed right:
Who might as well effected it by force;
But that men hold it wrong, what's wrought by might.
Offences vrg'd in publique are made worse:
The shew of iustice aggrauates despight.
"The multitude, that looke not to the cause,
"Rest satisfied, so it seeme done by lawes.

97

And now they diuerse articles obiect
Of rigor, malice, priuate fauourings,
Exaction, riot, falsehood, and neglect;
Crimes done, but sildome answered by Kings:
Which Subiectes doe lament, but not correct.
And all these faults, which *Lancaster* now brings
Against a King, must be his owne, when hee,
By vrging others sinnes, a King shall be.

98

For, all that was most odious was deuis'd,
And publisht in these articles abrode.
All th'errours of his youth were here compris'd,
Calamitie with obloquie to lode:
And more to make him publikely despis'd,
Libels, inuectiues, rayling rimes, were sow'd
Among the vulgar, to prepare his fall
With more applause and good consent of all.

99

Looke how the day-hater, *Mineruas* bird,*
Whil'st priuiledg'd with darknes and the night,
Doth liue secure t'himselfe, of others feard;
If but by chaunce discouered in the light,
How doth each little Fowle (with enuie stirr'd)
Call him to iustice, vrge him with despight;

* *The Owle is said to bee Mineruas bird.*

Summon the feathered flockes of all the wood,
To come to scorne the tyrant of their blood:

100

So fares this King, layd open to disgrace,
Whil'st euerie mouth full of reproche inuayes;
And euerie base detractor, in this case,
Vpon th'aduantage of misfortune playes:
Downe-falling Greatnes, vrged on apace,
Was followed-hard, by all disgracefull wayes;
Now in the point t'accelerate an end,
Whil'st miserie had no meanes to defend.

101

Vpon those articles in Parlement
So haynous made, inforc't, and vrg'd so hard,
He was adiudg'd vnfit for gouernment,
And of all regal powre and rule debarr'd:
For, who durst contradict the Dukes intent?
Or, if they durst, should patiently be heard?
Desire of change, old wrongs, new hopes, fresh feare,
Being far the *maior* part, the cause must beare.

102

Yet must we thinke, that some which saw the course
(The better fewe, whom passion made not blinde)
Stood careful lookers-on, with sad commorse,
Amaz'd to see what headlong rage design'd:
And, in a more considerate discourse
Of tragicall euentes, thereof diuin'd;
And would excuse and pittie those defects,
Which, with such hate, the aduerse parts obiects:

103

"Say'ing, better yeeres might worke a better care,
"And time might well haue cur'd what was amisse;
"Since all these faults fatall to Greatnes are,
"And worse deserts haue not beene punisht thus:
"But yet in this, the heauens, we feare, prepare
"Confusion for our sinnes, aswell as his;
"And his calamitie beginneth our:
"For, he his owne, and we abus'd his powre.

104

Thus murmur'd they; when to the king were sent
Certaine who might perswade him to forsake
And leaue his Crowne, and with his free consent
A voluntarie Resignation make;
Since that he could no other way preuent
These dangers which he else must needes partake:
For, not to yeeld, to what feare would constraine,
Would barre the hope of life, that did remaine.

105

And yet this scarce could worke him to consent
To yeeld vp that so soone, men hold so deare.
Why, let him take (sayd he) the gouernement,
And let me yet the name, the title beare:
Leaue me that shewe, and I wil be content;
And let them rule and gouerne without feare.
What, can they not my shadow now indure,
When they of all the rest do stand secure?

106

Let me hold that, I aske no other good:
Nay, that I will hold; *Henrie* do thy worst.
For, ere I yeeld my Crowne, I'le lose my blood;
That blood, that shall make thee and thine accurst.
Thus resolute a while he firmely stood,
Till loue of life, and feare of being forc't,
Vanquisht th'innated valour of his minde;
And hope, and friends, so wrought, that he resign'd.

107

Then to the Towre (where he remained) went
The *Duke,* with all the *Peeres* in company,
To take his offer with his free consent,
And this his Resignation testifie;
And thereof to informe the Parlement,
That all things might be done more formally,
And men thereby rest better satisfide;
As of an act not forc't, or falsifide.

108

And forth h'is brought vnto th'accomplishment,
Deckt with the Crowne in princely robes that day;

Like as the dead, in other Landes, are sent
Vnto their Graues, in all their best aray:
And euen like good, did him this ornament.
For, what he brought, he must not beare away;
But buries there his glory and his name,
Intomb'd both in his owne and others blame.

109

And there vnto th'assembly of these States,
His sorrow for their long indured wrong
Through his abus'd authority relates,
Excuses with confessions mixt among:
And glad he sayes, to finish all debates,
He was to leaue the Rule they sought-for long;
Protesting, if it might be for their good,
He would as gladly sacrifice his blood.

110

There, he his Subiectes all (in generall)
Assoyles and quites of oath and fealtie,
Renounces interest, title, right and all
That appertaind to kingly dignitie;
Subscribes thereto, and doth to witnesse call
Both heauen and earth, and God, & Saints on hie,
To testifie his act, and doth professe
To do the same with most free willingnesse.

111

Tis said, with his owne hands he gaue the Crowne
To *Lancaster,* and wisht to God he might
Haue better ioy thereof then he had knowne,
And that his power might make it his by right:
And furthermore he crav'd, of all his owne,
But life, to liue apart a priuate wight;
The vanity of Greatnes he had tri'd,
And how vnsurely standes the foote of pride.

112

This brought to passe, the Lords returne with speed,
The Parlement hereof to certifie;
Where, they at large publisht the Kings owne deed,
And forme of his resignement verbally:

And thereupon doth *Lancaster* proceede
To make his claime vnto the Monarchie;
And shewes the right he hath, both by descent,
And by recouerie, to the gouernement.

113

Which being granted, *Canterburie* rose
And animates them, by the sacred word,*
"In this their course: and by his Text, he showes
"How well they made their choyce of such a Lord;
"Who, as a man was able to dispose
"And guide the State: and how the royall sworde
"Ought to be at a mans commandement;
"Not at a childes, or one as impotent.

114

"Since, when the greatnes of his charge exceedes
"The smallnesse of his powers, he must collate
"The same on others: whence, sayes he, proceedes
"This rauenous expilation of the State;
"Whence no man any more the publike heedes,
"Then so much as imports his priuate state.
"*Our Health is from our head:* if that be ill,
"Distemp'red, faint, and weake, all the rest will.

115

"Then to the present, all his speach he drawes,
"And shewes what admirable parts abound
"In this braue Prince; being fit to giue them lawes,
"Fit for his valour, fit for iudgement sound.
And, *Lancaster,* indeed I would thy cause
Had had as lawfull and as sure a ground,
As had thy vertues, and thy noble hart,
Ordaind, and borne for an Imperial part.

116

Then had not that confus'd succeeding Age
Our fieldes ingrayn'd with bloud, our riuers dy'd
With purple-streaming woundes of our owne rage,
Nor seene our Princes slaughtred, Peeres destroyd.
Then hadst not thou, deare Countrie, com'n to wage

* *The Archbishop of Cant. takes his text out of the first booke of the Kings, cap. 9. Vir dominabitur in populo.*

Warre with thy selfe, nor those afflictions try'd
Of all consuming discorde here so long;
Too mightie now, against thy selfe too strong.

The ende of the second Booke.

The Argument of

the Third *Booke*.

Henrie, *the fourth, the Crowne established.*
The Lords, that did to Glosters *death consent,*
Degraded, do rebell, are vanquished.
King Richard, *vnto* Pomfret *Castle sent,*
Is by a cruell Knight there murthered,
After the Lords had had their punishment.
His Corps, from thence, to London *is conuayd;*
And there, for all to view, is open layd.

1

NOw risen is that Head, by which did spring
                                                          (rights;
The birth of two strong Heads, two Crownes, two
That monstrous shape, that afterward did bring
Deform'd confusion to distracted wights.
Now is attain'd that dearely purchast thing
That fill'd the world with lamentable sights:
And now, attain'd, all care is how to frame
Meanes to establish, and to hold the same.

2

  First, he attends to build a strong conceipt
Of his vsurped powre, in peoples mindes;
And armes his cause with furniture of weight:
Which easily the sword, and Greatnesse findes.
Succession, Conquest, and election straight
Suggested are, and prov'd in all their kindes.
More then ynough they finde, who finde their might
Hath force to make all, that they will haue, Right.

3

  Though one of these might verie will suffise
His present approbation to procure.
"But who his own cause makes, doth stil deuise

"To make too much, to haue it more then sure.
"Feare casts too deepe, and euer is too wise:
"No vsuall plots, the doubtfull can secure.
And all these disagreeing Claymes he had,
With hope to make one good of many bad.

4

Like vnto him that fears, and faine would stop
An inundation working-on apace,
Runs to the Breach, heapes mightie matter vp,
Throwes indigested burthens on the place,
Lodes with huge weights, the out-side, & the top,
But leaues the inner partes in feeble case;
Whil'st th'vnder-searching water, working-on,
Beares (proudly) downe, all that was idly don:

5

So fares it with our indirect desseignes,
And wrong contriued labors, at the last;
Whil'st working Time, and iustice vndermines
The feeble frame, held to be wrought so fast:
Then when out-breaking vengeance vncombines
The ill-ioyn'd plots so fayrely ouer-cast;
Turnes vp those huge pretended heapes of showes,
And all these weake illusions ouer-throwes.

6

But, after, hauing made his title plaine,
Vnto his Coronation he proceedes:
Which, in most sumptuous sort (to intertaine
The gazing vulgar, whom this splendor feeds)
Is stately furnisht, with a glorious traine:
Wherein, the former Kings he far exceedes;
And all t'amuse the world, and turne the thought
Of what & how 'twas done, to what is wrought.

7

And that he might on many props repose,
He strengths his owne, & who his part did take:
New Officers, new Councellors he chose:
His eldest sonne, the Prince of *Wales* doth make;

His second, Lord high Steward: and, to those
Had hazarded their fortunes for his sake,
He giues them charge, as merites their deseart;
And rayses them, by crushing th'aduerse part.

8

So that hereby, the vniuersall face
Of Court, with all the Offices of State
Are wholly chang'd, by death, or by disgrace,
Vpon th'aduantage of the peoples hate;
"Who, euer enuying those of chiefest place
"(Whom neither worth nor vertue, but their fate
"Exalted hath) doo, when their Kings doo naught
"(Because it's in their powre) iudge it their faute.

9

And in their steed, such as were popular,
And wel-deseruing, were aduanc't by grace.
Graue *Shirley,* he ordaines Lord Chancelor;
Both worthy for his vertues, and his race:
And *Norburie* hee appoints for Treasurer;
A man, though meane, yet fit to vse that place:
And others, t'other roomes; whom people hold
So much more lov'd, how much they loath the old.

10

And it behoues him now to doo his best
T'approue his vow, and oath made to the State:
And many great disorders he redrest;
Which alwayes Vsurpation makes the gate
To let it selfe into the peoples brest,
And seekes the publike best t'accommodate:
Wherein, Iniustice better doth then Right:
"For, who reproues the lame, must go vpright.

11

Though it be easie to accuse a State,
Of imperfection and misgouernment:
And easie to beget in people hate
Of present Rule, which cannot all content;
And fewe attempt it, that effect it not:

Yet, t'introduce a better gouernment
In steed thereof, if we t'example looke,
The vnder-takers haue beene ouer-tooke.

12

Then, against those he strictly doth proceed,
Who chiefe of *Glosters* death were guiltie thought;*
Not so much for the hatred of that deed:
But, vnder this pretext, the meanes he sought
To ruine such whose might did much exceed
His powre to wrong, nor else could well be wrought.
Law, Iustice, blood, the zeale vnto the dead,
Were on his side, and his drift coloured.

13

Here, many of the greatest of the Land
Accus'd were of the act,† strong proofes brought out;
Which strongly were refell'd: the Lords all stand,
To cleare their Cause, most resolutely stout:
The King, perceiuing what he tooke in hand
Was not with safety to be brought-about,
Desists to vrge their death, in any wise;
Respecting number, strength, friends, and allies.

14

Nor was it time now, in his tender raigne,
And infant-young-beginning gouernement,
To striue, with blood; when lenitie must gaine
The mightie men, and please the discontent.
"New Kings do feare; when old Courts farther straine:
Establisht States to all things will consent.
He must dispense with his will, and their crime,
And seeke t'oppresse and weare them out with time.

15

Yet not to seeme, but to haue some thing done,
In what he could, not as he would effect;
To satisfie the people (that begun,

* *The Nobilitie accused for the death of Thomas D. of Gloster.*
† *The Dukes of Surry, Excester, and Aumarle, the Earles of Salisburie, and Gloster, the Bishop of Carlile, Sir Thomas Blunt, and other, were the parties accused, for the death of the D. of Gloster.*

Reuenge of wrong and iustice to expect)
He caus'd be put to execution, one,
Who to performe this murther was elect;
A base companion, few, or none would misse:
Who first did serue their turne; and now serues his.

16

And, to abase the too high state of those
That were accus'd, and lessen their degrees,
Aumarle, Surry, Exceter, must lose
The names of Dukes, their titles, dignities,
And whatsoeuer profits thereby rise;
The Earles, their titles and their Signories:
And all they got in th'end of *Richards* raigne,
Since *Glosters* death, they must restore againe;

17

By this, as if by *Ostracisme,* t'abate
That great presumptiue wealth, whereon they stand.
For, first, hereby improvrishing their state,
He killes the meanes they might haue to withstand:
Then equals them with other whom they hate,
Who (by their spoyles) are rais'd to hie command;
That weake, and enuied, if they should conspire,
They wracke themselues, and he hath his desire.

18

Yet, by this grace (which must be held a grace;
As both they, and the world, are made beleeue)
He thinks t'haue dealt benignly in this case,
And left them state ynough, to let them liue;
And that the taking, from thē, meanes & place,
Was nothing, in respect what hee did giue:
But they, that knowe how their owne reckning goes,
Account not what they haue, but what they lose.

19

The Parlement, which now is held, decreed
What-euer pleas'd the King but to propound;
Confirm'd the Crowne, to him, and to his seed,
And by their oath their due obedience bound:

Which was the powre that stood him best in steed,
And made what-euer broken courses sound.
For, what he got by fortune, fauour, might,
It was the State that now must make his right.

20

Here was agreed, to make all more secure,
That *Richard* should remaine, for euermore,
Close-prisoner; least the Realme might chaunce indure
Some new reuolt, or any fresh vp-rore:
And, that if any should such broyle procure,
By him, or for him, he should die therefore.
So that a talke of tumult, and a breath,
Would serue him as his passing-bell to death.

21

Yet, reuerent *Carlile,* thou didst there oppose
Thy holy voyce, to saue thy Princes blood;
And freely checktst this iudgement, and his foes:
When all were bad, yet thou dar'dst to be good.
Be it inrold (that time may neuer lose
The memorie) how firme thy courage stood;
When powre, disgrace, nor death, could ought diuert
Thy glorious tongue, thus, to reueale thy heart.

22

"Graue, reuerent Lords, since that this sacred place
"Our *Auentine-Retire,* our holy hill
"(This place, soule of our State, the Realmes best grace)
"Doth priuiledge me speake what reason will:
"Let me but say my conscience in this case;
"Least sinne of silence shew my hart was ill:
"And let these walles witnesse, if you will not,
"I do discharge my soule, of this foule blot.

23

"Neuer shall this poore breath of mine consent,
"That he that two and twentie yeeres hath raignd
"As lawfull Lord, and King by iust descent,
"Should here be iudg'd, vnheard, and vnarraignd;
"By Subiects too (Iudges incompetent
"To iudge their King vnlawfully detaind)

"And vnbrought-foorth to plead his guiltless Cause;
"Barring th'Annoynted, libertie of lawes.

24

"Haue you not done inough, with what is done?
"Must needes disorder growe, from bad, to worse?
"Can neuer mischiefe end as it begunne,
"But being once out, must farther out, of force?
"Thinke you, that any meanes, vnder the Sunne,
"Can assecure so indirect a course?
"Or any broken cunning build so strong,
"As can hold out the hand of vengeance long?

25

Stopt, there, was his too vehement speech with speed,
And he sent close to warde, from where he stood;
His zeale vntimely, deem'd too much t'exceed
The measure of his wit, and did no good.
They resolute, for all this, do proceed
Vnto that iudgement could not be withstood:
The King had all he crav'd, or could compell:
And all was done; let others iudge, how well.

26

Now *Muse* relate a wofull accident,
And tell the blood-shed of these mightie Peeres,
Who (lately reconcil'd) rest discontent,
Griev'd with disgrace, remayning in their feares:
How-euer seeming outwardly content;
Yet th'inward touch, that wounded honor beares,
Rests closely rankling, and can finde no ease,
Till death of one side cure this great disease.

27

Meanes how to feele, and learne each others hart,
By th'*Abbots* skill of *Westminster* is found:
Who, secretly disliking *Henries* part,
Inuites these Lords, and those hee meant to sound;
Feasts them with cost, and drawes them on with art;
And darke, and doubtfull questions doth propound:
Then playner speakes; and yet vncertaine speakes:
Then wishes well; then off abruptly breakes.

28

My Lords, saith he, I feare we shall not finde
This long-desired King, such as was thought:
But yet, he may do well: God turne his minde:
Tis yet new dayes: but, Ill bodes new and nought:
Some yet speed well: though all men of my kinde
Haue cause to doubt; his speech is not forgot,
That Princes had too little, we too much.
God giue him grace: but, 'tis ill trusting such.

29

This open-close, apparent-darke discourse
Drew-on much speech: and euerie man replies:
And euery man addes heate: and words inforce
And vrge out wordes. For, when one man espies
Anothers minde like his, then ill breedes worse;
And out breaks all in th'end what closest lies.
For, when men well haue fed, th'blood being warme,
Then are they most improuident of harme.

30

Bewray they did their inward boyling spight;
Each stirring other to reuenge their cause.
One sayes he neuer should indure the sight
Of that forsworne, that wrongs both Land and lawes,
Another vowes the same; of his minde, right.
A third t'a point more neere the matter drawes;
Sweares, if they would, he would attempt the thing,
To chace th'vsurper, and replace their King.

31

Thus one by one, kindling each others fire,
Till all inflam'd they all in one agree:
All resolute to prosecute their ire,
Seeking their owne, and Countries cause to free;
And haue his first, that their blood did conspire.
For, no way else, they sayd, but this, could be
Their wrong-detained honor to redeeme:
Which, true-bred blood should, more then life, esteeme.

32

And let not this our new-made faithless Lord,
Sayth *Surry,** thinke, that we are left so bare
(Though bare inough) but we wil finde a sword
To kill him with, when he shal not beware.
For, he that is with life and will instor'd,
Hath, for reuenge, inough, and needes not care:
For, time brings meanes to furnish him withall:
Let him but wayte occasions as they fall.

33

Then, of the manner how t'effect the thing,
Consulted was: and in the ende agreed,
That a Maske, and common Reuelling,
Which was ordain'd, they should performe the deed;
For, that would be least doubted of the King,
And fittest for their safetie to proceed:
The night, their number, and the soddaine act,
Would dash all order, and protect their fact.

34

Besides, they might vnder the faire pretence
Of Tilts and Turnements, which they intend,
Prouide them horse, and armour for defence,
And all things else conuenient for their end:
Besides, they might hold sure intelligence
Among themselues, without suspect t'offend:
The King would thinke, they sought but grace in Court,
With all their great preparing in this sort.

35

A solemne oath religiously they take,
By intermutuall vowes protesting there,
This neuer to reueale; nor to forsake
So good a Cause, for danger, hope, or feare:
The Sacrament, the pledge of faith, they take:
And euerie man vpon his sword doth sweare,
By Knighthood, honor, or what else should binde;
To assecure, the more, each others minde.

* *Thom. late Duke of Surry.*

36

And when all this was done, and thought well done,
And euerie one assures him good successe,
And easie seemes the thing to euerie one
That nought could crosse their plot, or them suppresse:
Yet one among the rest (whose minde not wonne
With th'ouer-weening thought of hot excesse
Nor headlong carryed with the streame of will,
Nor by his owne election led to ill)

37

Iudicious *Blunt** (whose learning, valor, wit,
Had taught true knowledge in the course of things;
Knew dangers as they were, and th'humerous fit
Of ware-lesse discontent, what end it brings)
Counsels their heat, with calme graue words, and fit
(Words well fore-thought, that from experience springs)
And warnes a warier cariage in the thing;
Least blind presumption worke their ruining.

38

"My Lords, sayth he, I knowe your wisedomes such,
"As that of mine aduice you haue no need:
"I knowe, you knowe how much the thing doth touch
"The maine of all your states, your blood, your seed:
"Yet, since the same concernes my life, as much
"As his whose hand is chieftest in this deed,
"And that my foote must go as farre, as his;
"I thinke, my tongue may speake what needfull is.

39

"The thing we enterprize, I knowe, doth beare
"Great posibilitie of good effect;
"For-that so many men of might there are
"That venture here this action to direct:
"Which meaner wightes, of trust and credite bare,
"Not so respected, could not looke t'effect.
"For, none, without great hopes, will follow such
"Whose powre, and honor doth not promise much.

* *Sir Thom. Blunt.*

40

"Besides, this new, and doubtfull gouernment,
"The wauering faith of people vaine, and light,
"The secret hopes of many discontent,
"The naturall affection to the right,
"Our lawfull Sov'raignes life, in prison pent,
"Whom men begin to pittie now, not spight,
"Our well layd plot, and all, I must confesse,
"With our iust cause, doth promise good successe.

41

"But this is yet the outward fayrest side
"Of our desseigne: within, rests more of feare,
"More dread of sad euent yet vndescri'd,
"Then (my most worthy Lords) I would there were:
"But yet, I speake not this as to diuide
"Your thoughts from th'act, or to dismay your cheere;
"Onely to adde, vnto your forward will,
"A moderate feare, to cast the worst of ill.

42

"Danger, before, and in, and after th'act,
"You needes must graunt, is great, and to be waigh'd.
"Before; least, while we do the deede protract,
"It be by any of our selues bewraid:
"For, many being priuie to the fact,
"How hard it is to keepe it vnbetraid?
"When the betrayer shal haue life and grace,
"And rid himselfe of danger and disgrace.

43

"For, though some few continue resolute,
"Yet many shrink, which at the first would dare,
"And be the formost men to execute,
"If th'act, and motion at one instant were:
"But, intermission suffers men dispute
"What dangers are, and cast with farther care:
"Cold doubt cauils with honor, scorneth fame:
"And in the end, feare waighes downe faith, with shame.

44

"Then in the act, what perils shall we finde,
"If either place, or time, or other course,

"Cause vs to alter th'order now assign'd?
"Or that, then we expect, things happen worse?
"If either error, or a fainting minde,
"An indiscreet amazement, or remorse,
"In any at that instant should be found;
"How much it might the act, and all confound?

45

   "After the deede, the dangers are no lesse;
"Lest that, our forwardnes not seconded
"By our owne followers, and accomplices
"(Being kept backe, or slowe, or hindered)
"The hastie multitude rush-on, t'oppresse
"Confused weakenes, there vnsuccored;
"Or rayse another head, of that same race,
"T'auenge his death, and prosecute the case.

46

   "All this (my Lords) must be considered
"(The best and worst of that which may succeede)
"That valour mixt with feare, boldnesse with dread,
"May march more circumspect, with better heed.
"And, To preuent these mischiefs mentioned,
"Is, by our faith, our secrecie, and speed.
"For, euen already is the worke begun:
"And we rest all vndone, till all be done.

47

   "And though I could haue wisht another course,
"In open fielde t'haue hazarded my blood;
"Yet some are heere, whose loue is of that force
"To draw my life, whom zeale hath not withstood:
"But, like you not of your desseigne the worse.
"If the successe be good, your course is good:
"And ending well, our honor then begins.
"No hand of strife is pure, but that which wins.

48

   This sayd, a sad still silence held their mindes,
Vpon the feareful proiect of their woe;
But that, not long, ere forward furie findes
Incouraging perswasions on to goe.

We must (sayd they) we wil, our honour bindes,
Our safety bids, our fayth must haue it so:
We know the worst can come, 'tis thought vpon:
We cannot shift; being in, we must goe on.

49

And on in deed they went; but (ô!) not farre:
A fatal stop trauerst their headlong course;
Their drift comes knowne, and they discouered are:
For, some of many will be false, of force.
Aumarle became the man, that all did marre.
Whether through indiscretion, chance, or worse:
He makes his peace, with offring others blood;
And shewes the King, how all the matter stood.

50

Then lo, dismayde, confusion all possest
Th'afflicted troupe, hearing their plot describe.
Then runnes amaz'd distresse, with sad vnrest,
To this, to that, to flie, to stand, to hide:
Distracted terror knew not what was best;
On what determination to abide.
At last, Despaire would yet stand to the Sword,
To trie what friendes would doe, or fate affoord.

51

Then this, then that mans ayde, they craue, implore;
Poste here for helpe, seeke there their followers;
Coniure their friendes they had, labour for more,
Sollicite all reputed fauourers,
Who *Richards* cause seem'd to affect before:
And, in his name, write, pray, sende messengers;
To try what faith was left, if by this art
Any would step to take Afflictions part.

52

And some were found; and some againe draw back:
Vncertaine power could not it selfe retaine:
Intreate they may; authoritie they lacke:
And here, and there they march (but, all in vaine)
With desp'rate course; like those that see their wracke
Euen on the Rockes of death, and yet they straine

That death may not them idly finde t'attend
Their certaine last, but worke to meet their end.

53

And long they stand not, ere the chiefe, surpriz'd,
Conclude with their deare blood their tragedie:
And all the rest, disperst, run some disguis'd
To vnknowne coastes; some to the shores do flye;
Some to the woods, or whither feare aduis'd:
But running from, all to destruction hie.
The breach once made vpon a battered state,
Downe goes distresse; no shelter shroudes their fate.

54

And now what horror in their soules doth growe!
What sorrowes, with their friendes, and neere allies!
What mourning in their ruin'd houses now!
How many childrens plaints, and mothers cryes!
How many wofull Widowes left to bow
To sad disgrace! what perisht families!
What heires of hie rich hopes, their thoughts must frame
To base-downe-looking pouertie and shame!

55

This slaughter and calamitie fore-goes
Thy eminent destruction, wofull King.
This is the bloody Comet of thy woes,
That doth fore-tell thy present ruyning.
Here was thy ende decreed, when these men rose:
And euen with theirs, this act thy death did bring;
Or hastened, at the least, vpon this ground:
Yet, if not this, another had beene found.

56

Kings, Lords of times and of occasions, may
Take their aduantage, when, and how they list:
For, now the Realme, he thought in this dismay,
T'auoyd like mischiefes, neither would resist,
Nor feele the wound at all; since, by this way,
All future disturbations would desist;
The roote cut off, from whence these tumults rose,
He should haue rest, the Common-wealth respose.

57

He knew this time: and yet he would not seeme
Too quicke to wrath, as if affecting blood;
But yet complaines so farre, that men might deeme
He would 'twere done, and that he thought it good:
And wisht that some would so his life esteeme,
As ridde him of these feares wherein he stood:
And there-with eyes a Knight, that then was by;*
Who soone could learne his lesson, by his eye.

58

The man, he knew, was one that willingly
For one good looke would hazard soule and all;
An instrument for any villanie,
That needed no commission more at all:
A great ease to the King, that should, hereby,
Not neede in this a course of iustice call,
Nor seeme to wil the act: for, though what's wrought
Were his owne deed, he grieues should so be thought.

59

"So foule a thing (ô!) thou *Iniustice* art,
"That tort'rest both the dooer and distrest.
"For, when a man hath done a wicked part,
"How doth he striue t'excuse, to make the best,
"To shift the fault, t'vnburthen his charg'd hart,
"And glad to finde the least surmise of rest!
"And if he could make his, seeme others sin;
"What great repose, what ease he findes therein!

60

This Knight but yet, why should I call him Knight,
To giue impietie this reuerent stile?
Title of honour, worth, and vertues right,
Should not be giuen to a wretch so vile:
But pardon me, if I do not aright:
It is because I will not here defile
My vnstaind verse, with his opprobrious name,
And grace him so, to place him in the same.

---

* This Knight was Sir Pierce of Exton.

61

This caitife goes, and with him takes eight more
As desperate as himselfe, impiously bold
(Such villaines, as he knew would not abhorre
To execute what wicked act he would)
And hastes him downe to *Pomfret;* where, before,
The restless King, conuaide, was laid in hold:
There would he do the deed, he thought should bring
To him great grace and fauour, with his King.

62

Whether the soule receiues intelligence,
By her neere *Genius,* of the bodies end,
And so impartes a sadnesse to the sense
Fore-going ruine, whereto it doth tend:
Or whether Nature else hath conference
With profound sleepe, and so doth warning send
By prophetizing dreames, what hurt is neere,
And giues the heauie careful hart to feare:

63

How-euer, so it is, the now sad King
(Tost here and there, his quiet to confound)
Feeles a straunge waight of sorrowes, gathering
Vpon his trembling hart, and sees no ground;
Feeles sodaine terror bring cold shiuering;
Listes not to eate, still muses, sleepes vnsound,
His senses droope, his steady eyes vnquicke,
And much he ayles; and yet he is not sicke.

64

The morning of that day, which was his last,
After a wearie rest rysing to paine,
Out at a little grate his eyes he cast
Vpon those bordering hils, and open Plaine,
And viewes the towne, and sees how people past:
Where others libertie, makes him complaine
The more his owne, and grieues his soule the more;
Conferring captiue-Crownes, with freedome poore.

65

"O happie man, sayth hee, that lo I see
"Grazing his cattle in those pleasant fieldes!

"If he but knew his good (how blessed hee,
"That feeles not what affliction Greatnes yeeldes!)
"Other then what hee is, he would not bee,
"Nor change his state with him that Scepters wieldes:
"Thine, thine is that true life; That is to liue,
"To rest secure, and not rise vp to grieue.

66

"Thou sitst at home, safe, by thy quiet fire,
"And hear'st of others harmes; but feelest none:
"And there thou telst of Kings, and who aspire,
"Who fall, who rise, who triumphs, who do mone:
"Perhaps thou talkst of mee, and dost inquire
"Of my restraint, why here I liue alone,
"And pittiest this my miserable fall:
"For, pittie must haue part; enuie, not all.

67

"Thrice happy you that looke, as from the shore,
"And haue no venture in the wracke you see;
"No int'rest, no occasion to deplore
"Other mens trauailes, while your selues sit free.
"How much doth your sweet rest make vs the more
"To see our miserie, and what we bee!
"Whose blinded Greatnes, euer in turmoyle,
"Still seeking happy life, makes life a toyle.

68

"Great *Dioclesian* (and more great therefore
"For yeelding-vp that whereto pride aspires)*
"Reckning thy Gardens in *Illiria* more
"Then all the Empire, all what th'earth admires;
"Thou well didst teach, that he is neuer poore
"That little hath, but he that much desires;
"Finding more true delight in that small ground,
"Then, in possessing all the earth, was found.

69

"Are Kings that freedome giue, themselues not free,
"As meaner men, to take what they may giue?

* *Primus imperium communicauit, & posuit Dioclesianus: & in eo ponendo, dixisse fertur; Recipe Iupiter imperium, quod mihi commodasti.*

"What, are they of so fatall a degree,
"That they cannot descend from that, and liue?
"Vnlesse they still be Kings can they not bee,
"Nor may they their authority suruiue?
"Will not my yeelded Crowne redeeme my breath?
"Still am I fear'd? is there no way, but death?

70

Scarce this word, Death, from sorrow did proceed,
When in rusht one, and tels him, such a knight
Is new arriv'd, and comes from Court in speed.
What newes sayd he, with him, that traytrous wight?
What, more remouing yet? alas! what need?
Are we not farre ynough sent out of sight?
Or is this place, here, not sufficient strong
To guard vs in? or must we haue more wrong?

71

By this, the bloody troope were at the dore;
When-as a sodaine and a strange dismay
Inforc't them straine, who should go in before:
One offers, and in offring makes a stay:
An other forward sets, and doth no more:
A third the like, and none durst make the way:
So much the horror of so vile a deed,
In vilest mindes, deterres them to proceed.

72

At length, as to some great aduentrous fight,
This *Brauo* cheeres these bastards, all hee can;
And valiantly their courage doth incite,
And all against one weake vnarmed man:
A great exployte, and fit for such a knight;
Wherein, so much renowne his valor wan.
But see, how men that verie Presence feare,
Which once, they knew, Authority did beare.

73

Then, on thrusts one, and he would formost be
To shead anothers blood; but lost his owne:
For, entring in, as soone as he did see
The face of Maiestie, to him well knowne;

Like *Marius* Souldier at *Minternum,* hee
Stood still amaz'd, his courage ouer-throwne.
The King, seeing this, starting frō where he sate,
Out from his trembling hand his weapon gate.

74

Thus, euen his foes, who came to bring him death,
Bring him a weapon, that before had none;
That yet he might not idly lose his breath,
But die reueng'd, in action, not alone.
And this good chaunce, that thus much fauoureth,
He slackes not: for, he presently speedes one:
And, Lion-like, vpon the rest he flyes:
And here falles one; and there another lies.

75

And vp and down he trauerses his ground;
Now wardes a felling blowe, now strikes againe,
Then nimbly shiftes a thrust, then lends a wound,
Now backe he giues, then rushes-on amaine.
His quicke and ready hand doth so confound
These shamefull beastes, that foure of them lie slaine:
And all had perisht happily and well,
But for one act, that (ô!) I grieue to tell.

76

This coward Knight, seeing with shame and feare
His men thus slaine, and doubting his owne end,
Leapes vp into a chaire that (lo) was there,
The-while the King did all his courage bend
Against those foure, which now before him were,
Doubting not who behind him doth attend;
And plyes his hands vndaunted, vnaffeard,
And with good heart, and life for life he stird.

77

And whiles he this, and that, and each mans blowe
Doth eye, defend, and shift, being layd-to fore,
Backward he beares for more aduantage now,
Thinking the wall would safegard him the more;
When, lo, with impious hand, ô wicked thou,
That shamefull durst not come to strike before,

Behind him gav'st that lamentable wound,
Which layd that wretched Prince flat on the ground.

78

Now, proditorious wretch, what hast thou done,
To make this barbarous base assassinate
Vpon the person of a Prince, and one
Fore-spent with sorrow, and all desolate?
What great aduancement hast thou hereby wonne,
By being the instrument to perpetrate
So foule a deed? where is thy grace in Corte,
For such a seruice, acted in this sort?

79

First, he for whom thou dost this villanie
(Though pleas'd therewith) will not auouch thy fact,
But let the weight of thine owne infamie
Fall on thee, vnsupported, and vnbackt:
Then, all men else will loath thy treacherie,
And thou thy selfe abhorre thy proper act:
"So th'Wolfe, in hope the Lyons grace to win
"Betraying other beastes, lost his owne skinne.

80

But now, as this sweet Prince distended lay,
And him nor Life, nor Death, their owne could call,
(For, Life, remouing, rid not all away;
And Death, though entring, had not seis'd on all)
That short-tym'd motion had a little stay
(The mouer ceasing) though it were but small:
(As th'Organ-sound, a time, suruiues the stop,
Before it doth the dying note giue vp)

81

When lo, there streames a spring of bloud so fast,
From those deepe woundes, as all imbru'd the face
Of that accursed caytiue, as he past
(After the deed effected) through the place:
And therewithall those dying eyes did cast
Such an vpbrayding looke on his disgrace
(Seeming to checke so cowardly a part)
As left th'impression euen in his hart.

82

And this one King, most neere in bloud ally'd,
Is made th'oblation for the others peace.
Which peace yet was not hereby ratifi'd
So, as it could all future feares release.
For, though the other did forthwith prouide
To haue the rumour run of his decease,
By drawing the corps to London, where it was
Layd (three dayes to be seene) with open face:*

83

Yet, so great was this execrable deed,
As men would scarce therein belieue their eyes;
Much lesse their eares: and many sought to feed
The easie creditours of nouelties,
By voycing him aliue; how hee was freed
By strange escape out of his miseries:
And many did conspire now to relieue
Him dead, who had forsaken him aliue.†

84

And many suffred for his Cause, when now
He had none: many wisht for him againe,
When they perceiv'd th'exchange did not allow
Their hopes so much as they did looke to gaine,
By traffiquing of kings; and all saw how
Their full exspectances were in the wane.
They had a King was more then him before;
But yet a king, where they were nought the more.

85

And sure, this murthred Prince, though weake he was,
He was not ill; nor yet so weake, but that
He shew'd much Martiall valour in his place,
Aduentring oft his person for the State:
And might amongst our better Princes passe;

---

* *The Corps was conuayed from Pomfret to Londō: where it lay with open face in Paules, 3 dayes; and after a solemne obsequie, was had to Langley and there meanely interred.*

† *King Ric. bruted to be aliue after he was thus murthered: which begat a con-* [sic, /] *Conspiracie; for the which, Sir Roger Clarindon, supposed to be the base sonne of the blacke Prince was executed, with diuers Friers.*

Had not the flatterie, rapine, and debate
Of factions Lords and greedie Officers
Disgrac't his actions, and abus'd his yeares.

86

Nor is it so much Princes weakenesses,
As the corruption of their Ministers,
Wherby the Common-wealth receiues distress.
For, they, attending their particulars,
Make imperfections their aduantages
To be themselues both Kings and Councellors.
And, sure, this Common-wealth can neuer take
Hurt by weake kings, but such as we doo make.

87

Besides, he was (which people much respect
In Princes, and which pleases vulgarly)
Of goodly personage, and of sweete aspect,
Of milde accesse, and liberalitie;
And feastes, and shewes, and triumphs did affect,
As the delights of youth and iollitie:
But, here, the great profusion and expence
Of his reuenues, bred him much offence:*

88

And gaue aduantage vnto enmitie,
This grieuous accusation to prefer;
"That he consum'd the common Treasurie:
"Whereof he being the simple vsager
"But for the State (not in proprietie)
"Did alien at his pleasure, and transfer
"The same t'his minions, and to whome hee list;
"By which, the Common-wealth was to subsist.

89

"Whereby, sayd they, the poore concussed State
"Shall euer be exacted for supplyes.
Which accusation was th'occasion, that

* *Hee had in his Courte 1000. persons in ordinarie allowance of diet, 300. seruitours in
his Kitchin, aboue 300 Ladies Chamberers, and Landerers: His apparell was sumptuous;
and so was it generally in his time: hee had one Cote of gold and stone, valued at 30000.
markes. One enteruiew with the Fr. King at Ards, when his wife Isabel was deliuered
vnto him, cost 300000. markes.*

His successour by order nullifies
Many his Patents, and did reuocate
And reassume his liberalities:*
And yet, for all these wastes, these gifts and feasts,
He was not found a Bankrupt in his chests.†

90

But they, who tooke to Syndique in this sorte
The Actions of a Monarch, knew those things
Wherein the accoumpts were likely to fall short
Betweene the State of Kingdomes, and their Kings:
Which president, of pestilent import
(Had not the heauens blest thy indeuorings)
Against thee *Henry,* had beene likewise brought,
Th'example made of thy example wrought.

91

For, though this bountie, and this liberalness,
A glorious vertue be; it better fits
Great men, then kings: who, giuing in excesse,
Giue not their owne, but others benefits:
Which calles-vp manies hopes, but pleasures lesse;
Destroying far more loue, then it begets.‡
For, Iustice is their Virtue: that alone
Makes them sit sure, and glorifies the Throne.

The ende of the third Booke.

* *Hen. 4. reuoketh al letters patents of Annuities granted by K. Ed. and K. Ric. Ann. reg. 6.*

† *When he was first surpris'd in Wales, the D. of Lancaster had in Holt Castle 100000. markes in coyne, and 200000, markes in Iewels: and at his Resignation in the Towre, 300000 poūds in coyne, besides plate and Iewels.*

‡ *A Prince, excessiue in gifts, makes his subiects excessiue in sutes.*

The Fovrth *Booke*

THE ARGVMENT

King Henrie, *his excuses publishes*
For Richards *death; and truce doth intertaine*
With France. *The Scots, aggrieu'd for wrongs, address*
Themselues to warre; and are appeas'd againe.
The Welsh rebell. The Percies *practises*
(To part the State) are stopt, in battell slaine.
Continuall troubles still afflict this King;
Till Death an end doth to his trauailes bring.

1

THe bounds once ouer-gone, that hold men in,
They neuer stay; but on, from bad to worse.
"Wrongs do not leaue off there, where they begin;
"But, still beget new mischiefes in their course.
Now, *Henrie,* thou hast added to thy sinne
Of Vsurpation, and intruding force,
A greater crime; which makes that gone before
T'appeare more then it did, and noted more.

2

For, now thou art inforc't t'apologise
With forraine States, for two enormious things,*
Wherein, thou dost appeare to scandalise
The publike Right, and common Cause of Kings:
Which, though (with all the skill thou canst deuise)
Thou ouerlay'st with fayrest colourings;
Yet th'vnder-worke, transparent, shewes too plaine.
"Where open acts accuse, th'excuse is vaine.

3

And these defences, are but complements,
To dallie with confining Potentates;
Who, busied in their proper gouernments,
Do seldome tend th'affaires of other States:

---

* Commissioners are sent to forraine Princes, to excuse & iustifie the Kings proceedings.

Their wisedome, which to present powre consents,
Liue-dogges before dead Lyons, estimates:
"And no man more respects these publike wrongs,
"Then so much as t'his priuate state belongs.

4

Yet, most it seem'd the French King to import;
As sharer in his daughters iniurie:
"Though bloud, in Princes, links not in such sort,
"As that it is of any powre to tye,
Where their estates may seeme t'aduenture hurt;
Or where there is not a necessitie,
That doth combine them with a stronger chaine,
Then all these great Alliances containe.

5

For, though this King might haue resentiment,
And will, t'auenge him of his iniurie:
Yet, at that time, his State being turbulent,
Factious, and full of partialitie,*
And oftentimes he himselfe impotent,
By meanes of his Phreneticque maladie;
It was not likely, any good could rise
By vndertaking such an enterprise.

6

And therefore both sides, vpon entercourse
(As fitted best their present termes) agreed,
The former truce continue should in force,
According as it had beene fore-decreed
Vpon the match with *Richard;*‡ and a course
For *Isabel* (with all conuenient speed)
Prouided, with an honorable Traine
Suting her state, to be sent home againe.

7

Whome willingly they would haue still retain'd,
And matcht vnto the Prince:‡ but shee (though yong;

---

* In this time of Charles 6. began the ciuile warres in Fraunce, between the Dukes of Orleans, and Burgoigne.

† The Truce made with Ric. 2. renewd for 30. yeares: but broken the next yeare after, vpon their part; sending Iaques de Burbon, with forces into Wales, to the ayde of Glendour.

‡ The King labors to haue Q. Isabel matcht to his sonne Henry, Prince of Wales.

Yet sensible of that which appertain'd
To honor, and renowne) scornd any tongue
That offred such a motion; and disdaynd
To haue it thought, she would but heare that wrong
Mov'd to her, or her Lord, and husband dead,
To haue his murtherers race inioy his bed.

8

Besides; the French (doubting the Gouernment,
Thus gotten, would be subiect still to strife)
Not willing were to vrge her to consent
T'accept a troublous, and vncertaine life:
And, being returnd, she grew in th'end content
To be (at home) a Duke of *Orleance* wife;*
Scap't from such stormes of powre, holding it best
To be belowe her selfe, to be at rest.

9

And so hath *Henrie* assecur'd that side,
And therewithall his State of *Gasconie:*
Which, on th'intelligence was notifi'd
Of *Richards* death, were wrought to mutinie;†
And hardly came to be repacifi'd,
And kept to hold in their fidelitie:
So much, to him were they affectioned,
For hauing beene amongst them borne and bred.

10

These toyles abrode, these tumults with his owne
(As if the frame of all disioynted were,
With this disordred shifting of the Crowne)
Fell, in the reuolution of one yeare.
Beside; the Scotte (in discontentment growne,
For the detayning, and supporting here
The scourge of all this kindgome, *George Dunbar*)
With fire and sword, proclaymes an open war;

* *Queen Isabel was maried to Charles, sonne to Loyse, D. of Orleans.*

† *Thom. Percy E. of Worcester was sent into Gascony with 200. men at Armes and 400. Archers, to assist Sir Robert Knoles Lieutenant there: where he pacified that Country, being incensed by the French to reuolt vpon their discontentment for the death of King Ric. whom they especially loued for being borne at Burdeux.*

11

Taking their time, in these disturbances
And newnesse of a wauering Gouernment,
T'auenge them of their former grieuances,
And by our spoyles their fortunes to augment.
Against whose forces, *Henry* furnishes
A powrefull Army, and in person went;
But warres with a retyring enemy,
With much more trauaile then with victorie.

12

And, being (by sharp, deformed Winters force)
Caus'd to retire, he findes new stormes at home,
From other Coasts arysing; that prov'd worse
Then those, which now hee was returned from.
In *Wales,* a Cause of Law, by violent course,
Was (from a variance) now a warre become;
And *Owen Glendour,* who with *Gray* of late
Contests for priuate landes, now seekes a State.*

13

Whom to represse, he early in the Spring,
With all prouisions fit, doth forward set;
When streight his enemies (not purposing
To hazard battaile) to the mountaines get.
Where, after long and weary trauayling,
Without performing any great defeat,
He onely their prouisions wastes, and burnes,
And with some prey of Cattell home returnes.

14

Wherewith, the Rebell rather was the more
Incourag'd, then addaunted: and begun
T'aduenture farther then he did before;
Seeing such a Monarch had so little done,
Being com'n in person, with so great a powre,
And sodainely againe retyr'd and gone.
"For, in this case, they helpe, who hurt so small;
"And he hath nothing done, that doth not all.

* *Owen Glendour, an Esquire in North-Wales, contesting with the L. Gray of Ruthen,
for certaine landes which hee claymed by inheritance; and being not powerful inough
by his owne meanes to recouer them, procur'd force and made war vpon the L. Gray; and
after attempts for the principalitie of that Countrey. Ann. Reg. 2.*

15

But now* (behold) other new heads appeare,
New *Hidra's* of rebellion, that procure
More worke to doo, and giue more cause of feare;
And shew'd, that nothing in his State stood sure.
And these, euen of his chiefest followers were,
Of whome he might presume him most secure;
Who had th'especiall ingins beene, to reare
His fortunes vp, vnto the State they were.

16

The *Percies* were the men; men of great might,
Strong in alliance, and in courage strong:
Who now conspire; vnder pretence to right
Such wrongs, as to the Common wealth belong:
Vrg'd, either through their conscience, or despight,
Or finding now the part they tooke was wrong:
Or else Ambition hereto did them call,
Or others enuy'd grace; or, rather, all.

17

And such they were, who might presume t'haue done
Much for the king, and honour of the State;
Hauing the chiefest actions vnder-gone,
Both forraine and domesticall of late:
Beside that famous day of *Homeldon;*†
Where *Hotspur* gaue that wonderfull defeat
Vnto the Scottes, as shooke that kingdome more
Then many Monarchs armies had before.

18

Which might perhaps aduance their mindes, so farre
Aboue the leuell of subiection, as
T'assume to them the glory of that war;
Where all things, by their powre, were brought to passe:

---

* *Ann. Reg. 3.*
† *In this battell of Homeldon, the L. Hen. Percie, surnamed Hot-spur, accompanied with George Dunbar E. of March, ouerthrew the Scottish forces: where were slaine 23 Knights and 10000 of the Cōmons: the EE. of Fife, Murry, Angus, with 500. other of meaner degree, taken prisoners.*

They, being so mightie, and so popular,
And their command so spacious as it was,
Might (in their State) forget, how all these things
That subiects doo effect, must be their Kings.

19

And so fell after into discontent,
For-that the king requir'd to haue, as his,
Those Lords were taken prisoners; whome they ment
To hold still as their proper purchases:
Then, that he would not, at their sute, consent
To worke their Cosin *Mortimers* release,
Out of the Rebell *Owen Glendour's* hands;
Who held him prisoner, in disgracefull bands.

20

But be, what will, the cause; strong was their plot,
Their parties great, meanes good, the season fit,
Their practice close, their faith suspected not,
Their states far off, and they of wary wit:
Who, with large promises, so wooe the Scot
To aide their Cause, as he consents to it;
And glad was to disturne that furious streame
Of warre, on vs, that else had swallowed them.

21

Then ioyne they with the Welsh; who, now wel train'd,
In Armes and action dayly grew more great.
Their Leader, by his wiles, had much attaynd,
And done much mischiefe on the English State:
Beside, his prisoner *Mortimer* he gain'd,
From being a foe, to b'his confederate;
A man the King much fear'd: and well he might;
Least he should looke whether his Crowne stood right.

22

For, *Richard* (for the quiet of the State)
Before he tooke those Irish warres in hand,
About Succession doth deliberate:
And, finding how the certaine Right did stand,

With full consent this man did ordinate
The heyre apparent to the Crowne and Land;*
Whose competencie was of tender touch:
Although his might was small, his right was much.

23

With these, the *Percies* them confederat,
And (as three heads) conioyne in one intent:
And (instituting a Triumuirate)
Do part the Land, in triple gouernment;
Diuiding thus, among themselues, the State:
The *Percies* should rule all the North, from *Trent;*
And *Glendour, Wales;* the Earle of *March* should be
Lord of the South, from *Trent:* and so they 'gree.

24

Then, those faire bayts these Trouble-States still vse
(*Pretence of common good,* the Kings ill Course)
Must be cast forth, the people to abuse,
And giue their Cause, and them, the better force.
The king, for tyranny, they doo accuse,
By whom the State was growne from bad to worse;
A periur'd man, who held all faith in scorne:
Whose trusted Oathes had others made forsworne.

25

And, therewithal, the execrable act,
On their late murthered King, they aggrauate:†
How he imploy'd the dooers of the fact,
Whom afterwards hee did remunerate:
And dayly such taxations did exact,
As were against the Order of the State;
Presuming, those great summes hee did impose,
About his priuate vses to dispose:

* In the 9. yeere of the raigne of King Richard 2. was by Parlement ordained Roger E. of March heir apparent to the Crowne. This Roger was the sonne of Edmond Mortimer, who married Phillippa the only daughter of Leonel D. of Clarence, the third son of King Ed. 3. who by her had issue this Roger & Elizabeth: Roger had issue 4. children, all which, saue only Anne, dyed without issue: Anne was maried to Rich. E. of Cambridge, second sonne to Edmond D. of Yorke. This Rich. beheaded at Southhampton, had issue by Anne, Richard, surnamed Plantagenet, after Duke of Yorke.

† The Percies article against Hen. 4. Ann. Reg. 4.

26

And how he was inuironed with such
As had possest him; and in slanderous sort
Accus'd them so, as they durst not approche
To cleare themselues of such vniust report:
And, thereupon, they flatly disauouch
To yeld him more obedience, or support:
And, as t'a periurd Duke of *Lancaster*,
Their Cartell of Defiance they preferre;

27

Protesting, these obiections to make good,
With sword in hand, and to confirme and seale
Their vndertaking, with their dearest bloud,
As Procurators for the Common-weale:
And that vpon their Consciences it stood,
And did import their dutie and their zeale
Vnto the State, as Peeres to see redrest
Those miseries wherewith it was opprest.

28

Great seem'd their Cause: and greatly, too, did adde
The peoples loue thereto, these crymes impos'd;
That many gathered to the troupes they had,
And many sent them aide though vndisclos'd:
So that, the King, with all maine speed, was glad
Both by his remonstrances well compos'd,
And with his sword (his best defence) prouide
To right himselfe, and to correct their pride:

29

Divulging, first, a fayre Apologie
Of his cleere heart, touching the foule report
Of that assassinate: which vtterly
He doth abiure; protesting, in no sort
T'agree thereto, in will or priuitie:
And, how he had beene vsed to extort,
The State could witnesse best; by whose consent
Was granted what he had, in Parlement.

30

Which neuer was, but onely one supply,
In foure yeares troublous and expensiue Raigne:

And that, vpon extreame necessitie,
The safetie of the publicke to maintaine:
And that the *Percies* best could testifie,
How most that mony issued was, againe;
To whom the same was rendred, to the end
To warre the Scot, and Borders to defend:

31

And that the rest was, to the same effect
For which it was obtaynd, in like sort spent.
And where-as they did slanderously obiect,
How that they durst not hazard to present
In person their defences, in respect
He was incenst by some maleuolent;
It was most false: for, he knew no defence
They were to make, till now they made offence.

32

And how far, he had been, from cruelty,
Both *Wales,* and *Scotland* could him witnes beare;
Where, those effects of his great clemencie,
In sparing bloud, do to his cost appeare:
Much more, his subiects finde his lenitie;
Whose loue he seekes to haue, and not their feare.
"But thus, said he, they euer do pretend
"To haue receiv'd a wrong, who wrong intend.

33

Not to giue time vnto th'increasing rage,
And gathering furie, foorth hee marcht with speed;
Least more delay, or giuing longer age
To th'euill growne, it might the cure exceed.
All his best men at Armes, and Leaders sage,
All he prepar'd hee could; and all did need.
For, to a mighty worke thou goest, ô King,
That equall spirits, and equall powres shal bring.

34

There shall young *Hotspur,* with a fury led,
Ingrapple with thy sonne, as fierce as hee:
There Martiall *Worster,* long experienced
In forraine armes, shall come t'incounter thee.

There *Dowglas,* to thy *Stafford,* shall make head:
There *Vernon,* for thy valiant *Blunt,* shall be.
There, shalt thou finde a doubtfull bloudy day;
Though sickenesse keep *Northumberland* away.

35

Who yet reserv'd (though, after, quit for this)
Another tempest on thy head to rayse;
As if, still, wrong-reuenging *Nemesis*
Meant to afflict all thy continuing dayes:
And here this field hee happely doth misse,
For thy great good; and therefore well hee stayes.
What might his force haue done, being brought thereto,
When that already, gaue so much to doo?

36

The swift approche, and vnexpected speed,
The King had made vpon this new-rays'd force,*
In th'vnconfirmed troupes, much feare did breed,
Vntimely hind'ring their intended course:
The ioyning with the Welsh (they had decreed)
Was hereby dasht; which made their Cause the worse:
Northumberland, with forces from the North,
Expected to be there, was not set forth.

37

And yet, vndaunted *Hotspur,* seeing the King
So neere arriv'd; leauing the worke in hand,
With forward speed his forces marshalling,
Sets forth, his farther comming to withstand:
And, with a cheerfull voyce incouraging
His well experienc't and aduentrous Band,
Brings on his Army, eger vnto fight;
And plac't the same, before the King in sight.

38

"This day (saith he) my valiant trusty friendes,
"What-euer it doth giue, shal glory giue;

* *The K. hastened forward by George Dunbar, was in sight of his enemies lying in Campe neer to Shrewsburie, sooner then hee was exspected: for the Percies supposed he would haue stayed longer then hee did at Burton vpon Trent, for the comming of his Councell with other forces which were there to meete him. Whereupon they left to assaile the Towne of Shrewsbury; and prepared to encounter the kings forces, Ann. Keg. [sic] 4.*

"This day, with honor, frees our State, or endes
"Our misery with fame, that still shal liue:
"And doo but thinke, how well the same he spends,
"Who spends his blood, his Country to relieue.
"What? haue we hands, and shall we seruile bee?
"Why were swordes made? but, to preserue men free.

39

Besides, th'assured hope of victorie,
Which we may even fore-promise on our side,
Against this weake constrayned company;
Whom force and feare, not will and loue doth guide:
Against a Prince, whose foul impiety
The heauens doo hate, the earth cannot abide:
Our number being no lesse, our courage more,
No doubt we haue it, if wee worke therefore.

40

This sayd, and thus resolv'd, euen bent to charge
Vpon the King; who well their order view'd,
And wary noted all the course at large
Of their proceeding, and their multitude:
And deeming better, if he could discharge
The day with safetie, and some peace conclude,
Great proffers sendes of pardon and of grace
If they would yeeld, and quietnesse imbrace.*

41

Which though his feares might driue him to propose,
To time his businesse, for some other ende;
Yet, sure, hee could not meane t'haue peace with those,
Who did in that supreame degree offend:
Nor were they such, as would bee wonne with showes;
Or breath of oathes, or vowes could apprehend:
So that in honor, th'offers, he doth make,
Were not for him to giue, nor them to take.

* *The Abbot of Shrewsbury and one of the Clearks of the priuie seale were sēt from the K to the Percies to offer them pardon if they wold come to any reasonable agreement. Whereupon the E. of Worcester comming to the K. receiued many kind proffers: and promising to moue his Nephew therein, did at his returne, as is sayd, conceale them, and hastened on the battel; which was fought neer Shrewsbury. An. Reg. 4.*

42

And yet this much his courses doo approue,
He was not bloudy, in his Naturall;
And yeeld he did to more, then might behoue
His dignitie, to haue dispenst withall:
And, vnto *Worster*, hee himselfe did moue
A reconcilement to be made of all:
But *Worster*, know'ing it could not be secur'd,
His Nephews on-set (yet for all) procur'd.

43

Which seeing, the King (with greater wrath incenst)
Rage, against furie, doth with speede prepare.
And though, sayd he, I could haue wel dispenst
With this dayes bloud, which I haue sought to spare;
That greater glory might haue recompenst
The forward worth of these, that so much dare;
That we might good haue had by th'ouerthrowne,
And th'wounds we make, might not haue beene our owne:

44

Yet, since that other mens iniquitie
Calles-on the sword of wrath, against my will;
And that themselues exact this crueltie,
And I constrayned am this bloud to spill;
Then on, braue followers, on courageously,
True-harted subiects, against traytors ill:
And spare not them, who seeke to spoyle vs all;
Whose foul confused end, soone see you shal.

45

Forth-with, began these fury-mouing sounds,
The notes of wrath, the musicke brought from Hell,
The ratling Drums (which trumpets voyce confounds)
The cryes, th'incouragements, the shouting shrill;
That, all about, the beaten ayre rebounds
Confused thundring-murmurs horrible;
To robbe all sense, except the sense to fight.
Well hands may worke: the minde hath lost his sight.

46

O warre! begot in pride and luxurie,
The child of malice, and reuengeful hate;

Thou impious good, and good impietie,
That art the foul refiner of a State;
Vniust-iust scourge of mens iniquitie,
Sharpe-easer of corruptions desperate;
Is there no meanes, but that a sin-sicke Land
Must be let bloud with such a boysterous hand?

47

How well mightst thou haue, here, beene spar'd this day,
Had not wrong-counsaild *Percy* beene peruerse?
Whose forward hand, inur'd to woundes, makes way
Vpon the sharpest fronts of the most fierce:
Where now an equall furie thrusts, to stay
And backe-repell that force, and his disperse:
Then these assaile, then those re-chase againe,
Till stayd with new-made hils of bodies slaine.

48

There, lo that new-appearing glorious starre,
Wonder of Armes, the terror of the field,
Young *Henrie*,* laboring where the stoutest are,
And euen the stoutest forceth backe to yeeld;
There is that hand boldned to bloud and warre,
That must the sword, in wondrous actions, wield:
Though better, he had learnd with others bloud;
A lesse expence to vs, to him more good.

49

Yet here had he not speedy succour lent
To his indangered father, neere opprest,
That day had seene the full accomplishment
Of all his trauailes, and his finall rest:
For, *Mars*-like *Dowglas* all his forces bent
T'incounter, and to grapple with the best;
As if disdayning any other thing
To doo, that day, but to subdue a King.

50

And three, with fierie courage, he assailes;
Three, all as kings adornd in royall wise:
And each successiue after other quailes;

* *Prince Henry, at this Battel, was not 17 yeares of age.*

Still wondring, whence so many Kings should rise.
And, doubting lest his hand or eye-sight fayles,
In these confounded, on a fourth hee flyes,
And him vnhorses too: whom had hee sped,
He then all Kings, in him, had vanquished.

51

For *Henrie* had diuided, as it were,
The person of himselfe, into foure parts;
To be lesse knowne, & yet known euery where,
The more to animate his peoples harts:
Who, cheered by his presence, would not spare
To execute their best and worthyest parts.
By which, two special things effected are;
His safetie, and his subiects better care.

52

And neuer worthy Prince a day did quit
With greater hazard, and with more renowne,
Then thou didst, mighty *Henry,* in this fight;
Which onely made thee owner of thine owne:
Thou neuer proov'dst the Tenure of thy right
(How thou didst hold thy easie-gotten Crown)
Till now: and, now, thou shew'st thy selfe Chiefe Lord,
By that especial right of kings; the *Sword.*

53

And deare it cost, and much good bloud is shed
To purchase thee, a sauing victorie:
Great *Stafford* thy high Constable lyes dead,*
With *Shorly, Clifton, Gawsell, Caluerly,*
And many more; whose braue deathes witnessed
Their noble valour and fidelitie:
And many more had left their dearest bloud
Behind, that day, had *Hotspur* longer stood.

54

But he, as *Dowglas,* with his furie ledde,
Rushing into the thickest woods of speares,
And brakes of swordes, still laying at the Head
(The life of th'Army) whiles he nothing feares,

* *Edmond, E of Stafford, Constable of England.*

Or spares his owne, comes all inuironed
With multitude of powre, that ouer-beares
His manly worth: who yeeldes not, in his fall;
But fighting dyes, and dying kils withall.

55

What Arke, what trophey, what magnificence
Of glory, *Hot-spurre,* hadst thou purchas't here;
Could but thy Cause, as fayre as thy pretence,
Be made vnto thy Country to appeare!
Had it beene her protection and defence
(Not thy ambition) made thee sell so deare
Thy selfe this day; shee must haue here made good
An euerlasting Statüe for thy bloud.

56

Which thus misspent, thy Army presently,
(As if they could not stand, when thou wert downe)
Disperst in rout, betooke them all to flie:
And *Dowglas,* faint with wounds, & ouer-throwne,
Was taken; who yet wonne the enemie
Which tooke him (by his noble valour showne,
In that dayes mighty worke) and was preserv'd
With all the grace, and honor he deserv'd.

57

Worc'ster (who had escap't vnhappily
His death in battel) on a Scaffold dyes,*
The next day after, in the company
Of other chiefest of that enterprise.
And, so, the tempest of this mutinie
Became allay'd; and those great ieoperdies
Blowne-ouer in this sort, the Coasts well cleer'd,
But for one threatning cloud, that yet appear'd.

58

Northumberland (recouered) still out stands,
The principall of this great family
And faction; haueing *Berwike* in his hands,
With other holdes; strong by confed'racie

* *Tho. Percie E. of Worcester, with Sir Richard Vernon and the Baron of Kinderton,*
were taken in the Battell and beheaded.

With *Scotland;* mighty by his owne command:
And, likely now, his vtmost powre to trie,
T'auenge him on the ruine of his Bloud,
And ioyne with *Wales;* which yet vndanted stood.

59

Which mov'd the king (who had too much indur'd
In this dayes worke, to hazard new againe)
By all the aptest meanes could be procur'd
To lay to draw him in, by any traine.
And write he did, and vow'd, and him assur'd
(Vpon his princely word) to intertaine
With former grace if hee would but submit,
And come to yeeld th'obedience that was fit.

60

The Earle, be'ing now by this defeat dismay'd
(And fearing his confederates would fayle
With Fortune, and betray, rather then ayde,
Those who are downe; being for their owne auayle)
Relying on his Sov'raignes oath obay'd;
Which, with his tender griefs, did much preuaile:
And in hee came, and had no detryment,
But (for a shew) some short imprisonment.

61

The Parlement, that afterward insu'd,
Restor'd him t'all his dignities and landes.
And now none, but the Welsh, seem'd to seclude
The king, from hauing wholly in his hands
All peace within: and them he had pursu'd
While this braue army, with these ready bands,
Were yet on foot; could he but haue got pay
To hold them, and his charge of war defray.

62

But, that hee could not gaine, though all the wayes
That might be wrought, he labours to procure
Meanes to effect the same. But, those delayes,
And long protraction, which he must indure
By way of Parlement, so much betrayes
The opportunitie, that might secure

His vndertaking; as, the occasion, lost,
Draue both the State, and him, to greater cost.

63

For, now the Rebell, thus forborne, growes strong
Both in his reputation and successe:
For, hauing with his powre held out so long,
Many aduenture (with more forwardnesse)
To yeeld him ayd, and to support his wrong:
And forraine Princes (in his businesse
Whom hee sollicites) now wil lend their hand
To hould him vp;* seeing, himselfe can stand.

64

And thus he prospers; whiles, the King here spent
Much time to leuie treasure, to maintaine
His charge abrode: which, with that discontent,
That murmure, those denyals, hee doth gaine,
As that hee findes it euen as turbulent
To warre for it, as with it, all his Raigne;†
Though hee had those inforcements of expence,
Both for offence, retaynements, and defence.

65

For, here beside these troubles in the Land,
His large Dominions, held abrode, require
A plentiful and a prepared hand
To guard them; where so mightie men aspire
T'assaile, distract and trouble his Command,
With hopes, and promises, with sword and fire:‡
And then as deepe importes, his Coastes to cleere;
Which, by his neighbors, much infested were.

66

The *Flemings, Britaines,* with the *French* and all,
Attempt incursions, and worke much despight:

---

* *The Fr. K. sendes aide to Owen Glendour with 140. shippes, which landed at Milford Hauen. An. Reg. 6.*

† *An. Reg. 6. with much adoo the Laitie granted 2 fifteenes, vpon condition that the L. Furniuall should receiue all the mony, and see it to bee spent in the K. warres.*

‡ *The D. of Orleans with an Army of 6000. men entred into Guien, and beseiged Vergi, the space of 3, moneths, & return'd without obtaining it. An. Reg. 5. The Conte Cleremont, Sonne to the D. of Burbon, with Mon. de la Bret, wonne diuers Castles in Gasconie. The same time the Conte Sa. Paul inuadeth the Ile of Wight, with 1600. men.*

Orleance, for *Guien:* and here the Conte, Saint *Paul,*
For *Calais* labours, and the *Ile of Wight.**
Wherein, though neither had successe at all;
Yet *Cleremont* ouercame, and wonne by fight
Important Holdes, in *Gasconie* the-while,
And did the English much distresse and spoyle.

67

All which require prouisions to withstand:
And all are succord with great prouidence:
A Nauie, to secure the Seas, is mann'd,
And forces sent to Calais, for defence.†
And wherein other parts defectiue stand,
They are supply'd, with carefull diligence:
So that his subiects could not, but well knowe,
That what they granted, he did sure bestowe.

68

Nor did hee spare himselfe, nor his; but (bent
All-wholly vnto actiue Worthynesse)
The Prince of *Wales* vnto his Prouince sent;
Where, hee was sure hee should not take his ease:
His second sonne is, with the Earle of *Kent,*
Imploy'd (as Gouernour) to keep the Seas.
A third (though very yong) likewise sent forth
With *Westmerland,* attends vnto the North.‡

69

Thus were they bred, who after were to bee
Men amongst men: here, with these graue Adioynts
(These learned Maisters) they were taught to see
Themselues, to read the world, and keep their points.
Thus were they entred in the first degree
(And Accedence) of action; which acquaints
Them, with the Rules of Worth and Nobleness:
Which, in true Concord, they learn'd well t'expresse.

---

* *An. Reg. 6. The Cont Saint Paule besiegeth the Castle of Marke within 3. miles of Calais. The Brittaines vnder the conduct of the L. of Cassills spoyled and burnt the Towne of Plimmouth.*

 † *The K. sends 4000 men to Calais and 3000 to the Seas, vnder the conduct of his second sonne Tho. of Lancaster after D. of Clarence.*

 ‡ *Iohn, after D. of Bedford, sent with Ralph Neuile E. of Westmerland, into the North.*

70

And, whiles h'attends the State thus carefully,
The Earle of *Marches* children are conuay'd
Out of the Towre of *Windsor,* secretly;
Being prisoners there, not for their merit, lay'd;
But, for their Bloud; and to the ende whereby
This Chayne of Nature might be interlay'd
Betweene the Father and his high intents,
To hold him backe, to saue these innocents.

71

For which attempt (though it were frustrated
By their recouerie, who were got againe)
Aumarle (now Duke of *Yorke*) is chalenged,
By his owne sister, to haue layd that trayne;*
Who (late) her Lord, with others ruined,
In secretly betraying them, t'obtaine
His grace and peace: which yet contents him not.
For, Who hath grace and peace by treason got?

72

So much did loue, t'her executed Lord,
Predominate in this faire Ladies hart,
As in that region, it would not afford
Nature a place, to rest in any part
Of her affections; but that she abhord
Her proper blood, and left to doo the part
Of sisterhood, to doo that of a wife;
T'auenge a Husbands death, by Brothers life.

73

Vpon which accusation, presently
The Duke committed is, without much stirre
Or vulgar noyse; for that it tenderly
Did touch the secretst wounds of *Lancaster:*
When streight, another new conspiracie
(As if it were a certaine successor

---

* *The Lady Spencer, sister to Edward D. of Yorke, late wife to Tho. L. Spencer
(executed at Bristow, An. Reg. 1.) accused her brother to be the chiefe author of conuay-
ing away the E. of Marches sons out of the Towre of Windsor.*

Ally'd to this) ingendred in the North,
Is by th'Archbishop *Scroope* with power brought forth:*

74

And with faire zeale, and pietie, approv'd
To be for th'vniuersall benefit
And succour of the people, who (soone mov'd
By such perswaders, as are held vpright;
And for their zeale, and charitie belov'd)
Vse not t'examine if the Cause be right,
But leap into the toyle, and are vndon
By following them that they rely'd vpon.

75

Here, now aspersions, with new obloquies,
Are layde on old deserts; and future ill
On present suffrings, bruted to aryse,
That farther grieuances ingender wil
And then concussion, rapine, pilleries,
Their Catalogue of accusations fill.†
Which to redresse, they doo presume to make
Religion to auow the part they take.

76

And euen as *Canterburie* did produce
A Pardon to aduance him to the Crown;
The like now Yorke pronounces, to induce
His faction for the pulling of him down:‡
Whilst th'ignorant, deceiv'd by this abuse,
Makes others ends to be as if their owne.
But, what wold these haue don against the crimes,
Oppressions, ryots, wastes of other times?

77

Since now they had a Monarch, and a man,
Rays'd by his worth, and by their owne consent,

* *Hen. Percie E. of North. againe conspires against the K with Rich. Scroope Arch-*
bishop of Yorke, Tho. Mowbraie E Marshal, Tho. L, Bardolph, and others. They
assembled the Citizens of Yorke with the Country adioyning to take their part for the
commodity of the Realme.

  † *They divulge grieuous Articles against the King.*
  ‡ *The Archb. of York offers pardon to all that take their part against the King.*

To gouerne them, and workes the best he can
T'aduance the Crowne, and giue the State cōtent;
Commits not all to others care, nor ran
An idle course, or on his Minions spent.
"But, thus the Horse at first bites at the Bit;
"That after is content to play with it.

78

Growne to a mighty powre (attending now
Northumberland, with his prepared ayde)
The Bishop (by a *parle*) is, with a showe
Of combination, cunningly betrayed
By Westmerland:* whose wit did ouerthrowe,
Without a sword, all these great feares, and stayd
The mightiest danger, that did euer yet
Thy Crowne and State, disturbed *Henrie,* threat.

79

For which, this reuerent Priest with *Mowbray* dyes:
Who both, drawne on, with passion of despight,
To vndertake this fatall enterprise
(The one his brothers bloud-shed to requite;†
The other for his fathers iniuries)‡
Did wrong themselues, and did not others right.
For, who through th'eyes of their affections looke,
And not of iudgement, thus are ouer-tooke.

80

Whereof when newes came to *Northumberland*
(Who seldome other then of miserie
Seemes borne to heare; being euer behind hand
With Fortune, and his opportunitie)
To *Scotland* flyes: where, giuen to vnderstand
Of some intrapment by conspiracie,

---

* *The E. of Westmerland with Iohn D. of Lancaster, gathered an Armie against the conspiritours: whose power being too great for thē, the E. made semblance to ioyne with the Archb. for redress of such greuances as he pretended; and so circumuented and disfurnisht him of his forces. An. Reg. 6.*

† *The Archb. was brother to William Scroope E. of Wiltshire, Treasurer of England, before beheaded.*

‡ *Tho. Mowbray E. Marshall, sonne to the Duke of Norfolke, banished about the quarrell with H. Bullingbrooke.*

Gets into *Wales:* whence, hee aduentured
T'attempt another day; and lost his head.*

81

Whereby, once more those Parts are quieted,
When-as the King (who neuer had his brow
Seene free from sweat, nor hart from trouble rid)
Was, with suspicion that his sonne grew now
Too popular, and forward, so much fed
By wicked instruments (who well knew how
To gaine by Princes feares) as he thereby
Fell, in his griefe, to great extreamitie.†

82

Which when the vertuous Prince (who borne to bee
The module of a glorious Monarch) heard,
With humble protestations did so free
His fathers feares, and his owne honor cleer'd,
As that he plainely made the world to see
How base, Detraction, and Deceipt appeard;
And that a hart, so nobly built, could not
Containe (within) a thought, that wore a blot.

83

Wherewith, the king betakes him to some peace;
Yet to a peace, much like a sicke-mans sleep
(Whose vnrelenting paines do neuer cease;
But always watch vpon his weakenes keepe)
That neuer any Sabaoth of release
Could free his trauailes, and afflictions deepe:
But still his cares held working, all his life,
Till Death concludes a finall end with strife.

84

Whose Herald, Sickenes, being imploy'd, before,
With full commission to denounce his end;
And paine and griefe, inforcing more and more,
Besieg'd the Hold, that could not long defend;

---

* *The E. of North. returning out of Wales recouers new forces in Yorkeshire, and is with the L. Bardolph ouercome at Bramham Moore and slaine in the Battail, An. Reg. 9.*
† *The K. growes iealous of his sonne, Hen. Prince of Wales: who, with a better minde then fashion, came to his Father and cleared himself. An. Reg. 13.*

Consuming, so, al that resisting store
Of those prouisions Nature daign'd to lend,
As that the walles, worne thin, permit the Minde
To looke out thorow, and his frailty finde.

85

For, now (as if those vapors vanisht were,
Which heat of boyling bloud, and health, did breed,
To clowd the iudgement) things do plaine appeare
In their owne colours, as they are indeede;
When-as th'illightned soule discouers cleere
Th'abusing shewes of Sense, and notes with heed
How poore a thing is pride; when all, as slaues,
"Differ but in their fetters, not their Graues.

86

And, lying on his last afflicted bed,
Pale Death and Conscience both before him stand;
Th'one holding out a Booke, wherein he read
In bloudy lines the deedes of his owne hand:
The other shewes a glasse, which figured
An ougly forme of foule corrupted Sand;
Both bringing horror in the hiest degree,
With what he was, and what he soone should be.

87

Which seeing; all trembling, and confus'd with feare,
He lay a while, amaz'd with this affright:
At last, commands some, that attending were,
To fetch the Crowne, and set it in his sight.
On which, with fixed eye, and heauy cheere,
Casting a looke; O God, sayth he, what right
I had to thee, I now in griefe conceiue:
Thee, which with blood I held, with horror leaue.

88

And, herewithall, the soule (rapt with the thought
Of mischiefes past) did so attentiue wey
These present terrors, whil'st (as if forgot)
The dull oppressed body senselesse lay;
That he, as breathlesse quite, quite dead is thought;
When, lo, the sonne comes in, and takes-away

This fatall Crowne from thence, and out he goes;
As if impatient, longer time to lose.

89

To whom (call'd backe for this presumptuous deed)
The King (return'd from out his extasie)
"Began: O sonne, what needst thou make such speed
"To be before-hand with thy miserie?
"Thou shalt haue time ynough, if thou succeed,
"To feele the stormes that beat on Dignitie.
"And, if thou couldst but bee (be any thing)
"In libertie, then neuer be a King.

90

"Nay, Father; since your Fortune did attaine
"So high a Stand, I meane not to descend,
"Replyes the Prince: as if what you did gaine,
"I were of spirit vnable to defend.
"Time will appease them well, who now complaine,
"And ratifie our int'rest in the end.
"What wrong hath not continuance quite out-worne?
"Yeares make that right, which neuer was so borne.

91

"If so; God worke his pleasure, sayd the King:
"Yet thou must needs contend, with all thy might,
"Such euidence of vertuous deeds to bring,
"That well may proue our wrong to be our right:
"And let the goodnesse of the managing
"Raze out the blot of foul attaining, quite;
"That Discontent may all aduantage misse.
"To wish it otherwise, then now it is.

92

"And since my death my purpose doth preuent,
"Touching this *Holy warre* I tooke in hand
"(An action wherewithall my soule had ment
"T'appease my God, and reconcile my Land)
"To thee is left to finish my intent;
"Who, to be safe, must neuer idly stand:
"But some great actions entertaine thou still,
"To holde their mindes, who else wil practise ill.

93

"Thou hast not that aduantage by my Raigne,
"To ryot it, as they whom long descent
"Hath purchas't loue, by custome; but, with paine
"Thou must contend to buy the worlds content.
"What their birth gaue them, thou hast yet to gaine,
"By thine owne vertues, and good gouernment:
"So that vnlesse thy worth confirme the thing,
"Thou neuer shalt be father to a King.

94

"Nor art thou borne in those calme dayes, where Rest
"Hath brought asleepe sluggish Securitie:
"But, in tumultuous times; where mindes, addrest
"To factions, are invr'd to mutinie;
"A mischiefe, not by force, to be surprest,
"Where rigor still begets more enmitie:
"Hatred must be beguil'd with some new course,
"Where States are stiffe, and Princes doubt their force.

95

This, and much more, Affliction would haue say'd,
Out of th'experience of a troublous Raigne
(For which, his high desires had dearely pay'd
The int'rest of an euer-toyling paine)
But that this all-subduing Power here stai'd
His fault'ring tongue, and paine (r'inforc't againe)
Barr'd vp th'oppressed passages of breath,
To bring him quite vnder the state of Death.*

96

In whose possession I must leaue him now;
And now, into the *Ocean* of new toyles,
Into the stormie Maine (where tempestes growe
Of greater ruines, and of greater spoyles)
Set foorth my course (to hasten-on my vow)
Ov'r all the troublous Deepe of these turmoyles.
And, if I may but liue t'attaine the shore
Of my desired end, I wish no more.

The ende of the fourth Booke.

* *Ann. Dom. 14.12. the K. died in the 46. yeare of his age, when he had raigned 13 yeares 6 moneths; and left 4 sonnes; Hen. after him K. The D. of Clarence, Iohn D. of Bedford, and Humfrey D. of Gloster.*

The Fift *Booke*

THE ARGVMENT

Henry *the fift cuts off his enemie,*
The Earle of Cambridge, *that conspir'd his death.*
Henry *the sixt (married vnluckily)*
His, and his Countryes glorie ruineth.
Suffolke, *that made the match, preferd too hie,*
Going to exile, a Pirat murthereth.
What meanes the Duke of Yorke *obseru'd to gaine*
The worlds good-will, seeking the Crowne t'attaine.

1

CLose smothered lay the lowe depressed fire,
Whose after-issuing flames confounded all,
The whil'st victorious *Henry** did conspire
The wracke of *Fraunce,* that at his feete did fall:
Whil'st ioyes of gotten spoyles, and new desire
Of greater gaine, to greater deeds did call
His conquering troupes; that could no thoughts retaine,
Saue thoughts of glorie, all that actiue Raigne.

2

Whome here, me thinks (as if hee did appeare,
Out of the clowdy darkenes of the night)
I do behold approache with Martiall cheere,
And with a dreadful (and yet louely) sight:
Whose eye giues courage, and whose brow hath feare;
Both representing terror, and delight;
And stayes my course, and off my purpose breakes,
And in vpbrayding words thus fiercely speakes:

3

"Vngrateful times, that impiously neglect
"That worth, that neuer times againe shall shew;
"What? merites all our toyle no more respect?

* *Henry 5. began his raigne the 20 of March. An. 1412.*

"Or else standes Idlenesse asham'd to knowe
"Those wondrous Actions, that do so obiect
"Blame to the wanton, sinne vnto the slowe?
"Can *England* see the best, that she can boast,
"Lie thus vngrac't, vndeckt and almost lost?

4

"Why do you seeke for fained *Palladines*
"(Out of the smoke of idle vanitie)
"Who may giue glory to the true designes,
"Of *Bourchier, Talbot, Neuile, Willoughby?*
"Why should not you striue to fill vp your lines,
"With wonders of your owne, with veritie?
"T'inflame their ofspring with the loue of good,
"And glorious true examples of their Blood.

5

"What euerlasting matter here is found,
"Whence new immortall *Illiads* might proceed!
"That those, whose happie graces do abound
"In blessed accents, here may haue to feed
"Good thoughts, on no imaginarie ground
"Of hungry shadowes, which no profite breed;
"Whence, musicke-like, instant delight may growe;
"Yet, when men all do knowe, they nothing knowe.

6

"And why dost thou, in lamentable verse,
"Nothing but blood-shed, treasons, sinne and shame,
"The worst of times, th'extreame of ills, rehearse;
"To rayse olde staynes, and to renew dead blame?
"As if the mindes of th'euill, and peruerse,
"Were not farre sooner trained from the same,
"By good example of faire vertuous acts,
"Then by the shew of foul vngodly facts.

7

"Would God, our times had had some sacred wight,
"Whose words as happy as our swords had bin,
"To haue prepar'd for vs *Tropheis* aright,
"Of vndecaying frames t'haue rested in;
"Triumphant Arks, of perdurable might,

"O holy lines! that such aduantage win
"Vpon the Sieth of Time, in spight of yeares.
"How blessed they, who gaine what neuer weares!

8

"For, what is it to do, if what we do
"Shall perish neere as soone as it is donne?
"What is that glory wee attaine vnto
"With all our toyle, if lost as soone as wonne?
"A small requitall, for so great adoo,
"Is this poore present breath, a smoake soone gone;
"Or these dumb stones, erected for our sake:
Which, formless heapes few stormy changes make.

9

"Tell great *ELIZA* (since her dayes are grac't,
"With those bright ornaments, to vs deni'd)
"That she repaire what darknesse hath defac't,
"And get our ruyn'd deedes, reedifi'd:
"She in whose all-directing eye is plac't
"A powre, the highest powers of wit to guide;
"Shee may command the worke, and ouer-see
"The holy frame, that might eternall bee.

10

For, would Shee be content, that Time should make
A rauenous prey, vpon her glorious Raigne;
That Darkenesse, and the Night, should ouertake
So cleare a Brightnesse, shining without staine?
Ah! no: She fosters some (no doubt) that wake
For her eternitie, with pleasing paine.
And if shee, for her selfe, prepare this good;
Let her not so neglect those of her Blood.

11

This, that great Monarch, *Henrie*, seem'd to craue;
When (weighing what a holy motiue here
Vertue propos'd, and fit for him to haue,
Whom all times ought of dutie hold most deare)
I sigh't, and wisht that some would take t'ingraue,
With curious hand, so proud a worke to reare
(To grace the present, and to blesse times past)
That might, for euer, to our glorie last.

12

So should our well-taught times haue learn'd alike,
How faire shin'd Virtue, and how foul Vice stood;
When now my selfe am driuen to mislike
Those deedes of worth, I dare not vow for good:
I cannot mone who lose, nor prayse who seeke
By mightie Actions here t'aduance their Blood.
I must say, Who wrought most, least honor had:
How euer good the Cause, the deedes were bad.

13

And onely tell the worst of euerie Raigne;
And not the intermedled good report.
I leaue, what glorie Virtue did attaine
At th'euer-memorable *Agincort:*
I leaue to tell, what wit, what power did gaine
Th'assieged *Roan, Caen, Dreux;* or in what sort:
How Maiestie, with terror, did aduance
Her conquering foote, on all subdued *Fraunce.*

14

All this I passe, and that magnanimous King,
Mirror of vertue, miracle of worth;
Whose mighty Actions, with wise managing,
Forc't prouder boasting Climes to serue the North.
The best of all the best, the earth can bring,
Scarce equals him, in what his Raigne brought foorth;
Being of a minde, as forward to aspire,
As fit to gouerne what he did desire.

15

His comely body was a goodly seate,
Where Virtue dwelt most faire; as lodg'd most pure:
A body strong; where vse of strength did get
A stronger state to do, and to endure:
His life he makes th'example, to beget
Like spirit in those, he did to good inure;
And gaue, to *Worth,* such life, and liuelihood,
As if hee Greatnes sought, but to do good.

16

Hee as the Chiefe, and all-directing head,
Did with his subiects, as his members, liue;

And them to goodnesse forced not, but led;
Winning, not much to haue, but much to giue
(Deeming, the powre of his, his powr did spread)
As borne to blesse the world, and not to grieue;
Adorn'd with others spoyles, not subiects store:
No King, exacting lesse; none, winning more.

17

Hee, after that corrupted faith had bred
An ill inur'd obedience for Command;
And languishing luxuriousnes had spred
Weyward vnaptnesse ouer all the Land;
Those long vnordred troupes so marshalled,
Vnder such formall discipline to stand,
That euen his soule seem'd onely to direct
So great a body, such exployts t'effect.

18

He brings abrode distracted Discontent,
Disperst ill humors into actions hie;
And, to vnite them all in one consent,
Plac't the faire marke of glorie in their eye;
That, Malice had no leasure to dissent,
Nor enuie time to practise treacherie:
The present actions do diuert the thought
Of madnesse past, while mindes were so well wrought.

19

Here now were Pride, Oppression, Vsurie
(The canker-eating mischiefes of the State)
Call'd foorth to prey vpon the enemie;
Whil'st the home-burth'ned, better lightned sate:
Exactors did not, with a greedy eye,
Examine states, or priuate riches rate:
The silent Courts* warr'd not, with busie words;
Nor wrested law gaue the contentious, swords.

20

Now, nothing entertaines th'attentiue eare,
But stratagems, assaults, surprises, fightes;
How to giue lawes to them that conquered were,

* The Courtes of Iustice.

How to articulate with yeelding wightes:
The weake with mercie, and the proud with feare,
How to retaine; to giue deserts their rights,
Were now the Artes: and nothing else was thought,
But how to win, and maintaine what was got.

21

Nor here were any priuately possest
Or held alone imprisoned Maiestie,
Proudly debarring entraunce from the rest;
As if the prey were theirs, by victorie.
Here, no detractor woundes who merits best;
Nor shameless brow cheeres-on impietie.
Vertue, who all her toyle with zeale had spent,
Not here, all vnrewarded, sighing went.

22

But, here, the equally-respecting eye
Of Powre, looking alike on like deserts,
Blessing the good, made others good thereby;
More mightie, by the multitude of hearts.
The fielde of glorie, vnto all doth lie
Open alike; honour, to all imparts.
So that the onely fashion in request,
Was, to be good, or good-like, as the rest.

23

So much, ô thou Example, dost effect
(Being farre a better Maister, then Command)
That, how to do, by doing dost direct,
And teachest others action, by thy hand.*
"Who followes not the course, that kings elect?
"When Princes worke, who then wil idle stand?
"And, when that dooing good is onely thought
"Worthy reward; who will be bad for nought?

24

And had not th'Earle of *Cambridge*,† with vaine speed,

---

* —*Docet tolerare labores; Non iubet.*

† *Richard E. of Cambridge the second sonne to Edmond Langly, Duke of Yorke, maried Anne the daughter of Roger Mortimer Earle of March, descended from Lionnell D. of Clarence, the third sonne to K. Ed. 3. by whose right Richard D. of Yorke sonne to this E. of Cambridge, afterwards claymed the Crowne.*

Vntimely practiz'd for an others right,
With hope of aduance those of his proper seed
(On whome the Rule seem'd destined to light)
The Land had seene none of her owne to bleed,
During this Raigne, nor no aggreeued sight;
None the least blacknesse interclouded had
So faire a day, nor any eye lookt sad.

25

But now, when *Fraunce* perceiued (from afarre)
The gathering tempest, growing-on from hence,
Ready to fall, threatning their State to marre,
They labour all meanes to prouide defence:
And, practising how to preuent this warre,
And shut-out such calamities from thence,
Do foster, here, some discord lately growne;
To hold Ambition busied, with her owne.

26

Finding those humors which they saw were fit
Soone to be wrought, and easie to be fed,
Swolne full with enuie, that the Crowne should sit
There where it did (as if established)
And whom it toucht in Blood, to grieue at it;
They with such hopes and helps sollicited,
That this great Earle was drawne t'attempt the thing,
And practiseth how to depose the King.

27

For, being of mightie meanes to do the deed;
And yet of mightier hopes, then meanes to do:
And yet of spirit, that did his hopes exceed;
And then of Blood as great, to adde thereto:
All these, with what the gold of *France* could breed
(Being powers enow a clyming minde to woo)
He so imploy'd, that many he had wonne,
Euen of the chiefe the King reli'd vpon.*

28

The well-knowne right of th'Earle of *March* allur'd
A leaning loue: whose Cause he did pretend.

** The E. of Cābridge conspiring the death of the King, was with Hen Scroope Lord
Treasurer, & Sir Thomas Gray executed at South-Hampton. Ann. 3. Reg.*

Whereby, he knew that so himselfe procur'd
The Crowne for his owne children in the ende.
For, the Earle beeing (as hee was assur'd)
Vnapt for issue, it must needes descend
On those of his, being next of *Clarence* race;
As who, by course of right, should hold the place.

29

It was the time, when-as the forward Prince
Had all prepar'd for his great enterprize;*
And ready stand his troupes to part from hence,
And all in stately forme and order lyes,
When open Fame giues out intelligence
Of these bad complots of his enemies:
Or else, this time (of purpose) chosen is:
Though knowne before; yet let run-on, till this.

30

That this might yeeld the more to aggrauate
Vpon so foul a deed vntimely sought,
Now at this point, t'attempt to ruinate
So glorious a designe so forward brought,
Whil'st careful Virtue seekes t'aduance the State,
And for her euerlasting honor sought:
That though the Cause seem'd right, and title strong;
The time of dooing it, yet makes it wrong.

31

But, straight, an vnlamented death he had:
And straight were ioyfully the Anchors weighd:
And all flocke fast aboord, with visage glad;
As if the sacrifice had now beene payd,
For their good speed; that made their stay so sad,
Loathing the least occasion that delayd.
And, now, new thoughts, great hopes, calme seas, fair windes.
With present action intertaine their mindes.

32

No other crosse, ô *Henry,* saw thy dayes
But this, that toucht thy now possessed hold;

* *At Southhampton.*

Nor after, long, till this mans sonne assayes
To get, of thine, the right that he controll'd: *
For which, contending long, his life he payes.
So that, it fatal seem'd the father should
Thy winning seeke to stay and then his sonne
Should be the cause to lose, when thou hadst won.

33

Yet now in this so happy a meane-while,
And interlightning times, thy Virtues wrought,
That Discord had no leasure to defile
So faire attempts with a tumultuous thought:
And euen thy selfe, thy selfe didst so beguile
With such attention vpon what was sought,
That time affoords not now with feare or hate
Others to seeke, thee to secure thy State.

34

Or else, how easie had it beene, for thee,
All the pretendant race t'haue layd full lowe?
If thou proceeded hadst with crueltie,
Not suffering any fatall branch to growe:
But, vnsuspicious Magnanimitie
Shames such effectes of feare, and force, to showe;
Busied in free, and open Actions still
Being great: for, being good, hates to be ill.

35

And yet, such wrongs are held meete to be done,
And often for the State thought requisite:
As, when the publike good depends thereon,
When great iniustice is esteem'd great right:
But yet, what good with doing ill is won?
Who hath of blood made such a benefite,
As hath not fear'd, more after then before,
And made his peace the lesse, his plague the more?

36

Farre otherwise dealt this vndaunted King,
That cherished the ofspring of his foes;

---

* *Richard, Duke of Yorke, sonne to the E. of Cambridge, by Anne daughter to the Earle of March, made his claime, in 30. yeare of Hen. 6.*

And his Competitors to grace did bring:
And them, his friendes for Armes, and honors, chose;
As if plaine courses were the safest thing,
Where vpright goodnesse, sure, and stedfast goes,
Free from that subtile maskt impietie,
Which this depraued world calles policie.

37

Yet, how hath Fate dispos'd of all this good?
What haue these Virtues after times auail'd?
In what stead hath hy-raised Valour stood,
When this continuing cause of Greatnes fail'd?
Then, when proud-growne, the irritated blood,
Enduring not it selfe, it selfe assail'd;
As though that *Prowesse* had but learnd to spill
Much blood abrode, to cut her throat with skill.

38

How doth th'Eternall, in the course of things,
Immix the causes both of Good and Ill?
That thus the one, effects of th'other brings:
As what seemes made to blisse, is borne to spill?
What? from the best of Virtues glorie, springs
That, which the world with miserie doth fill?
Is th'end of happinesse, but wretchednesse?
Hath Sinne his plague, and Virtue no successe?

39

Either that is not good, the world holdes good:
Or else is so confus'd with ill; that we
(Abused with th'appearing likelihood)
Run to offend, whil'st we thinke good to bee:
Or else the heauens made man (in furious blood)
To torture man; Allotting no course free
From mischiefe long: Sending faire dayes that breed
But stormes; to make, more foul, times that succeed.

40

Who would haue thought, that so great victories,
Such conquests, riches, Land, and Kingdome gain'd,
Could not but haue establisht in such wise
This powrefull State, in state to haue remain'd?

Who would haue thought, that Mischiefe could deuise
A way, so soone to lose what was attain'd?
As if powre were but shew'd to grieue, not grace;
And to reduce vs into farre worse case.

41

With what contagion, *Fraunce,* didst thou infect
This Land, by thee made proud, to disagree?
T'inrage them so, their owne swordes to direct
Vpon them-selues, that were made sharp in thee?
Why didst thou teach them, here at home t'erect
Trophees of their blood, which of thine should bee?
Or was the date of thine affliction out,
And so (by course) was ours to come about?

42

But, that vntimely death of this great King,
Whose nine yeeres Raigne* so mightie wonders wrought,
To thee thy hopes, to vs despaire did bring;
Not long to keepe and gouerne what was got:
For, those that had th'affayres in managing,
Although their Countries good they greatly sought;
Yet, so ill accidentes vnfitly fell,
That their dessignes could hardly prosper wel.

43

An infant King doth in the State succeed,
Scarce one yeere old, left vnto others guide:†
Whose careful trust, though such as shew'd indeed,
They weigh'd their charge more then the world beside,
And did with dutie, zeale, and loue proceed;
Yet (for all what their trauaile could prouide)
Could not woo Fortune, to remaine with vs,
When this her Minion was departed thus:

44

But, by degrees first this, then that, regain'd,
The turning tide beares backe, with flowing chaunce
Vnto the Dolphin, all we had attain'd,

---

* Hen. 5. raigned 9. yeeres and ten moneths, and died in the 35 yeare of his age.
*† Hen. 6. scarce one yeere old when hee began his raigne, was committed to the charge
of the two good Dukes, Bidford and Gloster his Vncles.*

And filles the late lowe-running hopes of *Fraunce;*
When *Bedford* (who our onely hold maintain'd)
Death takes from vs, their fortune to aduance:
And then home-strife (that on it selfe did fall)
Neglecting forraine care, did soone lose all.

45

Neere three score yeeres are past since *Bullingbrooke*
Did first attaine (God knowes how iust) the Crowne:
And now his race, for right possessors tooke,
Were held of all, to hold nought but their owne:
When *Richard, Duke* of *Yorke,* begins to looke
Into their right, and makes his title knowne;
Wakening-vp sleeping Right (that lay as dead)
To witnesse, how his race was iniured.

46

His fathers end, in him, no feare could moue
T'attempt the like, against the like of might;
Where long possession now of feare, and loue,
Seem'd to prescribe euen an innated Right.
So that, To proue his state, was to disproue
Time, law, consent, oath, and allegeance quight:
And no way, but the way of blood there was,
Through which, with all confusion hee must passe.

47

And how much better for him, had it beene,
T'indure a wrong with peace, then with such toyle
"T'obtaine a bloody Right? since Right is sinne,
"That is ill sought, and purchased with spoyle.
But, this so wretched state are Kingdomes in,
Where one mans Cause, shall all the rest imbroyle:
And oft, t'aduance a Tyran to a Crowne,
Men run t'vndoo the State, that is their owne.

48

And yet that opportunitie, which led
Him to attempt, seemes likewise him t'excuse:
A feeble spirited King that gouerned,
(Who ill could guide the Scepter he did vse)
His enemies (that his worth maliced;

Who, both the Land, and him, did much abuse)
The peoples loue, and his apparant Right,
May seeme sufficient motiues to incite.

49

Besides; the now ripe wrath (deferd till now)
Of that sure and vnfayling *Iusticer,*
That neuer suffers wrong so long to growe,
And to incorporate with right so farre,
As it might come to seeme the same in showe
(T'incourage those that euill minded are
By such successe) but that at last he will
Confound the branch, whose root was planted ill.

50

Else, might the impious say (with grudging spight)
Doth God permit the Great to riot free,
And blesse the mightie though they do vnright,
As if he did vnto their wrongs agree?
And onely plague the weake and wretched wight,
For smallest faults, euen in the high'st degree?
When he, but vsing them for others scourge,
Likewise of them at lēgth the world doth purge.

51

But could not yet, for blood-shed, satisfie
The now well-ruling of th'ill-gotten Crowne?
Must euen the good receiue the penaltie
Of former sinnes, that neuer were their owne?
And must a iust Kings blood, with miserie
Pay for a bad, vniustly ouerthrowne?
Well; then we see, Right in his course must goe:
And men, t'escape from blood, must keepe it so.

52

And, sure, this King, that now the Crowne possest
(*Henrie* the sixt) was one, whose life was free
From that command of vice, whereto the rest
Of most these mightie Soueraignes subiects bee;
And numbred might haue beene, among the best
Of other men, if not of that degree:
A right good man, but yet an euill King;
Vnfit for what hee had in managing.

53

Of humble spirite, of nature continent:
No thought t'increase he had; scarce keep his owne:
For pard'ning apter, then for punishment,
He chokes his powre, to haue his bountie knowne.
Farre from reuenge, soone wonne, soone made content;
As fitter for a Cloyster then a Crowne:
Whose holy minde so much addicted is
On th'world to-come, that he neglecteth this.

54

With such a weake-good, feeble-godly King,
Hath *Richard, Duke* of *Yorke,* his Cause to trie:
Who, by th'experience of long managing
The warres of *Fraunce,* with supreame dignitie;
And by his owne great worth, with furthering
The common good against the enemie,
Had wrought, that zeale and loue attend his might,
And made his spirit equall vnto his Right.

55

For, now the *Duke* of *Bedford* beeing dead,
He is ordain'd the Regent to succeed
In *Fraunce* for fiue yeeres:* where, he trauayled
With ready hand, and with as carefull heed,
To seeke to turne backe Fortune (that now fled)
And hold vp falling power, in time of need:
And got and lost, and reattaines (againe)
That which againe was lost, for all his paine.

56

His time expir'd, he should for fiue yeeres more
Haue had his charge prolongd: but *Sommerset*
(That still had enui'd his command before)†
That place, and honor, for himselfe did get:
Which ads that matter to th'already store
Of kindled hate, which such a fire doth set
Vnto the touch of a confounding flame,
As both their bloods could neuer quench the same.

---

* *The D. of Yorke made Regent in Fraunce, after the death of the D. of Bedf.*
† *Edmond, Duke of Sommerset, a great enemie of the Duke of Yorke.*

57

And now the weaknesse of that feeble Head
(That doth neglect all care, but his soules care)
So easie meanes of practice ministred,
Vnto th'ambitious members, to prepare
Their owne desires, to what their humors led;
That all good actions coldly followed are,
And sev'rall-tending hopes do wholly bend
To other now, then to the publique end.

58

And, to draw-on more speedy miserie,
The King vnto a fatall match is led
With *Rayners* daughter, King of *Sicilie;**
Whom, with vnlucky starres, he married:
For, by the meanes of this affinitie,
Was lost all that his father conquered;
Euen as if *France* had some *Erynnis* sent
T'auenge their wrongs, done by the insolent.

59

This marriage was the Earle of *Suffolkes* deed,†
With great rewardes won to effect the same:
Which made him that hee tooke so little heed
Vnto his Countries good, or his owne shame;
It beeing a match could stand vs in no steed
For strength, for wealth, for reputation, fame:
But cunningly contriv'd for others gaine;
And cost vs more, then *Aniou, Mauns,* and *Maine.*

60

And yet (as if he had accomplished
Some mightie benefit vnto the Land)
He got his trauailes to be registred
In Parlement, for euermore to stand
A witnes to approue all what he did:
To th'end, that, if hereafter it were scand,

---

* *This Rayner was Duke of Aniou, & onely enioyed the title of the K. of Sicilia.*

† *William de la Pole E. of Suffolke, after created D. of Suff. the chiefest instrumēt in this mariage: which was solemnized, An. Reg. 23. betweene the King & the Lady Margaret, daughter to Rayner D. of Aniou; to whom was deliuered vp the Duchy of Aniou, & the County of Maine, vpon the conclusion of this match.*

Authoritie might yet be on his side;
As doing nought but what was ratifi'd:

61

Imagining, th'allowance of that Place
Would make that good, the which he knew was naught;
And so would his negotiation grace,
As none might think it was his priuate fault.
Wherein, though wit dealt wary in this case;
Yet, in the end, it selfe it ouer-raught.
Striuing to hide, he opened it the more;
His after-care, shew'd craft had gone before.

62

Deare didst thou buy, ô King, so faire a Wife,
So rare a spirit, so high a minde, the-while:
Whose portion was destruction; dowry, strife:
Whose bed was sorrow; whose embracing, spoyle:
Whose maintenance cost thee and thine, their life;
And whose best comfort, neuer was but toyle.
What *Paris* brought this booty of desire,
To set our mightie *Ilium* here on fire?

63

I grieue, I should be forc't to say thus much,
To blame her, whom I yet must wonder at;
Whose so sweete beautie, wit, and worth, were such,
As (Though she Fortune lost) she glory gat:
Yet doth my Countries zeale so neerely touch,
That here my Muse it doth exasperate;
Although vnwilling, that my pen should giue
Staine to that sex, by whom her fame doth liue.

64

For, sure, those virtues well deserv'd a Crowne.
And, had it not beene ours, no doubt she might
Haue beene among the Worthies of renowne,
And now sat faire with fame, with glorie bright:
But, comming in the way where sinne was growne
So foule and thicke, it was her chaunce to light
Amidst the grosse infection of those times;
And so came stain'd with black disgrace-full crimes.

65

For, some the world must haue, on whom to lay
The heauie burthen of reproche and blame;
Against whose deedes, th'afflicted may inuay,
As th'onely Authors, whence destruction came:
When yet, perhaps, 'twas not in them to stay
The current of that streame, nor help the same;
But, liuing in the eye of Action so,
Not hindring it, are thought to draw-on wo.

66

So much vnhappie do the Mightie stand,
Who stand on other then their owne defence,
When-as destruction is so neere at hand,
That if by weakenesse, folly, negligence,
They do not coming miserie withstand,
They shall be deemed th'authors of th'offence,
And to call in, that which they kept not out;
And curst, as they who brought those plagues about.

67

And so remaine for euer rigistred
In that eternall booke of Infamie;
When yet how many other causes led
As well to that, as their iniquitie?
The worst complots oft lie close smothered:
And well-meant deedes fall out vnluckily;
Whil'st the aggrieu'd stand not to waigh th'intent;
But euer iudge according to th'euent.

68

I say not this t'excuse thy Sinne, ô *Queene,*
Nor cleare their faults who mightie Actors are:
I cannot but affirme, thy pride hath been
A speciall meanes this Common-wealth to marre:
And that thy weyward will was plainely seene,
In vaine ambition, to presume too farre;
And that, by thee, the onely way was wrought
The Duke of *Gloster* to his death was brought:*

* *The pride and hautinesse of this Queene Margaret gaue the first originall to the mischiefs that followed by the death of Humfrey Duke of Gloster Protector.*

69

A man, though seeming in thy thought to sit
Betweene the light of thy desires and thee;
Yet did his taking thence plainely permit
Others to looke to that they could not see
During his life, nor would aduenture it:
When his Remoue quite made that passage free;
That, by his fall, thinking to stand alone,
Thou scarce could'st stand at all, when he was gone.

70

For, this *Duke* (as *Protector*) many yeeres,
Had rul'd the Land, during the Kings young age;
And now the selfe same charge and title beares,
As if hee still were in his pupillage:
Which, such disgrace vnto the Queene appeares,
That (all incenst, with an ambitious rage)
Shee doth conspire to haue him made-away;
As one, that stayd the Current of her sway:

71

Thrust thereinto, not onely with her pride;
But, by her fathers counsell and consent:
Who griev'd likewise, that any one beside,
Should haue the honor of the gouernment:
And, therefore, he such deepe aduice appli'd,
As forraine craft and cunning could inuent,
To circumuent an vnsuspecting wight,
Before he should discerne of their despight.

72

And many ready hands shee straight doth finde,
To ayde her deed, of such as could not brooke
The length of one mans office, in that kind;
Who, all th'especiall Charges vnder-tooke,
Rul'd all, himselfe: and neuer had the minde
T'impart a part with others; who would looke
To haue likewise some honor in their hands,
And griev'd at such ingrossing of Commands.

73

For, had he not had such a greedy loue
To intertaine his Offices too long,

Enuie had beene vnable to reproue
His acted life, vnless shee did him wrong:*
But, hauing liv'd, so many yeeres, aboue,
He grieues now to descend, to be lesse strong,
And kils that fame that virtue did beget;
Chose to be held lesse good, then seene lesse great.

74

    "For, could the mightie but giue bounds to pride,
"And weigh-backe Fortune, ere shee pull Them downe;
"Contented with inough, with honors satisfi'd,
"Not striuing how to make so much their owne,
"As to leaue nothing for the rest beside,
"Who seeme by their high-spreading ouer growne
"(Whil'st they themselues remaine in all mens sight,
"The odious marke of hatred and despight)

75

    "Then neuer should so many tragedies
"Burthen our knowledge, with their bloody end:
"Nor their disgrac't confounded families,
"From so high pride, to so lowe shame descend;
"But, planted on that ground where safetie lyes,
"Their braunches should to eternitie extend:
"But euer, they, who ouer-looke so much,
"Will ouer-see themselues; their state is such.

76

    Seuere he was,† and strictly did obserue
Due forme of Iustice towards euery wight;
Vnmoueable, and neuer won to swerue
For any cause, in what he thought was right:
Wherein, although he did so well deserue;
In the licentious, yet, it bred despight:
"So that euen Virtue seemes an Actor too,
"To ruine those, Fortune prepares t'vndoo.

77

    Now, such, being forward, who (the Queene well knewe)
Hated his might, and glad to innouate;
Vnto so great, and strong a partie grew,

---

* *Nil tam vtile, quàm breuem potestatem esse quæ magna sit.*
† *The Virtues of Humfrey D. Glocester.*

As it was easie to subuert his State:
And onely hope of alteration drew
Many to yeeld, that had no cause to hate.
"For, euen with goodnesse men growe discontent,
"Where States are ripe to fall, and virtue spent.

78

And, taking all the Rule into her hand
(Vnder the shadow of that feeble King)
The Duke sh'excludes from Office and Command,
And in the reach of enmitie doth bring,
From that respected height where he did stand
(When malice scarce durst mutter any thing):
And now the worst of him comes all reueal'd,
Which former feare, or rigor kept conceal'd.

79

Now is he taxed, that he rather sought
His priuate profit, then the publique good;
And many things presumptuously had wrought;
Other, then with our lawes, and customes stood:
As one, that would into the Land haue brought
The Ciuile forme, in cases touching blood;
And such poore Crimes: that shew'd, their spight was soūd;
But yet bewrayde, their matter wanted ground.

80

Yet serv'd they well the turne, and did effect
That which is easie wrought in such a case:
Where, what suborned *Iustice* shal obiect,
Is to the purpose, and must passe with grace;
And what the wretched bring, of no effect:
Whose haynous faultes his matter must deface.
"For, where Powre hath decreed to finde th'offence,
"The Cause is better still, then the defence.

81

A Parlement, at *Berry* summoned,
Dispatcht the deed, more speedily then well.*

* *The D. of Glocester comming to this Parlement from his Castle of the Viez in Wiltshire, was arrested by Iohn L. Beaumont high Constable, the Dukes of Buckingham and Somerset, with others; who appointed certaine of the Kings houshold to attend vpon him: but he died before he was brought to his answere, some say of sorrow, others of a Palsie, or an Impostume, An. Reg. 25. The D. of Suffolke was a principall instrument in this businesse.*

For, thither came the *Duke* without all dread,
Or ought imagining of what befell:
Where, now the matter is so followed,
That he conuented is, ere he could tell
He was in danger, or had done offence;
And presently to prison sent, from thence.

82

Which quicke, and sodaine action gaue no time
For men to weigh the iustice of the deed;
Whil'st looking onely on the vrged crime,
Vnto the farther drift they take no heed.
For, these occasions taken in the prime
Of courses new, that old dislikes succeed,
Leaue not behind that feeling touch of wrong.
Satietie makes passions still lesse strong.

83

And yet they seem'd some mutinie to doubt,
For thus proceeding with a man of might;
Consid'ring hee was popular and stout,
And resolute would stand vpon his Right:
And therefore did they cast this way about,
To haue him closely murdred out of sight;
That so, his trouble, and his death hereby,
Might come togither, and togither die:

84

Reckning it better, since his end is ment,
And must be wrought, at once to rid it cleare,
And put it to the fortune of th'euent;
Then by long doing, to be long in feare:
When, in such courses of high punishment,
The deed, and the attempt, like daunger beare:
And oft, things done (perhaps) do lesse annoy,
Then may the doing, handled with delay.

85

And, so, they had it straight accomplished.
For, next day after his commitment, he
Is dead brought forth; being found so in his bed:
Which was by sodaine sickenesse sayd to bee,

That had vpon his sorrowes newly bred;
As by apparant tokens men might see.
And thus ô Sickenesse, thou art oft beli'd;
When death hath many wayes to come, beside.

86

Are these the deedes, high forraine wittes inuent?
Is this that Wisedome whereof they so boast?
Well; then I would it neuer had beene spent
Heere, amongst vs, nor brought from out their coast:
Let their vile cunning, in their limits pent,
Remaine amongst themselues, that like it most:
And let the *North* (they count of colder blood)
Be held more grosse, so it remaine more good.

87

Let them haue fairer citties, goodlier soyles,
And sweeter fieldes, for beautie to the eye,
So long as they haue these vngodly wyles,
Such detestable vile impietie:
And let vs want their Vines, their Fruites the-whyles,
So that wee want not fayth and honestie:
We care not for those pleasures; so we may
Haue better hearts, and stronger hands then they.

88

Neptune, keepe-out, from thy imbraced Ile,
This foul contagion of iniquitie:
Drowne all corruptions, comming to defile
Our faire proceedings ordred formally:
Keepe vs meere English: let not craft beguile
Honor and Iustice, with strange subtiltie:
Let vs not thinke, how that our good can frame,
Which ruin'd hath the Authors of the same.

89

But, by this impious meanes, that worthy man
Is brought vnto this lamentable end.
And, now, that Current with maine furie ran
(The stop remov'd, that did the course defend)
Vnto the full of mischiefe, that began
T'a vniuersall ruine to extend;

That *Isthmus* fayling which the Land did keep,
From the intire possession of the Deepe.

90

And now the King, alone, all open lay;
No vnder-prop of Blood, to stay him by.
None, but himselfe stands weakely in the way
Twixt *Yorke,* and the affected sov'raignty:
Gone is that barre, that would haue beene the stay
T'haue kept him backe, from mounting vp so hie.
"But see (ah!) see: What state stand these men in,
"That cannot liue without, nor with their kin?

91

The *Queene* hath yet, by this, her full desire;
And now she with her Minion, *Suffolke,* raigns:
Now she hath all authoritie intire;
And all affayres vnto her selfe retains:
And onely *Suffolke* is aduanced hier,
He is the man rewarded, for his pains;*
He, that did her in stead most chiefly stand;
And more aduanc't her, then hee did the Land.

92

Which when they saw, who better did expect,
Then they began their error to descry;
And well perceiue, that onely the defect
Was in their iudgements, passion-drawne awry;
Found, formall rigor fitter to direct,
Then pride and insolent inconstancie.
"Better seueritie, that's right and iust,
"Then impotent affections, led with lust.

93

And thereupon, in sorrow thus complaine;
"What wondrous inconuenience do they feele,
"Where as such imbecillitie doth raigne,
"As so neglects the care of Common-weale?
"Where, euer one or other doth obtaine
"So high a grace thus absolute to deale;

* *De la Pole is created D. of Suffolke, Ann. Reg. 26. and is banished, and murthered, the next yeare after.*

"The-whilst th'aggreeued subiect suffers, stil,
"The pride of some predominating will?

94

"And euer, one remov'd, a worse succeedes:
"So that the best, that we can hope, is Warre,
"Tumults, and stirres, that this disliking breedes:
"The sword must mend, what Insolence doth marre.
"For, what rebellions, and what bloody deedes,
"Haue euer followed, where such courses are?
"What oft-remoues? what death of Counsailers?
"What murder? what exile of Officers?

95

"Witnesse the *Spencers, Gauestone,* and *Vere,*
"The mighty Minions of our feeblest Kings;
"Who euer Subiects to their subiects were,
"And onely the procurers of these things:
"When worthy Monarchs, that hold honour deare,
"Maister themselues, and theirs; which euer brings
"That vniuersall reuerence, and respect.
"For, who waighes him, that doth himselfe neglect?

96

"And yet our case is like to be farre worse;
"Hauing a King, though not so bent to ill,
"Yet so neglecting good, that giuing force
"By giuing leaue, doth all good order kill;
"Suffring a violent Woman take her course,
"To manage all, according to her will:
"Which, how she doth begin, her deedes expresse;
"And, what will be the end, our selues may ghesse.

97

Which after followed, euen as they did dread,
When now the shamefull losse of *Fraunce,* much grieues:*
Which vnto *Suffolke* is attributed;
As who in all mens sight most hatefull liues:
And is accus'd, that he (with lucre led)
Betraies the State, and secret knowledge giues

---

* *The Duchy of Normandy was lost, in the yeere 1449, after it had been held 30 yeeres
conquered by Hen. 5. Ann. Reg. 27.*

Of our designes; and, all that we did hold,
By his corruption, is or lost, or sold.*

98

And, as hee deales abroad, so likewise here,
He robs at home, the Treasurie no lesse;
Here, where he all authorities doth beare,
And makes a *Monopoly* of Offices:
He is inricht, h'is rais'd, and placed neare;
And onely he, giues consaile to oppresse:
Thus men obiect, whil'st many, vp in Armes,
Offer to be reuenged of these harmes.†

99

The *Queene,* perceiuing in what case she stoode
To lose her Minion, or ingage her State;
(After with long contention in her blood,
Loue and Ambition, did the Cause debate)
Shee yields to Pride: and rather thought it good,
To sacrifice her Loue vnto their hate;
Then to aduenture else the losse of all:
Which (by maintaining him) was like to fall.

100

Yet, seeking at the first to temporize,
She tries if that some short Imprisonment
Would calme their heat: when that would not suffize,
Then to exile him she must needs consent;
Hoping, that time would salue it in such wise,
As yet at length they might become content,
And shee againe, might haue him home at last,
When this first furie of their rage was past.

101

But, as he to his iudged exile went,
Hard on the shore he comes incountered
By some, that so farre off his Honour sent,

---

* *Articles obiected against de la Poole, Duke of Suffolke.*

† *At the Parliamēt at Leicester, the lower House besought the K. that such persons as assented to the rendring of Aniou and Maine, might bee duelie punished: of which fact, they accused as principals, the D. of Suffolke, the L. Say, Treasurer of Eng. with others. Wherevpon, the K. to appease the Commons, sequestred them from their offices & rooms; and after, banished the D. for 5 yeeres.*

As put his backe-returne quite out of dread:*
For, there he had his rightfull punishment,
Though wrongly done; and there he lost his head:
Part of his blood hath *Neptune,* part the Sand;
As who had mischiefe wrought by sea and land.

102

Whose death, when swift-wingd Fame at full conuaid
To this disturbed *Queene,* misdoubting nought;
Despight, and Sorrow such affliction laid
Vpon her soule, as wondrous passions wrought.
"And art thou Suffolke, thus, said she, betraid?
"And haue my fauours thy destruction brought?
"Is this their gaine, whom Highnesse fauoureth,
"Who chiefe preferd, stand as preferd to death?

103

"O fatall grace! without which, men complaine,
"And with it perish; what preuailes that we
"Must weare the Crowne, and other men must raigne,
"And cannot stand to be, that which we be?
"Must our owne Subiects limit and constraine
"Our fauours, wher-as they themselues decree?
"Must we, our loue, at their appointment, place?
"Do we commaund, and they direct our grace?

104

"Must they our powre, thus from our will, diuide?
"And haue wee might, but must not vse our might?
"Poore Maiestie, which other men must guide;
"Whose discontent can neuer looke aright:
"For, euer-more wee see those who abide
"Gracious in ours, are odious in their sight,
"Who would all-maistring Maiestie defeat
"Of her best graces; that is, to make men Great.

105

"But, well; We see, although the King be Head,
"The State will be the Heart. This Soueraigntie
"Is but in place, not powre; and gouerned

* *As the D. was sayling into France, hee was incoūtered with a ship of Warre, apper-taining to the D. of Excester: who tooke him, & brought him back to Douer: where his head was striken off, and his body left on the sands. Ann. reg. 27.*

"By th'equall Scepter of *Necessitie.*
"And we haue seene more Princes ruined,
"By their imoderat fauouring priuatly,
"Then by seuerity in generall.
"For, best h'is lik't, that is alike to all.

106

Thus stormes this Lady, all disquieted;
When-as farre greater tumults now burst out:
Which close and cunningly were practiced,
By such, as sought great hopes to bring about.
For, vp in Armes in *Kent* were gathered
A mighty insolent rebellious rout,
Vnder a dangerous Head; who, to deterr
The State the more, himselfe nam'd *Mortimer.**

107

The *Duke* of *Yorke,* that did not idle stand
(But seekes to worke on all aduantages)
Had likewise in this course a secret hand,
And hartned on their chiefest complices;
To try how here the people of the Land
Would (if occasion serv'd) b'in readiness
To aide that Line, if one should come in deed
To moue his Right, and in due course proceed;

108

Knowing himselfe to be the onely one,
That must attempt the thing, if any should:
And therefore, lets the Rebell now run-on
With that false Name, t'effect the best he could;
To make a way for him to worke vpon,
Who but on certaine ground aduenture would.
For, if the Traitor sped, the gaine were his;
If not, yet he stands safe, and blamelesse is.

109

T'attempt with others dangers, not his owne,
He counts it wisedome, if it could be wrought:

* *The Commons of Kent assembled thēselues in great nūber: and had to their Captaine Iack Cade, who named himselfe Mortimer, Cosen to the Duke of Yorke: with purpose to redresse the abuses of the gouernement.*

And t'haue the humour of the people knowne,
Was now that, which was chiefely to be sought.
For, with the best, he knew himselfe was growne
In such account, as made him take no thought;
Hauing observ'd, in those he meant to proue,
Their wit, their wealth, their cariage, and their loue.

110

With whome, and with his owne alliances,
He first begins to open (in some wise)
The Right he had; yet, with such doubtfulnes,
As rather sorrow, then his drift descries:
Complayning of his Countries wretchednes,
In what a miserable case it lies;
And how much it imports them to prouide
For their defence, against this womans pride.

111

Then, with the discontented he doth deale,
In sounding theirs, not vttering his intent;
As be'ing aduis'd, not so much to reueale,
Whereby they might be made againe content:
But, when they grieued for the Common-weale,
He doth perswade them to be patient,
And to indure; there was no other course:
Yet, so perswades, as makes their malice worse.

112

And then, with such as with the time did run,
In most vpright opinion he doth stand;
As one, that neuer crost what they begun,
But seem'd to like that which they tooke in hand:
Seeking all causes of offence to shun,
Prayses the Rule, and blames th'vnruly Land;
Works so with gifts, and kindely offices,
That, euen of them, he serues his turne no lesse.

113

Then, as for those, who were his followers
(Being all choyce men for virtues, or desearts)
He so with grace, and benefits prefers,
That he becomes the Monarch of their hearts.

He gets the learned, for his Counsaylers;
And cherishes all men of rarest parts:
"To whom, good done, doth an impressiō strike
"Of ioy and loue, in all that are alike.

114

And now, by meanes of th'intermitted warre,
Many most valiant men, impov'rished,
Onely by him fed and relieued are;
Onely respected, grac't, and honoured.
Which let him in, vnto their hearts so farre,
As they by him were wholly to be led.
"He onely treads the sure and perfect path
"To Greatnesse, who loue and opinion hath.

115

And, to haue one some certaine Prouince his,
As the maine body that must worke the feate,
Yorkeshire he chose, the place wherein he is
By title, liuings, and possessions great.
No Country hee preferres, so much as this:
Here, hath his Bountie, her abiding seat:
Here, is his Iustice, and relieuing hand,
Ready to all, that in distresse do stand.

116

What with his tenants, seruants, followers, friends,
And their alliances, and amities,
All that *Shire* vniuersally attends
His hand, held vp to any enterprize.
And thus farre, Virtue with her power extends:
The rest, touching th'euent, in Fortune lies.
With which accomplements, so mightie growne,
Forward he tends, with hope t'attaine a Crowne.

The ende of the fift Booke.

The Sixt *Booke*

THE ARGVMENT

The bad success of Cades *rebellion:*
Yorkes *open practise and conspiracie:*
His comming in, and his submission:
Th'effect of Printing and Artillerie.
Burdeux *reuolts; craues our protection:*
Talbot, *defending ours, dyes gloriously.*
The French warres end: and Yorke *begins againe;*
And, at S. Albones, Sommerset *is slaine.*

1

THE furious traine of that tumultuous rout,
Whom close sub-ayding power, and good successe,
Had made vnwisely proud, and fondly stout,
Thrust headlong on, oppression to oppresse;
And now, to fulnesse growne, boldly giue out,
That they the publique wrongs meant to redresse: *
"Formelesse themselues, reforming doe pretend;
"As if Confusion could Disorder mend.

2

And on they march, with their false-named Head,
Of base and vulgar birth, though noble fayn'd:
Who, puft with vaine desires, to London led
His rash abused troupes, with shadowes train'd:
When-as the King, thereof ascertained,
Supposing some small power would haue restrain'd

* *The Commons of Kent with their Leader Iacke Cade diuulge their many grieuances amongst which, That the King was driuen to liue onely on his Commons; & other men to inioy the Reuenues of the Crowne, which caused pouertie in his Maiestie, and the great payments of the people, now late granted to the King in Parlement. Also they desire, that the King would remoue all the false progeny and affinitie of the late D. of Suffolke which be openly knowne, and them to punish, and to take about his person the true Lords of his royall bloud; to wit, the mightie Prince the D. of Yorke, late exiled by the traytrous motion of the false D. of Suffolke, and his affinitie, &c. Also they craue that they who contriued the death of the high and mighty Prince, Humfrey D. of Glocester, might haue punishment.*

Disordred rage, sends with a simple crew
Sir *Humfrey Stafford;* whom they ouer-threw.

3

Which so increast th'opinion of their might,
That much it gaue to do, and much it wrought,
Confirm'd their rage, drew on the vulgar wight,
Call'd foorth the timorous, fresh partakers brought:
For, many, though most glad their wrongs to right,
Yet durst not venture their estates for nought:
But, see'ing the Cause had such aduantage got,
Occasion makes them stirre; that else would not.

4

So much he erres, that scornes, or else neglects
The small beginnings of arysing broyles;
And censures others, not his owne defects,
And with a selfe-conceite himselfe beguiles:
Thinking small force will compasse great effects,
And spares at first to buy more costly toyles:
"When true-obseruing prouidence, in warre,
"Still makes her foes, farre stronger then they are.

5

Yet this good fortune, all their fortune mard;
"Which, fooles by helping, euer doth suppresse.
For, wareless insolence (whil'st vndebard
Of bounding awe) runnes on to such excesse,
That following lust, and spoyle, and blood, so hard,
Sees not how they procure their owne distresse:
The better, lothing courses so impure,
Rather will like their wounds, then such a cure.

6

For, whil'st this wilde vnrained multitude
(Led with an vnfore-seeing greedy mind
Of an imagin'd good, that did delude
Their ignorance, in their desires made blind)
Ransacke the Cittie, and (with hands imbru'd)
Run to all out-rage in th'extreamest kind,
Heaping-vp wrath and horrour, more and more,
They adde fresh guilt, to mischiefes done before.

7

    And yet, se'ing all this sorting to no end,
But to their owne; no promis'd ayde t'appeare;
No such partakers as they did attend;
Nor such successes as imagin'd were;
Good men resolv'd, the present to defend;
Iustice, against them with a brow seuere:
Themselues, feard of themselues, tyr'd with excesse,
"Found, mischiefe was no fit way to redresse.

8

    And as they stand in desperat comberment,
Enuirond round with horror, blood, and shame:
Crost of their course, despayring of th'euent
A pardon (that smooth bait for basenesse) came:
Which (as a snare, to catch the impotent)
Beeing once pronounc't, they straight imbrace the same:
And, as huge snowy Mountaines melt with heat;
So they dissolv'd with hope, and home they get:

9

    Leauing their Captaine to discharge, alone,
The shot of blood, consumed in their heate:
Too small a sacrifice, for mischiefs done,
Was one mans breath, which thousands did defeat.*
Vnrighteous Death, why art thou but all one
Vnto the small offender and the great?
Why art thou not more then thou art, to those
That thousands spoyle, and thousands liues do lose?

10

    This furie, passing with so quick an end,
Disclos'd not those that on th'aduantage lay:
Who, seeing the course to such disorder tend,
With-drew their foote, asham'd to take that way;
Or else preuented, whil'st they did attend
Some mightier force, or for occasion stay:
But, what they meant, ill-fortune must not tell;
Mischiefe be'ing oft made good, by speeding well.

* *Anno Reg. 29.*

11

Put-by from this, the Duke of *Yorke* dessignes
Another course to bring his hopes about: *
And, with those friends affinitie combines
In surest bonds, his thoughts he poureth-out:
And closely feeles, and closely vndermines
The faith of whom he had both hope and doubt;
Meaning, in more apparant open course,
To try his right, his fortune, and his force.

12

Loue, and alliance, had most firmly ioynd
Vnto his part, that mighty Familie,
The faire distended stock of *Neuiles* kind;
Great by their many issued progenie:
But greater by their worth (that clearely shin'd,
And gaue faire light to their nobilitie)
So that each corner of the Land became
Enricht with some great *Worthy,* of that name.

13

But greatest in renowne doth *Warwicke* sit;
That braue King-maker *Warwicke;* so farre growne,
In grace with Fortune, that he gouerns it,
And Monarchs makes; and, made, againe puts downe.
What reuolutions, his first-mouing wit
Heere brought about, are more then too well knowne;
The fatall kindle-fire of those hot daies:
Whose worth I may, whose worke I cannot praise.

14

With him, with *Richard,* Earle of *Salisbury,*
Courtny and *Brooke,* and other his deare friends;

* *The D. of York, who at this time was in Ireland (sent thither to appease a Rebellion:
which hee effected in such sort, as got him & his linage exceeding loue and liking with that
people euer after) returning home, and pretending great iniuries to be offered him, both
whiles hee was in the K. seruice, & likewise vpon his landing in North-wales, combines
himself with Ric. Neuile E. of Salis. secōd son to Ralph, E. of Westmerland (whose
daughter hee had maried) & with Ri. Neuile the son, E. of Warw. with other his
especiall friēds, with whō he consults, for the reformation of the gouernment, after hee
had complained of the great disorders therein: Laying the blame, for the losse of
Normādy vpō the D. of Sommers. whom, vpon his returning thence, hee caused to be
arrested and committed.*

He intimates his minde; and openly
The present bad proceedings discommends;
Laments the State, the peoples misery,
And (that which such a pitier seldom mends)
Oppression, that sharp two-edged sword,
That others wounds, and wounds likewise his Lord.

15

"My Lords (saith he) how things are caried heere,
"In this corrupted State, you plainely see;
"What burthen our abused shoulders beare,
"Charg'd with the waight of imbecillitie:
"And in what base account all we appeare,
"That stand without their grace that all must be;
"And who they be, and how their course succeedes,
"Our shame reports, and time bewraies their deedes.

16

"*Aniou* and *Maine* (the maime that foule appeares;
"Th'eternall scarre of our dismembred Land)
"*Guien,* all lost; that did, three hundred yeares,
"Remaine subiected vnder our Commaund.
"From whence, mee thinks, there sounds vnto our eares
"The voice of those deare ghosts, whose liuing hand
"Got it with sweat, and kept it with their blood,
"To doe vs (thankless vs) their of-spring good:

17

"And seeme to cry; What? can you thus behold
"Their hatefull feete vpon our Graues should tread?
"Your Fathers Graues; who gloriously did hold
"That, which your shame hath left recouered?
"Redeeme our Tumbs, O spirits too too cold:
"Pull-backe these Towres, our Armes haue honored.
"These Towres are yours: these Forts we built for you:
"These walles doe beare our names; and are your due.

18

"Thus, well they may vpbraid our retchlesnes;
"Whil'st wee, as if at league with infamie,
"Ryot away, for nought, whole Prouinces;
"Giue-vp, as nothing worth, all *Normandie;*

"Traffique important Holdes, sell Fortresses
"So long, that nought is left but misery,
"Poore *Calais,* and these water-walles about,
"That basely pownd vs in, from breaking out.

19

"And (which is worse) I feare, we shall in th'end
"(Throwne from the glory of inuading Warre)
"Be forc't our proper limits to defend;
"Where, euer, men are not the same they are:
"The hope of conquest, doth their spirits extend
"Beyond the vsuall powres of valour, farre.
"For, more is he that ventureth for more,
"Then who fights, but for what hee had before.

20

"Put-to your hands, therefore, to reskew now
"Th'indangered State (deare Lords) from this disgrace:
"And let vs in our honour, labour how
"To bring this scorned Land in better case.
"No doubt, but God our action will allow,
"That knowes my right, and how they rule the place,
"Whose weakenesse calls-vp our vnwillingnesse;
"As opening euen the doore to our redresse.

21

"Though I protest, it is not for a Crowne
"My soule is moov'd (yet, if it be my right,
"I haue no reason to refuse mine owne)
"But onely these indignities to right.
"And what if God (whose iudgements are vnknowne)
"Hath me ordain'd the man, that by my might
"My Country shall be blest? If so it be;
"By helping me, you raise your selues with me.

22

Those, in whom, zeale and amity had bred
A fore-impression of the right he had,
These stirring words so much incouraged,
That (with desire of innouation mad)
They seem'd to runne-afore, not to be led;
And to his fire doe quicker fuell adde:

For, where such humors are prepar'd before;
The opening them, makes them abound the more.

23

Then counsell take they, fitting their desire:
(For, nought that fits not their desire is waigh'd)
The Duke is straight aduised to retire
Into the bounds of *Wales,* to leauie ayd:
Which vnder smooth pretence he doth require;
T'amoue such persons as the State betray'd,
And to redresse th'oppression of the Land;*
The charme, which Weakenesse seldome doth withstand.

24

Ten thousand, straight caught with this bait of breath,
Are towards greater lookt-for forces led:
Whose power, the King, by all meanes, trauaileth
In their arising to haue ruined:
But, their preuenting Head so compasseth,
That all ambushments warily are fled;
Refusing ought to hazard by the way,
Keeping his Greatnesse for a greater day.

25

And to the Citte straight directs his course;
The Cittie, seate of Kings, and Kings chiefe grace:
Where, hauing found his entertainement worse
By farre, then he expected in that place;
Much disappointed, drawes from thence his force,
And towards better trust, marcheth apace;
And downe in *Kent* (fatall for discontents)
Neere to thy bankes, faire *Thames,* doth pitch his tents.

26

And there, intrencht, plants his Artillerie;
Artillerie,† th'infernall instrument,

* *The D. of Yorke raiseth an Army in the marches of Wales, vnder pretext to remoue diuers Coūsellers about the King, and to reuenge the manifest iniuries don to the Commonwealth: & withal, he publisheth a declaratiō of his loyalty, and the wrongs done him by his aduersaries; offering to take his oath vpō the blessed Sacrament, to haue been euer true liege-man to the K. and so euer to continue. Which declaration, was written from his Castle of Ludlow, the 9 of Ianua. An. reg. 30. The 16 of Febru. the K. with the D. of Sōmerset, & other LL. set forward towards the Marches: but the D. of Yorke, took other waies, and made vp towards London.*

† *The vse of Guns, and great Ordinance, began about this time, or not long before.*

New-brought from hell, to scourge mortalitie
With hideous roaring, and astonishment:
Engine of horrour, fram'd to terrifie
And teare the Earth, and strongest Towres to rent:
Torment of Thunder, made to mocke the skies;
As more of power, in our calamities.

27

If that first fire (subtile *Prometheus* brought)
Stolne out of heauen, did so afflict man-kinde,
That euer since, plagu'd with a curious thought
Of stirring search, could neuer quiet finde;
What hath he done, who now by stealth hath got
Lightning and thunder both, in wondrous kinde?
What plague deserues so proud an enterprize?
Tell Muse, and how it came, and in what wise.

28

It was the time, when faire *Europa* sate
With many goodly Diadems addrest;*
And all her parts in florishing estate
Lay beautiful, in order, at their rest:
No swelling member, vnproportionate,
Growne out of forme, sought to disturbe the rest:
The lesse, subsisting by the greaters might;
The greater, by the lesser kept vpright.

29

No noise of tumult euer wak't them all:
Onely, perhaps, some priuate iarre within,
For titles, or for confines, might befall;
Which, ended soone, made better loue begin:
But no eruption did, in generall,
Breake downe their rest, with vniuersall sin:
No publique shock disioynted this faire frame,
Till *Nemesis* from out the Orient came;

---

* *This principall part of Europe, which contained the most florishing state of Christendom, was at this time in the hands of many seuerall Princes, and Commonwealths, which quietly gouerned the same: for, being so many, and none ouer-great, they were lesse attemptiue to disturbe others, & more carefull to keepe their owne, with a mutuall correspondēce of amitie. As, Italy had thē many more principalities & Commonwealths then it hath: Spaine was diuided into many kingdoms, France consisted of diuers free Princes: Both the Germanies of many more Gouernments.*

30

Fierce *Nemesis,* mother of fate and change,
Sword-bearer of th'eternall Prouidence
(That had so long, with such afflictions strange,
Confounded *Asias* proud magnificence,
And brought foule impious Barbarisme to range
On all the glory of her excellence)
Turnes her sterne looke at last vnto the West;
As griev'd to see on earth such happy rest.

31

And for *Pandora* calleth presently
(*Pandora, Ioues* faire gift, that first deceiv'd
Poore *Epimetheus* imbecillitie,
That thought he had a wondrous boone receiv'd;
By meanes whereof, curious Mortalitie
Was of all former quiet quite bereav'd):
To whom, beeing come, deckt with all qualities,
The wrathfull Goddesse breakes out in this wise;

32

Doost thou not see in what secure estate
Those florishing faire Westerne parts remaine?
As if they had made couenaunt with Fate,
To be exempted free from others paine;
At-one with their desires, friends with Debate,
In peace with Pride, content with their owne gaine,
Their bounds containe their minds, their minds appli'd
To haue their bounds with plentie beautifi'd.

33

Deuotion (mother of Obedience)
Beares such a hand on their credulitie,
That it abates the spirit of eminence,
And busies them with humble pietie.
For, see what workes, what infinite expence,
What monuments of zeale they edifie;
As if they would, so that no stop were found,
Fill all with Temples, make all holy ground.

34

But wee must coole this all-belieuing zeale,
That hath enioy'd so faire a turne so long;
And other reuolutions must reueale,
Other desires, other designes among:
Dislike of this, first by degrees shall steale
Vpon the soules of men, perswaded wrong:
And that abused Power,* which thus hath wrought,
Shall giue herselfe the sword to cut her throat.

35

Goe therefore thou, with all thy stirring traine
Of swelling Sciences, the gifts of griefe:
Go loose the links of that soule-binding chaine;
Inlarge this vninquisitiue Beliefe:
Call-vp mens spirits, that simplenes retaine:
Enter their harts, & Knowledge make the thiefe
To open all the doores, to let in light;
That all may all things see, but what is right.

36

Opinion Arme against Opinion growne:
Make new-borne Contradiction still to rise;
As if *Thebes*-founder, *Cadmus*, tongues had sowne,
In stead of teeth, for greater mutinies.
Bring new-defended Faith, against Faith knowne:
Weary the Soule with contrarieties;
Till all Religion become retrograde,
And that faire tire, the maske of sinne be made.

37

And, better to effect a speedy end,
Let there be found two fatall Instruments,
The one to publish, th'other to defend
Impious Contention, and proud Discontents:
Make, that instamped Characters may send
Abroad, to thousands, thousand mens intents;
And in a moment may dispatch much more,
Then could a world of Pennes performe before.

* *The Church.*

38

Whereby, all quarrels, titles, secrecies,
May vnto all be presently made knowne;
Factions prepar'd, parties allur'd to rise,
Sedition vnder faire pretentions sowne:
Whereby, the vulgar may become so wise,
That (with a self-presumption ouer-growne)
They may of deepest mysteries debate,
Controule their betters, censure actes of State.

39

And then, when this dispersed mischiefe shall
Haue brought confusion in each mysterie,
Call'd-vp contempt of states in generall,
Ripened the humor of impiety;
Then haue they th'other Engin, where-with-all
They may torment their selfe-wrought miserie,
And scourge each other, in so strange a wise,
As time or Tyrants neuer could deuise.

40

For, by this stratagem, they shall confound
All th'antient forme and discipline of Warre:
Alter their Camps, alter their fights, their ground,
Daunt mightie spirits, prowesse and manhood marre:
For, basest cowardes from a far shall wound
The most couragious, forc't to fight afarre;
Valour, wrapt vp in smoake (as in the night)
Shall perish without witnesse, without sight.

41

But first, before this generall disease
Breake foorth into so great extreamitie,
Prepare it by degrees; first kill this ease,
Spoyle this proportion, marre this harmonie:
Make greater States vpon the lesser seaze:
Ioyne many kingdomes to one soueraigntie:*
Rayse a few Great, that may (with greater power)
Slaughter each other, and mankinde deuour.

* *The many States of Christendome reduced to a few.*

42

And first begin, with factions to diuide
The fairest Land; that from her thrusts the rest,
As if she car'd not for the world beside;
A world within her selfe, with wonders blest:
Raise such a strife as time shall not decide,
Till the deare blood of most of all her best
Be poured foorth; and all her people tost
With vnkinde tumults, and almost all lost.

43

Let her be made the sable Stage, whereon
Shall first be acted bloodie Tragedies;
That all the neighbour States, gazing thereon,
May make their profite, by her miseries:
And those, whom she before had marcht vpon,
(Hauing, by this, both time and meane to rise)
Made martiall by her Armes, shall growe so great,
As (saue their owne) no force shall them defeat:

44

That when their power, vnable to sustaine
And beare it selfe, vpon it selfe shall fall,
She may (recouered of her wounds againe)
Sit and behold their Parts as tragicall:
For, there must come a time, that shall obtaine
Truce for distresse; when make-peace *Hymen* shall
Bring the conioyned aduerse powers to bed,
And set the Crowne (made one) vpon one head.

45

Out of which blessed vnion, shall arise
A sacred branch (with grace and glory blest)
Whose Virtue shall her Land so patronize,
As all our power shall not her dayes molest:
For, shee (faire shee) the Minion of the skies,
Shall purchase (of the high'st) to hers such rest
(Standing betweene the wrath of heauen and them)
As no distresse shall touch her Diadem.

46

And, from the Rockes of Safetie, shall descrie
The wondrous wracks, that Wrath layes ruined;
All round about her, blood and miserie,
Powres betray'd, Princes slaine, Kings massacred,
States all-confus'd, brought to calamitie,
And all the face of Kingdomes altered:
Yet, she the same inuiolable stands,
Deare to her owne, wonder to other Lands.

47

But, let not her defence discourage thee.
For, neuer one, but shee, shall haue this grace,
From all disturbs to be so long kept free,
And with such glorie to discharge that place.
And therefore, if by such a Power thou bee
Stopt of thy course, reckon it no disgrace;
Sith shee alone (being priuiledg'd from hie)
Hath this large Patent of her dignitie.

48

This charge the Goddesse gaue: when, ready straight
The subtill messenger, accompayned
With all her crew of Artes that on her wait,
Hastes to effect what she was counsailed:
And out she pours, of her immense conceit,
Vpon such searching spirits as trauayled
In penetrating hidden secrecies;
Who soone these meanes of miserie deuise.

49

And boldly breaking with rebellious minde
Into their mothers close-lockt Treasurie,
They Mineralls combustible do finde,
Which in stopt concaues placed cunningly
They fire: and fire, imprisoned against kinde,
Teares out a way, thrusts out his enemie;
Barking with such a horror, as if wroth
With man, that wrongs himselfe, and Nature both.

50

And this beginning had this cursed frame,
Which *Yorke* now planted hath against his King;*
Presuming, by his powre, and by the same,
His purpose vnto good effect to bring;
When diuers of the grauest Councell came,
Sent from the King, to vnderstand what thing
Had thrust him into these proceedings bad,
And what he sought and what intent he had.

51

Who, with words mildly-sharpe, gently-seuere,
Wrought on those wounds that must be toucht with heed;
Applying rather salues of hope, then feare,
Least corrasiues should desperat mischiefes breed.
And, what my Lord (sayd they) should moue you here,
In this vnseemely manner to proceed?
Whose worth being such, as all the Land admires,
Hath fairer wayes then these, to your desires.

52

Wil you, whose means, whose many friends, whose grace,
Can worke the world in peace vnto your will,
Take such a course, as shal your Blood deface,
And make (by handling bad) a good Cause, ill?
How many hearts hazard you in this case,
That in all quiet plots would ayde you still?
Hauing in Court a Partie farre more strong,
Then you conceiue, prest to redresse your wrong.

53

Phy, phy! forsake this hatefull course, my Lord:
Downe with these Armes; that will but wound your Cause.
What Peace may do, hazard not with the Sword:
Lay downe the force that from your force with-drawes;
And yeeld: and we will mediate such accord
As shal dispense with rigor and the lawes;
And interpose this solemne fayth of our
Betwixt your fault, and the offended Power.

* *The D. of Yorke being not admitted into the Citie passed ouer Kingstō Bridge, and so into Kent, an[d] on Brent heath neere Dartf. pight his fielde. The K. makes after, and imbatteled vpon Blacke heath: from whence he sendes the B.B. of Winchester and Ely with the E.E. of Salisbury & Warwike to mediat a peace.*

54

Which ingins of protests, and proffers kinde,
Vrg'd out of seeming griefe and shewes of loue,
So shooke the whole foundation of his Minde,
As they did all his resolution moue:*
And present seem'd vnto their course inclin'd,
So that the King would *Sommerset* remoue;
The man, whose most intolerable pride
Trode downe his worth, and all good mens beside.

55

Which, they there vow'd, should presently be done:
For, what will not peace-louers willing graunt,
Where dangerous euents depend thereon,
And men vnfurnisht, and the State in want?
And if with words the conquest will be won,
The cost is small: and who holds breath so scant
As then to spare, though with indignitie?
"Better descend, then end, in Maiestie.

56

And here-upon the Duke dissolues his force,
Submits him to the King, on publique vow:
The rather too, presuming on this course,
For-that his sonne, the Earle of *March,* was now
With mightier powers abroad: which would inforce
His peace; which else the King would not allow.
For, seeing not all of him, in him, he hath,
His death would but giue life to greater wrath.

57

Yet, comming to the King, in former place
(His foe) the Duke of *Sommerset* he findes:
Whom openly, reproching to his face,
Hee charg'd with treason in the highest kindes.
The Duke returnes like speeches of disgrace;
And fierie wordes bewray'd their flaming mindes:
But yet the triall was for them deferd,
Till fitter time allow'd it to be heard.

* *And finding the Kentish men not to answere his expectation, and the kings forces farre more then his, he willingly condescends to conditions of peace. Edmond D. of Sommerset of the house of Lancaster, descended from Iohn of Gante, was the especiall man against whom he pretended his quarrell.*

58

At Westminster, a Counsell, sommoned,
Deliberates what course the Cause should end
Of th'apprehended Duke of *Yorke;* whose head
Doth now on others doubtfull breath depend.
Law fiercely vrg'd his act, and found him dead:
Friends fayl'd to speake, where they could not defend:
Onely the King himselfe for mercy stood;
As, prodigall of life, niggard of blood.

59

And, as if angrie with the Lawes of death,
"Ah! why should you, sayd hee, vrge things so far?
"You, that inur'd with mercenarie breath,
"And hyred tongue, so peremptorie are;
"Brauing on him whom sorrow prostrateth:
"As if you did with poore Affliction warre,
"And prey on frayltie, folly hath betray'd;
"Bringing the lawes to wound, neuer to ayd.

60

"Dispense sometime with sterne seueritie:
"Make not the Lawes still traps to apprehend:
"Win grace vpon the bad, with clemencie.
"Mercie may mend; whom malice made offend.
"Death giues no thankes; but checkes authoritie:
"And life doth onely Maiestie commend.
"Reuenge dies not; Rigor begets new wrath:
"And blood hath neuer glorie; Mercy hath.

61

"And for my part (and my part should be chiefe)
"I am most willing to restore his state:
"And rather had I win him with reliefe,
"Then lose him with despight, and get more hate.
"Pittie drawes loue: blood-shed is natures griefe;
"Compassion followes the vnfortunate:
"And, losing him, in him I lose my power.
"We rule who liue: the dead are none of our.

62

"And should our rigor lessen then the same,
"Which we with greater glorie should retaine?
"No; let him liue: his life must giue vs fame;
"The childe of mercie newly borne againe.
"As often burials are Physicians shame;
"So, many deaths argue a Kings hard Raigne.
"Why should we say, The Law must haue her vigor?
"The Law kills him; but quits not vs of rigor.

63

"You, to get more preferment by your wit,
"Others to gaine the spoyles of miserie,
"Labour with all your powre to follow it;
"Shewing vs feares, to draw-on crueltie.
"You vrge th'offence, not tell vs what is fit;
"Abusing wrong-informed Maiestie:
"As if our powre, were onely but to slay;
"And that to saue, were a most dangerous way.

64

Thus, out of Pittie, spake that holy King:
Whom milde affections led to hope the best;
When *Sommerset* began to vrge the thing
With words of hotter temper, thus exprest:
"Deare soueraigne Lord, the Cause in managing
"Is more then yours; t'imports the publique rest:
"We all haue part; it toucheth all our good:
"And life's ill spar'd, that's spar'd to cost more blood.

65

"Compassion, here, is crueltie my Lord;
"Pittie will cut our throates, for sauing so.
"What benefite enioy we by the sword,
"If mischiefe shall escape to draw-on mo?
"Why should we giue, what Law cannot afford,
"To be'accessaries to our proper wo?
"Wisedome must iudge, 'twixt men apt to amend,
"And mindes incurable, borne to offend.

66

"It is no priuat Cause (I do protest)
"That moues me thus to prosecute his deede.
"Would God his blood, and mine, had well releast
"The dangers, that his pride is like to breed.
"Although, at me, hee seemes to haue addrest
"His spight; 'tis not the end hee hath decreed.
"I am not he alone, hee doth pursue:
"But, thorow me, he meanes to shoot at you.

67

"For, thus, these great Reformers of a State
"(Aspiring to attaine the Gouernment)
"Still take aduantage of the peoples hate,
"Who euer hate such as are eminent.
"(For, who can great affaires negotiat,
"And all a wayward multitude content?)
"And then these people-minions, they must fall
"To worke-out vs, to work themselues int'all.

68

"But note, my Lord, first, who is in your hand;
"Then, how he hath offended, what's his end:
"It is the man, whose Race would seeme to stand
"Before your Right, and doth a Right pretend:
"Who (Traitor-like) hath rais'd a mightie Band,
"With colour, your proceedings to amend.
"Which if it should haue hapned to succeed,
"You had not now sate to adiudge his deed.

69

"If oftentimes the person, not th'offence,
"Haue beene sufficient cause of death to some,
"Where publique safety puts in euidence
"Of mischiefe, likely by their life to come;
"Shall hee, whose fortune, and his insolence,
"Haue both deserv'd to die, escape that doome;
"When you shall saue your Land, your Crowne thereby;
"And since You cannot liue, vnlesse He die?

70

Thus spake th'aggrieued Duke, that grauely saw
Th'incompatible powers of Princes mindes;
And what affliction his escape might draw
Vnto the State, and people of all kindes:
And yet the humble yeelding, and the aw,
Which *Yorke* there shew'd, so good opinion findes,
That (with the rumor of his Sonnes great strength,
And French affaires) he there came quit at length.*

71

For, euen the feare t'exasperat the heat
Of th'Earle of *March,* whose forward youth and might
Well follow'd, seem'd a proud reuenge to threat,
If any shame should on his Father light:
And then desire in *Gascoyne* to reget
The glorie lost, which home-broyles hinder might,
Aduantaged the Duke, and sav'd his head;
Which, questionlesse, had else been hazarded.

72

For, now had *Burdeux* offered (vpon ayd)
Present reuolt, if we would send with speed.†
Which faire aduantage to haue then delay'd,
Vpon such hopes, had beene a shamefull deed.
And therefore this, all other courses stayd,
And outwardly these inward hates agreed;
Giuing an interpause to pride and spight:
Which breath'd, but to breake-out with greater might.

73

Whil'st dreadfull *Talbot,* terror late of *Fraunce,*
(Against the *Genius* of our Fortune) stroue,
The downe-throwne glorie of our State t'aduance;
Where, *Fraunce* far more then *Fraunce* he now doth proue:
For, friends, opinion, and succeeding chaunce
(Which wrought the weake to yeeld, the strong to loue)

---

* *The D. was suffred to go to his Castle at Wigmore.*
† *The Cittie of Burdeux send their Ambassadors offring to reuolt from the French part if ayd might be sent vnto them: whereupon, Iohn L. Talbot E. of Shrewsburie was imployed with a powre of 3000 men, and surprised the Cittie of Burdeux.*

Were not the same, that he had found before
In happier times; when, lesse would haue done more.

74

For, both the *Britaine,* and *Burgonian* now,
Came altred with our lucke, and won with theirs
(Those bridges, and the gates, that did allow
So easie passage vnto our affaires)*
Iudging it safer to endeuour how
To link with strength, then leane vnto despaires.
"And, who wants friends, to backe what he begins,
"In Lands far off, gets not, although he wins.

75

Which too well prov'd this fatall enterprize,
The last, that lost vs all we had to lose.
Where, though aduantag'd by some mutinies,
And pettie Lords, that in our Cause arose:
Yet those great fayl'd; whose ready quick supplies,
Euer at hand, cheer'd vs, and quail'd our foes.
Succours, from far, come seldome to our minde.
"For, who holds league with *Neptune,* and the winde?

76

Yet, worthy *Talbot,* thou didst so imploy
The broken remnants of disscattered power,†
That they might see it was our destiny,
Not want of spirit, that lost vs what was our:
Thy dying hand sold them the victorie
With so deare wounds, as made the conquest sowre:
So much it cost to spoyle who were vndon;
And such adoe to win, when they had won.

77

For, as a fierce courageous Mastiue fares;
That, hauing once sure fast'ned on his foe,
Lyes tugging on that hold, neuer forbeares,

* *The Dukes of Brittany and Burgundy were great meanes in times past for the Conquering of France.*

† *The E. of Shrewsburie accompayned with his sonne Sir Iohn Talbot, L. Lisle by the right of his wife, with the LL. Molins, Harrington, and Cameis, Sir Iohn Howard Sir Iohn Vernon & others, recouered diuers townes in Gascony: amongst other, the towne, and Castle of Chastillon in Perigent which the French soone after besieged.*

What force soeuer force him to forgo:
The more he feeles his woundes, the more he dares;
As if his death were sweet, in dying so:
So held his hold this Lord, whil'st he held breath;
And scarce, but with much blood, lets goe in death.

78

For, though he saw prepar'd, against his side,
Both vnlike fortune, and vnequall force,
Borne with the swelling current of their pride
Downe the maine streame of a most happy course:
Yet stands he stiffe, vndasht, vnterrifi'd;
His minde the same, although his fortune worse:
Virtue in greatest dangers being best showne;
And though opprest, yet neuer ouer-throwne.

79

For, rescuing of besieg'd *Chatillion*
(Where hauing first constraind the French to fly,
And following hard on their confusion)
Comes (lo) incountred with a strong supply
Of fresh-arriuing powers, that backe thrust-on
Those flying troupes, another chaunce to trie:
Who, double arm'd, with shame, and fury, straine
To wreake their foyle, and win their fame againe.

80

Which seeing, th'vndaunted *Talbot* (with more might
Of spirit to will, then hands of power to do)
Preparing t'entertaine a glorious fight,
Cheeres-vp his wearied Souldiers thereunto.
"Courage, sayth hee: those brauing troupes, in sight,
"Are but the same, that now you did vndo.
"And what if there be come some more then they?
"They come to bring more glory to the day.

81

"Which day, must either thrust vs out of all;
"Or all, with greater glorie, backe restore.
"This day, your valiant worth aduenture shall,
"For what our Land shall neuer fight for more.
"If now we faile, with vs is like to fall

"All that renowne which we haue got before.
"This is the last: if we discharge the same,
"The same shall last to our eternall fame.

82

   "Neuer had worthy men, for any fact,
"A more faire glorious Theater, then we;
"Whereon true Magnanimitie might act
"Braue deedes, which better witnessed could be.
"For, lo, from yonder Turrets, yet vnsackt,
"Your valiant fellowes stand, your worth to see,
"T'auouch your valour, if you liue to gaine;
"And if we die, that we di'd not in vaine.

83

   "And euen our foes (whose proud and powreful might
"Would seeme to swallow vp our dignitie)
"Shall not keep-backe the glory of our right;
"Which their confounded blood shall testifie:
"For, in their wounds, our goarie swords shall write
"The monumentes of our eternitie:
"For, vile is honor, and a title vaine,
"The which, true worth and danger do not gaine.

84

   "For, they shall see, when we (in carelesse sort)
"Shall throwe our selues on their despised speares.
"'Tis not despaire, that doth vs so transport:
"But euen true Fortitude, that nothing feares;
"Sith we may well retire vs, in some sort:
"But, shame on him that such a foul thought beares.
"For, be they more, let Fortune take their part,
"Wee'll tugge her too, and scratch her, ere we part.

85

   This sayd; a fresh infus'd desire of fame
Enters their warmed blood, with such a will,
That they deem'd long, they were not at the game;
And, though they marcht apace, thought they stood still,
And that their lingring foes too slowely came
To ioyne with them, spending much time but ill:
Such force had wordes, fierce humors vp to call,
Sent from the mouth of such a Generall.

86

Who yet, his forces weighing (with their fire)
Turnes him about, in pruiate, to his Sonne
(A worthy Sonne, and worthy such a Sire)
And telleth him, what ground hee stood vpon,
Aduising him in secret to retire;*
Considering how his youth, but now begun,
Would make it vnto him, at all, no staine:
His death small fame, his flight no shame could gaine.

87

To whom, th'aggrieued Sonne (as if disgrac't)
"Ah Father, haue you then selected me
"To be the man, whom you would haue displac't
"Out of the roule of Immortalitie?
"What haue I done this day, that hath defac't
"My worth, that my hands worke despis'd should be?
"God shield, I should beare home a Cowards name.
"He long enough hath liv'd, who dyes with fame.

88

At which, the Father, toucht with sorrowing-ioy,
Turnd him about (shaking his head) and sayes;
"O my deare Sonne, worthy a better day,
"To enter thy first youth, in hard assayes.
And now had Wrath, impatient of delay,
Begun the fight, and farther speeches stayes:
Furie thrustes on; striuing, whose sword should be
First warmed, in the wounds of th'enemie.

89

Hotly these small, but mightie-minded, Bands,
(As if ambitious now of death) doe straine
Against innumerable armed hands,
And gloriously a wondrous fight maintaine;
Rushing on all what-euer strength withstands,
Whetting their wrath on blood, and on disdaine;
And so far thrust, that hard 'twere to descry
Whether they more desire to kill, or dye.

* *The Lord Lisle was aduised by his father to retire him out of the battaile.*

90

Frank of their owne, greedy of others blood,
No stroke they giue, but wounds; no wound, but kills:
Neere to their hate, close to their work they stood,
Hit where they would, their hand obeyes their wills;
Scorning the blowe from far, that doth no good,
Loathing the cracke, vnlesse some blood it spils:
No wounds could let-out life that wrath held in,
Till others wounds, reueng'd, did first begin.

91

So much, true resolution wrought in those
Who had made couenant with death before,
That their smal number (scorning so great foes)
Made *Fraunce* most happie, that there were no more;
And Fortune doubt to whom she might dispose
That weary day; or vnto whom restore
The glory of a Conquest dearely bought,
Which scarce the Conqueror could thinke well got.

92

For, as with equall rage, and equall might,
Two aduerse windes combat, with billowes proud,
And neither yeeld; Seas, skies maintaine like fight
Waue against waue oppos'd, and clowd to clowd:
So warre both sides, with obstinate despight,
With like reuenge, and neither partie bow'd;
Fronting each other with confounding blowes,
No wound, one sword, vnto the other owes:

93

Whil'st *Talbot* (whose fresh ardor hauing got
A meruailous aduantage of his yeeres)
Carries his vnfelt age, as if forgot,
Whirling about, where any need appeares:
His hand, his eye, his wits all present, wrought
The function of the glorious Part he beares:
Now vrging here, now cheering there, he flyes,
Vnlockes the thickest troups, where most force lyes.

94

In midst of wrath, of wounds, of blood, and death,
There is he most, where as he may do best:
And there the closest ranks hee seuereth,
Driues-back the stoutest powres, that forward prest:
There makes his sword his way: there laboreth
Th'infatigable hand that neuer ceast;
Scorning, vnto his mortall wounds to yeeld;
Till Death became best maister of the Field.

95

Then like a sturdy Oke, that hauing long,
Against the warres of fiercest windes, made head,
When (with some forc't tempestuous rage, more strong)
His down-borne top comes ouer-maistered,
All the neere bordering Trees (hee stood among)
Crusht with his waightie fall, lie ruined:
So lay his spoyles, all round about him slaine,
T'adorne his death, that could not die in vaine.*

96

On th'other part, his most all-daring sonne
(Although the inexperience of his yeares
Made him lesse skild in what was to be done;
And yet did carrie him beyond all feares)
Into the maine Battalion, thrusting on
Neere to the King, amidst the chiefest Peeres,
With thousand wounds, became at length opprest;
As if he scorn'd to die, but with the best.†

97

Who thus both, hauing gaind a glorious end,
Soone ended that great day; that set so red,
As all the purple Plaines, that wide extend,
A sad tempestuous season witnessed.
So much adoe had toyling *Fraunce* to rend,
From vs, the right so long inherited:

* *The death of Iohn L. Talbot E. of Shrewsburie; who had serued in the warres of Fraunce most valiantly for the space of 30. yeeres.*
 † *The death of the L. Lisle, Sonne to this worthy E. of Shrewsburie.*

And so hard went we from what we possest,
As with it went the blood wee loued best.

98

Which blood, not lost, but fast lay'd vp with heed
In euerlasting fame, is there held deere,
To seale the memorie of this dayes deed;
Th'eternall euidence of what we were:*
To which, our Fathers, wee, and who succeed,
Doe owe a sigh, for that it toucht vs neere:
Nor must we sinne so much, as to neglect
The holy thought of such a deare respect.

99

Yet happy-hapless day, blest ill-lost breath,
Both for our better fortune, and your owne!
For, what foul wounds, what spoyl, what shamefull death,
Had by this forward resolution growne,
If at *S. Albons, Wakefield, Barnet-heath,*
It should vnto your infamie beene showne?
Blest you, that did not teach how great a fault
Euen Virtue is, in actions that are naught.

100

Yet, would this sad dayes losse had now beene all,
That this day lost: then should we not much plaine,
If hereby we had com'n but there to fall;
And that day, ended, ended had our paine:
Then small the losse of *Fraunce,* of *Guien* small;
Nothing the shame to be turn'd home againe,
Compar'd with other shames. But now, *Fraunce,* lost,
Sheds vs more blood, then all her winning cost.

101

For, losing warre abroad, at home lost peace;
Be'ing with our vnsupporting selues close pent;
And no dessignes for pride (that did increase)
But our owne throats, and our owne punishment;

* *1453. An. reg. 32. Thus was the Duchie of Aquitaine lost; which had remained in the possession of the Crown of England, by the space almost of 300 yeares. The right whereof came by the mariage of K. Hen. 2. with Elenor, daughter of Williā D. of Aquitaine. In this Duchie, are 4. Archbishops, 24. Bishops, 50. Earledomes, 202. Baronies, and aboue a 1000. Captainshippes, and Bayliwikes.*

The working spirit ceast not, though worke did cease,
Hauing fit time to practise discontent,
And stirre vp such as could not long lie still:
"Who, not imploy'd to good, must needes do ill.

102

And now this griefe of our receiued shame,
Gaue fit occasion, for ambitious care,
To draw the chiefe reproche of all the same
On such as obuious vnto hatred are,
Th'especiall men of State: who, all the blame
Of whatsoeuer Fortune doth, must beare.
For, still, in vulgar eares delight it breeds,
To haue the hated, authors of misdeeds.*

103

And therefore, easily, great *Sommerset*
(Whom enuie long had singled out before)
With all the vollie of disgraces met,
As th'onely marke that Fortune plac't therefore:
On whose ill-wrought opinion, Spight did whet
The edge of wrath, to make it pearce the more:
And grief was glad t'haue gotten now on whom
To lay the fault of what must light on some.

104

Whereon, th'againe out-breaking *Yorke* beginnes
To build new modules of his old desire.
And se'ing the booty Fortune for him winnes,
Vpon the ground of this inkindled ire,
He takes th'aduantages of others sinnes
To ayde his owne, and help him to aspire.
For, doubting, peace should better scanne deeds past,
Hee thinkes not safe, to haue his sword out, last:

* *Yorke procures the hatred of the people, against the Duke of Sommerset: and so wrought (in a time of the Kings sicknes) that hee caused him to be arrested in the Qu. great Chāber, and sent to the Towre of Lōdon; accusing him to haue been the occasiō of the losse of France: but the K. being recouered, he was againe set at liberty, Ann. reg. 32. The D. of Yorke, perceiuing his accusations not to preuaile against the D. of Som. resolues to obtaine his purpose by open war: and so being in Wales, accōpanied with his special friēds, assēbled an Armie, & marched towards Londō.*

105

Especially, since euery man (now prest
To innouation) doe with rancor swell:
A stirring humor gen'rally possest
Those peace-spilt times, weary of beeing well:
The weake with wrongs, the happy tyr'd with rest,
And many mad; for what, they could not tell:
The World, euen great with Change, thought it went wrong
To stay beyond the bearing-time, so long.

106

And therefore now these Lords confedered
(Beeing much increast in number and in spight)
So shap't their course, that gathering to a head,
They grew to be of formidable might:
Th'abused world, so hastily is led
(Some for reuenge, some for wealth, some for delight)
That *Yorke,* from small-beginning troups, soone drawes
A world of men, to venture in his Cause.

107

Like as proud *Seuerne,* from a priuat head,
With humble streames at first, doth gently glide,
Till other Riuers haue contributed
The springing riches of their store beside;
Where-with at length high-swelling, she doth spread,
Her broad-distended waters lay'd so wide,
That comming to the Sea, shee seemes, from farre,
Not to haue tribute brought, but rather warre:

108

Euen so is *Yorke* now growne, and now is bent
T'incounter with the best, and for the best.
Whose neere approach the King hastes to preuent,
With hope, farre off to haue his power supprest;*
Fearing the Cittie, least some insolent,
And mutinous, should harten on the rest

* K. Hen. sets forward frō Londō with 20000 mē of war, to encoūter with the D. of
Yorke; attended with Humf. D. of Buckingh. and Humfry his son, E. Stafford, Edm. D.
of Sōmers. Hen. Percy, E. of North Ia. Butler. E. of Wiltsh. & Ormond, Iasper, E. of
Pembrooke, the sonne of Owen Tewder, halfe brother to the K. Tho. Courtney, E. of
Deuonsh. Ioh. L. Clifford, the LL. Sudley, Barnes, Ross, & others.

To take his part. But hee so forward set,
That at *S. Albones* both the Armies met.

109

Where-to, their haste farre fewer hands did bring,
Then else their better leysure would haue done:
And yet too many for so foul a thing;
Sith who did best, hath but dishonour won:
For, whil'st some offer peace, sent from the King,
Warwicks too forward hand hath Warre begon;
A warre, that doth the face of Warre deforme:
Which still is foul; but foulest, wanting forme.

110

And, neuer valiant Leaders (so well knowne
For braue performed actions done before)
Did blemish their discretion and renowne
In any weake effected seruice more;
Bringing such powres into so straight a Towne,
As to some Citty-tumult or vp-rore:
Which, slaughter, and no battaile, might be thought;
Sith that side vs'd their swords, and this their throat.*

111

But this, on th'error of the King, is lai'd,
And vpon *Sommersets* desire t'obtaine
The day with peace: for which they longer staid
Then wisedome would, aduent'ring for the Maine:
Whose force, in narrow streets once ouer-laid,
Neuer recouerd head: but euen there slaine
The Duke and all the greatest Leaders are;
The King himselfe beeing taken prisoner.

*The D. of York, with the LL. pitched their battaile without the towne, in a place called Keyfield: and the K. power (to their great disaduantage) tooke vp the towne: where being assailed & wanting roome to vse their power, were miserably ouerthrowne & slaughtered. On the K. side, were slain Edm. D. of Sommers. who left behind him 3 sons, Hen.ry, Edm. & Ioh. Heere was also slaine, the E. of Northüberland, the E. Stafford, the L. Clifford, Sir Rob. Vere, with diuers others to the nüber of 5000: & on the LL. part, but 600. And this was the first battell at S. Albones, the 23 of May, Ann. reg. 33. The D. of Yorke, with other LL. came to the K. where hee was, and craued grace & for-giuenesse on their knees, of that that they had done in his presence, intending nothing but for the good of him and his kingdome: with whō they remooued to London; concluding there to hold a Parliament, the 9 of Iuly following.

112

Yet not a prisoner to the outward eye,
For-that he must seeme grac't with his lost day;
All things beeing done for his commoditie,
Against such men as did the State betray:
For, with such apt deceiuing clemencie
And seeming order, *Yorke* did so allay
That touch of wrong, as made him make great stealth
In weaker minds, with shew of Common-wealth.

113

Long-lookt-for powre thus got into his hand,
The former face of Court doth new appeare:
And all th'especiall Charges of Commaund,
To his partakers distributed were:*
Himselfe is made Protector of the Land.
A title found, which couertly did beare
All-working powre vnder another stile;
And yet the soueraigne Part doth act the while.

114

The King held onely but an emptie name,
Left, with his life: whereof the proofe was such,
As sharpest pride could not transpearce the same,
Nor all-desiring greedinesse durst touch:
Impietie had not inlarg'd their shame
As yet so wide, as to attempt so much:
Mischiefe was not full ripe, for such foul deedes;
Left, for th'vnbounded malice that succeedes.

The end of the Sixt Booke.

* *Ric. E. of Salisbury, made L. Chancelor, & the E. of Warwicke, Gouernour of Calice.*

The Seventh *Booke*

THE ARGVMENT

The King's repriz'd: Yorke, *and his side retires;*
And making head againe, is put to flight:
Returnes into the Land, his right requires:
Hauing regain'd the King, confirmes his right:
And, whil'st his rash improuidence aspires,
Is slaine at Wakefield, *by* Q. Marg'rets *might:*
Who, at S. Albones, *backe her Lord regaines;*
Is forc't frō thence: & March *the Crowne attaines.*

1

DIsordinate Authoritie, thus gaind,
Knew not at first, or durst not to proceed
With an out-breaking course; but stood restraind
Within the compasse of respectiue heed:
Distrust of friends, and powre of foes, detaind
That mounting will, from making too much speed:*
For, though he held the powre he longd to win,
Yet had not all the keyes to let him in.

2

   The Queene abroad, with a reuenging hand
(Arm'd with her owne disgrace, and others spight,
Gath'ring th'oppressed partie of the Land)
Held ouer him the threatning sword of might;
That forc't him, in the tearmes of awe, to stand
(Who else had burst-vp Right, to come t'his right)
And kept him so confus'd, that he knew not
To make vse of the meanes, which he had got.

* *The D. of York, in respect that K. Hen. for his holiness of life, and clemencie, was highly esteemed of the Commons, durst not attēpt any violēt course against his person: but onely labors to strengthen his owne partie: which he could not do, but by the oppression and displacing of many woorthy men: with committing other violencies, wherunto necessitie inforced him, for the preferment of his friends, which raisd a greater partie against him, then that he made.*

3

For, either by his fearing to restraine
The person of the King; or by neglect
Of guarding him with a sufficient traine,
The watchfull Queene, with cunning, doth effect
A practice that recouers him againe
(As one that with best care could him protect:)
And h'is conuaid to *Couentry,* to those
Who well knew how of Maiestie dispose.

4

Though this weake King had blunted thus before
The edge of Powre, with so dull clemencie,
And left him nothing else was gracious, more
Then euen the title of his Sov'raigntie;
Yet is that title of so precious store,
As it makes, golden, leaden Maiestie:
And where, or how-soeuer it doth fit,
Is sure t'haue the world attend on it.

5

Whether it be, that Forme, and Eminence,
Adorn'd with Pomp and State, begets this awe:
Or, whether an in-bred obedience
To Right and Powre, doth our affections drawe:
Or, whether sacred Kings worke reuerence,
And make that Nature now, which was first Law,
We know not: but, the Head will draw the Parts;
And good Kings, with our bodies, haue our harts.

6

For, lo, no sooner was his person ioyn'd
With this distracted body of his friends;*
But, straight the Duke, and all that faction find,
They lost the onely Engin for their ends:

---

* *The Queen, with her Party, hauing recouered the K. and withdrawing him far frō
Lon. (where they foūd the D. of Yorke was too much fauored by the Cittizens) grew to
bee very strong, by means that so many Ll. and much people, oppressed & discontented
with these proceedings of their enemies, resorted dailie vnto thē. Whervpon, the K.
sōmoned the D. & his adherents, to appeare before him at Couentry: but they, finding
their present strength not sufficient to make good their answer, retired thēselues into
seuerall parts. The D. of York withdrawes him to Wigmore, in Wales: the E. of Salisb.
into the North, the E. of Warw. to Calais.*

Authoritie, with Maiestie combin'd,
Stands bent vpon them now, and powrefull sends
Them summons to appeare, who lately held
That powre themselues, and could not be compeld.

7

Where-with confus'd, as either not prepar'd
For all euents; or se'ing the times not fit;
Or mens affections, failing in regard;
Or their owne forces, not of powre as yet:
They all retire them home; and neither dar'd
T'appeare, or to stand-out to answere it.
This vnfore-thought-on accident, confounds
All their dessignes, and frustrates all their grounds:

8

As vsually it fares, with those that plot
These machines of Ambition, and high pride;
Who (in their chiefest counsels ouer-shot)
For all things saue what serue the turne, prouide;
Whil'st that, which most imports, rests most forgot,
Or waigh'd not, or contemn'd or vndescri'd;
That some-thing may be euer ouer-gone,
Where courses shall be crost, and men vndone.

9

Yorke into *Wales, Warwicke* to *Calais* hies,
Some to the *North,* others to other parts;
As if they ran both from their dignities,
And also from themselues, and their owne harts:
"(The mind decay'd, in publique ieopardies,
"To th'ill at hand, onely it selfe conuerts)
That none would thinke, *Yorkes* hopes, being so neere dry,
Could euer flowe againe, and swell so hie.

10

And yet, for all this ebbing Chance, remaines
The spring that feedes that hope (which leaues men last):
Whom no'affliction so entire restraines,
But that it may remount, as in times past:
Though he had lost his place, his powre, his paines;
Yet held his loue, his friends, his title fast:

The whole frame of that fortune could not faile;
As that, which hung by more then by one naile.

11

Else might we thinke, what errour had it bin,
These parts thus sev'red, not t'haue quite destroy'd;
But that they saw it not the way to win.
Some more dependances there were beside:
Which, Age, and Fate, keeps vs rom looking in,
That their true Counsells come not right descri'd;
Which, our presumptuous wits must not condem:
They be'ing not ignorant; but we, of them.

12

For, heere, we looke vpon another Crown,
An other image of Nobilitie
(Which ciuile Discord had not yet brought down
Vnto a lower range of dignity);
Vpon a Powre as yet not ouer-flowne
With th'Ocean of all-drowning Sov'raintie.
These Lords, who thus against their Kings draw swords,
Taught Kings to come, how to be more then Lords.

13

Which well this Queene observ'd; and therefore sought
To draw them in, and ruine them with Peace;
Whom Force (she saw) more dangerous had wrought,
And did their powre and malice but increase:
And therefore, to the Citty hauing got,
A Counsell was convok't, all iarres to cease:
Where come these Lords at length; but yet so strong,
As if to doe, rather then suffer wrong.*

* Diuers graue persons were sent to the D. of York to mediat a reconciliation: and a
great Councell was called at London, Ann. reg. 36, to agree all differences: Whither cam
the E. of Salis. with 500. men, the D. of Yorke with 400. and was lodged at his house, at
Bainards Castle. The Dukes of Excester, and Somerset, with 800. men, lodged without
Temple Bar. The E. of Northū. the LL Egremōt & Clifford with 1500, & lodged without
the Cittie: The E. of Warwick from Calais with 600. men al in his liuery. The L. Mayor
kept continuall watch with 2000. men in armor during the treaty. Wherin by the great
trauaile & exhortation of the Archbishop of Canterbury, with other graue Prelates, a
reconciliation was concluded, and celebrated with a solēne procession. The E. of Warwicke
is set vpon by the Queenes seruants.

14

Here Scottish border broyles, and feares of *Fraunce*,
Vrg'd with the present times necessity,
Brought forth a suttle-shadowed countenance
Of quiet peace, resembling Amitie;
Wrapt in a strong and curious ordinaunce,
Of many Articles, bound solemnly:
As if those *Gordian* knots could be so ti'd,
As no impatient sword could them diuide:

15

Especially, whereas the selfe same ends
Concur not in a point of like respect;
But that each party couertly intends
Thereby their owne designments to effect:
Which Peace, with more indangering wounds, offends,
Then Warre can doe; that stands vpon suspect,
And neuer can be ty'd with other chaine,
Then intermutuall benefite and gaine.

16

As well by this concluded Act is seene:
Which had no power to holde-in minds, out-bent;
But quickly was dissolv'd and canceld cleene,
Either by *Warwicks* fortune or intent.
How euer vrg'd, the Seruants of the Queene
Assaulted his, as he from Counsell went:
Where, his owne person, egerly pursu'd,
Hardly (by Boate) escap't the multitude.

17

Which deed, most heynous made, and vrg'd as his,
The Queene (who soone th'aduantage apprehends)
Thought forthwith t'haue committed him on this:
But, he preuents, flyes North-ward to his friends,
Shewes them his danger, and what hope there is
In her, that all their ouerthrowes intends;
"And that these drifts, th'effects of this Peace are:
"Which giues more deadly wounding blowes, then war.

18

Strooke with his heate, began the others fire
(Kindled with danger, and disdaine) t'inflame:
Which hauing well prepar'd, to his desire,
He leaues the farther growing of the same,
And vnto *Calais* (to his strong retire)
With speed betakes him, to preuent the fame
Of his impos'd offence; least, in disgrace,
He might be dispossessed of that place.

19

Yorke straight aduis'd the Earle of *Salsbury*
T'addresse him to the King: and therevpon,
With other grieuances, to signifie
Th'iniurious act committed on his Sonne;
And there, to vrge the breach of th'Amitie,
By these sinister plots to be begun:
But, he so strongly goes, as men might ghesse,
He purpos'd not to craue, but make redresse.

20

Whom, the Lord *Audly,* hasting to restraine,
(Sent, with ten thousand men, well furnished)
Encountered on *Blore-heath;* where he is slaine,
And all his powre and force discomfited:*
Which chaunce, so opened and let-out againe
The hopes of *Yorke* (whom Peace had fettered)
That he resolues, what-euer should befall,
To set vp's Rest, to venture now for all.

21

Fury, vnti'd, and broken out of bands,
Runnes desp'rate presently to either head:
Faction and Warre (that neuer wanted hands
For Bloud and Mischiefe) soone were furnished:
Affection findes a side: and out it stands;
Not by the Cause, but by her int'rest led:
And many, vrging Warre, most forward are;
"Not that 't is iust, but only that 'tis Warre.

* *Iames Twichet L. Audly slaine at Bloreheath and his army discomfited by the E. of Salisb. with the losse of 2400. men. An. reg. 38.*

22

Whereby, the Duke is growne t'a mighty head
In *Shropshire,* with his Welsh and Northren ayde:
To whom came *Warwicke,* hauing ordered
His charge at *Calais;* and with him conuay'd
Many braue Leaders, that aduentured
Their fortunes on the side that he had lay'd:
Whereof as chiefe, *Trollop* and *Blunt* excell'd:
But, *Trollop* fayld his friends; *Blunt* faithfull held.*

23

The King (prouok't these mischiefes to preuent,
Follow'd with *Sommerset* and *Excester)*
Strongly appointed, all his forces bent,
Their malice to correct or to deterre:
And, drawing neere, a reuerent Prelate sent
To proffer pardon, if they would referre
Their Cause to Peace;† as being a cleaner course
Vnto their ends, then this foule barb'rous force.

24

"For, what a warre, sayd he, is here begun,
"Where euen the victory is held accurst?
"And who-so winnes, it will be so ill won,
"That though he haue the best, he speeds the worst.
"For, here your making, is, to be vndon;
"Seeking t'obtaine the State, you lose it first:
"Both sides being one, the bloud consum'd all one;
"To make it yours, you worke to haue it none.

25

"Leaue then with this, though this be yet a staine
"T'attempt this sinne, to be so neere a fall.
"The doubtfull Dye of warre, cast at the Maine,
"Is such, as one bad chaunce may lose you all.
"A certaine sinne, seekes an vncertaine gaine:
"Which, got, your selues euen wayle and pitty shall,
"No way, but Peace, leades out from blood and feares;
"To free your selues, the Land, and vs, from teares.

* *Sir Andrew Trollope, afterwarde fled to the King. Iohn Blūt remainde with the Lords.*

† *The King, beeing at Worcester, sends the B. of Salisbury to the LL. to induce them to peace, & to offer pardon.*

26

Whereto the discontented part replyes;
"That they, hereto by others wrongs inforc't
"Had no way else but these extremities,
"And worst meanes of redresse, t'auoide the worst.
"For, since that peace did but their spoyles deuise,
"And held them out from grace (as men diuorc't
"From th'honors, that their fortunes did afford)
"Better die with the sword, then by the sword.

27

"For, if pacts, vowes, or oaths, could haue done ought,
"There had enough been done: but, to no end
"Saue to their ruine, who had euer sought
"To'auoide these broyls, as grieuing to contend;
"Smothring disgraces, drawing to parts remote,
"As exil'd men: where now they were, to attend
"His Grace with all respect, and reuerence;
"Not with the sword of malice, but defence.

28

Whereby, they shewed, that words were not to win:
But yet the Pardon* works so feelingly,
That to the King, that very night, came-in
Sir Andrew Trollop, with some company,
Contented to redeeme his sinne with sinne;
Disloyalty, with infidelitie:
And, by this meanes, became discouered quite
All th'orders of th'intended next dayes fight.

29

Which so much vpon their weakened feares,
That presently their Campe brake vp, ere day;
And euery man with all his speed prepares,
According to their course, to shift their way.
Yorke, with his youngest Sonne, tow'ards *Ireland* beares;†
Warwicke to *Calais,* where his safety lay;

---

* The Bishop of Salisbury offred pardon, to all such as would submit themselues.
† The D. of York, with his youngest sonne the E. of Rutland, withdrew him into Ireland where he was exceedingly beloued.

To that sure harbor of conspiracie,
Enuies Retreit, Rebellions nursery.

30

Which fatall place, seemes that with either hand
Is made t'offend.* For, *Fraunce* sh'afflicts with th'one:
And with the other, did infest this Land;
As if ordained to doe good to none:
But, as a Gate to both our ills did stand,
To let-out plagues on vs, and int' her owne:
A part without vs, that small good hath bin;
But to keepe, lesse intire, the whole within.

31

And there, as in their all and best support,
Is *Warwicke* got, with *March* and *Salsbury;*
When all the Gates of *England,* euery Port,
And Shore close-shut, debarres their reentry;
Lockt out from all; and all left in that sort,
As no meanes seemes can ayde their misery.
This wound, giuen without blowe, weakens them more,
Then all their losse of blood had done before.

32

For, now againe vpon them frowningly
Stands Powre with Fortune, trampling on their States;
And brands them with the markes of Infamy;
Rebellions, Treasons, and Assassinats;
Attaints their Bloud, in all Posteritie;
Ransacks their Lands, spoiles their Confederats;
And layes so hideous colours on their crimes,
As would haue terrified more timorous times;

33

But, heere could doe no good: for why? this Age,
Being in a course of motion, could not rest,
Vntill the reuolution of their rage
Came to that poynt, whereto it was addrest.
Misfortune, crosses, ruine, could not swage
That heate of hope, or of reuenge, at least.
"The World, once set a-worke, cannot soone cease;
"Nor euer is the same, it is in peace.

* *The inconuenièces of Calais at that time.*

34

For, other motions, other int'rests heere,
The acting spirits vp and awake doe keepe:
"Faith, friendship, honour is more sure, more deere,
"And more it selfe, then when it is asleepe:
Worth will stand-out, and doth no shadowes feare:
Disgraces make impressions far more deepe;
When Ease, ere it will stirre, or breake her rest,
Lyes still, beares all, content to be opprest.

35

Yorke, and his side, could not, while life remain'd,
Though thus disperst, but worke and interdeale:
Nor any sword, at home, could keepe restrain'd
Th'out-breaking powres of this innated zeale.
This humor had so large a passage gain'd,
On th'inward body of the Common-weale;
That 'twas impossible to stop, by force,
This current of affections violent course.

36

Yet they at home (disorder to keepe forth)
Did all what powre could doe, or wit inuent;
Plac't, in th'auoided roomes, men of great worth;
Young *Sommerset,* with strength to *Calais* sent;*
Northumberland and *Clifford* to the North;
(Whereof They onely had the gouernment)
Defend all landings, barre all passages,
Striue to redresse the publique grieuances:

37

And, to this end, summon a Parlement:†
Wherein, when-as the godly King would not,
Vnto th'attainder of the Lords, consent;
The Queene in griefe (and in her passions hot)
Breakes out in speech, louingly violent:
"And what (saith shee) my Lord, haue you forgot
"To rule and be a King? Why will you thus
"Be milde to them, and cruell vnto vs?

Hen. the young D. of Sommers. was, in An. reg. 37, made Captain of Calais, & a priuie seal sent to the E. of Warwicke, to discharge him of that place: who, in respect he was made Captaine there by Parliament, would not obay the priuie seale.
† *The Parliament at Couentry.*

38

   "What good haue you procur'd by clemencie,
"But giuen to wilde presumption much more head?
"And now what cure, what other remedie
"Can to our desp'rat wounds be ministred?
"Men are not good, but for necessitie;
"Nor orderly are euer borne, but bred.
"Sad want, and pouertie, makes men industrious:
"But, Law must make them good, and feare obesquious.

39

   "My Lord; Hee gouerns well, that's well obayd:
"And temp'rat Rigour euer safely sits.
"For, as to him, who *Cotis** did vpbraid,
"And call'd his rigor, madnesse, raging fits;
"Content thee, thou vnskilfull man, he said,
"My madnesse keeps my Subiects in their wits:
"So, to like course my Lord, y'are forc't to fall;
"Or else you must, in th'end, vndoe vs all.

40

   "Looke but, I pray, on this deare part of you;
"This branch (sprung frō your blood) your owne aspect:
"Looke on this Childe, and think what shal ensue
"To this faire hope of ours, by your neglect.
Though you respect not vs, wrong not his due,
"That must his right, left you, from you expect;
"The right of the renowned *Lancaster,*
"His fathers fathers, and great grand-fathers.

41

   "Then turnes t'her sonne: O sonne! dost thou not see?
"He is not mov'd, nor toucht, nor weighes our teares.
"What shall I doe? What hope is left for me,
"When he wants will to help, & thou wantst yeares?
"Could yet these hands of thine but partners bee
"In these my labours, to keep-out our feares,
"How well were I? that now alone must toile,
"And turne, and tosse; and yet vndone the while.

* *Cotis, a Tyrant of Thrace.*

42

"I knowe, if thou could'st helpe, thy mother thus
"Should not beyond her strength endure so much;
"Nor these proud Rebels, that would ruine vs,
"Scape with their hainous treasons, without touch:
"I knowe, thou would'st conceiue how dangerous
"Mercy were vnto those, whose hopes are such;
"And not preserue, whom Law hath ouer-throwne,
"Sauing their liuely-hood, to lose our owne.

43

"But, sith thou canst not, nor I able am,
"Thou must no more expect of me, deare Son;
"Nor yet, in time to come, thy Mother blame,
"If thou, by others weakenesse be vndon.
"The world, with me, must testifie the same,
"That I haue done my best, what could be done;
"And haue not fail'd, with hazard of my life,
"The duetie of a mother and a wife.

44

"But well; I see which way the world will goe:
"And let it goe: and so turnes her about,
Full, with stout griefe, and with disdainefull woe;
Which, now, her words shut-vp, her lookes let-out.
The cast of her side-bended eye, did showe
Both sorrow and reproofe; se'ing so great doubt,
And no powre to redresse, but stand and vex,
Inmprisoned in the fetters of her sex.

45

Yet, so much wrought these mouing arguments
(Drawne from that blood, where Nature vrg'd her Right)
As his all-vpward tending zeale relents;
And, downeward to his State, declines his sight:
And so, to their Attainders he consents;*
Prouided, He, on their submission, might

* At this Parliament at Couentry, in the yeere 1459, in the 38 of Hen. 6. is Ric. D. of
Yorke, with his son Edw. and all his posteritie, and partakers, attainted, to the ninth
degree, their goods and possessiōs escheated, their tenants spoiled of their goods, the
Towne of Ludlow partaining to the D. of Yorke ransackt, and the Dutchess of Yorke
spoyled of her goods.

Out of his Princely powre, in his owne name,
Without a Parlement, reuoke the same.

46

Whil'st *Sommerset* with maine endeuour lay
To get his giuen (but vngot) gouernment,
The stout *Calisians* (bent another way)
Fiercely repell him, frustrate his intent:*
Yet takes he *Guines,* landing at *Whitsandbay:*
Where-as the swordes, hee brought, would not consent
To wound his foes: the fight no rancor hath:
Malice was friends: and Warre was without wrath.

47

Though hee their hands, yet *Warwicke* had their hearts:
To whom, both men and shipping they betray'd;
Whilst *Englands* (though debarred) shore imparts,
To him, her other-where intended ayde:
For, the Lord *Riuers,* passing to those parts,
T'haue fresh supplies vnto the Duke conuay'd;
At *Sandwich,* with his Sonne accompayned,
Staying for winde, was taken in his bed.†

48

Whose shipping, and prouisions, *Warwicke* takes
For *Ireland,* with his Chieftaine to conferre:‡
And within thirtie dayes this voyage makes,
And backe-returnes, ere knowne to haue beene there:
So that the heauens, the sea, the winde partakes
With him; as if they of his faction were;
Or that his spirit and valour were combin'd,
With destinie, t'effect what he design'd.

49

Which working, though without, and on the shore,
Reacht yet vnto the centre of the Land;
Searcht all those humors that were bred before;

* *Henrie D. of Sommerset with the LL. Audly, and Rosse attempted the towne of Calais, but were repulst; his people yeelding thēselues to the E. of War. and himselfe hardly escaped.*

† *The L. Riuers, and his sonne Sir Anthony Wooduill, were taken by Iohn Dinham, at Sandwich; whether they were sent to guard the towne, and supply the D. of Sommerset.*

‡ *The E. of Warwick sayled into Ireland to conferre with the D. of Yorke.*

Shakes the whole frame, whereon the State did stand;
"Affection, pittie, fortune, feare being more
"Farre off and absent, then they are at hand.
"Pittie becomes a traytor with th'opprest:
"And many haue beene rays'd, by being supprest.

50

For, they had left, although themselues were gone,
Opinion and their memorie behinde.
Which so preuayles, that nought could here be done,
But straight was knowne as soone as once design'd:
Court, Councell-chamber, Closet, all were won,
To be reuealers of the Princes minde:
So false is Faction, and so smooth a lyer,
As that it neuer had a side entire.

51

Whereby, th'exil'd had leasure to preuent,
And circumuent, what-euer was deuiz'd:
Which made, that *Faulconbridge,* to *Sandwich* bent,
That Fortresse and the Gouernour surpriz'd;*
Who, presently from thence to *Calais* sent,
Had his vnguiltie blood there sacrifiz'd:
And *Faulconbridge,* returning backe, relates
Th'affection here, and zeale of all estates.

52

Drawne with which newes, and with a spirit that dar'd
T'attempt on any likelihood of support;
They take th'aduantage of so great regard;
Their landing here secur'd them in such sort,
By *Faulconbridge;* the fatall bridge prepar'd
To be the way of blood, and to transport
Returning furie to make greater wounds
Then euer *England* saw within her bounds.

53

And but with fifteene hundred men do land,
Vpon a Land, with many millions stor'd:
So much, did high-presuming Courage stand

* *The L. Faulconbridge, sent to Sandwich, tooke the Towne and Sir Simon Monfort Gouernor thereof.*

On th'ayde, home-disobedience would afford.
Nor were their hopes deceiv'd: for, such a hand
Had Innouation ready for the sword,
As ere they neere vnto the Cittie drew,
Their powre beyond all former greatnesse grew.

54

Muse, what may we imagine was the Cause
That *Furie* workes thus vniuersally?
What humor, what affection, is it, drawes
Sides, of such powre, to this Nobilitie?
Was it their Conscience, to redresse the Lawes;
Or malice, to a wrong-plac't Sov'raintie,
That caus'd them (more then wealth, or life) desire
Destruction, ruine, bloud-shed, sword and fire?

55

Or was the Powre of Lords (thus inter-plac't
Betwixt the height of Princes, and the State)
Th'occasion that the people so imbrac't
Their actions, and attend on this Debate?
Or had their Greatnesse, with their Worth, imbas't
The Touch of *Royaltie* to so lowe rate,
As their opinion could such tumults moue?
Then Powre, and Virtue, you contagious proue.

56

And *Perianders* leuell'd Eares of Corne
Shew what is fittest for the publique Rest;
And that the hyest Minions which adorne
A *Common-weale* (and doo become it best)
Are *Zeale* and *Iustice, Law,* and *Customes,* borne
Of hye descent; that neuer do infest
The Land with false suggestions, claymes, affrights,
To make men lose their owne, for others rights.

57

But now, against this disproportion, bends
The feeble King all his best industrie:
And, from abrode, *Skales, Louell, Kendall,* sends,
To hold the Cittie in fidelitie;*

* *The King, from Couentry sendes the L. Skales, the L. Louel, the E. of Kendal, to London, with others, to keep the Cittie in obedience.*

The Cittie, which before (for others ends)
Was wrought to leaue the part of Royaltie:
Where, though the Kings commaund was of no powre;
Yet worke these Lords so, that they tooke the Towre:

58

And, from thence, labour to bring-in againe
The out-let will of disobediencie;
Send terror, threates, intreaties; but in vaine:
Warwicke, and *March,* are with all iollite
And grace receiv'd. The Citties loue did gaine
The best part of a Crowne: for whose defence,
And intertaining still, stayes *Salsburie,*
Whil'st *March,* and *Warwicke* other fortunes try;*

59

Conducting their fresh troupes against their King
(Who leaues a woman to supply his steed):
And neere *Northhampton,* both imbattailing,
Made, now, the very heart of *England* bleed:†
Where, what strange resolutions both sides bring,
And with what deadly rancour they proceed,
Witnesse the blood there shed, and fowlly shed;
That cannot, but with sighes, be registred.

60

There, *Buckingham, Talbot,* and *Egremont,*
Bewmont, and *Lucy;* parts of *Lancaster*
(Parts most important, and of chiefe account)
In this vnhappy day, extinguisht are.
There, the Lord *Grey,* (whose fayth did not amount
Vnto the trust committed to his care)
Betrayes his King, borne to be strangely tost;
And, late againe attain'd, againe is lost.‡

* The EE. of March, Warwike, and Salisburie, landing at Sandwich, were met by the
Archb. of Cant. who with his Crosse borne before him accompayned them to Londō An.
reg. 38. The affection which the Citie of London bare to the D. of Yorke was an especiall
meane for the raysing of that line, to the Crowne. The E. of Salisbury left to keepe the
Cittie.
† The Battell of Northhampton.
‡ The D. of Bucking. the E. of Shrewes. the L. Egremont, Iohn Vicont Bewmont, Sir
William Lucy slaine. The L. Edmond Grey of Ruthen who led the Vantguard of K.
Henrie withdrew himself and tooke part with the LL.

61

Againe is lost this out-side of a King*
Ordain'd for others vses, not his owne:
Who, to the part that had had him, could but bring
A feeble body onely, and a Crowne;
But yet was held to be the dearest thing
Both sides did labor-for, so much; to crowne
Their Cause with the apparency of might:
From whom, and by whom, they must make their Right;

62

When he himselfe (as if he nought esteem'd
The highest Crowne on earth) continues one;
Weake to the world: which, his Religion deem'd
Like to the breath of man; vaine, and soone gone:
Whil'st the stout Queene, by speedy flight redeem'd
The safety of her selfe, and of her Sonne:
And, with her, *Sommerset*† to *Durham* fled;
Her powres, supprest, her heart vnuanquished.

63

So much for absent *Yorke,* is acted here,
Attending *English* hopes, on th'*Irish* coast.
Which when, vnlookt-for, they related were,
Ambition (still on horse-backe) comes in poast,
And seemes with greater glory to appeare;
As made the more, by be'ing so long time lost:
And to the Parlement with state is led,
Which his associates had fore-summoned.

64

And, com'n into the Chamber of the Peeres,
He sets himselfe downe, in the chayre of State:
Where, such an vnexpected face appeares
Of an amazed Court, that gazing sate
With a dumbe silence (seeming, that it feares
The thing it went about t'effectuate)
As if the Place, the Cause, the Conscience, gaue
Barres to the words, their forced course should haue.

* *The King is conuaide to London, the Towre yeelded vp to the Lords, and the L. Skales who kept it, is murthred.*
† *The D. of Sommerset.*

65

Tis strāge, those times, which brought such hāds for blood,
Had not bred tongues to make good any side;
And that no prostituted conscience stood,
Any iniustice to haue iustifi'd
(As men of the forelone hope, onely good
In desperatest acts to be imploy'd)
And that none, in th'assembly there, was found,
That would t'ambitious descant giue a ground:

66

That euen himselfe (forc't of necessitie)
Must be the Orator of his owne Cause.
For, hauing viewd them all, and could espie
None proff'ring once to speake (all, in a pause)
On this friend lookes with an inuiting eye,
And then on that (as if he woo'd applause)
Holding the cloth of State still in his hand;
The signe, which he would haue them vnderstand.

67

But se'ing none moue; with an imperiall port,
Gath'ring his spirits, he ryses from his seat;
Doth, with such powre of wordes, his Cause support,
As seemes all others Causes to defeat.
"And, sure, who workes his Greatnesse in that sort,
"Must haue more powres, then those that are borne great:
"Such Reuolutions are not wrought, but when
"Those spirits doe worke, which must be more then men.

68

He argues first his Right, so long with-held
By th'vsurpation of the *Lancasters;*
"The Right of a direct Line, always held
"The sacred course of Blood; our Ancestors,
"Our Lawes, our reuerent Customes haue vp-held
"With holy hands. Whence, when disorder erres,
"What horrors, what confusion, do wee see,
"Vntill it be reduc't where it should bee?

69

"And how it prospers with this wretched Land,
"Witnesse the vniuersall miserie,

"Wherein (as if accurst) the Realme doth stand;
"Depriu'd of State, wealth, honor, dignitie;
"The Church, and Commons, vnderneath the hand
"Of violence, extortion, robberie;
"No face of order, no respect of Lawes:
"And thus complaynes of what himselfe is cause;

70

"Accusing others insolence, that they
"Exhausted the Reuenues of the Crowne:
"So that the King was forc't onely to prey
"Vpon his Subiects, poore and wretched growne:
"And that they now sought *Ireland* to betray,
"And *Calais* to the *French;* which hee had knowne,
"By th'intercepted notes of their owne hand,
"Who were the onely Traytors of the Land:

71

"And yet procur'd th'Attaynders most vniust,
"Of others guiltlesse and vnspotted blood;
"Who euermore had labour'd, in their trust
"And faithfull seruice for their Countries good:
"And who with extreame violence were thrust
"Quite out of all, spoyl'd of their liuelihood,
"Expos'd to all the miseries of life:
"Which they indur'd, to put-off blood and strife.

72

"But since (sayth he) their malice hath no ende,
"But t'end vs all, and to vndo the Land:
"(For which, the hatefull *French* gladly attend,
"And at this instant haue their swords in hand)
"And that the God of heauen doth seeme to bend
"Vnto our Cause, whereto the best men stand;
"And that this blood of mine, so long time sought,
"Reserued seemes, for some thing to be wrought;

73

"It rests within your iudgements, to vp-right,
"Or else to ruine vtterly the Land.
"For, this be sure, I must pursue my Right
"Whil'st I haue breath, or I and mine can stand.

"Thinke, whether this poore State, being in this plight,
"Stands not in need of some vp-raysing hand:
"Or whether 'tis not time we should haue rest,
"And this confusion, and our wounds redrest.

74

This said, he turnes aside, and out hee goes;
Leaues them to counsell what was to be done.
Where, though the most part gath'red, were of those
Who with no opposition sure would run;
Yet some, more temp'rate, offred to propose
That which was fit to bee considered on:
Who, though they knew his clayme was faire, in sight;
Yet thought, it now lackt the right face of Right;

75

Since, for the space of three score yeeres, the Crowne
Had beene in act possest, in three descents;
Confirm'd by all the Nobles of renowne,
The peoples suffrages, Oathes, Parlements;
So many Actes of State, both of our owne,
And of all other foraine Gouernments:
"That Wrong, by order, may grow Right by-this;
"Sith Right, th'obseruer but of Order is.*

76

"And then considring, first, how *Bullingbrooke,*
"Landing in *Yorkeshire* but with three score men,
"By the consent of all the Kingdome, tooke
"The Crowne vpon him, held for lawfull then;
"His Vncle *Yorke* and all the Peeres betooke
"Themselues to him, as to their Soueraigne; when
"King Richards wrongs, and his propinquitie,
"Did seeme to make no distance in their eye:

77

"Nor was without example, in those dayes:
"Wherein (as in all Ages) States do take
"The side of Publique Peace, to counterpayse
"The waight of wrong; which, time may rightfull make.

* *Non confirmatur tractu temporis, quod de iure ab initio non subsistit.*

"No elderhood, *Rufus* and *Henrie* stayes,*
"The imperiall Crowne of *England* t'vndertake:
"And *Iohn*, before his nephew *Arthur*, speedes;
"Whom, though depriv'd, *Henry* his sonne succeedes.

78

Edward the third, made Sov'raigne of the State,
Vpon his fathers depriuation, was:
All which, though seeming wrongs, yet fairely sate
In their succeeders, and for right did passe.
And if they could so worke, t'accommodate,
And calme the Peeres, and please the Populasse;
They wisht, the Crowne might, where it stood, remaine,
Succeeding inconuenience to restraine.

79

Thus th'auncient Fathers of the Law aduise;
Graue Baron *Thorpe* and learned *Fortescue:*
Who, though they could not fashion, otherwise,
Those strong-bent humors, which auersiue grew;
Yet seem'd to qualifie th'extreamities,
And some respect more to their Sov'raine drew;
That, during life, it was by all agreed,
He should be King, and *Yorke* should him succeed:

80

Which, presently enacted, was (beside)
Proclaym'd through-out with all solemnities;
And intermutually there ratifi'd
With protestations, vowes and oathes, likewise;
Built-vp, with all the strength of forme, t'abide
What-euer oppositions could aryse;
And might haue seem'd sure and authenticall,
Had all this bodie of the State beene all.

81

But *Trent*, thou keptst a part; *Thames* had not all:
The *North* diuided honor, with the *South:*
And like powre held like Greatnes seuerall:
Where other Right, spake with another mouth;
Another Heire, another Prince they call,

* *W. Rufus and Hen. 1. preferd before their elder brother.*

Whom naturall succession follow doth;
The branch of Kings, the true sonne of the Crowne:
To whom, no father can but leaue his owne.

82

The King, as husband to the Crowne, doth by
The wiues infeoffement hold; and onely here
Inioyes the same for life, by Curtesie;
Without powre to dispose in other-where
(After his death) but as th'authoritie,
Order, and custome of Succession beare:
And therefore *Henries* Act cannot vndo
The right of him, whom it belongs vnto.

83

And this vnnaturall intrusion, here,
Of that attainted Blood, out of all course,
Effected with confusion and with feare,
Must be reduc't to other tearmes, of force,
These insolencies Iustice cannot beare:
The sword (whereto they onely had recourse)
Must cut this knot, so intricately ty'd;
Whose vaine contriued ends are plaine descry'd.

84

Thus they giue-out; and out the sword in hand
Is drawne for blood, to iustifie the same:
And by a side, with many a Worthie, mand;
Great *Sommerset, Excester, Buckingham,*
With *Clifford, Courtney,* and *Northumberland*
(Lords of as mightie courage as of name)
Which all, against *Yorkes* forced courses, bend;
Who, hauing done, yet had not made an end:

85

But, to another worke, is forc't to go;
The last turmoyle lab'ring Ambition had:
Where Pride and Ouer-weening led him so
(For fortunes past) as made the issue sad:
For, whether safer counsell would or no,
His yet vnfurnisht troupes he desp'rat led
From *Sandall* Castle, vnto *Wakefield* Greene,
Against far mightier forces of the Queene.

86

Where, round inclos'd by Ambushments fore-lay'd,
Hard-working for his life (but all in vaine)
With number and confusion ouer-lay'd,
Himselfe and valiant *Salsbury* are slaine:
With whome, the most and dearest blood decay'd
Of his couragious and aduenturous traine:*
So short a life had those long hopes of his;
Borne not to weare the Crowne, he wrought for thus;

87

But, in the ryse of his out-springing lust,
Now in the last of hope, receiv'd this fall;
Now, that his working powres so far had thrust,
That his desires had but this step to all:
When, so neere home, he seem'd past all distrust,
This vnexpected wracke doth him befall:
This successor th'inheritor fore-goes;
The play-game made of Fortune, and his foes.

88

Whose young sonne, *Rutland* (made the sacrifice
For others sinnes, ere he knew how to sinne)
Brought only but to see this exercise
Of blood and wounds, endes ere he did beginne:
Whose teares, whose mone, whose lamentable cryes,
Could neither mercie nor compassion winne:
The branch of such a tree, though tender now,
Was not thought fit should any longer growe.

89

Which turning Chaunce, t'a long vngraced side,
Brings backe their almost quayled hopes againe;
And thrust them on, to vse the present Tide
And Flowe of this occasion, to regaine
Th'inthralled Monarch, and to vndecide
The late concluded Act they held for vaine;
And mooues their Armies, new refresht with spoyle,
For more confusion, and for more turmoyle:

* *The Battel of Wakefield, where the D. of Yorke is slaine: the E. of Salsburie taken
& beheaded at Yorke: Edmond E. of Rutland, youngest sonne to the D. of Yorke
murthered after the Battell, by the L. Clifford.*

90

Victoriously proceeding vnwithstood,
Till at S. *Albones Warwicke* forc't a stand:*
Where-as (to make his owne vndooing good)
The King is brought against himselfe to band:
His Powre and Crowne is set against his Blood;
Forc't on the side, not of himselfe, to stand.
Diuided King, in what a case thou art!
To haue thy hand, thus bent against thy hart.

91

And here this famous fatall place, againe,
Is made the stage of blood; againe these streets,
Imbru'd with slaughter, cov'red with the slaine,
Witness what desp'rat wrath with rancor meets.
But, Fortune now is in an other vaine;
Another side her turning fauour greets:
The King, heere lately lost, is now heere won;†
Still sure t'vndoe the side that he was on.

92

Warwicke, with other *Genius* then his owne,
Had heere to doe: which made him see the face
Of sad misfortune, in the selfe same Towne,
Where prosp'rous winning, lately gaue him grace:‡
And *Marg'ret* heere, this Martiall Amazon,
Was, with the spirit of her selfe, in place:
Whose labors, Fortune, euen to pittie, stir;
And, being a woman, could but giue it her.

93

The reputation and incouragement
Of *Wakefield* glory, wakened them to this.
And this seemes now the full accomplishment
Of all their trauell, all their combrances.
For, what can more disturbe this Gouernment,
When *Yorke* extinct, & *Warwick* conquered, is?

* *The 2. Battell at S. Albones.*
† *The King is againe recouered by the Queene.*
‡ *The E. of Warwick with the D. of Norffolk, put to flight, and Sir Iohn Grey slaine on the Kings side.*

Directing *Salsburie,* left without a head,
What rests there now, that all's not finished?

94

Thus, for the sicke, preseruing Nature striues
Against corruption, and the loathsome Graue;
When, out of Deaths colde hands, she backe repriues
Th'almost confounded spirits, she faine would saue:
And them cheeres vp, illightens, and reuiues;
Making faint Sickenesse, words of health to haue,
With lookes of life, as if the worst were past;
When strait come dissolution, and his last.

95

So fares it with this late reuiued Queene:
Whose Victories, thus fortunately wonne,
Haue but as onely lightning motions beene,
Before the ruine that ensu'd thereon.
For, now another springing powre is seene;
Whereto, as to the new arysing Sunne,
All turne their faces, leauing those lowe rayes
Of setting Fortune, which no Climer waighes.

96

Now is yong *March,* more than a Duke of *Yorke.*
For, youth, loue, grace and courage make him more.
All which, for Fortunes fauour, now do worke,
Who graceth freshest Actors euermore;
Making the first attempt, the chiefest worke
Of any mans designes, that striues therefore.
"The after-seasons are not so well blest.
"For, those first spirits make their first actions best.

97

Now as the *Libyan* Lion, when with paine
The wearie Hunter hath pursu'd his prey
From Rockes, to Brakes, from Thickets to the Plaine,
And at the point, thereon his hands to lay,
Hard-by his hopes, his eye vpon his gaine,
Out-rushing from his denne rapts all away:
So comes yong *March,* their endes to disappoint,
Who now were growne so neere vnto the point.

98

The loue of these important southerne parts,
Of *Essex, Surry, Middlesex,* and *Kent,*
The Queene had wholly lost; as they whose hearts
Grew ill affected to her gouernment,
Vpon th'vnciuile and presumptous parts,
Play'd by the Northerne troupes, growne insolent:
Whom, though she could not gouerne otherwise,
Yet th'ill that's wrought for her, vpon her lies.

99

So wretched is this execrable Warre,
"This ciuile Sworde: wherein, though all wee see
"Be foul, and all things miserable are;
"Yet most distresse-full is the victorie:
"Which is, not onely th'extream ruiner
"Of others; but, her owne calamity:
"Where, who obtains, what he would cannot do?
"Their powre hath part, who holpe him thereunto.

100

The Citty, whose good-will they most desire,
(Yet thereunto durst not commit their state)
Sends them not those prouisions they require;
Which seem'd restrained by the peoples hate:*
Yet *Marches* help farre off, and neere this fire
(To winne them time) forc't them to mediate
A reconcilement: which, well entertain'd,
Was fairely now growen-on, and neerely gain'd:

101

When, with a thousand tongs, swife-wing'd Fame coms,
And tells of *Marches* gallant Victories:
Who, what withstands, subdues; all ouercomes;
Making his way through fiercest enemies;
As hauing now to cast, in greater Summes,
The Reckning of his hopes, that mainly rise.
His fathers death, giues more life vnto wrath:
And vexed valour, greater courage hath.

* * The Queene, after the battaile of S. Albones, sent to the Maior of London for certaine prouisions: who willing to furnish hir therewithall, the Commons of the Cittie
stayed the same, and would not permit the carts to pass. Whereupon, the L. Mayor sent
to excuse himselfe, and to appease the displeasure of the Queene.*

102

And now, as for his last, his lab'ring worth
Works on the coast which on faire *Seuerne* lyes:
Whereto his Father (passing to the North)
Sent him, to leuie other fresh supplies:
But, hearing now what *Wakefield* had brought forth;
Imploring ayde against these iniuries,
Obtains from *Gloster, Worster, Shrewsburie,*
Important powres, to worke his remedie.

103

Which he, against *Pembrooke* and *Ormond,** bends;
Whom *Margaret* (now vpon her victory)
With all speed possible from *Wakefield* sends;
With hope to haue surpris'd him suddenly.
Wherein, though she all meanes, all wit extends,
To th'vtmost reach of wary policie;
Yet nothing her avayles: no plots succeed,
T'avert those mischiefes which the heauens decreed.

104

For, neere the Crosse ally'd vnto his name,
He crosst those mighty forces of his foes;†
And with a spirit, orday'nd for deeds of fame,
Their eager-fighting Army ouer-throwes:
Making all clear behind, from whence he came;
Bearing-downe, wholly, what before him rose;
Like to an all-confounding Torrent seemes:
And was made more, by *Warwicks* mighty streames.

105

With th'inundation of which Greatnesse, he
(Hauing no bounds of powre to keepe him backe)
Marcht to the Citie: at whose entrance free,
No signes of ioy, nor no applaudings lacke.‡

* *Iasper E. of Pēbrok, and Iames Butler E. of Ormond & Wiltshire.*

† *The battell of Mortimers cross when Owen Teuther, father to the E. of Pembrooke, who had married K Hen. mother was taken & beheaded.*

‡ *The E. of Warw. after his ouerthrow at S. Alb. retires with all the forces hee could make, and ioiness with the yong D. of York: comming to London, and receiued with all ioie, a great Councell who was presently called of the LL. spirituall and temporall: where King Henry was adiudged insufficient for the Gouernment of the Realme, and to be depriued of all regall authoritie; & the D. of Yorke elected for K. and after proclaymed by the name Edward the 4. the 4 of March, 1460. at the age of 18. And so Hen. 6. after he had raigned 38. yeares 8. moneths, was deposed.*

Whose neere approach, when this sad Queene did see,
(T'auoyde these rocks of her neere threatning wrack)
With her griev'd troupes North-ward she hence departs;
And leaues, to Youth and Fortune, these South-parts.

106

  Glory, with admiration, entring now,
Opened that easie doore to his intent,
As that there needes not long time to allow
The Right he had vnto the Gouernement;
Nor *Henries* iniuries to disauow,
Against his oath, and th'Act of Parlement.
"For, heere the speediest way he takes t'accord
Difference in law, that pleades it with the Sword.

107

  Gath'red to see his mustred Companies,
Stoode all the flocking troupes of *London* streets;
When *Faulconbridge,* with gentle feeling, tries
How strong the pulse of their affection beates;
And (reckning-vp the grieuous miseries,
And desolation, which the Country threats)
Askt them, whom they would haue to be their King,
To leade those troupes, and State in forme to bring.

108

  Whereto, with such an vniuersall showt,
The Earle of *March,* the multitude replyes,
As the rebounding Eccho streight through-out
(From Towre to Towre reuerberated) flyes
To th'eares of those great Lords, who sate about
The consultation for this enterprise.
Whose care is sav'd, which most they stood vpon:
For, what they counsell how to doe, is done.

109

  And nothing now, but to confirme him king,
Remaines (which must not long remaine) to do.
The present heate doth strait dispatch the thing,
With all those solemne rites that long thereto:
So that, what *Yorke,* with all his trauayling,
Force and intrusion, could not get vnto,

Is now thus freely layd vpon his sonne;
Who must make faire, what fowlly was begunne.

110

Whose end, attayn'd, had it here made an end
Of foule destruction, and had stay'd the bloud
Which *Towton, Exham, Tewksbury* did spend
With desp'rate hands, and deeper wounds withstood;
And that none other Crowne, brought to contend
With that of his, had made his seeme lesse good;
How had this long-afflicted Land been blest!
Our sighes had ended, and my *Muse* had rest.

111

Which now (but little past halfe her long way)
Stands trembling at the horrors that succeed;
Weary with these embroylements, faine would stay
Her farther course, vnwilling to proceed:
And, faine to see that glorious holy-day
Of Vnion, which this discord reagreed;
Knowes not as yet, what to resolue vpon;
Whether to leaue-off here, or else go-on.

The end of the seauenth Booke.

The Eightth *Booke*

THE ARGVMENT

King Edward, *Powre against King* Henry *led;*
And hath at Towton-field the victory.
From whence, King Henry *into Scotland fled:*
Where he attempts his States recouery;
Steales into England; is discouered;
Brought Prisoner to the Towre disgracefully.
And Edward, *whiles great* Warwick *doth assay*
A Match in France, marries the Lady Grey.

1

ON yet, sad Verse: though those bright starres, from whence
Thou hadst thy light, are set for euermore;
And that these times do not like grace dispense
To our indeuours, as those did before:
Yet on; since She, whose beames do reincense
This sacred fire, seemes as reseru'd in store
To raise this Worke, and here to haue my last;
Who had the first of all my labours past.

2

On (with her blessed fauour) and relate,
With what new bloud-shed, this new chosen Lord
Made his first entry to th'afflicted State,
Past his first Act of publique, with the sword,
Ingor'd his new-worne Crowne, and how he gat
Possession of affliction, and restor'd
His Right vnto a Royall miserie;
Maintained with as bloudy dignitie.

3

Shew, how our great Pharsalian Field was fought
At *Towton* in the North;* the greatest day

* *Edward beeing proclaimed, and acknowledged for King, presently sets forward towards the North, to encounter with K. Hen. 6. who in York-shire had assembled a puissant armie, of neere 60000. men, and at a place called Towton, about 4. miles from Yorke, both their powers met: where was foght the greatest battaile our stories mention, in all these ciuill wars. Where both the Armies consisted of aboue a 100000. men, & all of our own nation.*

Of ruine, that dissension euer brought
Vnto this Kingdom: where, two Crownes did sway
The worke of slaughter; two Kings Causes wrought
Destruction to one People, by the waie
Of their affections, and their loyalties;
As if one, for these ills, could not suffise.

4

Where *Lancaster* and that couragious side
(That noble constant Part) came furnished
With such a Powre, as might haue terrifi'd
And ouer-run the earth; had they been led
The way of glory, where they might haue tri'd
For th'Empire of all *Europe,* as those did
The Macedonian led into the East;
Their number being double, at the least.

5

And where braue *Yorke* comes as compleatly mand,
With courage, valour, and with equall might;
Prepar'd to trie with a resolued hand,
The metall of his Crown, and of his Right:
Attended with his fatall fier-brand
Of Warre, *Warwicke;* that blazing starre of fight,
The Comet of destruction, that portends
Confusion, and distresse, what way he tends.

6

What rage, what madness, *England,* do we see?
That this braue people, in such multitude
Run to confound themselues, and all to be
Thus mad for *Lords,* and for meere Seruitude.
What might haue been, if (Roman-like, and free)
These gallant Spirits had nobler ends pursu'd,
And strayn'd to points of glory and renowme,
For good of the Republique and their owne?

7

But, here no *Cato* with a Senate stood
For Common-wealth: nor here were any sought
T'emancipate the State, for publique good;
But onely, headlong, for their faction wrought.
Here, euery man runs-on to spend his bloud,

To get but what he had already got.
For, whether *Pompey,* or a *Cæsar* wonne,
Their state was euer sure to be all one.

8

And, first, before these fatall Armies met,
Had forward *Warwicke* lay'd the passage free,
At *Ferry Brigges:** where the Lord *Clifford* (set
With an aduentrous gallant companie
To guard that streight, *Yorkes* farther march to let)
Began the Scene to this great Tragedie;
Made the first entrance on the Stage of blood:
Which now, set wide for wounds, all open stood.

9

When, *Edward* to exhort his men began,
With words, whereto both spirit and Maiestie
His pers'nage gaue; for-that he was a man
(Besides a King) whose Crowne sate gracefully:
Com'n is the day, sayd he, wherein who can
Obtaine the best, is Best: this day must try
Who hath the wrong, and whence our ills haue beene:
And tis our swords must make vs honest men.

10

For though our Cause, by God and men allow'd,
Hath in it honor, right, and honestie:
Yet all, as nothing, is to be avow'd,
Vnless withall, we haue the victorie.
For, Iustice is (we see) a virtue proud,
And leanes to powre, and leaues weake miserie.
And therefore, seeing the case we now stand in,
We must resolue either to dy or winne.

11

So that if any here doth finde his heart
To fayle him, for this noble worke, or stands
Irresolute this day; let him depart,
And leaue his Armes behind, for worthier hands.
I knowe, enow will stay to doo their part,
Here to redeeme themselues, wiues, children, landes,

* *The L. Clifford slaine at Ferry Briggs.*

And haue the glory that thereby shall rise,
To free their Country from these miseries.

12

But here, what needed wordes to blowe the fire
In flame already, and inkindled so
As when it was proclaym'd, they might retire
Who found vnwillingnes to vnder-goe
That ventrous worke; they all did so conspire
To stand out Fortune, that not one would goe,
To beare away a hand from bloud; not one
Defraud the Field of th'euill might be done.

13

Where *Warwicke* too (producing, in their sight,
An argument, whereby he did conclude
There was no hope of safetie, but by fight)
Doth sacrifize his horse, to Fortitude:*
And thereby did the least conceipt of flight,
Or any succour, by escape, exclude;
"Se'ing, in the streight of a necessitie,
"The meanes to win, is t'haue no meanes to flye.

14

It was vpon the twi-light of that day
(That peacefull day) when the Religious beare
The Oliue-branches as they go to pray,
(And we, in lieu, the blooming Palme vse here)
When both the Armies, ready in array
For th'early sacrifize of blood, appeare
Prepar'd for mischiefe, ere they had full light
To see to doo it, and to doo it right.

15

Th'aduantage of the time, and of the winde
(Which, both, with *Yorke* seeme as retayn'd in pay)
Braue *Faulconbridge*† takes hold-on, and assign'd
The Archers their flight-shafts to shoote away:
Which, th'aduerse side (with sleet and dimnesse, blinde,
Mistaken in the distance of the way)

* *The E. of Warwike, before the Battayle began, with his own hands killed his horse.*
† *William Neuile, L. Faulconbridge, after created E. of Kent.*

Aunswere with their sheafe-arrowes; that came short
Of their intended ayme, and did no hurt.

16

But, gath'red by th'on-marching Enemy,
Returned were, like clowdes of steele; which powre
Destruction downe, and did new-night the sky;
As if the Day had fayl'd to keepe his howre.
Whereat, the ranged horse breake-out, deny
Obedience to the Riders, scorne their powre,
Disrank the troupes, set all in disarray,
To make th'Assaylant owner of the day.

17

Thus, thou peculiar Ingine of our Land
(Weapon of Conquest, Maister of the Field)
Renowmed Boaw (that mad'st this Crowne command
The towres of *Fraunce,* and all their powres to yeeld)
Art made at home to haue th'especiall hand
In our dissensions, by thy worke vp-held:
Thou first didst conquer vs; then rays'd our skill
To vanquish others; here our selues to spill.

18

And now how com'st thou to be out of date,
And all neglected leav'st vs, and art gone?
And with thee, th'ancient strength, the manly state
Of valor, and of worth, that glory wonne?
Or else stay'st thou, till new-priz'd shot abate?
(That neuer shall affect what thou hast don)
And onely but attend'st some blessed Raigne,
When thou and Virtue shalt be grac't againe.

19

But, this sharp tempest draue *Northumberland,*
(Who led the vant-guard of king *Henries* side)
With eger heat ioine battaile, out of hand;
And this disorder, with their swords to hide.
Where, twice fiue howres, these furious armies stand;
And Fortunes Ballance weigh'd on neither side;

Nor either did but equall bloud-shed gayne,
Till *Henries* chiefest leaders all were slaine.*

20

Then, lo, those spirits, which from these heads deriue
Their motions, gaue off working; and, in haste,
Turne all their backs to Death, and mainely striue
Who from themselues shall run-away most fast.
The after-flyers on the former driue:
And they againe, by the pursuers chac't,
Make bridges of their fellowes backs, to pass
The Brooks and Riuers, where-as danger was.

21

Witnes O cleare-stream'd *Cock:* within whose banks,
So many thousand, crawling, helpless lay,
With wounds and wearinesse;† who, in their rankes,
Had valiantly behav'd themselues that daie:
And might haue had more honour, and more thankes
By standing to their worke, and by their stay.
"But men, at once, life seeme to loue and loath;
"Running to lose it, and to saue it both.

22

Vnhappy *Henrie,* from a little Hill,
Plac't not far off (whence he might view the fight)
Had all th'intire full prospect of this ill,
With all the scattered slaughter, in his sight:
Saw how the victor rag'd, and spoil'd at wil,
And left not off when all was in his might:
Saw, with how great adoo himselfe was wonne;
And with what store of blood Kings are vndone.

23

We are not worth so much, nor I, nor he,
As hath beene spent for vs, by you this day,
Deare people, said he: therefore, O, agree,

* In this battaile of Towton on K. Hen. side, were slaine Hen Percy E. of North. the
EE. of Shrewsbury and Deuonshire. Iohn L. Clifford, the LL. Bewmond, Neuile,
Willouhby, Wells, Roos, Grey, Dacres, Fitz-hugh, Molineux, Beckingham: Knights, the 2.
base sons of Hen. Holland D. of Excester, Richard Percie, Geruase Clifton, Andrew
Trollop. &c.
† The whole number slaine were accompted, by some, 33000. by others, 35091.

And leaue off mischiefe, and your malice stay.
Stay, *Edward*, stay. They must a People bee,
When we shall not be Kings: and it is they,
Who make vs with their miseries. Spare them,
For whom thou thus dost seeke a Diadem.

24

For me, I could be pleas'd t'haue nought to doe
With Fortune; and content, my selfe were ill,
So *England* might be well; and that t'vndoe
Me, might suffice the sword, without more ill.
And yet perhaps, these men, that cleaue vnto
The parts of Princes, with such eger will,
Haue likewise their owne ends, of gaine or hate,
In these our strifes, and nourish this debate.

25

Thus stood he (drawing lines of his discourse)
In contemplation;* when, more needfully,
It did import him to deuise a course,
How he might shift for his recouery:
And had beene taken had not some by force,
Rescu'd, and drawne him off, more speedilie;
And brought him vnto *Yorke,* in all maine poste:
Where he first told his Queen, the daie was lost.

26

Who, as compos'd of that firme temp'rature
Which could not bend to base complaynts, nor wayle
As weakenes doth (fore-knowing how t'indure)
Fayl'd not her selfe, though Fortune did her fayle;
But, rather casts-about how to procure
Meanes to reserue her part, and to preuaile
Of that poore time, left her to saue her owne;
As one though ouer-come, not ouer-throwne:

27

Now, when she had of fatall *Lancaster*
Seene all the pillars crusht and ruined,
That vnder-set it; all that followed her

---

* *Queen Margaret with her sonn were in the City of Yorke, expecting the euent of*
this Battaile.

Of those heroicke personages, dead,
Saue onely *Sommerset,* and *Excester*
(Who from this last destruction hardly fled)
And saw all lost, and nothing in her might,
But onely that which must be sav'd by flight:

28

Now, when there was no North left, of their owne,
To draw vnto; no side, to gather head;
No people to be rays'd, t'an emptie Crowne;
Nor yet the ground their owne, whereon they tread.
Nor yet your faith (worthy of all renowne)
Constant *Northumbrians,* firme continued:
And, though you could not render succors fit
Vnto your Sov'raigne, you would saue him yet;

29

And be (as few men, in this world, are) true
Vnto affliction, and to miserie:
And would not basely purchace and renew
Your peace, and safetie, by disloyaltie:
But wrought, that though the Victor did pursue,
With greedy care and egre industrie,
To haue surpriz'd him; yet was all in vanie,
Till he recouered *Berwicke,* with his Traine.

30

Where now, he was at some more vacancie
To vnderstand, and see himselfe vndone:
Which, in this sodaine-comming misery,
He had no leasure to consider-on.
And now suruaies he that poore company,
Attending on himselfe, his wife, and sonne;
Sees how that all the State, which serv'd his Crowne,
Was shut within the walls of one small towne:

31

Beholds there, what a poore distressed thing,
A King without a people was; and whence
The glory of that Mightinesse doth spring,
That ouer-spreds (with such a reuerence)
This vnder-world: whence comes this furnishing

And all this splendor of Magnificence:
He sees, what chayre so-euer Monarch sate
Vpon, on Earth, the People was the State.

32

And yet, although he did contayne no more
Then what he saw; yet saw a peece so small
Could not containe him. What he was before,
Made him vncapable of any wall,
To yeeld him succour now: he must haue more,
Then onely this small Holde, or none at all.
And therefore, this (se'ing it auayl'd him not,
Nor could he keepe) he renders to the Scot;*

33

As th'Earnest, to confirme and ratifie
The league betweene them two, newly begun.
Whereof to make more sure and faster tye,
He promist, too, th'alliance of his sonne:
And all that might secure their amity,
With willingnesse, on either side was done.
And heere they practise, all they can deuise,
To turne reuenge vpon their Enemyes.

34

Thus, *England,* didst thou see the mightiest King
Thou euer hadst (in Power and Maiesty
Of State, and of Dominions: gouerning
A most magnificent Nobility;
With an aduent'rous people, flourishing
In all the glories of felicitie)
Chac't from his kingdom, forc't to seeke redresse
In parts remote, distrest and succourlesse.

35

Now *Bullingbrook,* these miseries, heere showne,
Doo much vnlode thy sinne; make thy ill, good.
For, if thou didst by wrong, attaine the Crowne,
T'was without cryes; it cost but little bloud:
But, *Yorke,* by his attempt hath ouer-throwne

* Hen. 6 deliuers the towne of Berwicke to the K. of Scots.

All the best glorie wherein *England* stood;
And did his state by her vndooing winne:
And was, though white without, yet red within.

36

And thus he hath it: and is now to deale
For th'intertaining and continuance
Of mens affections; and to seeke to heale
Those foul corruptions, which the maintenance
Of so long wars bred in the Common-weale.
He must remunerate, prefer, aduance,
His chiefest friendes; and prosecute, with might,
The aduerse part; doo wrong, to doo men right:

37

Whil'st Martiall *Margaret,* with her hopefull Sonne,
Is trauailing in *France* to purchase ayde;
And plots, and toiles, and nothing leaues vndone;
Though all in vaine. For, being thus ouer-layd
By Fortune and the Time, all that is done
Is out of season. For she must haue stay'd
Till that first heate of mens affections (which
They beare new Kings) were laid, and not so much.

38

When they should finde, that they had gayn'd no more,
Then th'Asse, by changing of his Maisters, did;
(Who still must labour as he vs'd before)
And those expectancies came frustrated,
Which they had set vpon th'imagin'd score,
Of their accounts; and had considered,
How that it did but little benefite
The Doues; To change the Falcon, for the Kite.

39

And yet braue Queene, for three yeares of his Raigne,
Thou gau'st him little breathing time of rest;
But still his miseries didst entertaine
With new attempts, and new assaults addrest:
And, at thy now-returne from *France* againe,
(Suppli'd with forces) once more gatheredst

An Army for the Field, and brought'st, to warre,
The scattered parts of broken *Lancaster*.*

40

And once againe, at *Exham*, ledst them on
With Scots, and French t'another bloody day;
And there beheldst thy selfe againe vndone,
With all that Rest, whereon thy fortunes lay.
Where, *Somerset* (late to King *Edward* gone,
And got his pardon) hauing scap't away,
With noble *Percie*, came to bring their blood
Vnto thy side, whereto they first had stood.

41

Where, the Lords, *Molines, Rosse,* and *Hungerford*,
With many else of noble Families,
Extinguisht were; and many that daies sword
Cut-off their names, in their posterities.
Where fled, againe, their lucklesse followed Lord;
And is so neere pursu'd by th'enemies,
As th'Ensigne of his Crowne was seiz'd vpon,
For him who had before his Kingdome wonne;

42

And shortly after, too, his person gat.
For, he, now wearied with his long exile,
And miseries abrode, grew passionate,
With longing to returne t'his natiue soyle.
And se'ing he could not do the same, in State;
He seekes, disguis'd in fashion, to beguile
The world a time, and steale the libertie
And sight of his deare Country, pruiately:

43

As if there were, for a pursued King,
A couert left on earth, wherein to hide;
When Powre and Iealousie are trauailing,

* *Queene Margaret, furnished with a great power of Scots and French, to the number of 20000, with her husband entred into Northumberland, took the Castle of Bambrough and after came forward to the Bishoprick of Durham. Wher Hen. Bewfort D. of Somerset who had lately beene reconciled to K. Ed. 4. ioined with them, and also brought thither with him Sir Ralph Percie, a man of great courage & worth: who were taken in the battaile of Exham, and executed in An. 3. Ed. 4. 1464.*

And lay to catch affliction, on each side.
Misfortune serues, we see, for euery thing.
And soon he comes, God knows, to be descry'd:
And *Edward* hath the booty he desir'd:*
For whose establishment, all things conspir'd.

44

Yet, long it was not, ere a fire began
To take, in th'inwardst Closet, where he lay'd
The treasure of his chiefest trust; and ran
From thence, through al his State, before it staid.
For, be'ing a King, who his whole fortunes wan
With others handes, must many leaue vnpay'd:
And could not fill vp that vast greedinesse
Of Expectation, which is bottomlesse:

45

Though he did all the best that in him lay
(As a most actiue Prince) to satisfie
The int'rest of their trauayles, and defray
The bands contracted twixt his soueraignty
And the Republick: seeking to allay
All greeuances; re-order equity;
Reform the Barres, that Iustice did abuse;†
Lay easie on the State, as new Kings vse.

46

As he, who, hauing found great Treasury,
The first yeare offers, with most gratefull cheere,
A sheepe of gold, to *Iunoes* deïty;
And next, of siluer, for the second yeare;
The third, of brasse; and then, neglectiuely,
Nothing at all: So those respects, which were
Borne of a present feeling, mov'd him most;
But soon were with their times and motiues lost.

47

And, what his bounty could not recompense,
He payes with honors, and with dignities.

---

* *King Hen. was taken in Lancashire, and brought to London, with his legs bound to the Stirops, hauing, in his company, onlie Doctor Manning, Deane of Windzor, with another Diuine: who were taken with him and committed to the Tower.*

† *K. Ed. 4. sate on the Kings Bench, in open Court, 3 daies together, in Michaelmas Terme An. 2. of his raigne, to vnderstand how his lawes were executed.*

And (more to angle the beneuolence,
And catch the loue of men, with curtesies)
He oft would make his dignity dispense
With his too lowe familiarities;
Descending, from his Sphere of Maiesty,
Beneath himselfe, very submissiuely.

48

And when he had dispos'd, in some good traine,
His home affaires; he counsells how t'aduance
His forraine correspondence, with the chaine
Of some alliance that might countenance
His Greatnesse, and his quiet intertaine.
Which was thought fittest with some match, of *France;*
To hold that Kingdome, from subayding such
Who else could not subsist, nor hope so much.

49

Nor was it now a time to haue contrast
With any forrain mighty Potentate;
But keep the outer doores of each side fast,
Hauing so much to doo within his State.
And, therevpon, was *Warwicke* (by whose cast
All must be wrought) imploy'd to mediate
A present Marriage, to be had betweene
Him, and the sister of the yong French Queene.*

50

Which was not long, nor hard to bring to passe
Where like respects met in a point alike.
So that the same as euen concluded was,
And all as done; Lady and friends all like:
When Loue, the Lord of Kings (by whom must passe
This Act of our Affections) tooke dislike
That he was not made priuy thereunto;
And therefore, in his wrath, would all vndoe.

* *The Earle of Warwicke was sent into France to treat of a mariage between King
Edward and the Ladie Bona, daughter to Loyse D. of Sauoy, and sister to the La. Carlote
Queene of France: which was there agreed vpon; and Monsieur Damp Martin with
others appointed to be sent into Eng. for the full accomplishing thereof.*

51

For, whiles this youthfull Prince, at his disport
In *Grafton* woods, retyr'd from publick care,
Attending how his sute in *France* did sorte
(Whereon his cogitations onely were)
He comes, at home, surpris'd in other sort;
A neerer fire inflam'd his passions heere;
An English Beautie, with more worth indu'd
Then *France* could yeeld, his royall heart subdu'd.*

52

A wofull widdow, whom his quarrell had
(As it had many moe) made desolate,
Came to his Court, in mournfull habit clad,
To sue for Iustice, to relieue her state.
And entring as a suppliant all sad;
With gracefull sorrow, and a comely gate
She past the Presence: where, all eyes were cast
On her more stately presence, as she past.

53

Her lookes, not let-abrode (but carefully
Kept in, restraind) held their reseruednesse:
Obseruing none but her owne dignity,
And his, to whom she did her selfe addresse.
And, drawing neere his royall Maiesty,
A blush of reuerence, not bashfulnesse,
Lightned her louely cheeks, and downe she kneeles;
Giues her Petition, for the wrongs she feeles.

54

And, in deliv'ring it, lifts vp her eyes
(The mouingst Mediatours shee could bring)
And strait withdrawes them, in submissiue wise;
Not fixing them directly on the King:
Who, mov'd with her sweet fashion, bade her rise,
With gentle language full of comforting;
Read her request: but thought not what he read.
The lines, hee view'd, her eyes had figured.

* *But in the mean time, (the first of May) the K. maried the La. Elizabeth Grey,*
daughter to the Dutchess of Bedford, late wife to Sir Iohn Grey slaine at S. Albones on
King Henries part.

55

Then paus'd a while, and mus'd; as if he weigh'd
The substance of her sute. The which, God wote,
Was not the thing he mus'd. And, hauing stay'd,
Seem'd to read on againe; but yet reades not:
And still a stealing side-cast looke conuai'd
On her sweet face; as if he had forgot
To be else-where, then where he did behold:
And thought not what he did; but what he would.

56

But, least his sodaine passion might haue, there,
More witnesses then he would wish to haue;
He tooke vp his desires, which posting were
Beyond their stages; and this answere gaue:
Madam, we will our selfe take time to heare
Your Cause at large: wherein we wil you haue
No other reference, but repaire to vs:
Who will accommodate this businesse.

57

She, that expected present remedie
(Hearing this dilatory answer) thought,
The King found scruple in the equitie
Of her request; and thereupon he sought
To put her to delayes of Court, whereby
She might be tyr'd and in the end get nought.
And that, which her opinion made more strong,
Was that he studied, and was mute, so long.

58

Which forc't from her these wordes: My Lord,
Let not my being a *Lancastrian* bred
Without mine owne election, disafford
Me right, or make my Cause disfigured;
Since I am now the subiect of your sword:
Which God hath (with your Right) established,
To doo vs right: and let not what wee were,
Be now the cause to hurt vs as we are.

59

Ladie, mistake me not: neuer did I
Make war with women, nor vs'd womens war,

Reuenge; but prosecuted honestly
My Right, not Men. My quarrels ended are,
With my obtayning of the victorie.
And (Lady) knowe, your Cause mouses me thus far,
As you shall finde, sayd hee, I doo desire
To doo you greater right then you require.

60

   With this, they part; both, with their thoughts full charg'd:
She, of her sute in hand; and he of her:
Wherein, he spends that night, and quite discharg'd
All other cogitations; to confer,
First, how he might haue her estate inlarg'd:
Then, in what sort her seruice to prefer
Vnto his new exspected Wife and Queene:
Then, how to maske his loue, from being seene.

61

   For, yet, Lust was not growne to that degree
To haue no limits; but that shame kept-in
The greatest Greatnes, from this being free
To hold their Wantonness to be no sinne.
For, though Kings cannot ouer-maistred bee,
They will be ouer-lookt, and seene within:
And, though they could their weaknesses make sure;
Yet crymes, though safe, can neuer be secure.

62

   Sometimes, he thinks it better to prouide
A place retyr'd, and haue her from the Court:
And then, with what pretentions he might hide
His priuat comming, and his oft resort:
Then, by his Queene, if it should be espi'd,
How he might cleare with her, and stop report.
And thus consumes the night: and if hee slept,
He slept those thoughts that with these passions kept.

63

   The morning being com'n (and glad he was
That it was com'n) after so long a night
He thought would haue no morning (time did passe

So slowe, and his desires ran-on so light)
A messenger with speed dispatched was,
Of speciall trust, this Lady to inuite
To come t'his presence; though before the time
That Ladies rise: who rarely rise betime.

64

Yet soone shee hastes: and yet that soone seem'd long,
To him whose longing went so swift a pase:
And frets, that such attyring should belong
To that which yeelds it selfe sufficient grace;
Consid'ring how these ornaments may wrong
The set of beautie: which, we see, doth grace
Th'attire it weares, and is not grac't thereby;
As be'ing that onely, which doth take the eye.

65

But now, be'ing com'n, that quarrell of delay
Streight ended was: her presence satisfies
All, what Expectance had layd out for stay:
And he beheld more sweetnesse in her eyes,
And saw her more then she was yesterday:
A cheerliness did with her hopes arise,
That lamped cleerer then it did before,
And made her spirit, and his affections, more.

66

When, those who were about him, presently
Vayded the roome, and left him to confer
Alone with his faire Suter priuatly
(As they who to his courses conscious were)
And he began: Madame, the remedie
Which you (in your Petition) sue-for here,
Shall be allow'd to th' vtmost that you craue,
With th'expedition you would wish to haue.

67

And here I haue another sute to you:
Which if you please to grant, wee both shall now
Rest equally content. Wherewith, there grew
That sodaine alteration in her brow,

As all were ouer-cast; and so with-drew
That freedome from her lookes (least they should 'low
More then her heart might meane) as they reflect
A narrower and a carefuller aspect.

68

That when he saw this barrier of dislike
Thus inter-set, to keepe his forwardnes
Backe from presumptiue pressing; it did strike
That reuerence, as it staide him to expresse
His farther will. And she replies: 'Tis like,
When Kings to subiects sue, they meane no less
Then to command; nor must they be withstood;
For-that good Kings will seeke but what is good.

69

And, in that faire respect, your Maiestie,
According to your will, both must and may
Command my seruice; most reuerently
Your royall pleasure euer shall obey.
With which word, *pleasure* (though it doubtfully
In that hard fastnesse of condition lay,
Vnder the locke of goodnesse) he was cast
In hope, he might obtaine the same at last.

70

And thus reioynes; My pleasure only shall
Be, Madame, for your good; please it but you
To make it so. And, here to tell you all,
I loue you; and therein I tell you true.
What honour may by Kings affections fall,
Must light vpon your fortunes, as your due.
And though *France* shall a Wife, for fashion, bring:
You must be th'onely mistress of the King.

71

Streight might you see, how Scorne, and Feare, & Shame
(All intermixt in one aspect) returne
The message of her thoughts, before words came.
And first, within her brow, in state sate Scorne;
Shame in her Cheekes; where also Feare became
An In-mate too; and both appeare, by turne:

Blushes did paleness, paleness blushes chace;
As scorning, fearing, shaming such disgrace.

72

She scornes to be addeem'd so worthlesse-base
As to bee mov'd to such an infamie.
She shames to thinke, that ought, within her face,
Should breed th'opinion of immodestie.
Shee feares the fatall daunger of the place,
Her 'loneness, and the powre of Maiestie:
And so (confus'd) in feare, in shame, in scorne,
This Aunswere to his Motion doth returne:

73

My sov'raigne Lord, it grieues me that you deeme,
Because I in this sort for Iustice sue,
I would the same with mine owne wrong redeeme,
And by dishonour reobtaine my due:
No: I would hate that right, which should but seeme
To be beholding to a wanton view
Or motiue of my person, not my Cause;
That craues but right, from Iustice, and your lawes.

74

And knowe, great Monarch, that I more doo waigh
My Distaffe with mine honour, then I doo
The mightiest Scepter, King did euer sway
Vpon the earth, or Nations bow'd vnto.
I owe subiection; which I humbly pay,
With all the outward seruice I can doo:
But, Sov'raigne, in the region of my hart
I raigne sole Queene; no King can force a part.

75

Here, Feare a little interpos'd a touch,
To warne her violence to temporize
With Powre, and State: and she concludes her speach,
With crauing pardon in more humble wise;
Yet, in proud humble wise: which shew'd, how much
She did her honor aboue Greatnes prize.
And so, being full of what she did conceiue,
Desires to be dismist, and takes her leaue.

76

Here, *Mary Pembrooke* (by whose generous brow
And noble graces, I delineat
These shapes of others virtues) could I showe
In what a desperat and confus'd estate
She left this disappointed King; and how
Loue and Ambition in their glory sate,
And tyranniz'd on his diuided hart,
Warring each other with a powrefull part.

77

How first, Loue vnderneath his Colours brought
The strength of all her gracefull worthinesse;
And sets them in th'aduantage of his thought,
Vpon the side of Youth and Wantonnesse:
Then how Ambition, that for glory wrought,
Comes with his State, his Crowne, and Powrfulnes,
And plants her on the side of prouidence,
To beat vnfit Affections off from thence.

78

But, I must ouer-goe these passages;
And hasten-on my way, to ouer-take
Mine endes, in sad and grauer businesses;
Whereof I shall to you relation make:
And yet my zeale here forc't mee thus t'expresse
Elizabeth, for our *Elizaes* sake;
Who grac't the *Muses* (which her Times became):
For, they who giue them comfort, must haue fame.

79

And I must tell you now, when this great fight
Of counter-passions had beene throughly try'd,
How in the ende the victorie did light
Vpon Loues forces, as the stronger side;
And beat downe those respects of benefite,
Of honor, greatnes, strength, and all beside;
And neuer graunted rest vnto his strife,
Till mariage rites had her confirm'd his wife.

80

Which, that place, where he saw her first, saw donne,
Ere he remov'd his foot: for, Loue is stil

In haste, and (as a Lord, that rules alone)
Admittes no Counseller, in good nor ill.
For, He and Kings gladly giue eare to none,
But such as smooth their wayes, and sooth their will.
And who will not desire to giue his voyce
(Be what it will) to prayse a Princes choyce?

81

Which was (indeed) in virtue, beautie, grace,
And all but fortune, worthy of his bed:
And in that too, had hee but liv'd the space
T'haue seene her plentious issue fully bred;
That they might haue collated strength and grace
On her weake side: which (scornd and maliced)
Lay-open vndefenc't, apt to b'vndon
By proud vsurping Powre, when he was gon.

82

But now, when fame of this home-chosen Match
Arriu'd in *France* (for there it did arriue,
Ere they could heere attend to make dispatch
T'impart the same to *Warwick,* or contriue
Some colour that in any sort might fetch
Him fayrely off, and no dishonor giue)
It so much stird the humors in those parts,
As marr'd the whole complexion of their hearts.

83

The *French* King scornes such an indignity.
Warwick disdaines imployment in this case.
The Queene (inrag'd) with extreame vehemency,
Stormes at her sisters and her owne disgrace.
The Lady *Bona* takes most tenderly
To be so mockt, with hope of such a Place:
And all blame *Warwick,* and his fraud condem;
Whil'st he himselfe, deceiu'd suffers with them:

84

And could not (by all meanes might be deuiz'd)
Vntaste them of this violent disgust;
But that they still held, something lay disguis'd
Vnder this treaty. So that now he must

Bring-home his reputation cauteris'd
With th'idle marke of seruing others lust
In friuolous imployments, or be sent
Out of the way to colour some intent.

85

"Which, to himselfe, made him, with griefe inueigh
"Against distemp'red kings: who often are
"Ill warrants for their owne affaires; and waigh
"Their lusts, more then their dignity, by far:
"And what a miserie they haue that sway
"Their great designes; what danger, and what care;
"And often must be forc't, be'ing at their becks,
"To crack their reputation, or their necks.

86

"How their high fauours like as fig-trees are,
"That growe vpon the sides of rocks; where they
"Who reach their fruit, aduenture must so far
"As t'hazard their deep down-fall and decay.
"Their grace, not fixt; but, as a blazing star
"Burnes out the present matter, and away:
"And how the world could too wel witnesse beare,
"That both their loues and hates like dangerous were.

87

Thus he complaynes, and makes his home-retire;
All disappointed of his purposes.
For, hoping, by this Match, to hold intire
That Lady, with her great alliances;
And haue the King more firm to his desire,
By managing of both their bus'nesses;
He, by this Match (thus made without his mean)
Comes barr'd from al those tying int'rests cleane.

88

For, well he knew, that all his seruice past
Was past; and would not be a future tye
To hold him in, vnlesse that he could cast
To introduce some neere necessity
Of his imployment, that were like to last,
And shut-out all other concurrency.

Without which, nor his Greatnes, nor his Wits,
Could ward him from the Kings vnconstant fits.

89

Which more perplext him, and in neerer sort,
Then what *France* might by his ambassage ghesse,
Or *England* deeme. But, being arriu'd at Cort,
He drawes a Trauerse 'twixt his greeuances;
Lookes like the time: his eye made not report
Of what he felt within: nor was he lesse
Then vsually he was, in euery part;
Wore a cleere face, vpon a clowdy hart:

90

Congratulates the Queene; commends the King
For his rare choice; protesting her to be
Far beyond all, the world beside could bring
To fit his liking; and that he did see
The Lady *Bona* was a peeuish thing,
Sullayne, and proud; and would in no degree
Haue pleas'd his humor, or in any sort
Haue satisfi'd the Ladies of this Cort.

91

And, after hauing finisht all the rite
Of complement and interuisiting;
He humbly craues dismission that he might
Retire a while, t'attend the managing
And setting of his country-bus'nesse right;
Whereby the better to attend the King:
From whom he parts; and neuer seem'd more deere,
More grac't, nor yet himselfe of fre'er cheere.

92

First, *Warwicke*-Castle (that had seldome knowne
The Maister there) he visits; and from thence
Goes t'other goodly Mannours of his owne.
Where, seene with ioy, with loue, with reuerence;
(King of him selfe,) he findes that there is show'n
The vse of life, the true magnificence,
T'inioy his Greatnesse: which, at Corte, in vaine
Men toyle-for, and yet neuer doo attaine.

93

Which, his religious Confessor (who best
Could cast, with what a violent accesse,
This feuer of Ambition did molest
His still-sick minde) takes hold-on; to addresse
(Vpon th'aduantage of this little rest)
Some lenitiues, t'allay the firynesse
Of this disease; which (as a maladie,
Seiz'd in the Spirits) hath seldom remedy.

94

"And thus sets on him: See, my Lord, how heere
"Th'eternall Prouidence of God hath brought
"You to the Shore of safetie (out of feare)
"From all the waues of misery, that wrought
"To ouer-whelm you; and hath set you cleare,
"Where you would bee; with hauing (which you sought
"Through all these hazards of distresse) a King
"Of your owne making and establishing.

95

"And now, my Lord, I trust you will sit downe,
"And rest you, after all this passed thrall,
"And be your selfe (a Prince within your owne)
"Without aduent'ring any more at all
"Your state in others Bottomes; hauing knowne
"The dangers that on mighty Actors fall;
"Since, in the foot of your accompts, your gaynes
"Come-short to make euen reck'ning with your paines.

96

"Inioy now what you wrought-for, in this sort
"(If great-mens Endes be to enioy their Endes)
"And knowe, the happiest powre, the greatest port,
"Is onely that which on it selfe depends.
"Heere haue you State inough to be a Cort
"Vnto your selfe; here, where the world attends
"On you, not you on it, obserued sole:
"You, else-where but a part, are heere the whole.

97

"Th'aduantages of Princes, are (we see)
"But things conceiu'd imaginarily.

"For, euery state of fortune, in degree,
"Some image hath of principalitie:
"Which they inioy more naturall and free,
"Then can great Powers, chain'd with observancie,
"And with the fetters of respect still ty'd;
"Being easier far to follow then to guide.

98

"And what are Corts, but Camps of misery?
"That doo besiege mens states, and still are prest
"T'assaile, prevent, complot, and fortifie;
"In hope t'attaine, in feare to be supprest:
"Where, all with shewes, and with apparancie,
"Men seeme, as if for stratagems addrest:
"Where, Fortune, as the Woolfe, doth still prefer
"The fowlest of the traine that followes her.

99

"And where, fayres hopes are lay'd (as ambushments)
"To intercept your life, and to betray
"Your liberty to such intanglements,
"As you shal neuer-more get cleare away:
"Where, both th'ingagements of your owne intents,
"And others recknings, and accounts, shall lay
"Such waights vpon you, as you shal not part,
"Vnlesse you breake your credit, or your heart.

100

"Besides: as exiles, euer from your homes
"You liue perpetuall in disturbancy;
"Contending, thrusting, shuffling for your roomes
"Of ease or honor, with impatiency:
"Building your fortunes, vpon others tombes,
"For other then your owne posterity.
"You see, Corts few aduance; many vndoo:
"And those they do aduance, they ruine too.

101

"And therefore now, my Lord, since you are heere,
"Where you may haue your rest with dignitie;
"Worke that you may continue so: and cleare
"Your selfe, from out these streights of misery.

"Hold your estate and life, as things more deare
"Then to be throwne at an vncertainty.
"Tis time, that you and *England* haue a calme;
"And time, the Oliue stood aboue the Palme.

102

    Thus the good Father, with an humble thought
(Bred in a Cellularie lowe retyre)
According to his quiet humor, sought
T'auert him from his turbulent desire;
"When the great Earle began: Father, I note
"What you with zeale aduise, with loue require:
"And I must thanke you, for this care you haue,
"And for those good aduertisements you gaue.

103

    "And truely, Father, could I but get free
"(Without being rent) and hold my dignitie;
"That Sheep-cot, which in yonder vale you see
"(Beset with Groues, and those sweet Springs hard-by)
"I rather would my Palace wish to bee,
"Then any roofe, of proudest Maiestie:
"But, that I cannot dooe; I haue my part:
"And I must liue, in one house, with my hart.

104

    "I knowe, that I am fixt vnto a Sphere
"That is ordayn'd to moue. It is the place
"My fate appoints me; and the region where
"I must, what-euer happens, there, imbrace.
"Disturbance, trauaile, labor, hope and feare,
"Are of that Clime, ingendred in that place.
"And action best, I see, becomes the Best.
"The Starres, that haue most glorie, haue no rest.

105

    "Besides: it were a Cowards part, to fly
"Now from my Holde, that haue held out so well;
"It be'ing the Station of my life, where I
"Am set to serue, and stand as Sentinell:
"And must, of force, make good the place, or dy,
"When Fate and Fortune (those great States) compell.

"And then, we Lords in such case euer are,
"As peace can cut our throats as well as war.

106

"And hath her griefes, and her incombrances:
"And doth with idle rest, deforme vs more
"Then any *Magha* can, or sorceresse,
"With basely wasting all the Martiall store
"Of heat and spirit (which graceth Manlinesse)
"And makes vs still false images adore:
"Besides profusion of our faculties,
"In grosse dull glutt'ny, vap'rous gourmandise.

107

"And therefore since I am the man I am,
"I must not giue a foote, least I giue all.
"Nor is this Bird within my breast so tame,
"As to be fed at hand, and mockt with-all.
"I rather would my state were out of frame,
"Then my renowne should come to get a fall.
"No, no: th'vngratefull boy shall neuer think,
"That I, who him inlarg'd to powre, will shrink.

108

"What is our life, without our dignitie?
"Which oft, we see, comes lesse by liuing long.
"Who euer was there worth the memorie,
"And eminent indeed, but still dy'd young?
"As if worth had agreed with destinie,
"That time, which rightes them, should not doo thē wrong
"Besides; Old-age doth giue, by too long space,
"Our soules as many wrinkles as our face.

109

"And as for my inheritance and state
"(What euer happen) I wil so prouide
"That Law shall, with what strength it hath, collate
"The same on mine, and those to mine ally'd:
"Although I knowe, she serues a present State,
"And can vndoo againe what shee hath ty'd.
"But, that we leaue to him, who poynts-out heyres:
"And howsoeuer, yet the world is theirs.

110

"Where, they must worke it out; as borne to run
"Those Fortunes, which as mightie Families
"(As euer they could be) before haue donne.
"Nor shall they gaine, by mine indignities,
"Who may without my courses be vndonne.
"And who-so makes his State, and life, his tyes
"To doo vnworthily, is borne a slaue:
"And let him with that brand go to his Graue.

111

Here, would the reuerent Father haue reply'd,
That it were far more Magnanimitie,
T'indure, then to resist: that we are ty'd
As well to beare the inconueniencie
And straynes of Kings and States; as to abide
Vntimely raynes, tempests, sterilitie,
And other ills of Nature that befall:
Which we, of force, must be content withall:

112

But that a speedy messenger was sent
To shewe, the D. of *Clarence* was hard-by.
And, thereupon, *Warwicke* breakes-off, and went
(With all his traine attending formally)
To intertaine him, with fit complement;
As, glad of such an opportunitie
To worke vpon, for those high purposes
He had conceiv'd in discontentednes.

The ende of the eightth Booke.

Variants

BOOK I

Head-title: THE ARGVMENT OF THE FIRST BOOKE. 95, 01   [The
ciuile warrs ⌐/ betweene the hou=/ses of york & / Lanaster [*sic*] MS
Argument: MS om.

1.8   whil'st 95   right MS, 95   throwen 95
2.1   thee / you
  2   Deare people too too . . . Blood?
  4   thy / your   stood;
  5   might you . . . woe MS   [woe? 95, 01
  6   you . . . your Nephewes good,
  7   Yours
  8   The *Perenei,* and *Alps, Aquitayne,* and *Rheine.*
3.1   And yet what 01   [And yet ô God we haue no cause to plaine MS, 95
  2   the quiet calme we ioy
  3   thee / you MS
  4   for that no
  5   but / then 01   finde then vnite MS, 95 (corr. to: finde then to vnite, "Faults
      Escaped" 95)
  8   which no age
4.1   Thou sacred Goddesse   [O sacred MS, 95
  2   great worke I now entend
  4   the < that MS–D
  5   latter
  7   Strengthen thy Subiect strange thinges to rehearse

5.   And thou *Charles Montioy* borne the worldes delight,
      That hast receiu'd into thy quiet shore
      Mee tempest-driuen fortune-tossed wight,
      Tir'd with expecting, and could hope no more:
      And cheerest on, my better yeares to write
      A sadder Subiect, then I tooke before;
      Receiue the worke I consecrate to thee
      Borne of that rest, which thou dost giue to mee.
6.4   and how it past MS
7.2   Iudge the true progresse: here vouchsafe   [here bigin MS, 95
  8   growne full   grow out
8.2   Gloss: *mat* Grosart suggests *mat* [*ched*]; perhaps *met* is more likely. Gloss om.

      Ten Kings had now raignd of the *Norman* race
      With variable fortune, turning chaunce,
      All in two hundreth sixtie one yeares space,
      When *Edward* third of name and first of *Fraunce*

Possest the Crowne in Fortunes highest grace;
And did to greatest state, his state aduance,
When England might the largest limits see,
That euer any King attaind but hee.

After 8:   9
       For most of all the rest, toyld in vnrest,
What with wrong titles, what with inward broyle,
Hardlie a true establishment possest
Of what they sought with such exceeding toyle:
For why their power within it selfe opprest,
Scarce could break forth to greatnes al that while;
Such wo the childhood of this state did passe
Before it could attaine to what it wasse.
       [1   For all the rest toild in their own vnrest MS
       3   Hardlie / Neuer MS
       6   could / would MS

9(=10).1   Gloss: *William the Conquerour.* MS om.
       3   Altring the lawes, chaunging the forme
       4   And placing barbarous Customes he had brought:
       6   with grieuous taxes tyranie had sought,
       7   Scarce layde th'assured grounds to build vpon .
       8   The chaunge so hatefull in such course begon.

   10.1   the selfe same wayes   Gloss: *William Rufus.* MS om.
       2   great outworne with Warre, or slaine in peace
       3   Onely vpon depressed weaknes prayes
       4   And treades downe what was likeliest to increase:
       5   Those that were left, being left to wofull dayes,
       6   Had onely powre to wish for some release:
       7   Whilst giuing
       8   himselfe was after slaine.

   11.1   *Henrie* his brother raignes when he had donne   Gloss: *Henry. 1.* MS om.
       3   The *Norman Duke* the Conquerours first sonne,
       4   Lightens in shew, rather
       5   Those greeuaunces, his fatall race begunne,
       7   Whose sonnes being drownd for whom he did prepare

   12.2   Gloss: *King Stephen.* MS om.
       3   Raysing such tumults as
       5   State / Realme
       8   Conclude some hope, of quiet; to take breath.   [concludes MS

   13.1   Gloss: *Henry 2.* MS om.
           The sonne of *Maud* (from *Saxon* bloud deriu'd
       By mothers line) succeedes th'vnrightfull King
       Henrie the second, in whose raigne reuiu'd
       Th'oppressed state, and first began to spring,
       Who if he had not beene so too long liu'd
       T'haue seene th'affliction that his age did bring
       By his vngodly Sonnes; most happie man,
       For they against him warr'd, for whom he wan.
           [5   And ô if . . . beene too MS, 95
           7   then happie MS, 95

After 13(=14):   15

 All *Ireland, Scotland,* th'Iles of *Orcades,*
Poytiers, Guienna, Brittany hee got,
And leades foorth sorrow from it selfe, to thease,
Recouers strength at home so feeble brought:
Giues courage to the strong, to weaker ease;
Ads to the state what *England* neuer sought:
Who him succeed (the forraine bloud out growne)
Are home-borne Kings, by speech and birth our owne.
 [8 and / by MS

16

 Loe hitherto the new borne State in teares,
Was in her raw and wayling infancie,
During a hundred two and twentie yeares
Vnder the hand of strangers tyrannie:
And how some better strength and youth appeares,
Which promises a glad recouerie:
For hard beginnings haue the greatest States
What with their owne, or neighbourers debates.
 [8 neighbors fierce MS

17

 Euen like to *Rheine,* which in his birth opprest
Strangled almost with Rocks and mightie Hils,
Workes out a way to come to better rest,
Warres with the Mountaines, striues against their wils:
Bringes foorth his streames in vnitie possest,
Into the quiet bed he proudlie fils,
Carrying that greatnes which he cannot keepe
Vnto his death and buriall in the deepe.
 [8 deepe: 95

18

 So did the worldes proud *Mistres Rome* at first
Striue with a hard beginning, warr'd with need;
Forcing her strong Confiners to the worst,
And in her blood her greatnes first did breed:
So *Spaine* at home with *Moores* ere foorth it burst
Did practize long and in it selfe did bleed:
So did our state begin with her own woundes
To try her strength, ere it enlarg'd her boundes.

14(=19).1 Gloss: *Richard. 1.* MS om.
 1 But now comes Richard to succeed his sire,
 3 His fathers limits bound not his desier:
 4 He spreades the English Ensignes in the East,
 5 And whilst his vertues would haue raisd him higher
 6 Treason and Malice, his great actions ceast:
15.2 Gloss: *K. Iohn.* MS om.
16.1 Gloss: *Henry. 3.* Hen. 3. < om. MS–D
 8 And kept his owne, yet did his owne appease MS, 95 [appease: MS
17.1 Gloss: *Edward. 1.* Ed. 1 < om. MS–D
18.2 Gloss: *Edward. 2.* Ed. 2 < om. MS–D
 8 fortunate. 95

19.1 Gloss: *Edward. 3.* Ed. 3 < om. MS—D
   2 rebrings backe
   7 Could greatnes haue but kept what he had got,
   8 It was enough he did, and what he wrought.
20.1 Gloss: Ed. the black prince, who dyed before his father. < om. MS—D
21.3 Gloss: *Rich. 2.* MS om.
22.7 Second of name; a name in two accurst   [a man in MS
23.4 And / That
   5 calamitie was rife
   6 As / That MS
   7 Time would
24.2 Gloss om.
25.1 Gloss om.
   3 and what h'had done
   7 The other *Edmond Langley,* whose mild spirit   Gloss om.
   8 Affected quiet and safe delight.   [a safe MS, 95
26.1 did interpose his proud vnrest   Gloss om.
   2 *Thomas* of *Woodstocke,* one most violent,
   3 Impatient of commaund, of peace, of rest,
   4 Whose brow would shew, that which his hart had ment
   5 His open malice and repugnant brest
   6 Procur'd much mischiefe by his discontent:
   7 the charge of King and State,
   8 Till by himselfe he might it ordinate.
27.4 such / so MS
   8 doth on / vpon MS
28.3 Which is the thing that Kingdomes doth transport,   [O this is that which
      Kingdomes MS, 95
   4 The plague the heauens do for iniustice threate   [This plague MS,
      95   [heauens for MS
   5 When children rule, who euer in this sort
   6 Confound the State, their auncestors did get;
29.2 Where / For
30.1 Whether it were that they which had the charge   [Now whether twere that MS
   2 Permit / Suffred   [Suffer MS
   6 presumed to take the raigne
   7 We will not saie: but now 95   [I know not; but as now he lendes his eare MS
   8 And youthfull counsell willingly doth heare. MS
31.4 easiest
32.2 These ill / The kinges MS
   5 his nature . . . meeke
33.4 all togither
   5 withall
   6 this confus'd disordering

34.   And sure the King plainely discouereth
         Apparant cause his Vncles to suspect;
         For *Iohn* of *Gaunt* was sayd to seeke his death
         By secret meanes, which came not to effect:
         The Duke of Gloster likewise practiseth
         In open world that all men might detect
         And leagues his Nobles, and in greatest strength
         Rises in armes against him too at length.
         [6   may detect MS
          8   at the length. MS   Gloss om.

35.   Vnder pretence from him to take away
      Such as they sayd the State oppressors were,
      To whom the Realme was now become a pray:
      The chiefe of whom they nam'd was *Robert Vere*
      Then Duke of Ireland; bearing greatest sway
      About the King, who held him onely dere:
      Him they would haue remoou'd and diuers more,
      Or else would neuer lay downe armes they swore.
        [2   states MS, 95
        4   namd Robte *De Vere* MS   Gloss om.

36.8 And there arrest the   [their MS   Gloss om.
37.1 Who soone, with many others had their   [Which MS, 95
    2 All put to death without the course   [Cruelly slaine without MS, 95
    3 For / And   broyles / warres MS, 95
    4 through / for
    5 for MS   those / the   doth MS
    6 such as. / those whom
    7 though themselues are wrong'd and often forst
    8 Yet for they can doe most are thought the worst.
38.1 And yet I doe not seeme herein to excuse   [t'excuse MS
    3 Which
    4 But onely blame the course held in the thing   [course of managing MS, 95
    5 too well grac'd
    6 And wanton fauorits MS   mischiefe euer bring
    7 And this Experience euen her selfe doth speake 01   [So that concluding I may
       boldly speake MS, 95
39.4 vttwardlie < vtterlie MS–D
    6 nor MS
    7 still / now MS, 95
    8 must not be drawne
40.2,7 Glosses om.
    8 greater / mortall MS
41.3 Hauing himselfe a busy stirring minde   [busy / working MS, 95
    5 Whether he
    6 that   State / boundes MS, 95
    8 strong; 95, 01   [strong: MS
42.1 But / Or 95, 01   [Wee cannot certaine gesse, but this is sure MS
43.1 now to further this
    2 The great Earle of *S. Paule*   Gloss om.
    3 From *Charles* of *Fraunce* vnto the young Queene sent
    4 Both to see her, and salute 01   [To see both her and MS, 95
44.1 the suttle Earle foorthwith   [soone MS, 95
45.3 Easier you
46.3 require MS
    5 how   tuch (commas om.)
    7 That
    8 Be still thought
47.3 So shall you hereby scape
    8 Strangled or poison'd secret let him be.
48.3 Whom you may wisely order in such kind
    4 That you may such confessions then exact,
    5 As both you may appease the peoples
    6 And by . . . much aggrauate the

50(=55). MS, 95 om.

   2 Gloss om.

51(=56 in 01 <=55 in MS,95).2 Gloss: *Mowbray after . . . of murthering the . . . Calice.*
        MS, 95 om.

            And long it was not ere he apprehendes
            The Duke, who close to *Calice* was conuei'd,
            And th'Earles of *Arundell* and *Warwicke* sendes,
            Both in close prisons strongly to be laid;
            And soone the Duke his life vnquiet endes,
            Strangled in secret ere it was bewraide;
            And Arundell was put to publike death,
            But warwicke by great meanes he banisheth.   MS, 95

52(=57). MS, 95 om.

   3 gigenerous
   8 offence.

  53. MS, 95 om.

   3 a strange / strange fond

54(=59<=56).1 And for his person he procures a guard MS, 95

   5 hereof / had now   [hath MS

55.1 his vncles albeit in MS, 95

   2 For that no remedy they could deuise MS, 95

   3 sorrowes

   4 vttwardlie MS

56.1 bounde MS

57.1 standing on himselfe

   4 Whilst MS

58.1 being MS

   6 Gloss om.

59.1 and whilst all sylent grieue at what is donne   [sylent / in themselues   [at
        om. MS

   2 being / then

   3 And worthily great Iohn of *Gaunts* first sonne   Gloss om.

   5 In sad discourse vpon this course begun

   6 Which he to *Mowbray* Duke of Norfolke told   Gloss om.

60. Gloss: *Froisart. Pol. Virg. & Hal, deliuer it in this sort: but Walsinghame reportes
      it otherwise.* MS. om   [*but . . . otherwise* 95 om.

            The faythles Duke that presently takes hold
            Of such aduantage to insinuate
            Hastes to the King, peruerting what was told,
            And what came of good minde he makes it hate:
            The King, who might not now be so controld
            Or censur'd in his course, fretting thereat,
            For Herford sendes, who doth such wordes denie,
            And craues the combate of his enemie.
         [5 who / that MS, 95   not so now MS
          6 much frets thereat; MS, 95
          7 Sendes for the Duke, MS, 95

  61. Om.

62(=66<=63).1 Which straight was graunted

   2 When both

   3 To right each other as th'euent should finde,

   4 And now both euen at poynt of combate were,

   6 and so stayes them 95, 01   [Gives signe, proclaymes, they cease, staies y^em there
      MS

    7   As better now aduisd what way to take
    8   most certaine o1   [his assured MS, 95
  63.1 lightlie MS
  64.4 Gloss om. MS, 95
  66.2 O how the MS, 95
  67.6 saide MS
  68.1 t'abide 95, o1
  69.1 Ah MS, 95   whom / that
    7   Yet one daie ô we MS, 95
  70.4 But would as oft change as they change their will MS, 95
  72.1 oft < ought MS–D
    4   as well MS
    5   Se'ing . . . chaunce o1   [Seeing how . . . change MS, 95
  73.5 would / will MS
    8   warre? o1   [warre. 95   [thvniustest warr. MS
  74.7 and / at MS
  76.6 Fitter
  77.1 Gloss om.
  78.1 Certaine it is
    4   Be'ing MS
    7   But beeing now 95, o1
  79.3 dazeleth the clearest
    7   have MS
    8   That (least suspected) ruine
  80.7 Cnsuming o1
  82.6 no course else
    7   Realms
  84.1 And MS, 95
    5   which / that MS
    7   wert / wast MS
  85.1 Lord / King
    2   spirit MS
  86.1 Who / For MS, 95
    2   He doth with cunning traine and pollicy MS, 95
    6   Gloss om.
  87.1 Comd
    4   reuerent / wofull
    5   A naked goodly   Gloss om.
    6   rent-white
    8   it seem'd shee sayd:
  88.1 whether MS
    5   O whither thus MS, 95   [whether . . . run? MS
    7   bloodshed, ô what broyles
  89.8 in o1
  90.2 sigh'd
    5   The / Tho 95 (corr. to The, "Faults Escaped" 95)
  92.2 Laboring MS   sprite 95
    6   that / wch corr. to y^t MS—not D
93–9(=97–103<=94–100). MS om.
  94.7 And ô in such a case who is it will 95
    8   ill.
  95.8 more.
  96.2 th'intended 95
  97.2 low deepe-buried

98.7   For ô what 95
   8   intend? 95
99.2   That cannot sound
   4   Holding   which / that
   5   Wondring how strange twas wrought, how close begun,
   6   And thinke all actions else did tend to that,
   7   When ô how 95
   8   Making the happy wiser
100(=[94] in MS).1   The morning sonne he first salutes wth blood MS   Gloss om.
   5   that
101.2   And th'Archbishop of Canterbury shew'd   Gloss om.
102.5   Gloss om.
103.8   wrought: MS
105.2   inform'd < informed MS—D
   5   Gloss: *The Duke . . . Yorke.* MS om.
   7   Gloss om. MS
106.1   had < om. MS—D   Armie / forces MS, 95   Gloss om.
   3   forces / people MS, 95
   4   B'ing 95   [Being MS
107.8   lament. MS
108.4   wise: 01   wise? 95   [wise MS
   5   noble / lawfull
   6   enemies: 01   [enemyes MS
   8   rage? 01
110.4   dissolation MS
111.4   far < their MS—D
112.7   th'end MS
113.8   night.
115.1   earth / Earle 01
116.2   Disordered mortalitie
   4   declare ! (turned semicolon) 01
   5   In fearefull signes to signifie the Woe MS
117.5   doe . . . make way
   7   Making our   [o^r< om. MS—D
After 117(=121<=118=[111]):

122

Or do the conscience of our wicked deedes
Apply to sinne the terrour of these sightes,
Hapning at the instant when commotion breedes
Amazing only timorous vulgar wights,
Who euer aggrauating that which feedes
Their feares, still finde out matter that affrightes,
Whillst th'impious fierce, neglecting feele no touch,
And waigh too light what other feare so much?
   [3   th'instant MS
   8   much.   MS, 95

123

No, no, th'eternall power that guides this frame,
And serues him with the instruments of heauen
To call the earth and sommon vp our shame,
By an edict from euerlasting giuen;
Forbids mortalitie to search the same:
Where sence is blind, and wit of wit bereauen,

Terror must be our knowledge, feare our skill,
T'admire his worke, and tremble at his will.
  [1   Ah no MS, 95

118(=124<=121=[114]).1 And   this / thiese MS
    4   thou / ô MS, 95
End-title: 95 om. [*Finis* MS

Book II

Head-title: THE ARGVMENT OF THE SECOND BOOKE. 95, 01   [The
Second Canto MS

 2.1   *O Percy* how by MS, 95   Gloss: *This . . . Worster, and brother . . . Northum-*
       berland. MS om.
   7   obraid
 3.2   oft < ought MS—D
 5.1   Now *Maiestie* forsaken, all alone 01   [O *Maiestie* left naked all alone MS, 95
   2   But . . . thy right
   3   Sawst those . . . thy 01   [Those gallant . . . thy MS, 95
   5   Th'amazing 95, 01 (corr. to amuzing, "Faults Escaped" 95)
   6   state / cares
   7   Are MS, 95
   8   Thy selfe . . . thy selfe . . . bereft? 01   [bereft. 95   [bereft MS
 6.5   saftie < fortune MS—D
 7.1   As stately
   8   deuowre.
 8.2   Gloss om.
   7   What never he ymaginde   MS
11.5   turne the head
   7   with / by MS
   8   fled
12.7   neuer 01   ["never" underlined in text, "=newer" written in print-hand in
       margin MS—D(?)
   8   rarely men keepe / rare performed MS, 95
13.1   Which seeing this
   5   who / that MS, 95
14.7   th'humatous 01   [the humorous MS
16.7   Kings / to

After 16, in MS only: [17]
       What hath my raigne deservd to bee thus leaft?
       How could my faultes to so great measure rise?
       Whoe hath committed so iniurious theaft
       Vpon my Love t'abuse it in this wise?
       How came I so of honor cleane bereaft?
       Whoe hath made me so hatefull to yor eyes?
       Is all the good forgott that I have done
       Onlie the bad if any thought vpon?

                 [18]
       O call to mynde that I am hee yor King,
       Whose bounty had no boundes, rewardes no end,
       Tis I that never spared any thing

That might the Maiestie of Court commend:
Tis I that all that wch my Realme did bring
Vpon my Realme most willingly did spend
If any thing my officers did ill,
Adiudg it as their fault not to my will.

17(=[19]).1   O if MS, 95
    5   state / stay MS   [ô why should you distrust MS, 95
    6   The gaine of glory whereto age appiers MS
    7   hath MS
18.1   sees . . . sees / knowes . . . knowes MS   ["while" (carried over below the line)
       stricken out and "while" in Daniel's hand substituted above MS–D
    4   Smothd MS
    7   Euen made a pray onely vnto a few
    8   vp / that would / might . . . others MS   [shewe
19.4   but with shewes
    5   misshapen letter at end of "huge" corrected MS–D   [vnproportion'd < vnpro-
       portioned MS–D
    6   Betwixt MS
20.6   *Maiestie imparts* 95

After 20:   21
          Hence, hence I see, and to my griefe I see,
       Th'vnreconcileable disunion
       Is growne betweene m'aggraued Realme and mee,
       And by their fault, whose fayth I trusted on:
       My easie nature tractable and free,
       Soone drawne to what my Counsell would haue done,
       Is thus betrayde by them and my neglect,
       Easiest deceiud where least I did suspect.
          [1   O hence MS, 95
           3   betwixt m'aggrieued MS

21(=22=[24]).4   And talk with him about the MS   Gloss om.
    8   hate. o1   [hate, 95   [hate: MS
22–9   See above, pp. 57–8.
22.3   and   o9a, 23a
    7   And / and . . . resto'rd   o9a, 23a
23.1   he a parley doth exhort 95, o1   [ple Ms
    2   the King to leaue that vncooth place MS
    3   and   o9a, 23a   a comfortable cheere MS
    5   the publique MS, 95
    6   and   o9a, 23a
    8   host . . . Ostage MS
24.4   so / of MS
    6   *Maiestie withstood* 95
25.1   h'in MS, 95, o1   [he'in o9, o9a, 23a
    2   And doth confer . . . staying MS, 95
    3   That fortune leaft MS
    6   Good / True MS   Gloss: Y^e Byshop of Carlile. < om. MS–D
    7   that good Earle of Salisbury MS   Gloss om. MS
26.1   O *Time* commit not MS, 95
    2   Vppon the holy faith of these good men MS, 95
    4   worthy of our pen MS, 95
    5   magnanim'ous 95   must / shalt MS   Gloss om. all eds. except o9a, 23a

6   in o9a, 23a   thy constant honour then MS, 95
8   in all men pittied o1   [that all MS, 95
27.1 Nor Conscience would that I MS, 95, o1
2   The memorie of thee, most o1   [O *Jenico,* thy memory so cleere MS, 95
    Gloss: Jenico a Gascoyn seruant to King Ric. yᵗ wore his liuery when all men
    forsooke him. < om MS–D
3   be'ing . . . wish / with . . . *Gascony* o1   [being . . . *Gascony* MS, 95
4   the / that MS   we hold so deere MS, 95
5   So *England* should MS, 95   small / poore MS
6   Wholy her owne, and shee no partner heere MS, 95
7   good < fame MS–D
28.2 Gloss: Th'Earle of Salisbury. < om. MS–D   95, o1 om.
7   Nothing but MS, 95, o1
8   and o9a, 23a   call, / all. o9 (corr. to call. in "Faults Escaped" o9)   [call. 95,
    o1, o9a, 23a—though all eds. after o9 retain "Faults Escaped."
29.4 t'obrayd MS, 95, o1
6   against o9a, 23a
8   and o9a, 23a
30.3 (That . . . hold) MS
4   choose MS
7   those / the MS
8   chiefly / only MS
32.1 h'will neuer
6   relieue: (turned semicolon)
33.7 obrayding
8   whom / that MS, 95
34.6 altogither
35.2 fate < might MS–D
4   hate < slight MS–D
6   state < right MS–D
36.8 right?
37.1 Bushop MS   Gloss: Yᵉ Bishop of Carlile: < om. MS–D
39.4 On / In MS
40.8 your / the MS
41.4 the glorie of this good
8   all right MS
43.8 farther but 95, o1
44.3 doeing MS
7   Gloss om. MS
45.1 oath my Lord I thinke in conscience
7   buy / by MS
47.1 out / euen
2   all men spake but as MS
6   Safety (His om.)
8   all ridd of MS
48.2 neighbou'ring 95, o1   [neighboring MS
5   in < om MS–D
49.5 th'one
6   tho'ther MS
8   arose MS
53.8 truth was dreames, & < om. MS–D   were < was MS–D   truthe < trueth
    MS–D (see p. 43)
54.6 great / fowle
8   As though MS obrayd

55.1 hee / you MS
   7 that liue in sun-shine of delightes
   8 And flie the winter when affliction lightes.
56.7 Which when he saw, and in his sorrow waid   [and wth discretion weighd MS
   8 Thus out of griefe vnto himselfe he sayd: [said. MS, 95

After 56(=57=[59]):   58
      O faythlesse *Cosen,* here behold I stand
      Spectator of that act my selfe haue playd,
      That act of Rule which now vpon thy hand
      This wauering mutability hath layd:
      But *Cosen,* know the fayth of this false land
      Stands sworne to me, that fayth they haue betrayd
      Is mine, mine is the rule, thou dost me wrong
      T'vsurpe the gouernment I held so long.
      [5 But / And MS
       7 mine, time mine the MS, 95
       8 held / hould MS

             59
      And when thou hast but tride what I haue found,
      Thou mayst repent t'haue bought commaund so deare,
      When thou shalt find on what vnquiet ground
      Greatnesse doth stand, that standes so high in feare:
      Where infinite occasions do confound
      The peace of minde, the good thou look'st for here:
      How fatall is th'ascent vnto a Crowne,
      Frõ whence men come not downe, but must fall downe.
      [3 upon how slippery MS
       6 good / ioy MS
       7 How / O MS, 95   tha'scent MS

MS only: [62]
      And that corrupting breath of smooth deceipt
      That soothes the eare wth choyce of pleasing thinges
      Did first marr me, I perisht wth that baite
      wch me this shame, and thee this fortune bringes
      Thease daungerous guests that now vpon thee waite
      Thinking best living vnder newest kinges
      Will use thee thus, or labor so to doe
      And in short tyme will seeke to chaung thee to
      [2 choyce < coyce MS–D

             60
      And you that cherish fat iniquitie,
      Inriching sinne, with store, and vice with gaine
      By my disgrace, see what you get thereby
      To raise the bad, to make the good complaine:
      These vipers spoyle the wombe wherein they lie,
      And haue but impudence a grace to gaine,
      But bodyes and bold browes, no mindes within
      But minde of ill, that knowes but how to sin.
      [1 And / O MS, 95
       3 Bee learnd by mee see MS
       7 But / Great MS
       8 ill / lust MS

MS only: [64]
    Thease doe preoccupate the heart the eye
    And grace of mighty men that might doe good
    And thease doe put backe blushing honesty
    That grieves when vertue is not vnderstood
    Theas doe disgrace the grace whereon they ly
    And doe defile the worth of reverent bloud
    And murder the opynion of the best
    W^{ch} doe thease idle manners most detest

61

    And for the good which now do take thy part
    Thou mayst reioyce, for th'others I am glad
    To thinke they may in time likewise subuart
    The expectation which of thee men had:
    When thou shalt finde how difficult an art
    It is to rule and please the good and bad:
    And feele the grieuance of this fatall sort,
    Which still are borne for Court, or made in Court.

57(=62=[66]).1 More griefe had sayd: when loe the Duke he saw
       [more had hee said MS
    2 Entring the Castle come to parley there,   [parle MS, 95
    3 Which makes him presently from thence withdraw
    4 Into a fitter place some other where:
    5 His fortune now inforst an yeelding awe
    6 To meete him, who before in humble feare   [who / that MS
    7 glad, t'haue stayd
    8 respectiue / attendant
  58.1 The Duke when come
    3 of wronge which reuerence did bring
    5 downe euen at his entering
  59.1 began / thus sayde
    2 both vnlookt for, and vnsent vnto
    3 presumed to come hither now:
    4 But this your wrong and rigor draue me to:
    5 And being come, I purpose now to show
    6 You better how to rule, and what to do:
    7 You haue had time too much to worke our ill,   [tyme (to much) MS
    8 But now redresse is planted in our will.
  60.1 As you shall please deare
    2 You haue me in your powre: I am content
    3 And I am pleasd, if my disgrace may bring   [I reioyce . . . shall bring MS
    4 Good to my Countrey which I euer ment: [never MS
    5 But yet God graunt your course held in this thing,   [your / the MS
    6 Cause not succeeding ages to repent.
    7 they left: the Duke had haste to go,
    8 end the matter so.
  61.1 Straight / And MS
    2 The Duke sets forward as they had decreed,
  63.2 shootes . . . claps, hands thrusts MS
  64.2 never thought could bee MS
  65.5 O what MS, 95
  66 ff. Misnumbered 67 ff. CT

66.7 Had < And MS—D
    8 was.
67.   MS om.
68(=73=[76]).1 & < om. MS—D   notes / views MS
    5 desire MS   as / was
    8 shootes
69.6 s'vpright < vpright MS—D
    7 bowes: deare Lord with . . . grace: 95, 01   [bowes (deare Lord) with . . . grace?
       MS
    8 face? 95, 01   [face. MS
70.1 eye? 95, 01   [eye, MS
    6 Sweet / Poore MS
71.5 i'st 95, 01
72.1 Ah / O MS, 95
    5 What? / O MS, 95
73.6 this? MS
    7 lookes MS
    8 past.
74.3 At length love-sharpened eyes MS
75.1 saide shee MS
76.7 And let desire MS
77.1 see but himselfe MS
    5 lovelie face MS
79.3 prize 95, 01
    5 tis true tis hee MS
    6 Alas tis hee tis my owne Lord MS
80.1 heart / soule
    2 it / him   stops / layes   way / key
    3 Raignes all alone a Lord without controule
    4 So long till greater horror threatneth:
    5 And euen in danger brought to loose the whole,
    6 H'is forst come foorth, or els to stay with death,
    7 Opens a sign and lets
81.2 & < om. MS—D (?)
    7 thother MS   then'his < then his MS—D
82.3 past 01
    5 whilst MS
    8 spake. 95, 01   [spake: MS
83.1 What / O MS, 95   mee ¿ (turned question mark) 01
    5 And / O MS, 95
    6 retorne < om. MS—D
    8 that / and MS   King. 01
After 83(=88=[91]), in MS only:

[92]
Our sad attempt was that to take in hand,
To conquere others, and to loose thyne owne
And seeking more to add vnto thy land
To leave thy land and to forgoe thy crowne
Whiles thou their mischiefe didst not vnderstand
Being there victorious here art overthrowne
Wicked ungratefull people so to deale
Against your faith your king and common weale.

[93]

O was there none that wth respective eye
would once vouchsafe to looke vpon their Lord?
Deservd hee no regard in passing by?
No not the least applause by signe or word?
well London thou that sawst this iniury
Thy streetes may rue the grace they did afford,
To bee the stage vnto this wicked act
And curse the causes and bewaile the fact.

84(=89=[94]).1 And ô my Lord MS
 86.3   be / goe MS
    5   deere . . . morne MS
 87.2   ô lets not MS, 95
 88.1   close and secrete MS
 89.3   th'obrayding
    7   Lookes angerlie about as bent to chide MS
    8   spide MS
 90.2   o welcome deare he saies? MS, 95   [sayes MS
    4   eyes MS
After 91(=[101]). End-title: *Finis* MS. This concludes the manuscript.

After 94(=99):   100
        And could not Maiestie be ruined
        But with the fearefull powre of her owne name?
        And must abusd obedience thus be led
        With powrefull titles to consent to shame?
        Could not confusion be established
        But forme and order must confirme the same?
        Must they who his authoritie did hate,
        Yet vse his stile to take away his state?
        [1 And / Ah 95 (Henceforward all variants from 01 are in 95.)

95(=101).1 Order ô how predominant 95
    7   then / ô 95
    8   wrong?
 97.1   now doth Enuie
    4   but not to b'answered
    5   maie complaine but
 99.1   Gloss om.
    5   O how each 95
    8   blood.
102.7   And did or might their grieued hartes to ease
    8   Vtter their sorrowes in like termes as these.

After 102(=108):   109
        What dissolute proceedinges haue we here?
        What strange presumptuous disobedience?
        What vnheard fury voyde of awe or feare,
        With monstrous vnexampled insolence?
        Durst Subiects euer here or any where
        Thus impiously presume so fowle offence,
        To violate the power commaunding all,
        And into iudgement Maiestie to call?
        [6 offence?
        8   call.

110

Fame hide it close and do not carrie word
To after-comming ages of our shame,
Blot out of Bookes, and rase out of Record
All monuments, memorials of the same:
Forget to tell how we did lift our sword,
And enuious idle accusations frame
Against our lawfull Sou'raigne, when we ought
His end and our release haue stayd, not sought.
    [1 O fame conceale and

103(=111).1 Since better
    5 yet / ô 95
104.1 grieued they
    2 persuade and vrge him on
    3 To . . . and make with free
    4 make om.
    5 Seeing he
    6 The danger of his owne confusion
105.7 What / O 95
107.2 in company, / attended on:
    4 And testifie his resignation:
    6 might more formally be done:
    7 men might rest more satisfide thereby,
    8 As not done of constraint, but willingly.
108.1 he's o1
    8 for euermore in others
110.7 And all this did he but t'haue leaue to liue,
    8 The which was all he crau'd that they would giue.
111.1 Tis / This (corr. to Tis, "Faults Escaped") CT
112.2 T'acquaint the Parlament with what is done
    4 And manner of his resignation:
    5 When Canterburie vrgd them to proceed   Gloss: *Thomas Arundell Bishop of*
       Canterbury.   [*Thomas* om. 95
    6 Forthwith vnto a new election,
    7 And *Henry* make his claime both
    8 And resignation to
113–14. Om.
115(=121).1 Who there with full and generall applause
    2 Is straight proclaimd as King, and after crownd,
    3 The other cleane reiected by the lawes,
    4 As one the Realme had most vnworthy found.
    5 And yet ô *Lancaster,* I would
    7 noble heart / glorious worth
    8 For Empire borne, for Gouernment brought foorth:
116.1 not ô that sad succeeding 95
    2 Our . . . our / Her . . . her
    3 our / her
    4 our / her   slaughtred / slaine
    5 come
End-title: Om.

After 116(=122):   123
    Whereby the bloud of thirteene battels fought

About this quarrell, fatall to our land,
Haue been reseru'd with glory to haue brought
Nations and Kingdomes vnder our command:
And all that which thy sonne* and thou had got,
With glorious prayse had still been in our hand,
And that great Worthy last of all thy name†
Had ioynd the Westerne *Empire* to the same.

   * *K. Hen. 5.*
   † *K. Hen. 8.*

[1 So had the
  5 So should all that thy   Gloss om.
  6 had / haue
  7 Gloss om.

124

So should his great imperiall Daughter now
Th'admired glorie of the earth, hereby
Haue had all this nere bordring world to bow
To her immortalized Maiestie:
Then proud *Iberus* lord not seeking how
T'attaine a false-conceiued Monarchie,
Had kept his barraine boundes and not haue stood
In vaine attempts t'inrich the Seas with bloud:
  [8 bloud.

125

Nor interpos'd his greedie medling handes
In other affayres, t'aduance his owne:
Nor tyrannisd ouer so many landes
From late obscuritie so mightie growne.
But we with our vndaunted conquering Bandes
Had led our Ensignes vnto landes vnknowne,
And now with more audacious force began
To march against th'Earths-terror *Ottoman.*
  [6 led / lent

After 125, in 95 only: 126
Where thou (*O worthy Essex*) whose deare blood
Reseru'd from these sad times to honour ours,
Shouldst haue conducted Armies and now stood
Against the strength of all the *Easterne Powres:*
There should thy valiant hand performd that good
Against the barbarisme that all deuoures,
That all the states of the redeemed *Earth*
Might thee admire, and glorifie thy birth.

127

Thence might thy valor haue brought in despight
Eternall *Tropheis* to *Elizas* name,
And laid downe at her sacred feete the right
Of all thy deedes and glory of the same.
All that which by her powre, and by thy might
Thou hadst attaind to her immortall fame

Had made thee wondred here, admir'd a farre
The *Mercury* of peace, the *Mars* of warre.

126

Where thou my Lord, the glorie of my Muse
Magnanimous *Mountioy,* th'ornament of men,
Hadst had a large and mightie fielde to vse
Thy holy guiftes and learned counsels then:
Whole landes and Prouinces should not excuse
Thy trusty fayth, nor yet sufficient been
For those great vertues to haue ordered
And in a calme obedience rendered.

   [126(=<128).1   And thou
     2   Pure-spirited *Mountioy*
     8   rendered / gouerned

127

Nor had my Muse so sad a subiect tooke,
Composing bloudie accents of these times:
Nor told of woundes that grieued eyes might looke
Vpon th'horror of their predicessors crimes:
Bur rather glorious triumpes vndertooke,
And registred in euerlasting rimes
The sacred Tropheis of ELIZABETH
T'haue kept the wonder of her worth from death.

   [1   had I then at solitary brooke
    2   Sate framing bloudy
    4   the horror of their fathers
    5   rather a more glorious subiect tooke
    6   To register
    7   Tropheis / glories

After 127(=<129):   130

And likewise builded for your great designes
O you two worthies bewties of our state,
Immortall tombes of vnconsuming lines
To keepe your holie deedes inuiolate:
You in whose actions yet the image shines
Of ancient honor neere worne out of date,
You that haue vertue into fashion brought
In these neglected times respected nought.

   [<130. Misnumbered 136

128

But whither am I carried with the thought
Of what might haue beene, had not this been so?
O sacred *Fury* how was I thus brought
To speake of glory that must tell of wo?
These acted mischiefes cannot be vnwrought
Though men be pleasd to wish it were not so.
And therefore leaue sad Muse th'imagin'd good,
For we must now returne againe to blood.

            The end of the second Booke.
   [128(=<131. End-title om.

Book III

Argument 5 *Is murthered there. The* Percies *making head*

  6 *Against the King, receiue the punishment.*

  7 *And in the end a tedious troublous raigne*

  8 *A grieuous death concludes with care, and paine.*

2.1 Striuing at first to

  2 his weake cause, in apt-abused mindes,

  3 He deckes his deed with colours of deceit

  4 And ornamentes of right, which now he findes:

  6 their / three

  7 inough he findes, that findes his might

  8 they / he

3.1 All these he hath, when one good would suffize

  2 The worlds applause, and liking to procure,

  6 The doubtfull can no vsuall plots indure:

  7 These selfe-accusing titles all he had,

  8 Seeking to

4.1 Like foolish he that

  7 Thinking for that the outward forme seemes strong

  8 Tis sure inough, and may continue long.

After 4:   5

      But when the vnderworking waues come on,

      Searching the secrets of vnfenced wayes,

      The full maine *Ocean* following hard vpon,

      Beares downe that idle frame, skorning such stayes;

      Prostrates that frustrate paines as if not done,

      And proudly on his silly labors playes,

      Whilst he perceiues his error, and doth finde

      His ill proceeding contrary to kinde.

5(=6).2 wrong-contriued

  3 time or Iustice

  4 The feeble ground-worke craft thought laid so fast

  7 huge / strong

6.1 But well he thought his powre made all seem plaine

  2 And now t'his

  4 splendor / error

  5 Is furnisht with a stately-glorious

7.8 Seeking all meanes t'oppresse the aduerse

8.1 All Counsellers vnto the former King,

  2 All th'officers, and Iudges of the state,

  3 He to disgrace, or els to death did bring,

  4 Lead by his owne, or by the

  5 Who euermore by nature mallicing

  6 Their might whom not their vertues, but

  7 hath, whom when Kinges do what's naught   [who 95

  8 it's / tis   tis thought their fault.   [faut. 95

9.1 And plac'd for these such

  2 Belou'd of him, and in the peoples grace,

  3 Learned graue *Shirley* he makes Chancellor,

  4 One of great spirit, worthy his worthy race:

  5 And *Clifford* he ordaines Lord *Treasuror,*

6   A man whose vertues well deseru'd that place:

7   Others to other roomes (whom

8   loathd 95   old)

10-11. Om.

12(=11; misnumbered 17 in 95).2 Gloss: *of Thomas of Woodstocke Duke*   95 om.

8   shadowed.

13.2 Gloss: *for . . . Gloster* om. 95

14.4 men / wight

15.5 one om.

6   One that to do this

7   A base meane man whom few

16.5 honour with it goes

18.1 Yet / And   which yet must be a

3   He doth himselfe secure and them deface,

4   Thinking not rigor that which life doth giue:

5   But what an error was it in this case

6   To wrong so many, and to let them liue?

7   But errors are no errors but by fate,

8   For oft th'euent make foule faults fortunate.

19.5 And ô b'it sinne t'examine now this deed

6   How iust tis done, and on how sure a ground?

7   Whether that Court may change due course or no,

8   Or ought the Realme against the Realme can do?

21.4 dar'st

6   courage / vertues

22.2 *Our Auentine, retire* (corr. to our Auentine retyre, "Faults Escaped") 95

5   say / speake 01   O let me speake 95

23.5 too / two 95

24(=23).

Haue you not done inough? blush, blush to thinke,
Lay on your harts those hands; those hands too rash,
Know that this staine that's made doth farther sinke
Into your soules then all your blouds can wash,
Leaue with your mischiefe done and doe not linke
Sin vnto sin, for heauen, and earth will dash
This ill accomplisht worke ere it be long,
For weake he builds that fences wrong with wrong.   95

25.8 we will not say how

27.2 *Abbots* skill / *Abbot* now

30.8 chaste 95

32.2 Gloss om. 95

5   but stoor'd 95

7   withall / with all   01 time will fit and furnish all the rest 95

8   but euen attend, and doe his best 95

33.4 shall b'ordaind 95   deed? 01

34.8 with 01

37.1 Sober, milde *Blunt* 95

2   iudgement 95

41.4 my / ô 95

42.7 grace and life 95

8   and of strife. 95

45.7 an other 01

47.1 though / ô 95   an other 01

53.2 *Conclude* 95
54.   (All exclamation points question marks.)
  1   And / o 95
  7   what 01
56.1 May om.
  2   May take th'aduantage
  3   Realme with these rebellions
  4   Vext, and turmoyled, was thought would not resist
  5   wound, when like confusions
  6   Should by this meanes be stayd, or quite supprest,   [stayd, as all men wist 95
  7   The cause be'ing once cut off, that did molest,
  8   The land should haue her peace, and he his rest.
59.4 O how he striues 95
  8   O what repose 95   therein?
60.1 yet / ô 95
  5   But / O 95
63.1 now sayd 01
  7   steedie
65.7 Thine / O 95
66.7 O know tis others sin not my desart 95
  8   And I could wish I were but as thou art. 95
67.3 intr'est 01   No sorrow 95
  7   O blinded greatnes! thou with thy turmoyle 95
  8   mak'st 95
After 67(=66), in 95 only:

67

But looke on mee, and note my troubled raigne,
Examine all the course of my vext life;
Compare my little ioyes with my long paine,
And note my pleasures rare, my sorrowes rife,
My childhood spent in others pride, and gaine,
My youth in daunger, farther yeares in strife,
My courses crost, my deedes wrest to the worst,
My honour spoild, my life in daunger forst.

68

This is my state, and this is all the good
That wretched I haue gotten by a crowne,
This is the life that costes men so much bloud
And more then bloud to make the same their owne,
O had not I then better beene t'haue stood
On lower ground, and safely liu'd vnknowne,
And beene a heards man rather then a king,
Which inexperience thinkes so sweet a thing.

68(=67=<69).1 O thou great Monarch, and 95
  2   skorning that   Gloss: *Dioclesian the Emperor.* .01 om.
  4   took'st those sweet retires 95
  5   that ô he is not 95
After 68(=<69), in 95 only:

70

But what do I repeating others good
To vexe mine owne perplexed soule the more?

> Alas how should I now free this poore bloud
> And care-worne body from this state restore?
> How should I looke for life or liuely-hood
> Kept here distrest to die, condemnd before
> A sacrifice prepared for his peace
> That can but by my death haue his release?

69(=68=<71).3   What / O 95
  70.1   had sorrow vttered,
    2   But in   such / how
    3   Is come from Court, his name deliuered
    4   with him sayd he . . . trayterous
    5   more remoues? Must we be farther led?
    6   not sent inough yet out
    7   Or hath this place not strength sufficient
    8   or haue they worse intent?
  71.8   hinders them
  72.1   great assault the Knight
    2   Cheeres vp his fainting men all that he
    5   exployt worthy a man of might,
    6   Much honour wretch wherein thy valor
    7   Ah poore weake Prince, yet men that presence feare
  73.7   startes vp from where
  74.1   who / that
  75.6   lies
  76.5   which / that
  77.7   wofull deadly wound
    8   Which / That   most sweete Prince

78(=77=<80).
> Monster of men, what hast thy fury done
> Vnto an ouerpressed innocent,
> Lab'ring against so many, he but one,
> And one poore soule with care, with sorrow spent?
> Could thine owne eyes indure to looke vpon
> Thy handes disgrace, or didst thou then relent?
> But what thou didst I will not here deuine
> Nor staine my thoughtes to enter into thine.
>   [1   ô what hast thou here done
>   5   O could thy eies

79(=78=<81).
> But leaue thee wretch vnto blacke infamie,
> To darke eternal horror, and disgrace,
> The hatefull skorne to all posteritie:
> The out-cast of the world, last of thy race,
> Of whose curst seed, nature did then deny
> To bring foorth more, her faire workes to deface:
> And as asham'd to haue produc'd that past,
> She stayes her hand, and makes this worst, her last.

After 79(=78=<81):   79
> There lyes that comely body all imbrude
> With sacred blood, amidst the foule he shed:
> Those holly streames became with that vile, rude

Vnhallowed staynes confusdly interspred:
Ah why was Grossenes with such grace indude,
To be with that sweet mixture honoured?
Or seru'd it but as some vile graue, ordaynd
Where an imbalmed corps should be contaynd?
    [2   sacred / that pure   amidst the / mixt with that
    3   O that those sacred streames with such vile
    4   matter should be mingled!
    5   Ah / O

80(=<83).1 Those faire distended limmes all trembling lay,
    2 Whom yet nor
    3 remou'd had not rid all away,
    4 seas'd not yet on all
    5 motion (that soone finish shall
    6 The mouer ceasing) yet a while doth stay
    8 vp:
81.   So holdes those organs of that goodly frame,
The weake remaines of life a little space,
But ah full soone cold death possest the same,
Set are those sun-like eyes, bloudlesse that face,
And all that comely whole a lumpe became,
All that faire forme which death could scarce disgrace
Lyes perisht thus, and thus vntimely fate
Hath finisht his most miserable state.

82.1 this / thus
    3 Now onely one, both name and all beside
    4 Intirely hath, pluralitie doth cease:
    5 He that remaines, remaines vnterrifide
    6 With others right; this day doth all release:
    7 And hencefoorth he is absolutly King,
    8 No Crownes but one, this deed confirmes the thing.   Gloss om.
III.83–IV.14 in CT om. all other eds. Bk. III in 95, 01 = Bks. III and IV in 09, 23.

BOOK IV

15(=III.83=<86).1 And yet new Hydraes loe, new heades appeare   Gloss om.
    2 T'afflict that peace reputed then so sure,
    3 And gaue him much to do, and much to feare,
    4 And long and dangerous tumultes did procure
    5 these / those
    7 Who whether not so grac'd or so preferd
    8 As they expected, these new factions stird.
16.3 That thus conspire
    4 The crooked courses they had suffered long
    5 Whether their conscience vrged them, or
    6 Or that they saw the
    7 Or that ambition
17–19. Om.
20(=85=<88).1 What cause so euer were, strong
    2 th'occasion fit
    5 draw in the Scot

6   he likes and yeeldes to it

7   Not for the loue of them, or for their good,

8   But glad hereby of meanes to shed our blood.

21.1   who fitly trainde

2   And all in armes vnder a mightie head

3   Great *Glendour,* who long warr'd, and much attaind,   Gloss: *Owen Glendour.*

4   Sharpe conflictes made, and many vanquished:

5   With whom was *Edmond Earle* of *March* retaind

6   Being first his prisoner, now confedered,

22(=87=<90; 87 ff. misnumbered 97 ff. in 01).6   Gloss: Cambridge, sonne   95 om.

7   Then iudge if this the King might nearely touch   [And iudge 95

8   were small   [wes small 95   being much

23.2   conioyne / they league

8   so / thus

24.1   those two helpes which still such actors finde,

2   Kinges disgrace,

3   Doth fit their course, and draw the vulgar minde

4   To further them, and ayde them in this case:

5   The King they accusd for cruell, and vnkinde,

6   That did the State, and Crowne, and all deface;

7   who / that

25.1   Besides the odious detestable act

2   Of that late   Gloss om.

3   Making it his, that so had will'd the

4   That he the doers did

5   And then such taxes dayly doth exact

6   That were

7   And with all these, or worse, they him assaild,

8   Who late of others with the like preuaild.

After 25(=90):   101 (i.e. 91)

Thus doth contentious proud mortalitie

Afflict each other, and it selfe torment:

And thus dost thou, mind-tortring Miserie,

Restles Ambition, borne in discontent,

Turn and retosse with vile iniquitie,

The vnconstant courses frayltie did inuent:

And foulst faire order, and defilst the earth,

Fostring vp warre, father of blood and dearth.

[3   dost / ô

5   Turn'st and retossest with iniquity

26-7.   Om.

28(=92=<95).2   impos'd / rehearst

4   many more do flocke from coastes disperst;

5   But when the King had heard these newes so bad,

6   Th'vnlookt for dangerous toyle more nearly pierst,

7   For bent t'wards *Wales* t'appease those tumults there

8   H'is for'st diuert his course, and them forbeare.

29-32.   Om.

33(=93=<96).2   marcht / hastes

8   To such a field that power to power

34.   Gloss: *The Earle of Northumberlans sonne.*   [*The son to the Earle of North-*
ūberland. 95

2   Meete with thy forward sonne
3   warlike
35.4   Did meane t'afflict . . . continuall
5   here / yet   doth / might
7   brought / ioynd
36.2   Gloss om.   *Reg. / Keg.* CT
6   dasht / stopt   Cause / part
37.2   arriu'd / approch'd
6   By his great spirit his well imboldned Band
7   Bringes a strong Host of firme resolued might,
8   And plac'd his troupes
38.1   my faithfull valiaunt   [my / ô 95
7   Our holie cause, our freedome, and our right,
8   Sufficient are to moue good mindes to fight.
39.2   That . . . even promise
7   our / but
8   What need we doubt, if wee but worke
40.3   wary / carefull   course / forme
8   Gloss om.
41-2.   Om.
43(=101=<104).1   But this refusd, the King with wrath incensd
3   And ô saith he, though I could haue dispensd 95
7   might honor had
8   owne o1   [owne. 95
44.5   my maisters

After 44(=102):   113 (i.e. 103)
         Straight moues with equall motion equall rage
      The like incensed armies vnto blood,
      One to defend, an other side to wage
      Foule ciuill warre, both vowes their quarrell good:
      And too much heate to blood doth now inrage
      Both who the deed prouokes, and who withstood,
      That valor here is vice, here manhood sinne,
      The forward'st handes doth the least honor winne.
      [3   another
       5   Ah too
       8   the / ô

45(=104=<107).1   But now begin
2   that musicke
6   Thundring confused, murmurs
8   sight.
46.2   of wrath, and of dissention:
3   Horrible good; mischiefe necessarie,
4   The foule reformer of confusion
5   mens / our
6   Cruell recurer of corruption:
7   Ah that these sin-sicke states in need should stand
      [Ah / O 95
8   To be . . . hand!
47.   Gloss: *The Prince of Wales.*
1   And how well hadst thou here beene   [And ô how well thou hadst beene 95
3   Whose young vndaunger'd hand now rash, makes way
6   rebeat-backe

7 chace backe
48.3 Gloss: *Henry the sonne who was after Hen. 5.*   95 om.
7 But better hadst thou
8 him / thee
49.1 Hadst thou not there lent present speedy ayde
2 To thy . . . nearely tyrde
3 Whom fierce incountring *Dowglas* ouerlayd,
4 That day had there his troublous life expirde:
5 Heroycall courageous *Blunt* arayd   Gloss: *Which was sir Walter Blunt.*
6 In habite like as was the King attirde,
7 And deemd for him, excusd that fate with his,
8 For he had what his Lord did hardly misse.

50.   For thought a King, he would not now disgrace
         The person then suppos'd, but Princelike shewes
         Glorious effectes of worth that fit his place,
         And fighting dyes, and dying ouerthrowes:
         Another of that forward name and race,*
         In that hotte worke his valiant life bestowes,
         Who bare the Standard of the King that day,
         Whose colours ouerthrowne did much dismaye.

         * *Another Blunt which was the kings Standard bearer.*

51-2. Om.
53(=110=<113).1 and ô much bloud
2 this loosing victorie
3 Disturbed King: yet hast thou conquered   [O trauayld king 95   Gloss om.
4 A doubtfull day, a mightie enemie:
5 But yet what woundes, what famous worth lyes dead,   [yet / ô 95
6 That makes the winner looke with sorrowing eye,
7 Couragious *Stafford* lost, that much had wrought,
8 And valiant *Shorly* who great glory got.   Gloss: *Sir Hugh Shorly.*

54.   Om.
55(=111=<114).
         Such wracke of others blood thou didst behold,
         Furious young *Hotspur,* ere thou lost thine owne,
         Which now once lost, that heate in thine waxt cold,
         And soone became thine Armie ouerthrowne,
         But why had not this spirit this courage bold,
         Been in some better cause so hylie showne,
         That we might not thus violently then
         Haue tearmed that rage, which valour should haue ben.
         [2 O furious *Hotspur*
         4 thine / thy
         5 And ô that this great spirit
         6 Had in some good cause bene rightly showne
         7 So had not we thus
56-82. Om.

83(=112=<115).1 But now the King retires him to his peace,
2 A peace much like a feeble sick
3 (Wherein his waking paines
4 Though seeming rest his closed eyes doth keepe)
5 For neuer peace could euer so release   [neuer / ô no
6 His intricate turmoyles, and sorrowes deepe

7 still / that   cares kept waking
8 Continue on, till death conclude the strife.
84.1 imploy'd / sent
5 And so consum'd all that imboldning store
6 Of hot gaine-striuing blood, that did contend,
7 Wearing the wall so thin, that now the
8 Might well looke thorow
85.1 When loe as if the vapours
3 the sence, that nothing might appeare
4 Vnto the thought, that which it was in deed)
5 The lightened soule began to see more cleere
6 How much it was abusd, and
7 The plaine discouered falsehood open layd,
8 Of ill-perswading flesh that so betrayd.
86.2 Where death
8 soone / straight
87.1 all confusd, trembling with
2 as ouerthrowne in sprite
7 my soule doth now conceiue
8 held / got

After 87(=116):   127 (i.e. 117)
    Wert thou the cause my clyming care was such
    To passe those boundes, nature, and law ordaind?
    Is this the good which promised so much,
    And seemd so glorious ere it was attaind?
    Wherein was neuer ioy, but gaue a touch
    To checke my soule, to thinke how thou wert gaind
    And now how do I leaue thee vnto mine?
    Wherein is dread to keepe, death to resigne.
      [8   which it is

88(=118=<121).1 With this the soule rapt wholy with
    2 Of such distresse, did
    3 Her present horror
    4 oppressed / consumed
    5 And now as
    6 the / his
    7 This / The
    8 impatient / vnwilling

After 88:   129 (i.e. 119)
    And whilst that sad confused soule doth cast
    Those great accountes of terror and distresse,
    Vppon this counsell it doth light at last,
    How she might make the charge of horror lesse,
    And finding no way to acquit thats past,
    But onely this, to vse some quicke redresse
    Of acted wrong, with giuing vp againe
    The Crowne to whom it seem'd to appertaine.

                    130 (i.e. 120)
    Which found, lightned with some small ioy, shee hyes,
    Rouses her seruantes that dead sleeping lay,
    (The members of her house) to exercise

One feeble duetie more, during her stay:
And opening those dimme windowes, he espies
The crowne for which he lookt, was borne awaie:
And all-aggrieu'd with the vnkind offence,
He causd him bring it backe, who tooke it thence.
    [5 dimme / darke
     8 who / that

89(=121=<124).1 whom (excusing his presumptuous deed,
   2 By the supposing him departed quite)
   3 He sayes: [said: 95   needes thee
   4 Vnto that care, where feare exceedes thy right,
   5 And where his sinne, whom thou shalt now succeed,
   6 Shall still vpbraide thy'inheritance of might?
   7 And if thou canst liue, and liue great, from woe
   8 Without this carefull trauaile; let it goe.
90.5 who / that
91.2 And thou o1   [And ô do thou contend 95
92.2 sacred warre
93.8 Thou canst not be the father
94.8 stiffe / strong
95.4 Th'int'rest
   6 paine r'inforc'd againe,
   7 And cut off all the passages
   8 Gloss om.
96.6 Ou'er o1   [O're 95
End-title: Om.
After 96(=128=<131; misnumbered 113):

139 (i.e. 129)

Helpe on ô sou'raigne *Muse,* helpe on my course,
If these my toyles be gratefull in thy eyes;
Or but looke on, to cheare my feeble force,
That I faint not in this great enterprize:
And you great Worthyes you, that take remorse
Of mine estate, and helpe my thoughts to rise,
Continue still your grace, that I may giue
Ende to the worke, wherein your worth may liue.
    [5 you ô worthy you
     6 my estate
End-title: *The end of the third Booke.* 95 om.

BOOK V

Head-title: THE ARGVMENT OF THE FOWRTH BOOKE.
Argument.3   *sixt marryed vnlickely,*

1.3 Whilst thou . . . didst   Gloss: *Henry 5.*
 4 thy feete
 7 Thy
 8 But   actiue / working

After 1:   2
What do I feele here now in passing by
These blessed times that I am forst to leaue?

What trembling sad remorse doth terrefie
M'amazed thoughts with what I do conceiue?
What? doth my pen commit impietie
To passe those sacred *Tropheis* without leaue?
And do I sinne, not to salute your ghostes
Great Worthies, so renown'd in forraine coastes?
　　[1　here / ô

2(=3).1　Who do I see out of the darke appeare,
　　2　Couered almost with cloudes as with the night,
　　3　That here presents him with a
　　4　seeming of dreadfull　　　[Seeming 95
　　8　speakes.
　5.1　O what eternall matter 95
　　8　But when
　7.1　O that our 95
　　8　who / that　　weares.
　8.1　What is it ô to 95
　10.1　For / O 95
　　8　O let her not neglect 95
　11.　Gloss: *Hen. 5.* 95
　12.3　am / haue
　　6　Actions to aduaunce
　15.5　Making his life th'example
　　6　in vre
　　7　Most glorying to aduaunce true vertuous blood
　16.1　Who as
　17.4　Feeble
　　5　Yet he those long . . . so led 95
　19.5　Ease was not suffered with
　　6　T'examine . . . wealthes to rate
　　7　Gloss om. 95
　21.1　And here were none that　　[Here ô were 95
　24.1　Gloss: This Richard, sonne to the D. of Yorke Earle of Cambridge maried . . .
　　　Crowne. 95 om.
　　2　vntimely 01
　　3　t'aduaunce 95
　　4　the / yet
　25.1　perceiuing
　26.8　practises
　27.5　these / which
　　8　Gloss om.
　28.1　the Earle 95
　30.2　vntimely / so vilely
　　3　point / time
　　4　glorious great designes
　　7　seem'd / were 95
　31.1　And
　　8　Whith 95
　33.4　attempts 01　　　Gloss: *Vntill Richard . . . Hen. 6.* 01　　*Richard Duke of Yorke.*
　　　95
　　7　feare / care
　34.1　Else ô 95

After 34(=35):   36
     Which how much were it to be still, requir'd
     In all of might, if all were like of minde:
     But when that all depraued haue conspird
     To be vniust, what safetie shall they finde
     (After the date of vertue is expird)
     That do not practize in the self-same kinde,
     And countermine against deceite with guile?
     But ô what mischiefe feeles the world the while?
     [1 Which ô how much it were to be requir'd

35(=37).4 great . . . great / most . . . most
    5 yet / ô 95
38.1 How / O 95
   2 So mixe 95
39.6 And that no course is free
   7 And that faire dayes do breed
40.1 that / but 95
   2 conguestes 01
   7 As greatnes were
41.2 The
   8 was ours by course
42.2 Gloss om. 95
43.2 Gloss om. 95
   8 thus
44.8 forrainge 01
45.7 sleeping-wrong
46.5 to
47.1 O then yet how much better had 95
   5 What madnes, vnconstrained to begin
   6 To right his State, to put the State in broyle?
   7 Iustice her selfe may euen do wrong in this,
   8 No warre be'ing right, but that which needfull is.
48.4 guide / vse 01   Vnworthy of the 95
49.3 neuer / neuers CT
50.1 spright
   5 wights 95
   6 highest 95
   7 others to scourge
51.1 yet / ô 95
   7 due course must rightly goe   [Then ô I see due 95
   8 And th'earth must trace it or else purchase woe. 95
52.4 many mightie
53.1 Humble of spirite, by nature patient   [Milde, meeke of 95.
   2 t'increase, or scarse to keepe   [scarse keepe 95
   3 Apter for pardoning
   4 Seeking his bountie, not his powre t'haue knowne
   8 this 95
54.1 weake, goode, feeble, godly
55.3 Gloss om.
56.3 Gloss: *The Duke . . . to the . . . Yorke & had euer enuied his prefermēt.* 95
58.7 if / in 01
59.1 Earle / Duke   Gloss om.
   5 Being a

7 contriv'd . . . others / contriued . . . their
8 To cost   Gloss: *Which were deliuered vp to her father vpon the match.*
60.8 ratifide.
63.1 that I am forst
  2 whom / that
  4 As euerlasting admiration gat
  6 As it doth here my Muse exasperate o1   [That I am drawne to say I know
    not what 95
  7 Vnwilling that . . . should euer giue   [And yet ô that 95
64.3 Haue matcht the worthiest that the world hath knowne
  7 the / that
65.1 And
66.1 doth
  6 be thought . . . the offence
  8 as those, that
67.3 yet / ô
  7 aggrieued . . . t'weigh 95
68.2 who / that
  8 brought. Gloss: *Humfrey Duke of Gloster Protector.*   [*Protector* om. 95
70.5 With 95
  8 As who the course of her maine will doth staie.
71.3 That   one / else
72.4 That to himselfe th'affaires all wholly tooke:
  5 And ruling all, had neuer any minde
  6 who / that
73.1 And
  2 Of still continuing of his charge too
  4 vnlesse / without   Gloss om.
74.1 O could 95
  8 despight.
75.1 Then should not ô so 95
  7 those that
76.1 Gloss om.
  8 to vndoo.
77.1 Those thus prouided whom the Queene well knew,   [knew 95
  4 As easie t'was to ouerthrow
78.6 Whilst
  7 When straight the
80.7 th'offence. o1
81.2 Gloss om.
  5 Whereas the   [Where as 95
82.8 Sacietie
83.3 Seeing he was most
  8 dye.
85.2 that day . . . committing
  5 sorrowes gathered
86.3 O then 95
  5 O let their cunning 95
88.7 how / that
90.7 see in what a state   [ô in 95
91.6 Gloss om.
  7 instead
93.2 O what great 95

8   will. 95
97.1   Thus well they deem'd what after followed
2   Gloss om.
5   He with the enemie confedered
7   Of all our strength; that all
98.5   h'is / His CT
8   Gloss om.
100.3   would calme
8   this rage
101.4   Gloss om.
102.2   Vnto the trauaild Queene
5   O God (sayth she) and art thou thus betraid
103.3   Thus beare the title of a Soueraigne
4   And suffred not to
5   O must our subiects 95
6   where as
104.1   Must / Will 01   O will they then our powre, and will 95
3   which / that
5   who / that

After 104(=106):   107
         Deere Suffolk, I beheld thy wofull cheere,
     When thou perceiu'd no helpe, but to depart:
     I saw that looke wherein did plaine appeare
     The lamentable message of thy hart,
     That seemd to say: O *Queene,* and canst thou beare
     My ruine so? the cause whereof thou art:
     Canst thou indure to see them worke their will,
     And not defend me from the hand of ill?
          [1   ô I saw thy
           2   perceiu'dst

                              108
         Haue I for thee aduentured so much,
     Made shypwracke of my honor, fayth and fame?
     And doth my seruice giue no deeper touch
     To thy hard hart, better to feele the same?
     Or dost thou feare, or is thy weakenesse such,
     As not of force to keepe me from this shame?
     Or else now hauing seru'd thy turne of mee,
     Art well content my ouerthrow to see?

                              109
         As if my sight did read vnto thy minde
     The lecture of that shame thou wouldst forget,
     And therefore peraduenture glad to finde
     So fit occasion, doth it forward set:
     Or else thy selfe from dangerous toyle t'vnwind,
     Downe on my necke dost all the burthen let;
     Since Kinges must haue some hated worse then they,
     On whom they may the waight of enuy lay.

105(=110; misnumbered 114 in 95).1   No *Suffolke,* none of this, my soule is cleere
      2   Farre from the thought of such impietie: [Without the 95

    3 Yet must I needes confesse, that too much feare,
    4 Made me defende thee less couragiously:
    5 Seeing more Princes euer ruind were
106.1 Thus in her passion loe she vttered
    2 When as
    8 Gloss: *Iacke Cades rebellion in Kent, who named himself Mortimer.* 95 om.
107.4 chief accomplices
    5 here / that 95
    8 proceed
108.6 That 95
109.3 humor / honor (corr. to humor, "Faults Escaped") 95
111.3 be'ing aduis'd / being sure
112.2 He doth in most vpright opinion stand
    4 what still they
    8 lesse, 01
113.1 who / that
    5 gets / drawes
    7 whow 01
114.8 hath; 01
116(=121).
End-title. *fift / fourth*

Book VI

Head-title: THE FIFT BOOKE OF / THE CIVILL WARRES / betweene
the two Howses of / *Lancaster* and *Yorke.* [The Fyft Booke of the Ciuill / VVarres
betweene 95   [The fift Booke of the Ciuill warres / betweene the two Houses of
Lancaster / and *Yorke.* 95a

1.6 Gloss om.
2.1 Gloss: *Iacke Cade.*
6.1 Eor 95
  8 Adding fresh
7.1 And seeing yet all this draw to no end

After 7:   8
       Like when a greedy Pyrat hard in chaze
    Pursuing of a rich supposed prize,
    Workes for the windes, plyes sayles, beares vp a pace,
    Our-runnes the cloudes, scoures after her that flyes:
    Pride in his hart, and wealth before his face,
    Keepes his hands wrought, and fixed keepes his eyes
    So long, till that ingag'd within some straight,
    He falles amid his foes, layd close in wayt:

                          9
       Where all too late, discouering round about
    Danger and death, the purchase of his hast;
    And no backe flying, no way to get out,
    But there to perish, or to yeeld disgrac't;
    Cursing his error, yet in th'error stout:
    He toyles for life, now charges, now is chac't:
    Then quailes, and then fresh courage takes againe,
    Striuing t'vnwind himselfe, but all in vaine.

8(=10).1 So standes this rout in
   4 A / When   for / of
   5 Pardon (the snare
   8 get. 95, 95a
11.2 Gloss: This Rebellion was thought to be fostred by some friend of the Duke of
      Yorke, . . . Ireland, sent . . . euer after: But now returning . . . wales. The D.
      of York combines . . . whose . . . married, . . . Warwicke. Rest of gloss om.
      95, 95a om.
12.3 distended / discended (corr. to distended, "Faults Escaped") 95, 95a
   7 A mightie partie for a mightie cause
   8 By their vnited amitie hee drawes.

After 12(=14):   15
         For as the spreading members of proud *Po,*
         That thousand-branched *Po,* whose limmes embrace
         Thy fertile and delicious body so
         Sweete *Lombardie,* and beatifies thy face:
         Such seemd this powreful stocke, from whence did gro
         So many great discents, spreading their race,
         That euery corner of the Land became,
         Enricht with some great *Heroes* of that name.
         [4 beautifies 95a

13(=16).2 braue / great
  14.2 his most assured friendes   Gloss: *The E. of Deuonshire and the L. Cobham.*
      95, 95a om.
   7 two-edged / double edged (corr. to two edged, "Faults Escaped") 95, 95a
  15.1 Lords / Lord (corr. to Lords, "Faults Escaped") 95, 95a
  16.1 (the maime / (O maine (corr. to O mayme, "Faults Escaped") 95, 95a
   2 Eternall scarre 95, 95a
   3 And Guien's lost 95, 95a
   8 good. 95, 95a
  17.1 O how can you behold 95, 95a
  18.1 obrayd 95, 95a
   5 important / strong
   8 pounds 95, 95a
  19.5 The / Where
  21.7 blest, if so it be;   [blest; if so it be, 95, 95a
  22.1 In those whom
   5 runne before
  23.7 Gloss om.
  24. Gloss: *Anno Reg. 30. The first Sulleuation of the D. of Yorke.* 95, 95a om.
  25.3 Where finding of
  26.2 Gloss: *The vse . . . time.*   95, 95a om.
  27.1 that / the o1   O if the fire 95, 95a
   6 thunder, both in
   8 wise? o1
  28.2 vvith 95   Gloss om.
   4 order at
   8 vpright, o1
  29.2 iarrs 95, 95a
   8 came.
  31.8 wise. o1   [wise: 95, 95a

32.8 beautifide: o1
33.4 pietie? o1   [pietie: 95, 95a
     7ʼ so / if 95, 95a
34.7 And th'abused power that such a power hath got,   [th'abus'd 95, 95a   Gloss
      om.
35.1 thou therefore
     5 whom darkenesse doth detaine
36.2 to / so 95, 95a
     5 like defended
37.6 intent CT
38.7 They / Hee
     8 their / his
39.3 of all states generall 95, 95a
     7 in the strangest wise
40.8 withnesse o1
41.6 Gloss om.
43.8 defeat.

After 45(=48):   49
         Though thou shalt seeke by all the meanes thou may
         And arme impietie, and hell and all,
         Stirre vp her owne, make others to assay,
         Bring fayth disguisd, the power of *Pluto* call,
         Call all thy craftes to practise her decay,
         And yet shall this take no effect at all:
         For shee secure (as intimate with fate)
         Shall sit and scorne, those base dissignes of hate.

47(=51).2 one, / on, o1   [none 95, 95a
     8 of eternitie.
48.3 vvith 95   Artes / crafts
     5 mimens 95, 95a
49.6 away 95a
50.2 hath now planted   Gloss om.
51.8 desires?
52.6 still,
     8 wrong? o1
53.3 vvhat 95
     4 Fly from the
54.4 they / it   Gloss: And finding . . . then his. Edmond . . . Gante. 95, 95a om.
55.7 tho 'gainst his dignitie,
     8 end in 95, 95a
58.1 sommoned / gathered
     3 the apprehended o1
     5 act / death o1   [deed 95, 95a
59.2 Ah! / and
     8 ayd, o1
61.5 is / as 95, 95a
62.5 burials, is
63.8 dangerons 95
64.4 thus / thys 95, 95a
     7 touches
65.3 enioy we / shall we haue
     6 To'be'accessaries 95, 95a

66.6 his end 95, 95a
67.1 For this course euer they deliberate,
   2 Which do aspire to reach the gouernment,
   3 Still / To
   4 Who / Which   such as / those that
   5 manage great affayres of state
69.6 doome?
   8 die. 01
70.1 Thus / Thys 95a
   8 Gloss: *Suffred . . . Wigmore.* 95, 95a om.
71.8 hazarded, 01
72.2 Gloss om.
73.4 where 01   [vvhere 95
   7 that / as
74.4 Gloss: *The Dukes . . . Burgundie.*
75.8 and / or 95, 95a
76.2 Gloss om.
83.5 goared 95, 01   [gored 95a
85.3 game / same
   4 march'd, they thought they yet stood still
   5 came. 95
   6 so ill 95, 95a
86.1 Who weighing yet his force and their desire
   4 Tells him the doubtfull ground they stood vpon
   5 Gloss: *The Lord Lisle.*
   6 Seeing his youth but euen now begun
87.3 whom / which 95, 95a
   8 I haue liu'd enough, if I can die with fame,   [fame. 95, 95a
88.2 Turnes 95, 95a
   8 th'enemie, 01
89.1 Bands, / Bands. CT; comma from 01   [Bands 95, 95a
90.5 blow, from far that   [blow from 95a
91.2 Who / That
   5 So working, that Fate knew not how dispose 01   [Sith these made doubtfull how
       Fate would dispose 95, 95a
   8 can thinke worth ought. (corr. to could thinke well gote, "Faults Escaped") 95, 95a
92.8 owes.
93.1 ardor / spirit
94.2 whereas 95, 95a
   6 hands . . . rest,
95.8 Gloss in roman. 95, 95a om.
96.4 Yet did thrust him on beyond   [did it thrust 95, 95a
   5 Flying into the maine Battallion   [rest of line om.
   8 Gloss om. 95, 95a
98.4 Gloss om.
   7 Who must not sinne
99.6 be showne 95, 95a
   7 faute 95, 95a
100.3 come
102.1 this / the 95, 95a
   3 They draw (corr. to To draw "Faults Escaped") 95, 95a
   4 obuious vnto hatred / naturally hated
   5 Seeing them apt to bear the greatest blame,

6   That offices of greatest enuy beare
7   And that in
8   Gloss om.
103.4   As the maine marke Fortune had plac'd therefore
5   hard-wrought
7   Griefe being glad
104.2   models
3   Se'ing the faire bootie
5   He takes / Taking 95, 95a
7   For / And 95, 95a
8   last. 01
105.1   sith 95, 95a
3   generally
8   loug. 95 (turned n)
106.3   gathering / drawing
4   Began to grow to be of fearefull might
5   so hastie gathered
107.   Gloss om.
6   discended (corr. to distended "Faults Escaped") 95, 95a
8   warre.
108.4   Seeking t'haue had his povver, farre off supprest   [far of 95, 95a   Gloss: *The
first Battle at S. Albones the 23. of May Anno. Reg. 33.*   95, 95a om.
7   hee / h'is
109.1   Where-to / Whether
4   Since
110.1   Neuer did valiant
3   Blemish the reputation of renowne
5   To bring such
8   Sith / Where   Gloss om.
111.1   But this on Warwicks wrath must needes be layd
3   they / he 95, 95a
4   would, or then was for his gaine
6   euen there / fowlly 01   but there came slayne 95, 95a
7   The Duke / Himselfe 01   Both he and all the Leaders els besides; 95, 95a
Gloss: *Edmond D. of Somerset slaine, who left behind him 3. sonnes, Henry, Edm.
& Iohn. Here was also slaine the E. of Northum. and the L. Clifford.* 95, 95a om.
8   beeing / is 01   himselfe alone a prisoner bides. 95, 95a
112.   Gloss: *Anno Reg. 34.* 95, 95a om.
1   A prisoner, though not to th'outward eye   [the outvvard 95, 95a
3   be'ing 95a
6   seeming-order 95, 95a
113.2   Court straight altered   [now altered 95, 95a
3   All the supremest charges
4   were contributed 01   [Were to his ayders straight contributed 95, 95a   Gloss
om. 95, 95a
6   which onely couered
8   Which th'only greatest part   [Which yet the greatest 95, 95a
114.4   Nor once all-seeking Fortune durst to tuch; 95, 95a
5   inlarged shame
7   such a deede 95, 95a
8   horrors that succeed.
End-title. *Sixt / fift*
This concludes 95, 99.

Book VII

N.B.: Henceforward, variants are from 01 only.

Head-title: THE SIXT BOOKE OF / THE CIVILL WARRES / betweene
the two Houses of / *Lancaster* and *Yorke.*

Argument 1 *repriz'd* / *repriu'd*

  1.1 DIsordinate / Vnnatural
    6 Gloss om.
    8 not all / he not   key
  3.1 For whether by not daring
    3 him, whom he held weake, or vaine
    4 Or that the Queene
    7 And / But
  4.1 For though this feeble King   before om.
    3 more om.
    4 Then / But
    5 store om.
    8 t'attend
  5.7 Or what it is, the
    8 And with our bodyes Kings must haue
  6.2 Gloss om. except as given below, 9.2
    6 Standes now upon them, and
    7 Summons for them t'appeare
  7.1 either / whether
    8 groundes.
  8.3 Who / That
    7 ouer-gone / left vndone
  9.2 Gloss: *The D. of Yorke flyes to . . . North.*
    7 se'ing *Yorkes* hopes so
    8 That they would euer swell againe so hye.

After 9:   10

      So humble *Rodon, Wainsteedes* sweete delight,*
    That waters *Mountioyes* solitarie rest,
    Be'ing checkt with Sommers heate, shrinkes out of sight
    Downe in his narrow bed, as quite supprest,
    That lately Swolne with forrayne-ayding might,
    Ran boundlesse ouer all, and all possest:
    And now so feeble growne, hath left no more
    Then scarse sustaynes his variable store.

       * *Rodon the Riuer by Wainsteed.*

10(=11).1 So now seem'd Yorke; and yet for all remaynes
    3 no affliction
    5 place / State
 11.2 distry'de
 12.6 drowning / winning
    7 thus t'wards kings abus'd their swordes
 13.6 Summons a Parlament all
    8 Gloss om. except as given below, st. 16.
 14. Gloss: *Anno Reg. 36.*
 15.4 desiguments
    8 Then mutuall vtilitie and gaine.

16.   Gloss: *The Earle . . . seruantes.*
19.3   As by way of complainte, to signifie
  6   To be by these sinister plots begun
20.4   Gloss: *The Lord Audly slaine at Bloreheath by the E. of Salisburie.*
21(=22).   ʒ2 (turned digit)
  2   desp'rate / headlong
  4   was soone furnished
  8   't is / t'is
22.3   To whom / Whither
  8   But th'one betrayd their cause: Gloss: *Sir Andrew Trollop fled . . . Lords.*
23.5   And neare them came
  7   Gloss: *The B. of Salisburie.* Rest of gloss om.
24.6   t'obtaine / to winne
25.1   this b'a too great staine
27.3   Saue / But
28.2   so feelingly / s'effectually   Gloss om.
  8   fight:
29.1   wakened (possibly the better reading)
  5   Gloss om.
30.2   Is / Sh'is   Gloss om.
  3   infect
31.4   r'entry
32.1   For now upon them standes imperiously
  2   Fortune and Powre, with all the States grace on
  4   Treason, Conspiracie, Rebellion
  5   Degrades, depriues them of abilitie
  6   B'Attayndor, and by confiscation
  7   And sets a hideous face vpon their crimes
  8   As / Which   times.
34(=35, misnumbered 34).
  1   Other occasions, other intre'sts heare
  6   Disgrace receiues
  7   ere it will / rather than
36(=37).1   home all their best meanes brought forth
  2   Disordred broyles t'appease, or to preuent
  4   Young / Great   strength / powre   Gloss om.
  8   grieuances.
37.1   Gloss om.
38.7   Sad want / Famine
39.2   And I see temprat rigor safely sitts
  3   did vpbraid / once obrayd
  7   So, to like / And to this   my Lord / you see
40.1   but, I pray, / but (my lord)
41.8   b'vndone
45.2   blood, Nature ought stand vpon
  3   tending / bended
  4   Lookes somewhat downe t'a selfe tuition
  5   Gloss: posteritie attainted . . . degree. Rest of gloss om. *Ludlow / Ludlom* CT
  6   As that himselfe, on   might om.
  7   Out of / Might by
46.4   Gloss om.
47.8   Gloss: Woodvill, taken . . . Dinham. Rest of gloss om.
50 ff. (=51 ff.). Misnumbered 49 **ff.** CT
51.3   to / towards

4   Gloss in roman.

54.1 may / shall

2 Fury runnes out thus

3 humour / Virtues

5 eminence who waighd no lawes

6 Or the as-yet vnstrayn'd vp Sou'raigntie

7 Which had this disproportion in the partes

8 Of might to draw, diuert, and gouerne hartes?

55.1 Or did th'opinion of a powre wrong plac'd

2 Cause this infectious sicknesse of the State

3 That men rather then wealth, or life, imbrac'd

4 Destruction, ruine, bloodshed, and debate

5 their Virtues, and their

6 Maiestie to this lowe rate?

7 Then Virtu'and Worth, you proue contagious,

8 And Honour out of square, growes dangerous.

56.1 And / Where

2 Yeeld Princes safetie, and the peoples

3 Whilst next to Kinges are plac'd (Kings to adorne)

4 These (as the Minions who are fauored best)

5 Religion, Law, Statutes, Customes

7 suggestions, titles, claymes

8 Nor seeke for Crownes, whereat Ambition aymes.

57.3 And, from abrode / From Couentry

4 Gloss: The K. sendes . . . London. Rest of gloss om.

6 Royaltie / Maiestie

7 Where, though / And where

8 Towre.

58.2 disobedience

4 iollitie / reuerence

5 grace / ioy   The Citties / This place, this

7 intertaining / holding   Gloss: The E. of Salisbury left to keepe the citie.

8 try. Gloss om.

59.1 Leading their new got troupes

2 Who had t'a womans care resignd his heed

60.8 Gloss: The D. . . . slayne. Rest of gloss om.

61.4 Only a feeble body and

5 Which yet was that they held the only thing

6 And both sides labord for so

62.1 When / Whilst

7 Gloss om.

63.2 Stay'ng still for *English*

4 Ambition fayles not, to be here in poost

5 seemes / comes

6 Which seemes to be made more, by be'ing long lost

64.1 come

2 him . . . Estate

5 as it seemes it feares

65.2 Did not breed

6 b'imployde

8 ground.

67.3 doth

6 he that is

8 spirits worke
68.8 Till it b'againe reduc'd
69.5 The Church opprest, the Laytie' vnder the hand
  8 cause
70.2 S'impayred the
  3 That euen the
  4 growne: / growne) CT
  8 land.
71.5 who / yet
  8 indurd t'avoyd, bloodshed, and strife.
72.8 Seemes as reseru'd to be for something wrought:
73.7 Or / And
  8 this / haue
74.4 Who sure would make no opposition
  6 Matter worthy consideration
  7 his right, was such in
  8 Yet seem'd not now t'haue the . . . Right.
75.4 Peoples assent, oathes, Parlaments
  8 Since   Gloss om.
76.6 when om.
  7 King Richards / The others
  8 Seemd then . . . eie.
77(=78, misnumbered 77). 5 Gloss: W. Rufus . . . brother. Hen. 3. succeeds in the
      kingdome after the depriuation of his father, and the election of Lewes.
  8 succeedes,
78.1 third enters vnto the State
  2 was om.
  3 fairely / rightly
  4 In th'after body of succession
  5 to accommodate
  6 All thinges to each mans satisfaction
  8 Farther confused mischiefes to
79.4 auersiue / a way-ward
  6 And to that godly King some reuerence drew
  7 That they at length, during his life agreed
80.1 presently / solemnly
  2 Proclaym'd with ioyfull acclamations
  4 By oathes, vowes, protestations
  5 Built with all strength of forme, as to abide
  6 All whatsoeuer oppositions
81.8 T'whose child, no   leaue / loue
82.5 death / life
83.1 this / the   here om.
  3 Onely effected with confusion
  5 insolencies may not thus go on
84.3 many'a
  5 With om.
  6 courage / spirites,
  7 Who
  8 Who, though h'had done, he had . . . end.
86.6 Gloss: *The Battel . . . Yorke: the E. . . . . Battle.*   Rest of gloss om.
  8 thus.
87.2 had this foule fall

89.8   turmoyle.
91.6   tendring
    7   Gloss: *is* om.
92.4   Gloss: *Kings | Queenes*
93.3   now eu'n th'accomplishment
    6   & om.
    7   left om.
95.1   And so it fares   late om.
    2   thus / so
96.8   their / the
97.1   as / like
99.4   most of all is eu'n the
    7   cannot what he would, do;
    8   who / that

After 99(=100)   101
        Which causd that she not long her conquest ioy'd
      Nor long imbrac'd her Lords redemption,
      Who now with passion wholly ouerioy'd
      Triumphes t'haue lost the day, to be so wonne,
      Blessing their care, praising their faithfull ayde;
      Embracing now his wife, and now his sonne,
      Whom there with many others else he knights,
      Who for him, held against him fiercest fights.

             ·   102
        Thus he that lately of another side
      Was brought of force to be of their intent,
      Recarried with the current of the tide,
      Is backe return'd t'his proper element:
      Th'vnvoluntary bonds seeme as vntide;
      For forc'd t'offend h'is almost innocent:
      N'agreement, that necessity constraines,
      Longer than the necessitie, remaines.

100(=103).4   Gloss om.
    8   gain'd.
101.8   vexed / this last   greatest
102.3   Whither, when *Yorke* set forward for the North
    4   Hee's sent to
    8   remedie;
104.1   Christened by his owne name
    3   borne for eternall fame
    8   Whereinto runne *Warwicks* dispiersed streames.
105.4   Gloss om.
    7   unto the North departs
    8   Leauing to
106.1   now / thus
    3   that / now   allow / discusse
    5   Nor *Henries* dealing most iniurious
108.2   all generally cryes
    3   streight / all
109.1   Nothing, but now to crowne this chosen King
    8   Borne to make

After 109(=112):   113
     In whom appeare all Maiesties best partes
     Both pers'nage, bloud, vertue, powre and wit,
     Which in the throne and kingdome of mens hartes,
     Onely make princes gloriously to sit,
     And which, now to recure the broken parts,
     Of a dis-ioynted Rule, were onely fitte,
     To whom my verse now vowes of honor brings,
     This is my side, my Muse must hold with kings.

110(=114).1 But had this end attaind, here
    3 *Towton | Saxton*
    6 this of thine   his / thine
    8 rest / ceast
111.1 but in the midst of her
    3 with blood and slaughter
    4 to / would
    6 hath agreed,
    7 And knowes not yet
End-title: FINIS.   This completes o1.

Book VIII

N.B.:   Book VIII appeared first in o9, sheets of which were used for 23. There are
       no more variants.

  3.6 one / our CT   (corr. in "Faults Escaped," CT R4ᵛ).
26 ff. misnumbered 25 ff.
35.3 didst / did didst CT
37.6 out / out out CT

Notes

Title-page motto

Aetas prima canat veneres, extrema tumultus;
Bella canam, quando scripta puella mea est.

(Propertius, *Elegies, II.x.7.*)

"Let youth sing of loves, age of war's alarms; I shall sing of wars, since my love has already been celebrated." Daniel's Muse, in her "youth," had sung of Delia and Rosamond. See I.5.4n.

To her sacred Maiestie

Appeared in 1601–02; deleted in 1609. Both Corser (p. 41) and Grosart (*1*, xxiv) unaccountably say that this refers to Queen Anne. The sentiments as well as the date show that it could be meant only for Elizabeth. Contrast the Epistle Dedicatory to Queen Anne prefixed to *Coll. Hist. Eng.*, 1618.

9–16 See VI.44–6.

17–18 This is possibly a basis of the legend that Daniel was made "Laureat" upon the death of Spenser.

22–3 blessed Vnion . . . sacred Concord: The marriage of Henry VII of Lancaster with Elizabeth of York. See Dedication, p. 67, and VI.44–5. This is the official Tudor interpretation of English history, which Daniel took over from the chroniclers.

29–30 vainely entertaine . . . ydle shadowes: Daniel's continual criticism of the Elizabethan stage. See Apology to *Philotas*.

To the Right Honorable . . .

Prefixed to 1599 *Poeticall Essayes*. Mountjoy is mentioned in *CW*, I.5, II.128, and VII.10n. of this edition.

To the Right Noble . . .

First appeared in 1609. See beginning of Book VIII.

The Right Noble Lady: "Sidney's sister, Pembroke's mother"; Daniel's chief patroness and literary coworker in the Wilton Circle.

4–5 the one: Book VIII. the other: Book III split into III and IV, with added material. See Variants.

16 purpose: In general, the same plan as Shakespeare's history plays, from *Richard II* to *Richard III*. Daniel never got beyond Edward IV.

26–28 the Historie . . . our common Annalles: See above, Sources, pp. 1–7.

31 Famae [sic] . . . : Nunc fama rerum standum est, ubi certam derogat vetustas fidem (Livy, *Ab Urbe Condita*, VII.vi.6). "As it is, one must hold by the tradition, where antiquity will not allow us to be certain."

339

40 Poets: Sidney had made this point in the *Defense of Poetry*. See also Spenser's distinction between poets historical and historiographers, in the Letter to Raleigh prefixed to *The Faerie Queene*.

58 censure: estimate.

62 credulous: Those favorably disposed to a "suspension of disbelief."

64 *14* yeares: Isabel was actually seven years old when Richard married her in 1396, and not yet eleven when he was led captive into London. See I.40.7, and p. 11 above.

67–70 this Harmony of words . . . a language fitting Lightnes and Vanitie: Note the shift in emphasis by Milton; in writing "that other harmony of prose" he feels that he has but the use of his left hand.

79 Historie of *England,* from the Conquest: Daniel brought this up only to the end of Edward III, at which point the *Civil Wars* had begun in detail.

Book I

1–3 Compare the opening lines of Lucan's *Pharsalia* (*De bello civili*):

> Of war I sing, war worse than civil, waged over the plains of Emathia, and of legality conferred on crime; I tell how an imperial people turned their victorious right hands against their own vitals; how kindred fought against kindred; how, when the compact of tyranny was shattered, all the forces of the shaken world contended to make mankind guilty; how standards confronted hostile standards, eagles were matched against each other, and pilum threatened pilum.
>
> What madness was this, my countrymen, what fierce orgy of slaughter? . . . it was your duty to rob proud Babylon of her trophies over Italy, did you choose to give to hated nations the spectacle of Roman bloodshed, and to wage wars that could win no triumphs? Ah! with that blood shed by Roman hands how much of earth and sea might have been bought . . . Ere this the Chinese might have passed under our yoke . . . If Rome has such a lust for unlawful warfare, let her first subdue the whole earth to her sway and then commit self-slaughter; so far she has never lacked a foreign foe. But, if now . . . Italy bristles with thorn-brakes, and her soil lies unploughed year after year . . . these great disasters are not due to proud Pyrrhus or the Carthaginian; no other sword has been able to pierce so deep; the strokes of a kindred hand are driven home.
>
> Still, if Fate could find no other way for the advent of Nero . . . then we complain no more against the gods: even such crimes and such guilt are not too high a price to pay. . . . Rome owes much to civil war, because what was done was done for you, Caesar. (Loeb Classical Library, trans. by J. D. Duff, London, Heinemann; New York, Putnam, 1928.) See also Shakespeare's indebtedness to Daniel, p. 18 above.

1.4–8 The deliberate overuse of antithetical structure is decorous here, being descriptive of the conditions of civil dissension. Cf. I.115.7–8, VIII.71.7–8. See Pope's *Rape of the Lock,* I.101–2:

> Where wigs with wigs, with sword-knots sword-knots strive,
> Beaux banish beaux, and coaches coaches drive.

Daniel was a neo-classicist and was esteemed in the early 18th century.

3.3 happie gaine: The notion of a *felix culpa* adumbrated in this stanza is a good example of how Daniel added to and combined his sources. Even the prone-to-moralize Hall had gone no further in this connection than to state that "there can be no vnion or agrement but in respect of a diuision." Daniel superimposed the sentiment in the last paragraph quoted from Lucan, above. Milton, who also wrote English history and desired to be "doctrinal and exemplary to a nation," and who was doubtless familiar with Daniel's work (see VI.26.39n.), set this idea in its larger context in *PL*, XII.469–78.

4.1   Anticipates Milton's transcending the pagan muses: *PL*, I.6–23.

4.8   life to my verse: Probably means longevity rather than vivacity.

5.1   Charles Blount, Lord Mountjoy, later Earl of Devonshire, one of Daniel's patrons. See dedicatory sonnet, p. 66 above. The "quiet shore" is probably Wanstead, which Mountjoy purchased from Essex in 1599; see VII.10n. Mountjoy died in 1606; see Daniel's *Funerall Poeme*.

5.4   grauer tones: See title-page motto, n. Spenser also cheered him on, publicly, in *Colin Clout* (1594):

> Yet doth his trembling Muse but lowly flie,
> As daring not too rashly mount to hight,
> And doth her tender plumes as yet but trie
> In love's soft laies and looser thoughts delight.
> Then rouze thy feathers quickly, DANIELL,
> And to what course thou please thy selfe advance.
> But most me seemes thy accent will excell
> In tragick plaints and passionate mischance.

But the opinion was not unanimous: witness Everard Guilpin in *Skialetheia* (1598), Satire VI:

> *Daniel* (as some holds) might mount if he list,
> But others say that he's a Lucanist.

Meres, in *Palladis Tamia* (1598), judged that "as Lucan hath mournfully depainted the ciuil wars of Pompey and Caesar: so hath Daniel the civill wars of Yorke and Lancaster, and Drayton the civill wars of Edward the second and the Barons." (See Grosart, *4*, xi, for his, Hales' and Gosse's ideas of what "Lucanist" means; also sources, pp. 6–7 above, and Coleridge on Lucan, VI.26 ff.n.) And Thomas Freeman the epigrammatist, *Rubbe and a Great Cast* (1614), Epigram 69:

> *Ad Sam. Danielem ut Ciuile bellum perficiat.*

> I see not (Daniel) why thou shouldst disdaine
> If I vouchsafe thy name amongst my mirth;
> Thy *AEtas prima** was a merry vaine,
> Though later Muse tumultuous in her birth;
> Know, here I praise thee as thou wast in youth;
> *Venereous*, not mutinous as now;
> Thy Infancie I loue, admire thy growth,
> And wonder to what excellence 'twill grow:
> When thou shalt end the broils thou hast begun,
> Which none shall do, if thou shalt leaue vndone.

* *Aetas prima canat veneres postrema tumultus*: Master *Daniels* Mott prefixed to most of his Workes.

Henry Chettle is encouraging (*England's Mourning Garment*, 1603):

> He that so well could sing the fatal strife
>   Between the royal Roses, white and red,
> That prais'd so oft Eliza in her life,

His muse seems now to die, as she is dead:
Thou sweetest song-man of all English swains,
Awake for shame! honour ensues thy pains.

And Richard Barnfield in *A Remembrance of some English Poets* (1598) called *CW* "that rare Worke, *The White Rose and the Red.*" But two other contemporaries demurred: Drayton, "To my most dearely-loved friend Henery Reynolds Esquire, of Poets & Poesie" (1627?):

Amongst these *Samuel Daniel,* whom if I
May speake of, but to sensure doe denie,
Onely haue heard some wiseman him rehearse,
To be too much *Historian* in verse;
His rimes were smooth, his meeters well did close,
But yet his maner better fitted prose

and Edmund Bolton, "*Hypercritica;* or a Rule of Judgment for writing, or reading our History's" (1610?): "The Works of *Sam. Daniel* contain'd somewhat aflat, but yet withal a very pure, and copious *English,* and words as warrantable as any Mans, and fitter perhaps for Prose than Measure." The next generation found more to praise. William Hemminge (*Elegy on Randolph's Finger, c.* 1630–32) speaks of

the pithy Danyell whose salt lynes afford
A wayghty sentence In each little word

and John Owen's *Epigram 46* (1633), *Ad Sam. Daniel* Poetam, goes thus:

Cui calamum tractas dextra, gladiumque sinistra?
Est tibi Mars laevus, dexter Apollo tuus.

6.7–8 See V.5. Daniel uses these terms in the spirit of Sidney's *Defense.* He is here emphasizing the historical aspect of Spenser's "poet historical"; see *FQ,* II. ix–x.

10.7 giuing Beastes: taking land away from the nobles and making it into royal hunting preserves.

12.2 Preuents: comes before, usurps the rightful place of. Gloss. tumultuarily: A form used at this period with special reference to riotous troops.

12.6 partiall: partisan, factious.

14.6 Despight: spitefulness, animosity.

15.4 rigour: heavy-handedness, tyranny.

15.7 conuented: charged with a crime.

15.7–16.4 (variant) Cf. Holinshed, end of reign of Henry II.

16.8 appease: pacify, reduce to quiescence.

17.6 ingenerate: produce; "Experience of those times ingenerate worthy mindes" is parallel to "ordered Raigne breedes plenty of mighty spirits." Anacolutha were not considered blemishes in Elizabethan verse writing.

18. Edward II's reign is the subject of Drayton's *Barons Wars,* which is modelled in considerable part on Daniel.

22.2 addrest: well ordered.

22.3 Neuer more Princes: Edward III had seven sons.

25.1 *Iohn:* Better known as John of Gaunt, father of Henry IV.

26.3 ouer-thwart: perverse, obstructionist.

33.3 Minions naught: good-for-nothing court favorites.

35.7   sequestered: impeached.

35.8   Gloster's league swore they would kill Vere and his associates.

36.7–8   A precedent for Prince Henry's striking the Lord Chief Justice in his very seat of judgment. See Shakespeare, 2 *Henry IV*, V.ii.80.

38.   See *Richard II*, III.iii.179.

40.2   The Queen: Anne of Bohemia.

40.7   young daughter: Isabel was seven years of age; Richard was twenty-nine.

41.6   articles: Richard's truce with Charles VI of France, which did not regain lands to which the English laid claim.

42.8   attache: arrest.

43.7   sulleuate: incite to an uprising.

44–9   An example of how Daniel "vsed that poeticall licence, of framing speaches to the persons of men according to their occasions." His materials were as follows; Froissart:

> The king of England failed not to inform the earl of St. Poule of the state that his country was in, and how he always found his uncle the duke of Gloucester hard and rebellious against him, and shewed him all things that he knew. When the earl of St. Poule heard the king speak in this manner, he was much astonished, and said that it ought not to be suffered, and added—Sir, if you suffer this they will destroy you: it is said in France that the duke . . . draws the hearts of the young men of the realm to his part, for they desire war rather than peace; so that if the war begin to stir, the aged wise men would not be heard nor believed, for reason, right, and justice, have no place nor regard where evil reigns; therefore provide against the evil before it is too late: it were better you had them in danger than they you. These words . . . sunk deeply in the heart of the king, and caused him sore to muse . . . [Gloucester] quoth . . . It is very probable that some false traitors have counselled the king to the same . . . these Frenchmen are very subtile, and can craftily execute their plans, and by degrees pursue their intents, and will give largely to bring about their purpose . . . The king . . . declared that the rumour was unfounded, for it was no such thing; but for truth, he said the earl of St. Poule had come into England with no other design but recreation, and was sent hither by the French king to see him and the queen his wife; the king said there was no other correspondence between them, and that the king swore, by the faith that he owed to God and to the crown of England, and said he wondered greatly what could give rise to such a report.

Polydore Vergil:

> Per eos dies uenit in Angliam Guido comes diui Pauli missus a Carolo, ut officij ac amoris gratia, eius uerbis Isabellam filiam & Ricardum salutaret. Rex multa conferendo aperit comiti, quemadmodum dux Glocestriae summa ope nitatur, ut bellum Carolo inferatur. & quia id ex animi sententia obtinere nōdum potuerat, populum ad seditionem solicitet, quo domi bellum ardeat, quod foris gerendū summe concupiuerat. Item narrat eūdem ducē iniussu suo, bene multos ex suis domesticis & amicis, affecisse supplicio, ac denique sibijpsi exitium machinari. Haec ubi comes accepit, subito respondit, non esse diutius tantum iniuriarum patiendum, sed continuo uindicandum, similque praecauendum malum, quod omnino futurum esset, nisi mature obuiam iretur. His comitis uerbis Ricardus permotus . . .

Walsingham omits the incident, as does Stow later. Hall's chronicle begins after it. Holinshed:

> The earle of saint Paule at his last comming into England to receiue king Richards oth for obseruing the truce, had conference with the king of diuerse matters. The

king by waie of complaint, shewed vnto him how stiffe the duke of Glocester was
in hindering all betwixt the realmes of England & France, but also procuring trouble
at home, by stirring the people to rebellion. The earle . . . hearing of this stout demeanor of the duke, told the king that it should be best to prouide in time against
such mischiefs as might insue thereof, and that it was not to be suffered, that a
subiect should behaue himselfe in such sort toward his prince. The king marking
his woords, thought that he gaue him good and faithfull counsell, and therevpon determined to suppresse both the duke and other of his complices . . . And as it
commeth to passe that those which suspect anie euill, doo euer deeme the woorst;
so he tooke euerie thing in euill part . . .

By his amplifications, by inserting the word "cunningly," by implicitly accepting
Gloucester's estimate of the crafty foreigner as responsible for the English king's
decision, Daniel has added a dimension to the outline given in his sources, as
well as translating reported speech into the vividness of *viva voce* remarks. See
VI.72.3–4n.

46.2 commorse: compassion.

46.3 Princes blood-shed: others' blood shed *by* princes.

46.4 by force: by the unjust exercise of power.

46.5 giues such a tuch: stirs up so much feeling.

47.1 "And often, because of this, the case (against the criminal) may be
thwarted."

48.6 fact: deed (usually in Daniel, as here, a criminal act).

49.6 assaies: tries to attain (to).

50.2 Gloss: the LL. of the league with Gloster: the Lords Appellant.

52.3 degenerous: degenerate, base.

53.8 "Which disturbs the public tranquillity" (?).

57.2 "Beyond the bounds of any sanction that he has to be regardful of."

57.8 "That subjects should be governed by advice; kings may do what they
will."

58.4 Sooth'd: encouraged, humored.

58.6 Gloss: *Nihil est* . . . : "There is nothing which power cannot believe of
itself, when it is praised as being equal to the gods" (Juvenal, *Satires*, IV.70). See
Jonson, *Sejanus*, Act I:

> O what is it proud slime will not believe
> Of his own worth, to have it equal prais'd
> Thus with the gods?

60, 61. Gloss (variants): Note how Daniel proceeds: no authority in *MS;* justification by authority of three chroniclers in 95; leaves original stanza, but qualifies
with Walsingham note, 01; decides on a compromise version, eschews all authority,
09. The main point of difference concerns who accused whom. Froissart, Polydore,
Hall, and the *Mirror for Magistrates* (following Hall) say Herford was the indiscreet malcontent, Mowbray the taciturn confidant, talebearer, and original appellant. Walsingham is very succinct and factual: "Circa praesens tempus appel-
lavit Dux Herfordiae Ducem Northfolchiae, de quibusdam verbis per eum dictis,
quae in Regis dedecus redundabant." Holinshed, who also has Herford as the
appellant, is much more circumstantial and makes it explicit that Herford had
first accused Mowbray in Parliament before the matter got to the king. Stow
follows Holinshed. Fabyan has Herford as appellant. This, of course, is Shakespeare's version; and modern historians, discounting the chroniclers and depend-

ing chiefly on Parliamentary records where they are available, agree with the latter account. See, e.g., C. Oman, *The Political History of England, 4,* 141–3, and Appendix I, "On Authorities." Oman ignores Froissart, Hall, Holinshed, and Stow, discounts Polydore Vergil, but declares Walsingham valuable. Daniel in his changes maintains his original order of accusation but softens the impeachment of Mowbray as a malicious sycophant and confidence-breaker.

61.6–7   menacing . . . wrong: "threatening to be revenged for the alleged wrong."

64.4   Gloss: This comment appears only in Walsingham. This, and the last note, might indicate that Daniel checked through Walsingham at the time when he was revising for the edition of 1601.

64.8   "And such a foe as now he considered Herford to be."

65.6–8   See *Richard II,* I.iii.208–12.

68.7   confiners: inhabitants.

70.3   comport: bear, be satisfied with.

71.1   When-as: whereas, at the same time.

71.6   apt-diuided: prone to division (?).

73.3–4   See *Richard II,* V.i.55–6.

74.5   considerate: prudent, cautious (in Daniel, with overtones of pusillanimity).

76.2   Transported: carried away.

76.4   naught: morally and legally wrong.

77.1   I know not how: The "wild Irish," who had been insufficiently "appeased" in 1394, were rising again. Daniel may have adapted this disclaimer from Hall: "In this ceason kyng Richard sailed into Irelande as diuers authores testifie, but what he did there is no parte of my processe, whiche dependeth on the sequele of this deuisiõ."

77.3   appease: pacify, put down by force.

78.7   now he was exil'd: Walsingham reports that, on the death of John of Gaunt, Richard declared Herford's banishment perpetual and seized his lands.

80.8   lackt: felt the need of.

81.1   Ill-perswading want: poverty, which tempts men to do wrong. (The capital letter introduced in 09 helps point up Daniel's almost invariable object-noun : transitive-verbal sequence in the use of the compound epithet.)

81.3   Loosenes . . . religion bindes: A play on the literal meaning of the supposed root *re-ligare,* to bind; see I.102.2–4, "alliance," "intelligence," "Religion." Fealty to a sovereign was a religious duty: see "vngodly" (I.85.6) and "binde" (I.91.5); "sinnes," "faith" (I.97).

82.3   See IV.92, V.18–19, VI.101, and *2 Henry IV,* IV.v.203–16.

83.   See *Richard II,* III.ii.107–10.

86.6   Gloss: Both these figures occur in Holinshed, qualified with "some say," "other report," etc.

87 ff.   This episode is Daniel's contribution. Cf. *2 Henry IV,* III.i.

89.6   that long, Impietie did: "that long, which Impietie did."

89.7–8   See *Richard II,* III.iii.88.

91.2   smooth: gloss over, whitewash. (I.102.5: cover up the rough spots of.)

91.8   When-as: at such a time when.

97.3   conferre: bring together for comparison, "cf."

97.5–6   "That our times might not be provided with a precedent for evil-doing in remembered crimes of the past; but, perturbed (cast down?) by our own shame."

98.4   See *2 Henry IV*, III.i.72–4. Henry invokes what Milton was to call "Necessity, the tyrant's plea."

98.7   sort to: are directed toward, are found to result in.

99.8   (variant) the happy: the successful.

100.1   Gloss: This is almost verbatim from Holinshed.

101.   Derived solely from Stow.

102.6   discusse: judge.

106.4   closely: secretly, unbeknownst.

106.7   amas'd: thrown into consternation.

107–18.   See the end of Lucan's *Pharsalia,* Book I.

117.2   Respect: take cognizance of.

118.4   See *Richard II,* III.iii.97.

Book II

1.3   attendes: exerts himself (in contrast to "late great mighty Monarch," who received obedience automatically).

1.7–8   See *Richard II*, III.ii.217–18.

2.   Most of the chroniclers have it thus, but Walsingham exonerates Worcester: "[Richard] dimisit igitur familiam, monens per Senescallum, Dominum Thomam Percy, ut se reservarent ad tempora meliora."

5.5   amuzing: misleading.

7.5   with pompe of Waters, vnwithstood: Quoted in line 4 of Wordsworth's sonnet, "It is not to be thought of."

9.2   Without the compasse: beyond the possibility.

11.5   that idle feare to stay: to check that unwarranted fear.

14.7   humorous: capricious, peevish.

17.7–8   See Shakespeare's *King Henry V,* who quotes his father as "happy, having such a son That would deliver up his greatness so Into the hands of justice." (*2 Henry IV,* V.ii.110–12.)

18.1   (wo worth the while): "Evil betide the time!" This parenthetical padding of the verse was introduced in the *Shepherds Calendar* by Spenser—see January, l.8, and May, ll.193–4 which, E.K. points out, is "a patheticall parenthesis, to increase a carefull hyperbaton."

21.1–2   The multiplicity of names by which Henry is called may be confusing. His father was John of Gaunt (i.e. Ghent, where he was born), Duke of Lancaster. Henry was born at Bolingbroke Castle, hence that appellation; by his marriage to Mary Bohun, coheiress with the Earl of Derby and Herford, he acquired those titles; and upon his father's death, despite Richard's attainder and disinheritance of him, he was acclaimed Duke of Lancaster by the lords who joined his revolt. Hall sums it up: "Henry Plantagenet borne at Bolyngbroke in the Countie of Lyncolne, duke of Lancastre and Herfford erle of Derby, Lecester and Lyncolne sonne to Iohn of Gaunt duke of Lancastre . . . was published, proclaymed & declared kyng of England and of Fraunce, and lorde of Irelāde . . . sacred, enoynted and crouned king by the name of kyng Henry the fourth."

23.8   ost . . . ostage: The vicarious nature of Christ's sacrifice and the similar notion of a pledge enter into this play on words.

26.5   Gloss: Auncitor: ancestor. The story of "Perkin a Lee" is found only in Holinshed, among Daniel's usual sources.

27. Holinshed: "Ienico Dartois a Gascoigne [gloss: 'A constant seruant'] that still ware the cognisance or deuise of his maister king Richard, that is to saie, a white hart, and would not put it from him, neither for persuasions nor threats; by reason whereof, when the duke of Hereford vnderstood it, he caused him to be committed to prison within the castell of Chester. This man was the last (as saieth mine author) [Stow calls Stephen Scrope 'mine authour' for this section] which ware that deuise, and shewed well thereby his constant hart toward his maister, for which it was thought he should haue lost his life, but yet he was pardoned, and at length reconciled to the dukes fauour, after he was king."

27.1 "Nor will my conscience allow that I should injure."

29.1–3 craggie Rocks . . . trusty Mountaines: Suggested by Holinshed's "craggie mounteine" in describing the place of ambush. The substance of this speech about the position for defense or escape is attributed in Stow to the Archbishop of Canterbury speaking to Henry. See also *Richard II*, III.ii.23–6. This was one of the passages marked along the margin of Wordsworth's copy of the 1717 edition of Daniel. See Cecil C. Seronsy, "Wordsworth's Annotations in Daniel's *Poetical Works*," *Modern Language Notes, 68* (1953), 403–6.

36.3–4 "His crime [treason] is capital: and he will not scruple to break his word if thereby he can save his life."

37.2 quiet did affect: was desirous of peace.

39.4 this poore promontorie: Conway, in the northwest corner of Wales.

42.2 affect: aim for.

44.7 Others law: Amnesty was an *act* of oblivion, not a law in the statutory sense. The words *law* and *lex* are probably used here to mean "a legal act which may be considered a precedent."

46.8 Feare, that's wiser: Commas did not necessarily indicate nonrestrictive clauses in Elizabethan practice.

48 ff. An example of Daniel's working-up of prosaic materials. Holinshed:

> The king keeping on his waie, had not ridden past foure miles, when he came to the place where the ambushes were lodged, and being entred within danger of them, before he was aware, shewed himselfe to be sore abashed. But now there was no remedie: for the earle being there with his men, would not suffer him to returne, as he gladlie would haue doone if he might; but being inclosed with the sea on the one side, and the rocks on the other, hauing his aduersaries so neere at hand before him, he could not shift awaie by any meanes, for if he should haue fled backe, they might easilie haue ouertaken him, yer he could haue got out of their danger. And thus of force he was then constrained to go with the earle, who brought him to Rutland, where they dined, and from thence they rode vnto Flint to bed.

Shakespeare seems to have remembered this passage; compare the imagery in *Richard II*, II.i.44–63, and *King John*, II.i.23–9. See also below, VI.43 and 90–1. Stanzas 48–9 marked in Wordsworth's copy. See II.29.1–3n.

54.4 A hundred thousand men: a round number for "a great many men"— taken from Stow. Walsingham: "numeroso valde."

55.5 Preacing: pressing.

56.4 preuents: anticipates.

57.8 respectiue: respectful, assiduous.

58.5 astonishing: (simulated) awe and dismay.

59(variant). Daniel got this first version from Stow; he revised it from Holinshed.

59.8 of force: by necessity.

61–5. Based on Holinshed. Froissart gives a completely different story: "without making any alteration or diminution whatever in respect to the royal dignity." Henry "proceeded on horseback in company with the king, and they frequently talked together." Henry led Richard to London by back ways, to avoid crowds, and took him to the Tower without going down the Watling Street or through the city of London. Stow describes the journey down the Watling Street, enumerating the towns; then, he says, Richard was handed over to the Londoners two miles out of the city; he was taken to Westminster, then to the Tower by water. Henry entered London "by the chiefe gate."

66 ff. See Dedication.6o ff., and p. 11 above. This episode is entirely Daniel's invention and seems to have been the basis for *Richard II*, II.ii, III.iv.96–9, V.i, V.ii.1–40.

68.3 the chiefe: the important personages.

77.7 conferr'd: compared.

82.4 interpoint: punctuate.

101.2 haynous: This comment is to be found in Hall, and in Holinshed copying him.

106–7. There seems to be no warrant for Daniel's attributing this desire to Richard.

113.2 Gloss: *Vir dominabitur* . . . : "This man shall rule over my people"— the story of the selection of Saul to be king of Israel, 1 Kings 9:17 (in the King James version, 1611, 1 Samuel 9:17; Daniel might have changed to conform, if he had revised again after 1609). Froissart and Walsingham mention this, and Holinshed gives the whole sermon (from Fabyan). The Archbishop was wrenching the text somewhat, emphasizing *vir:* "a man shall haue lordship and rule of the people, and not a child . . . In sted of a child wilfullie doing his lust and pleasure without reason, now shall a man be lord and ruler . . ."

114.2 collate: bestow.

114.4 expilation: pillaging.

(123 ff.) These stanzas, which form a spirited though wistful peroration to Book II, were deleted in 1609, presumably because the glory and hegemony of England thwarted by the Civil Wars is projected in terms of the Tudor line culminating in Elizabeth—something which would not go down very well with James Stuart or Queen Anne. And by 1609 Daniel himself had pretty well succeeded in transferring his enthusiasms to the new regime.

Daniel's invincible chauvinism is nowhere better exemplified: st. (124–5) achieve a truly Stogumber-like simplicity (see Shaw's *Saint Joan*).

(123).1 thirteene battels: Shrewsbury, 21 July 1403; Bramham Moor, 19 February 1408; first St. Albans, 22 May 1455; Blore Heath, 22 September 1459; Northampton, 10 July 1460; Wakefield, 30 December 1460; second St. Albans, 17 February 1461; Towton, 29 March 1461; Hexham, 15 May 1464; Edgcott, 26 July 1469; Barnet, 14 April 1471; Tewkesbury, 3 May 1471; Bosworth, 22 August 1485.

(123).3 Haue: should have. See st. 116 and variants; the assortment of auxiliaries (have, had, should have, should—and sometimes merely implied) all perform the function of apodoses to the original contrary-to-fact protasis in 115.5–6. See also (128).2.

<126,<127,(126),<130: The Essex stanzas were deleted in 1601–02, of course, in view of his disgrace and execution in February 1601. Mountjoy, who was white-

washed in the Essex affair, was currently successful as Lord Deputy in Ireland but was being watched closely: hence, perhaps, the cautious change from "gouerned" to "rendered" and the substitution of "magnanimous" for the touchy "pure-spirited." Mountjoy died in 1606. See VII.10n.

<127.1   in despight: notwithstanding any opposition.

<130.3   vnconsuming: undying.

Book III

Argument.5–8(variant)   These changes correspond to the rearrangement of material in Books III and IV in 09. See variants, III.83 ff.

9.5(variant)   Apparently revised from Holinshed, who says Norbury was made Lord Treasurer, and Clifford Privy Seal. Stow: Shirley, Chancellor; Clifford, Keeper of Privy Seal.

13.3   refell'd: refuted.

15.5   one: John Hall, King Richard's servant.

15.7   companion: low, ignoble person; gangster; *cf.* "fellow."

16.5   A rare slip in which Daniel, in revising for grammatical consistency or more exact diction, provides a new B rhyme instead of an A.

17.1   *Ostracisme:* In the original sense of banishment accompanied by confiscation.

22 ff.   See *Richard II,* IV.i.114–49.

22.2   *Auentine-Retire:* One of the hills of Rome, bearing a temple of Diana which was a kind of political sanctuary.

28.4   nought: bad, unsuitable.

28.5   men of my kinde: the clergy.

28.7   Henry said this when he was still Earl of Derby, according to the chroniclers.

30.4   that forsworne, that: that perjured man, who.

34.5   See *Richard II,* IV.i.328.

37–47.   Another speech "framed" by Daniel.

37.3   humerous: capricious.

37.4   ware-lesse: reckless.

55.2   wofull King: Richard.

56.3   he: Henry.

57.   See *Richard II,* V.iv.

61.5   *Pomfret:* Pontefract, a castle in Yorkshire, where Richard was imprisoned.

64.6   complaine: bewail the loss of.

64.8   Conferring: comparing.

65–70.   See *Richard II,* V.v.

73.5   *Marius* Souldier: Caius Marius, Roman officer. Plutarch:

> The magistrates . . . of Minturnae consulted together, and determined not to delay any longer, but immediately to kill Marius; and when none of their citizens durst undertake the business, a certain soldier . . . went in with his sword drawn to him. The room itself was not very light, that part of it especially where he then lay was dark, from whence Marius' eyes, they say, seemed to the fellow to dart out flames at him, and a loud voice to say, out of the dark, "Fellow, darest thou kill Caius Marius?" The barbarian hereupon immediately fled, and leaving his sword in the place rushed out of doors, crying only this, "I cannot kill Caius Marius." (Dryden's translation, revised by Clough.)

75.1   trauerses: crisscrosses; a technical fencing term.

75.7   happily and well: That is, from Richard's and the narrator's point of view.

78.1   proditorious: traitorous.

78.9   See *Richard II,* V.vi.38–44, and p. 15n. above.

79.2   auouch thy fact: acknowledge having a part in your criminal deed.

79.6   proper: own.

87–9.   Glosses: All these figures are taken from Holinshed and Stow, except that they give the number of "persons in ordinary allowance of diet" as "ten thousand." Although in transcribing the figures a zero might have been lost (see note to VI.108.4 Gloss), it may be that even Daniel found this estimate impossibly high. Shakespeare accepts it (*Richard II,* II.i.282–3).

88.6   alien: transfer ownership, embezzle.

89.1   concussed: extorted from by violence.

89.8   Gloss: *the D. of Lancaster had:* That is, Henry seized these assets of Richard's.

90.1   tooke to Syndique: undertook (or took it upon themselves) to censure.

90.5   president: precedent.

Book IV

3.2   confining: living in, and concerned only with, their own territory.

3.7   respects: pays attention to.

5.6   his Phreneticque maladie: Charles VI was regularly incapacitated by "midsummer madness."

15.2   *Hidra's:* The Hydra was a water serpent with nine heads, which kept growing back as fast as they were lopped off. This is one of Daniel's favorite images for rebellion.

20.7   disturne: divert.

22.6   Gloss: Daniel, apparently following Holinshed, has confused the various Marches and Mortimers (as also has Shakespeare, 1 *Henry IV,* I.iii.80–4). Philippa and Edmund Mortimer had *two* sons; the elder, Roger Earl of March, was the one designated by Richard as his heir; however, he died in 1398. *His* eldest son, Edmund Earl of March, was next in line, and was the king-designate according to the Yorkists. His uncle, the younger son of Phillippa and Edmund Mortimer, was also named Edmund Mortimer; he it was who was captured by Glendower and who later married the latter's daughter. This Edmund's sister Elizabeth (Kate, in Shakespeare), was the wife of Henry (Hotspur) Percy. See genealogical table II in *Oman;* also, Wilson's edition of 1 *Henry IV,* pp. 128–9.

22.7   "Whose sufficiency to assume the crown would not bear rough handling." This is a reversal (economically achieved by using the noun for the verb) from the previous idea in 95 and 01: "And [Then] you may judge how difficult it would have been for Richard to disvalue Mortimer's claim" [?].

26.8   Cartell: challenge.

30.1   supply: a grant of money, by Parliament, for the maintenance of the Crown.

34.1–2   See *Richard II,* II.iii.36–42; 1 *Henry IV,* I.i.78–92, V.iv.59–101.

36.3   vnconfirmed: inexperienced.

36.5–6   See 1 *Henry IV,* IV.i.124–7.

43.7   by th'ouerthrowne: by virtue of having overcome an enemy. This is

Daniel's normal conviction that Englishmen automatically derive good (and are entitled to it) by making wounds, provided that it is someone else's blood that is shed. See, e.g., 48.5–8; or compare IV.54–5 with VI.81–5, 89–99.

48. See 1 *Henry IV,* IV.i.97–103.

49–51. See 1 *Henry IV,* V.iv.29–50.

54. As to the death of Hotspur, Daniel follows the chroniclers, most of whom say he was killed by "other" of the king's side; Walsingham says flatly "dubium cujus manu"; Polydore, however, has him taken alive but cut down immediately with a battle-ax.

55(variant). See 2 *Henry IV,* I.i.50.

64.6 Gloss: fifteenes: two grants of supply, each being provided by a tax amounting to one-fifteenth of the value of personal property.

69.6 Accedence: entry into, assumption of responsibility.

73.8 Gloss: commodity: advantage.

74.7 toyle: trap.

75.5 concussion: violent extortion. pilleries: plundering.

76.2 him: Henry; see I.101–2.

81.8 Gloss: a better minde then fashion: "a better disposition than was attributed to him" (?); "a mind better than was indicated by his current behavior and/or get-up" (?). Holinshed: "the like traine had beene sildome seene repairing to the court at any one time in those daies. He was apparelled in a gowne of blew satten, full of small oilet holes, at euerie hole the needle hanging by a silke thred with which it was sewed. About his arme he ware an hounds collar set full of S S of gold, and the tirets likewise being of the same metall." Stow says the account of his "strange apparel" is from the translator of Titus Livius, who "was informed by the earle of Ormond, an eie witnes of the same."

83.5 Sabaoth: sabbath, rest after toil. See Spenser, *FQ,* VII.viii.2.8–9, *Var. Ed.,* and note; also, D. C. Allen, *Modern Language Notes, 64,* 93–4.

84. See 2 *Henry IV,* IV.iv.118–20., and pp. 22–3, 32 above. Daniel too liked this image well enough to salvage it for his revamped ending of Book IV in 1609; and he had adapted it to the description of Mountjoy's death in the *Funerall Poeme Vppon the Death of the late noble Earle of Deuonshyre* (1606):

> Although the feruor of extremity
> Which often doth throw those defences downe,
> Which in our health, wall in infirmity,
> And open lay more then we would haue knowne.
> Yet did no idle word in him bewray
> Any one peece of nature ill set in,
> Those lightnesses that any thing will say
> Could say no ill of what they knew within
>
> .   .   .   .   .   .
>
> And when his spirit and tongue, no longer could
> Do any certaine seruices beside,
> Euen at the point of parting, they vnfolde
> With feruent zeale . . .

J. R. Lowell (*Writings,* Boston, 1869, *3,* 156) says that Waller "has lived mainly on the credit of . . . and of a single couplet,

> The soul's dark cottage, battered and decayed
> Lets in new light through chinks that Time hath made,

in which the melody alone belongs to him, and the conceit, such as it is, to Samuel Daniel. . . . Waller has made worse nonsense of it in the transfusion."

84.2   denounce: announce.

84.3   inforcing: forcing themselves in.

86.3,5   Th'one: Conscience. The other: Death. Cf. *hic, ille*.

87.   See 1 *Henry IV*, IV.iii.105.

92.   See 2 *Henry IV*, IV.v.212–15.

(129).5 you ô worthy you (95) : Probably Mountjoy. you great Worthyes you (01) : Probably Mountjoy plus Egerton, perhaps also the Countess of Cumberland. The dedication to the Countess of Pembroke superseded this stanza, and it was omitted in 09.

Book V

1.3   Gloss: 1412: So Hall; other chroniclers and modern historians say 1413. Cf. "Certaine Advertisements to the Reader" prefixed to *Coll. Hist. Eng.*: "The Computation of Times is not of so great moment, figures are easily mistaken; the 10. of July, and the 6. of August, with a yeare ouer or vnder, makes not a man the wiser in the businesse then done, which is onely that hee desires."

2.5   feare: a fear-inspiring frown.

2.6   "The latter producing terror, the former delight."

4.4   Lords and captains, Henry's comrades-in-arms in the French wars.

5.5–8   See I.6.7–8 and n.

16.6   the world: That is, of course, the totality of Englishmen; to spoil others was an English prerogative, and its success an adornment.

18–19.   See I.82–3 and n.

20.4   "How to impose terms upon surrendering persons."

28.2   pretend: assert.

31.4   sacrifice: An allusion to the story of Iphigenia at Aulis.

33.2   interlightning: alleviating (?).

34.2   pretendant: claimant to the throne.

36.1–4   The Earl of March and the Duke of York were entrusted with important posts in the French wars; Henry Percy, son of Hotspur, was brought back from hiding in Scotland and restored to the earldom of Northumberland.

41.   See *Richard II*, II.i.44–63; *King John,* II.i.23–4. Cf. also V.88–9, II.48–9.

44.3   the Dolphin: Charles of Valois, Dauphin (first-born son of the king) of France, later crowned Charles VII through the efforts of Joan of Arc.

45.1–2   three score yeeres: Bolingbroke became Henry IV in 1399. In this section of the book Daniel ranges back and forth from about 1435 (death of the Duke of Bedford) to about 1455 (first battle of St. Albans).

46.   See VI.14.6n.

46.4   prescribe: imply by virtue of long-standing custom or usage.

56.5   th'already store: This use of "already" as a temporal adjective has not been found anywhere by the compilers of the NED. Daniel was a sufficiently bold innovator on occasion, as had been his master Spenser: see *Shepherds Calendar,* May. l.9, "in euery where," which E.K. calls "a straunge, yet proper kind of speaking."

59.8   *Mauns:* The town and fortress of Le Mans, in Maine.

61.1   th'allowance of that Place: the ratification of Parliament.

61.6   ouer-raught: overreached.

62.2   the-while: meanwhile.

74.2   waigh-backe: counterpoise.

76 ff.   Daniel follows the Yorkist chroniclers, who perpetuated the idea of the "good Duke Humphrey" and of Suffolk as a "flagitious" traitor. Modern historians have generally reversed this estimate. See, e.g., C. L. Kingsford, *Prejudice and Promise in XVth Century England*, ch. 6.

79.3–6   ". . . that he had caused men adiudged to dye, to be put to other execution, then the law of the land had ordered or assigned" (Hall, *Henry VI*, Ann. xxv.)

80.   See *Philotas*, 1384–99; *Cleopatra*, 645–70.

81.2   Gloss: *Impostume:* abscess.

81.6   conuented: summoned to appear to face charges.

82.8   still: always.

83.1   doubt: suspect, be apprehensive of.

86–8.   Compare *Delia*, sonnet 53.

87.5   the-whyles: for as long as necessary.

90.4   the affected sov'raignty: York's possession of the crown at which he aimed.

95.1–2   the *Spencers:* Hugh and Hugh Despenser, father and son, later favorites of Edward II. *Gauestone:* Piers Gaveston, boyhood friend and first favorite of Edward II. (On these two, see I.18 and Marlowe, *Edward II*.) *Vere:* Robert de Vere, Earl of Oxford, favorite of Richard II; see I.35.

101.4   Gloss: Coleridge note: "Considering the style of this poem, & how it is pitched, it is unpardonable in the author to have put the particulars of Suffolk's Death in a *Note;* & yet have inserted a stanza unintelligible without it. Concerning the abuse of *Notes* in modern works an Essay might be written usefully." (Lamb, 2, 171.) Coleridge's judgment may be somewhat modified by our knowing that the stanza was not "inserted" but was in all the editions; whereas the gloss (in fact, all the Suffolk glosses) was provided only in 1609. May this be due to Daniel's having by then seen *2 Henry VI*, IV.iv?

102 ff.   Coleridge note:

> This is the most inappropriate Speech in the whole Work: it is indeed so very much out of character, that, I should not be surprized if some thing of nearly the same import were to be in our old English or Latin chronicles / for Daniel is a man of excellent good sense, and had he had to *invent* a speech for the Queen, would, I would fain think, have entered decently, at least *Racinishly* if not Shakespearianly, into her character—and yet meeting the speech in the shape of history would have [been] seduced by it's coincidence with his own modes of reflection to have inserted & versified it. The recommencement of the narration, 'Thus *storms* the Lady', is truly *humorous*. Like a Phlegmatist, who conversing with his Lip-brother, the Pipe, in his Mouth, observed—I know, I'm too-apt-to speak—pre—cip—cipi—cipitately. (Lamb, 2, 172–5.)

Stanzas 62–78, 91, and 99 ff. provide some material for assessing Daniel's idea of Queen Margaret's "character." Coleridge was not aware of the original presence of four and a half stanzas following 104, nor that until 1609 106.1 read "Thus in her passion loe she vttered"; these changes seem to uphold his criticism. I have not found an exemplar for the speech in any of Daniel's usual chronicle sources.

113–14.   Coleridge note:

> It is perhaps worth noticing as an excellence suited to the style of the Poetry (what-

ever may be thought of that) that the accents and scansion of Daniel's Lines more assist the reading of the sense, than in any work, I know. If the Line runs ill to you, you may be sure, you have not read it in it's exact sense. The whole represents a grave easy man talking seriously to his friends. Sometimes too he breaks up, for a moment, the feeling of versification; but never by a *contradiction to* it, but by heightening the feeling of conversation ex. gr. by putting 3 important words in the most important Line of an aphorism; as if at each of the 3 words the Speaker gave a wise nod aided by the motion of the forefinger, "To *greatness,* who *Love* and *Opinion* hath." (Lamb, 2, 175.)

Coleridge has placed an "x" before and after 113.2 and has written "1," "2," and "3" respectively under "Greatness," "Love," and "Opinion" in 114.8. (Seronsy, p. 108.) See also VI.46.4n.

116.7   accomplements: reinforcements.

Book VI

1.2   close sub-ayding power: power giving secret encouragement and assistance.
1.3   fondly stout: foolishly resolute.
2.5   Coleridge note: "I do not recollect to have seen this word elsewhere, accented as a Paeon Secundus⌣̄ ⌣ ⌣/ but it gives the meaning & brings out the *sensorium*-syllable far better than the present anapestic or Paeon tertius emphasis. What is '*tain'd*' or '*tained?*'" (Lamb, 2, 178.) Coleridge has marked the line and scanned the final word thus: "aˇscē̄rtaˇinēd."
3.8   Occasion: fortunate eventuality.
5.3–4   "For, reckless insolence (so long as it is not held in check by the restraining power of respectful fear)."
(8).7   some straight: some narrow channel.
9.1–2   discharge . . . the shot: pay the reckoning.
10.5   preuented: forestalled.   attend: wait for.
10.6   occasion: favorable opportunity.
14.2   Thomas Courtney, Earl of Devonshire; Edward Brooke, Lord Cobham.
14.6   Coleridge note:

> We can not too highly praise the strain of political morality thro' this Work. No Success, no Heroism ever makes the Author forget the immutable Right & Wrong. And if it be objected, that the Right to the Throne is confounded with the right to common property, to an estate or house, yet still this was the Creed of those ages / as much the Creed of Henry the IVth & Vth as Richard the Second—yet Daniel was not *blinded* by it so as to overlook the guilt of involving a nation in civil war in an old tho' rightful claim—see p. 155, Stanza 46 [i.e. V.46]. (Lamb, 2, 182.)

(15).   This stanza perhaps supplies corroboration for Daniel's Italian journey; Lombardy is the district where lived Guarini, whom Daniel is thought to have visited. See M. Eccles, *Studies in Philology, 34,* 148–67.

16.1   Coleridge note: "In the first Line of Stanza 16. of this Book is a Pun in it's right place & passion. Had Puns never been used less judiciously than in this Instance & that of the fallen Angels in the 6th Book of Paradise Lost, they would still have been considered as Beauties." (Lamb, 2, 183.) The pun is doubtless intended—the word was "O maine" in the text of 95, 95a, and was corrected to "O mayme" in the "Faults Escaped"; there is perhaps some connection also between stt. 16–17 here and parts of 2 *Henry VI,* I.i. But Coleridge's doctrine is surely esoteric.

18.1 retchlesnes: heedlessness.

24.1 Ten thousand: So Holinshed; again, probably a round number. Hall says "a greate hoste"; Polydore, "exercitū bene magnum."

24. Gloss (variant): *Sulleuation:* insurrection.

25.7 fatall for discontents: Kent had also been the cradle of the Peasants' Revolt against Richard II in 1381 led by Wat Tyler, Jack Straw, and John Ball.

26.2,7 ff. On this whole passage, cf. Milton's description of the use of artillery as invented in hell, as an *ersatz* retort to God's thunderbolts (*PL*, VI.469–634); especially he might have owed to Daniel such passages as 630–2:

> eternal might
> To match with thir inventions they presum'd
> So easy, and of his Thunder made a scorn

and 498–506:

> Th'invention all admir'd, and each, how hee
> To be th'inventor miss'd, so easy it seem'd
> Once found, which yet unfound most would have thought
> Impossible: yet haply of thy Race
> In future days, if Malice should abound,
> Some one intent on mischief, or inspir'd
> With dev'lish machination might devise
> Like instrument to plague the Sons of men
> For sin, on war and mutual slaughter bent.

Coleridge note:

> But the passage vexes me: it has spoilt, and discharactered, the poem, the best of it's kind in any language: for spite of a few dazzling Passages in the Pharsalia it is as much superior to Lucan's (meâ quidem sententiâ) as the steady staid gait of manhood to the all-sort-of motions of a Hobbitihoy, or as plain and often deep sense to stoical declamations. The Pharsalia is really a Hobbitihoy poem—neither man nor boy. It is to me just what I should have expected from a youth well educated & of strong natural Talents at 19: and great works might have followed if he had lived / but more probably, if the work had been composed in his head, & forgotten by himself. For no man is proof against the popularity of his own writings. —But in this long [passage] what vexes one is, that the whole might so well have been said in the Author's own person, the philosophy being shallow indeed & short-sighted (a cowardice of present evil is the character of the writers of that age) but it is of a piece, it harmonizes, and in the morally, tho' not *intellectually* (for that is scarcely possible) nobler aera that succeeded even Milton fell into the nonsense of abusing Fire-arms. (Lamb, 2, 186–93.) See Seronsy, p. 110.

26.4 astonishment: thundering. See *PL*, I.266, "astonisht," literally, "thunderstruck"; 281, "astounded and amaz'd."

28. Coleridge note: "A theory framed in fancy (in strictness, not θεωρια, but ἀθεωρια, or at best ἡμιθεωρια) never fails to produce a distortion of faith. Consult the contemporary historians of the twelfth and thirteenth centuries and compare them with Daniel's flattering statement." (Note in Anderson's *British Poets* volume; quoted in T. M. Raysor, *Coleridge's Miscellaneous Criticism*, p. 238; cf. also Seronsy, p. 110, nn. 13–14.)

29.3 confines: borders.

30 ff. Coleridge note: "Nothing can be more *out of keeping*, as the painters say, than the introduction of these fictions in so grave and prosaic, tho' rhymed, history. They read like a stupid lie, told in cold blood, for lying's sake." (Raysor, p. 239.) J. H. Roberts ("A Note on Samuel Daniel's Civile Wars," *Modern Language Notes, 41,* 1926, 48–50) sees this passage, which "gives to Nemesis the new role of predestinator," as conflicting with the earlier view of Nemesis as "righteous retribution," and he accounts for it by the fact that Daniel "was undoubtedly writing his sixth book just during or just after the Lambeth Conference [of 1595], where the issue of predestination was clearly defined." If so, this may have something to do with Daniel's desire to exonerate Henry IV of personal blame.

30.3–6 Probably with reference to Tamburlaine, who had confounded the kingdoms of Asia. He died *c.* 1406.

31.3 Epimetheus imbecillitie: Epimetheus ("afterthought"), Prometheus' brother, unthinkingly accepted the beautiful Pandora and her box.

33.6 edifie: build.

34–41. See Satan's climactic argument in the temptation of Eve, *PL,* IX.679–733. This regret for the destruction of faith by rationalism has been regularly decried by certain humanists as anti-intellectual; Daniel's contemporary Bacon was to be the prophet and high priest of a resurgence of the scientific spirit to which we owe the modern world. Coleridge (see also his note to stt. 22 ff. above) was emphatically on the side of the moderns; he glosses here: "The Poets of Elizabeth & still more of James's time had a half in half hankering for Popery— we see it in Spenser, in Drayton, in Massinger In dignity of moral character they were wofully inferior to the succeeding age—a fact honorable to Liberty, & therefore to human nature." (Lamb, 2, 189.)

36.3 Cadmus: Planted the teeth of the dragon he had killed; armed men sprang up and began fighting among themselves. As well as founding Thebes, Cadmus was credited with introducing the alphabet and other fatal tools of civilization. Europa was his sister.

Another indication that Milton was acquainted with this passage in Daniel is his admission, in *Areopagitica,* "I know that they [books] are as lively, and as vigorously productive, as those fabulous dragon's teeth, and being sown up and down, may chance to spring up armed men."

36.5 (variant) like defended: defended merely because it is liked (?). This is one of Daniel's less happy compound epithets; he evidently felt it to be too obscure himself.

36.8 tire: head ornament, hairdress. (Perhaps an allusion to "tiara," the pope's triple crown?)

37.2 two fatall Instruments: Guns were in use in Europe considerably earlier than this period; in fact, there is mention of artillery of a sort at the Battle of Crécy. But "great ordnance" did come into general use only with the development of corned or grained gunpowder in the first quarter of the 15th century. Shakespeare speaks of artillery being used at the Battle of Holmedon (1402) in 1 *Henry IV,* I.i.57 and I.iii.59–64. Holinshed says the Scots were defeated by the "violence of the English shot," but this refers (as his source, Walsingham, makes clear) to archery.

Printing from movable type began in Europe shortly before the middle of the 15th century (see McKerrow, *Intro. to Bibl.,* App. I). Both printing and artillery are mentioned by Hall, Holinshed, and Stow in this general context of their chronicles; the development, however, and the ruefulness, seem to be Daniel's own contribution. Shakespeare, quite possibly with this in mind, has Hotspur parody the courtier who talked "so like a waiting gentlewoman Of guns and drums and wounds—God save the mark!—

> that it was great pity, so it was,
> This villainous saltpetre should be digged
> Out of the bowels of the harmless earth,
> Which many a good tall fellow had destroy'd
> So cowardly; and but for these vile guns,
> He would himself have been a soldier.

See also above, pp. 23–4.

38–9. Milton, again, may have been aware of this argument, although as a revolutionary he discounts it: "For when God shakes a kingdom with strong and healthful commotions to a general reforming, 'tis not untrue that many sectaries and false teachers are then busiest in seducing . . ." (*Areopagitica.*)

40. This argument, though really illogical unless it includes all weapons (even swords), had been used ever since Diomedes complained about Paris' bow-inspired valor (*Iliad,* Bk. XI). See also VIII.18n.

42.8 vnkinde: Coleridge note: "the etymon of *Kinde* is here preserved, & unkind = unnatural." (Lamb, 2, 191.)

44.6–8 The marriage of Henry VII with Elizabeth of York.

46.4 Coleridge note: "See p. 192, 1. 14 [i.e. this line]—where there are 3 emphatic and 3 subemphatic words." (Lamb, 2, 175.)

48.5 conceit: store of ideas.

49. Cf. *PL,* VI.478–87, 509–20, 552–3.

(49).4 Bring fayth disguisd: cause loyalty (and/or keeping one's word ?) to be so disfigured through dissimulation as to be unrecognizable (?). Or perhaps an allusion to the activities of the Jesuits, who worked clandestinely in England after being outlawed; they were regularly denounced as impious, crafty hellhounds in the pay of the devil.

50.1–2 frame: engine (artillery).   planted: erected, emplaced.

50.2 Gloss: pight: pitched.

52.6 plots: projects.

53.4 that from your force with-drawes: that takes away from your real effectiveness.

54.1 ingins: ingenious snares.

54.4 Gloss: answere his expectation: come up, in numbers, to his expectation.

55.8 in Maiestie: in matters pertaining to kingship.

58.5 "The law rigorously called attention to his deed as a crime, and adjudged him liable to capital punishment."

59–63. These words of the king, and even the attitude which prompted them, are provided by Daniel; nothing in the chronicles.

59.5 Brauing: treating contumeliously. See *Philotas,* 1482 ff.:

> O do not so insult vpon calamity;
> It is a barberous grosnesse, to lay on
> The weight of scorne, where heauy misery
> Too much already weighs mens fortunes downe:
> For if the cause be ill I vndergo,
> The law, and not reproch, must make it so.

68.6 With colour: using a pretext.

72.3–4   This attitude toward treachery (on the part of another country, and in favor of England) should be compared with the remarks about France's complicity in Cambridge's plot against Henry V (V.25–7) and the pious sentiments expressed in V.86–8. Again see Shaw's Stogumber, and the explanation of the urbane Warwick: "[Treachery] does not mean in England what it does in France. In your language traitor means betrayer: one who is perfidious, treacherous, unfaithful, disloyal. In our country it means simply one who is not wholly devoted to our English interests." (*Saint Joan,* sc. iv.)

77.1   fierce courageous Mastiue: the fierceness, at least, was concurred in by the French; however, they chose a more pejorative animal appellation for him, "the mad bull." French mothers used his name as a bogey-word to frighten their children into obedience.

80.5   brauing: insulting.

82.1   fact: deed.

90.1   Frank: generous.

93.   Coleridge note:

> . . . a fine stanza [see Seronsy, pp. 107–8]. What is there in description superior even in Shakespeare? Only that Shakespeare would have given one of his *glows* to the first line, and flattered the mountain top with his sovran eye—instead of that poor—
>
> "A marvellous advantage of his years."
>
> But this, however, is Daniel—and he must not be read piecemeal. Even by leaving off, and looking at a stanza by itself, I find the loss. (Raysor, *Misc.,* p. 236. Raysor reads "surer" for "sovran": see Seronsy, p. 105, n. 3.)

95.8   Gloss: 30. yeeres: The chroniclers say twenty-four, perhaps because he was first heard of being driven out of Orleans by Joan of Arc in 1429. His death occurred in 1453.

99.   Coleridge note: "A Stanza obscure from mismanagement of syntax—a defect, of which there is scarce a second example in our 'well-languaged Daniel,' as Spenser most appropriately, as to the fact, calls him, tho' the phrase stands in contrast to the sense—Southey. rarely will the English tounge admit [of] participles of substantives." (Lamb, 2, 208–9.) Seronsy (p. 111, n. 1) points out that the epithet comes from William Browne's *Britannia's Pastorals,* Bk. II, song 2; and notes that the "of" in Coleridge's last line is lined through.

101.5   Seronsy, p. 111: "Coleridge scans 1. 5 as follows: 'The wŏrkĭng Spĭrĭt ceās'd nŏt, thŏ' Wōrk dĭd cēase'."

Coleridge note:

> A whole Book might be written, neither diffuse or uninstructive, on the metrical excellence of the 5th line of the CIst Stanza. The pause after Spirit compels a stress on ceas'd, & so makes Ceas'd not, by addition of the pause after not, = to a spondee—a fine effect after the Tribrach, or ⌣⌣⌣—
> Spirit, Body, money, honey, & two or 3 more perhaps which I do not recollect, are remnants of genuine *metre* in our language—they are, at least always may be, Pyrrhics, i.e. ⌣⌣ = —: as a a [*sic*] delicate Ear may instantly perceive & prove that accent, contrary to the almost universal opinion, shortens the syllable on which it rests; for in these words there is an equal accent on both syllables—hence they are both short—The wŏrkĭng Spĭrĭt (a pause equal to u) cēas'd nōt, thō Wōrk dĭd cēase. N.B. This is a valuable remark. (Lamb, 2, 209.)

102.4   obuious vnto: standing in the way of.

105.4   Coleridge note (Lamb, 2, 210): "either (or = to) spoilt." The word appears "spilt" or "spylt" in all editions; Coleridge's meaning is acceptable, unless he intends (led on by the context of ll. 4–5) to include the connotation (later than Daniel) of "spoiled child."

106.6 Coleridge note: "two Paeon quarts with an anapest interposed, 14 instead of 15, the pauses more than making up the deficient time / so very much more indeed, that I cannot but admire the metrical Judgement of the Poet." (Lamb, 2, 211.) Seronsy (p. 111) observes, "Coleridge refers to his previous notes on Daniel's metrical skill, 'p. 192 & 175', scans the line '◡◡◡–/◡◡–/◡◡◡–/' ".

108.4 Gloss: Polydore as usual gives no figures for the numbers of the troops; Hall says York had "a greate power" and the king "an host"; Holinshed gives the king "aboue two thousand men of warre," and York "not past three thousand men (as some write." As to the number killed: Hall, "viij.M. men and more"; Holinshed, "in all to the number of eight thousand, as Edward Hall saith in his chronicle: if there escaped not a fault in the impression, as 8000 for 800, sith hundreds in verie deed would better agree with the number of the kings whole power, which he brought with him to that battell, being not manie aboue two thousand, as by writers appeareth." Daniel's "20000" in the king's army may also have been a fault in the impression. Oman finds about 3,000 men on each side, and that "not more than 120 persons in all perished, possibly as few as sixty." (*Pol. Hist. Eng., 4, 367.*)

110.5 straight: narrow. St. Albans was little more than a few straggling houses lining the Watling Street, the main road to London from the north.

111.4 aduent'ring for the Maine: taking a chance on gaining the most important point (victory through parley?). See VII.25.3n.

112.3 commoditie: advantage.

112.7 make great stealth: steal into the affections.

Book VII

Argument 1 repriz'd: recaptured.

1 ff. Coleridge note:

> In the mind of a man like Daniel, neither Priest or Lawyer, too honest to falsify a notion of Duty, and too good by nature to stifle a sense of general misery, this mistake (common to all his Contemporaries except Buchanan, Knox, & Raleigh) (I speak of Authors) of the Jus Individui de re individuâ for the Munus Individui *propter* rem publicam occasioned a civil war, bloodless indeed, yet as perplexed as that which the same mistake called into action by ambition produced in the *real* world. See Judge Foster's excellent animadversion on Hales concerning Kings de jure & de facto. (Lamb, 2, 216–17.)

On Foster see Seronsy, p. 112, n. 17.

1.4 respectiue heed: careful caution.

5.1,3,5 Coleridge note: "for 217, V. [i.e. p. 217, st. 5, in Lamb, vol. 2] a fine stanza." (Lamb, vol. 2, 3d flyleaf, verso.)

> Is it from any hobby-horsical Love of our old writers (and of such a passion respecting Chaucer, Spenser, and Ben Jonson, I have occasionally seen glaring proofs in one the string of whose shoe I am not worthy to unloose), or is it a real Beauty, the interspersion, I mean (in stanza poems) of rhymes from polysyllables—such as Eminence, Obedience, Reverence? To my ear they convey not only a relief from

variety, but a *sweetness* as of repose—and the understanding they gratify by reconciling Verse with the whole wide extent of good Sense. Without being distinctly
conscious of such a notion, having it rather than reflecting it, (for one may think
in the same way as one may see and hear), I seem to be made to know that I need
have no fear; that there is nothing excellent in itself which the Poet cannot express
accurately and naturally, nay no good word. (Lamb, vol. 2, 4th flyleaf, verso.)

See also Seronsy, pp. 107–8.

8.2 Coleridge note: "The word [Machines] was pronounced, sometimes,
Matchins, sometimes Mackins, from m̄achiña." (Lamb, 2, 218.)

9.6 it selfe conuerts: pays attention to.

(10). Mountjoy had purchased Wanstead from Essex in 1599. Daniel may well
have been accustomed to retire thence to write, even when it was Essex's: see
"solitary brooke," II.(129).1, and I.5.1. There is probably a pun on "Sommers
heate": Edward Somerset, Earl of Worcester, was in the opposite faction to
Mountjoy after the Essex rebellion. Cf. Spenser, *Prothalamion,* 67, "Yet were
they [Somerset's daughters] bred of Somers-heat." See p. 33 above, and L. Michel,
"Sommers heate again," *Notes and Queries,* vol. *195,* no. 14, 8 July 1950, pp. 292–3.

(10).3 checkt: Grosart (2, 261) prints "deckt," which has no authority and
makes no sense. Since the stanza does not appear elsewhere since 1602, this ghost
word must have thoroughly mystified any modern reader.

13.8 Gloss: Holinshed says the Lord Mayor's force was 5,000 men.

18.6–7 "to forestall the rumor of the offence imputed to him."

19.3 signifie: declare.

20.8 set vp's Rest: A favorite Elizabethan expression, taken from the card
game pinero, meaning "play this hand, with these cards." Take a stand, determine. Cf. *Romeo and Juliet,* IV.v.6, V.iii.110. The implication is chiefly that of
consolidating one's resources in preparation for attack: Antony, in North's
Plutarch, "determined to set up his rest, both by sea and land" where a literal
translation of the Greek would be simply "determined to attack by land and sea
at once."

21. Again, as an example of the influence of Hall's didacticism in historical
writing and of Daniel's metamorphosis of his materials:

> As fier beying enclosed in a strayte place, wil by force vtter his flāme, and as the
> course of water astricted & letted will flow and brust out in continuance of tyme:
> so thys cācard crocodryle and subtle serpēt, could not lōg lurk in malicious hartes,
> nor venemous stomackes, but in cōclusion she must (according to her nature) appere
> & shewe her selfe. For after this apparant cōcord, and intrinsecall discord, accordyng
> to the very nature of dissimulacion, diuers noblemen of byrthe, but not stable of
> worde, putting from them honor, trought and honestie forgat their othe, and brake
> their promisse, & aduanced forth the banner of displeasure, and the flagge of malice.
> So a man may se, that such persons, regard neither their awne peculiar profite, nor
> the publique wealth of their natiue countrey, nor yet passe of an othe, or promise
> brekyng, to whom discord is pleasant, and discencion is delectable. (Beginning of
> Ann. Reg. xxxvii.)

21.5 Affection: partisanship.

22.3–4 "having confirmed and re-established his command."

25.3 Maine: a number called by the caster before the dice were thrown.

28.2 feelingly: working upon susceptibilities; effectually.

32.5(6) Attaints, Attayndor: "The legal consequences of judgement of death or outlawry, in respect of treason or felony, viz. forfeiture of estate real and personal, corruption of blood, so that the condemned could neither inherit nor transmit by descent, and generally, extinction of all civil rights and capacities." (*NED.*)

32.7 colours: interpretations.

36.3 th'auoided roomes: the offices vacated by the attainted Yorkists.

36.6 That is, the people of the North would obey only their feudal lords (?).

37–44. This episode is not found in the chroniclers. See 3 *Henry VI*, II.ii.9 ff., and I.i.230 ff.

41.4 Prince Edward was six years old at the time of this Parliament, when he was declared the official heir to the throne.

44.7 vex: scold.

55.8 contagious: Apparently, here, in the pejorative sense only; see original version of ll. 7–8 in variants.

56.1 *Periander:* Tyrant of Corinth, *c.* 625 B.C. He sent a messenger to Thrasybulus, tyrant of Miletus, to ask the best way to maintain his power. Thrasybulus led the messenger through a field of corn (i.e. wheat), cutting off the tallest ears— implying that Periander should level his nobles.

57.5–6 For example, Bolingbroke's coup against Richard II.

58.8 Gloss: This is found only in Stow.

59.2 steed: stead, place.

62.2 continues one: maintains his former attitude.

65.8 descant giue a ground: provide a basic theme upon which to sing variations.

68–73. Daniel takes considerable liberties with York's oration as reported by Hall and abridged by Holinshed.

76.7 his propinquitie: Bolingbroke's kinship to the royal family (?).

76.8 make no distance: constitute no disqualifying barrier (?).

79.2 *Thorpe:* Thomas Thorpe, speaker of the House of Commons, later Baron of the Exchequer; a staunch Lancastrian. *Fortescue:* Sir John, Chief Justice of the King's Bench and writer on English law; a Lancastrian, persecuted for his loyalty, he finally changed sides.

81. Queen Margaret had fled northward after the battle, taking Prince Edward with her.

81.1 *Trent:* A continuation of the Humber, traditional dividing line between the north and the south of England; cf. "Northumberland."

82.2 infeoffement: Granting of a holding on condition of subservience.

85.8 far mightier forces: Hall and Holinshed say the queen had 18,000, "or, as some write," 22,000; York, not fully 5,000. As usual, these figures are undoubtedly exaggerated.

87.7 fore-goes: predeceases.

89.5 vndecide: nullify, invalidate.

91.8 This irony is found in Hall and copied by Holinshed.

92.1–2 with other *Genius* then his owne: Obscure; possibly means he was hampered by the presence of and irresponsibility of the king or that he was confronted for the first time by a spirit and military genius equal to his own. Contrast line 6, Margaret's happy condition, at one with herself and allied with Fortune.

93.4 trauell: travail.

110.3(and variant) *Towton:* Usually called the Battle of Towton, it was actually fought between Towton and Saxton, and closer to the latter.

BOOK VIII

1.3–4   See the Epistle "To the Prince" prefixed to *Philotas*. Book VIII appeared first in 1609.

1.5–2.1   This is a little obscure. "She" seems to be Elizabeth's successor as inspiration of Daniel's Muse; but Queen Anne did not have the "first of all his labors past." The Countess of Pembroke, Daniel's early and apparently continuing patroness, seems to fill the description best; the poem was dedicated anew, to her, in 1609 when the verse dedication to Elizabeth was deleted.

3.1   Pharsalian Field: Scene of the Battle of Pharsalus, the decisive conflict between Pompey and Caesar. Treated in Book VII of a poem by Lucan, *De Bello Civili*, concerning the struggle between Caesar and the Senate; the poem is usually, though without authority, called the *Pharsalia*. Daniel took this poem as his overall model; he was dubbed the "English Lucan" by his friend Camden and a "Lucanist" by Edward Guilpin, and Meres continued the ascription in *Palladis Tamia*. See Sources, pp. 6–7, and I.1–3n.

3.2   Gloss: "The force under [the Lancastrians'] command must have been very large: the chroniclers, in their habitual exaggeration, speak of 60,000 or 100,000 men. Perhaps so many as 15,000 or 20,000 may have been present. The Yorkists were decidedly inferior in numbers" (Oman, p. 406). Hall on this occasion seems to have backing: "Kyng Edward, whose whole army, they that knew it, and payed the wages, affirme to xlviii. M. vi. C. &. lx persons," but he does not identify the paymasters. Oman ignores Hall, as he "is demonstrably wrong in many points" (p. 408n.)

4.7–8   Plutarch: "[Alexander's] army, by their computation who make the smallest amount, consisted of thirty thousand foot, and four thousand horse; and those who make the most of it, speak but of forty-three thousand foot, and three thousand horse."

5.8   what way he tends: Both "wherever he goes" and "depending on his aspect" (in the technical astrological sense).

7.1   *Cato:* Roman champion of taxation against corruption and extravagance, and implacable foe of the republic's rival, Carthage.

7.7   *Pompey, Cæsar:* rivals for the dictatorship of Rome.

14.1–4   that day: Palm Sunday, 29 March 1461. Polydore Vergil says that King Henry would rather not fight on Palm Sunday, "quo potius orandum, quam pugnandū sibi statuerat," but was forced to by his soldiers, who, according to their nature, were impatient of delay.

Daniel seems to be connecting the carrying of olive branches with the idea of peacefulness. According to St. John the people carried palm branches on the first Palm Sunday (the other evangelists say "branches from the trees"). In the Palm Sunday liturgy, branches of palm are said to signify victory over the prince of death, and the olive the advent of spiritual unction through Christ; also spoken of is the olive brought to Noah by the dove. Olive or other trees were often used in countries where palm was unavailable; in Jerusalem either was acceptable; in Rome olive branches are still distributed to the people.

15.3–7   flight-shafts: Light, well-feathered arrows for long-distance shooting. sheafe-arrowes: Arrows carried in a bundle or quiver (for close-in, rapid-fire shooting?). Falconbridge, according to Hall, had ordered his archers to provide themselves with one round of flight-arrows.

18.   Cf.VI.40 and n. It seems somewhat illogical to praise the bow and damn the gun, when both are "equalizers" in that they allow a coward to kill a brave man at a safe distance; but Daniel possibly means that the difference lies in the personal strength required to draw the longbow. The crossbow was sometimes called a "gun" or "artillery."

19.8 Gloss: Number slain: Verbatim from Stow; Hall and Holinshed say 36,776.

22–6. See *3 Henry VI*, II.v.1–54, and p. 27 above.

25.2 Gloss: expecting the euent: awaiting the outcome.

29.8 recouered: reached.

30.1 vacancie: leisure.

33.4 alliance: i.e. matrimonial; Prince Edward was betrothed to the daughter of the Scottish king.

35.1–4 Hartley Coleridge (*Essays and Marginalia*, London, 1851, 2, 13): "This expression savours not of Daniel's usual wisdom. Bolingbroke's usurpation cost all the blood. I am always provoked when I hear of "*The bloodless Revolution of '88*," as if it were not the aftermath of the great rebellion, and as if there had been no blood shed at Killiekrankie, the Boyne, Londonderry, Aghrim, Sherrif Moor, Preston Pans, or Culloden,—not to speak of the noble lives that perished on the scaffold, on the tree, to them not ignominious, and of the bloody wasteful foreign war, of which that dirty business was at least a co-cause."

35.8 "And though displaying the white rose as his emblem, was bloody-minded."

45.7 Gloss: From Stow.

48.7 subayding: secretly backing.

49.1 contrast: contention, strife.

52.7 past the Presence: made her entrance into the king's formal reception.

52.8 presence: demeanor.

54.8 figured: adorned, embellished (?).

55–75 See *3 Henry VI*, III.iii.

56.8 accommodate: adjust, take care of.

72.8 Motion: suggestion.

76.1–3 Daniel got the story, and a good many of the details of Elizabeth's "brow" and graces, from Hall and Holinshed but much elaborated it and gave it his characteristic speaking voice. In order to see how much was contributed by his image of Mary Pembroke, cf. Hall: "But now consider the old prouerbe to be true yᵗ saieth: that mariage is destinie . . . for she was a womā more of formal countenaunce, then of excellent beautie, but yet of such beautie & fauor, that with her sober demeanure, louely lokyng, and femynyne smylyng (neither to wanton nor to humble) besyde her toungue so eloquent, and her wit so pregnant, she was able to rauishe the mynde of a meane person, whē she allured and made subiect to her, yᵉ hart of so great a king . . . she so wisely, and with so couert speache aunswered and repugned . . ." Holinshed takes this over, changing a few expressions, and adds to the description of the hotness of Edward's fiery love the fact that he had once attempted to seduce the daughters of Warwick, for he "loued well both to behold and also to feele faire damsels."

78.6 Elizabeth, for our Elizaes sake: For another collation of Elizabeths, see Spenser's *Amoretti*, sonnet 74.

80.6 sooth: flatter, encourage, justify.

81.5 collated: gathered.

84.5   cauteris'd: seared, branded.

84.6   th'idle marke: the stigma of a trifler.

85.2   distemp'red: lacking in order and self-control, capricious.

87.7   mean: offices as go-between.

88.6   concurrency: competition.

89.4   a Trauerse 'twixt: a screen in front of.

93–111.   This colloquy is entirely Daniel's contribution. Compare Warwick's
point of view with that of Ulysses in *Ulysses and the Syren.*

95.2   thrall: servitude, bondage.

95.7   foot: tally, balance.

96.3   port: social station.

101.8   Oliue: symbol of peace.   Palme: symbol of victory in war.

102.2   Cellularie: monastic, hermitlike.

106.3   *Magha:* Oriental witch.

106.7   profusion: wasteful expenditure.

109.3   collate: bestow.

111.6   sterilitie: barrenness (leading to poor harvests).

112.2   the D. of *Clarence:* Edward's brother George, who here broke his alle-
giance to join Warwick and married his daughter. Later, at the Battle of Barnet,
he deserted Warwick and went back over to Edward's side.

The ende of the eightth Booke:

The poem was never finished. What with the battles of Barnet, Tewekesbury,
and Bosworth Field, the rise and fall of Richard III, sundry plots, murders, and
executions, and the final merger of the two houses establishing the Tudor dynasty,
there was plenty of suitable material to fill the classic twelve books. But Daniel was
side-tracked into writing his prose *History* (the "design" of which, like that of *CW,*
was not finished either), and never got back to the *Civil Wars.* At the end of the
Epistle prefixed to *Philotas* as published in 1605, Daniel wrote

> And yet I grieue for that vnfinisht frame
> Which thou deare Muse didst vow to sacrifice
> Vnto the bed of Peace, and in the same
> Designe our happinesse to memorize,
> Must, as it is, remaine, though as it is:
> It shall to after-times relate my zeale
> To Kings, and vnto right, to quietnesse,
> And to the vnion of the Common-weale.
> But this may now seeme a superfluous vow,
> We haue this peace; and thou hast sung enow,
>   And more then will be heard, and then as good
>   As not to write, as not be vnderstood.

This was deleted in 1607; perhaps he was encouraged to go on—but he wrote just
the one more book. See I.5.4n.

Index to Introduction and Notes